815   SAU.   8694

9 25

D1222185

The Observer's
Basic Civil Aircraft Directory

THE OBSERVER'S

BASIC CIVIL AIRCRAFT DIRECTORY

COMPILED BY WILLIAM GREEN
AND GORDON SWANBOROUGH

FREDERICK WARNE & CO LTD   London
FREDERICK WARNE & CO INC   New York

Published by Frederick Warne & Co Ltd 1974
© *Pilot Press Ltd 1974*

LIBRARY OF CONGRESS CATALOG CARD
No 73-89831

ISBN 0 7232 1525 1

Filmset and printed in Great Britain
by BAS Printers Limited, Wallop, Hampshire
813.374

Introduction

Together with its companion volume *The Observer's Basic Military Aircraft Directory*, the *Basic Civil Aircraft Directory* provides a comprehensive and compact reference source to the world's most important and most widely-used aircraft. Like the two volumes of similar titles but smaller format published in 1967, these *Basic* directories supplement but do not replace the annual *Observer's Book of Aircraft* which, now in its 23rd year of publication, surveys the latest aircraft each year and reports on the newest variants of existing types that have appeared in the preceding twelve months or are expected to appear during the currency of the particular edition.

The purpose of the present volume is somewhat different, being to provide in the handiest possible fashion a guide to the characteristics of the aircraft in commercial and civil use throughout the world, with airlines, government agencies, air taxi operators, business corporations, flying clubs, private owners and agricultural operators. This brief necessarily excludes certain new types that have been built or are building as prototypes but for which no firm pro-

duction plans exist at the time of going to press. On the other hand, the inclusion of types that are in service though no longer in production extends the scope of the book "backwards" to encompass designs that first emerged as many as 40 years ago.

By their nature, many commercial aircraft have working lives of 20 years or more, while the smaller private-owner types may remain airworthy for twice as long, thanks to the tender care often expended on them by their enthusiastic owners. To include *every* such type still to be found airworthy in some odd corner of the world or other would have extended the contents of this volume to unacceptable limits and have defeated the aim of compactness; therefore, only those older types still flying in reasonably large numbers are included. In some cases, arbitrary decisions have been made to include or exclude specific types based primarily on the probability of such types being seen with regularity by the majority of the book's users.

In a few cases, the same basic aircraft types have been included in both this volume and its *Military* companion, but such duplication has been avoided so far as conveniently possible by including those types (mostly the larger transports and some trainers) that have dual military/civil rôles only in the volume appropriate to their major application.

The aircraft in this volume—196 fixed-wing types and 32 helicopters—have been grouped according to ten categories of primary function, and the arrangement within each of these categories is alphabetical by manufacturers. This arrangement makes for the easiest possible comparison of similar aircraft types, but should not be taken to imply that specific aircraft are applicable only to those functions: for example, some business aircraft are used as third-level airliners, many of the aircraft listed in the sport and touring section are also operated as business or utility transports or for agricultural duties, and so on.

Numerous aircraft described in this volume have been produced in two or more versions—in some cases perhaps a dozen or more—and often with major external differences. Wherever space permits, the details given under the headings "Power plant", "Performance", "Weights" and "Dimensions" cover a representative spread of variants and the photographs and silhouettes have been selected to illustrate different external features of the variants.

All silhouettes are the work of Dennis I Punnett and are the copyright of Pilot Press Ltd. Credits for the photographs supplied by private individuals appear on page 224.

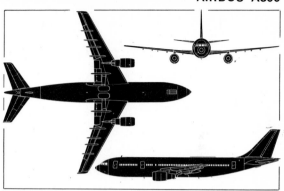

Both photograph and silhouette depict the Airbus A.300B2, the initial production variant that entered service with Air France in Spring 1974

Country of Origin: France/Germany/UK.

Type: Short- to medium-range airliner.

Power Plant: Two (initial standard) 49,000 lb st (22 260 kgp) General Electric CF6-50A or (from 1975) 51,000 lb st (23 133 kgp) CF6-50C turbofans.

Performance: (CF6-50C engines) Max cruising speed, 582 mph (937 km/h) at 25,000 ft (7 620 m); best economy cruise, 554 mph (891 km/h); max operating ceiling, 35,000 ft (10 700 m); range with max payload (B2), 1,500 mls (2 410 km), (B4), 2,100 mls (3 370 km); range with max fuel, (B2), 3,100 mls (5 000 km), (B4), 3,915 mls (6 300 km).

Weights: Basic operating (B2), 186,810 lb (84 740 kg), (B4), 191,330 lb (86 790 kg); max payload (B2), 70,000 lb (31 750 kg), (B4), 77,630 lb (35 210 kg); max take-off (B2), 302,000 lb (137 000 kg), (B4), 330,700 lb (150 000 kg).

Dimensions: Span, 147 ft 1¼ in (44,84 m); length, 175 ft 11 in (53,62 m); height, 54 ft 2 in (16,53 m); wing area, 2,799 sq ft (260,0 m²).

Accommodation: Flight crew of three and typical one-class layouts for 281 seats (eight abreast) or up to 331 at reduced pitch.

Status: First and second prototypes (to B1 standard) flown on 28 October 1972 and 5 February 1973 respectively. First and second production aircraft to B2 standard flown on 28 June and 20 November 1973 respectively. Certification in March 1974 with deliveries starting May 1974. Total airline orders and options by June 1974: Air France, six B2 (plus 10); Lufthansa, three B2 (plus four); Iberia, four B4 (plus eight); TEA, one B1; SATA, one B4; Air Siam, two B4; Transbrasil, two B4; Sterling, three B4.

Notes: In addition to Aérospatiale in France and the Deutsche Airbus consortium of German aerospace companies, the A300 production embraces Hawker Siddeley in the UK, Fokker-VFW in Holland and CASA in Spain. The first two prototypes are of the initial B1 type with shorter fuselage, now superseded by the B2 described above, which has been ordered by Air France and Lufthansa (part of the ATLAS group of companies). The B4 is dimensionally similar but has increased fuel capacity and operates at higher weights; the first order for this variant was placed by Iberia, with the first example being No 9 on the production line. Other airlines that have ordered this version include Air Siam, Transbrasil and Sterling Airways.

BOEING 707-320

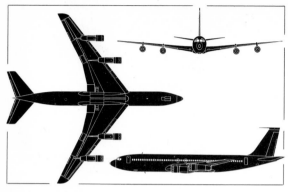

The photograph (above) shows a Boeing 707-3D3C in the colours of Alia, the Royal Jordanian Airline, and the silhouette depicts a Boeing 707-320C

Country of Origin: USA.

Type: Long-range airliner.

Power Plant: Four (-320) 15,800 lb st (7 167 kgp) Pratt & Whitney JT4A-3 or -5 or 16,800 lb st (7 620 kgp) JT4A-9 or 17,500 lb st (7 945 kgp) JT4A-11, (-420) 17,500 lb st (7 945 kgp) Rolls-Royce Conway 508 turbojets (-320B, -320C) 18,000 lb st (8 165 kgp) JT3D-3 or 19,000 lb st (8 618 kgp) JT3D-7 turbofans.

Performance: Max cruising speed (-320, B, C), 600 mph (965 km/h); (-420), 603 mph (970 km/h); best economy cruise (-320B, C), 550 mph (886 km/h); initial rate of climb, (-320B, C), 4,000 ft/min (20,3 m/sec); service ceiling (-320B, C), 39,000 ft (11 885 m); range with max payload (-320), 4,600 mls (7 400 km) (-420), 4,720 mls (7 580 km), (-320B), 6,240 mls (10 040 km), (-320C), 4,300 mls (6 920 km); range with max fuel (-320), 6,790 mls (10 927 km), (-420), 6,955 mls (11 193 km), (-320B, C), 7,475 mls (12 030 km).

Weights: Basic operating (-320), 132,627 lb (60 158 kg), (320B), 141,100 lb (64 000 kg), (-320C), 138,610–146,000 lb (62 872– 66 224 kg); max payload, (-320, -420), 40,053 lb (18 165 kg), (-320B), 53,900 lb (24 448 kg), (-320C passenger), 84,000 lb (38 100 kg), (-320C cargo), 91,390 lb (41 453 kg); max take-off (-320, -420), 312,000 lb (141 520 kg), (-320B, -320C), 333,600 lb (151 315 kg).

Dimensions: Span (-320, -420), 142 ft 5 in (43,4 m), (-320B, -320C), 145 ft 8½ in (44,42 m); length, 152 ft 11 in (45,6 m); height, (-320, -420) 41 ft 8 in (12,7 m), (-320B, -320C) 42 ft 5½ in (12,94 m); wing area, (-320, -420) 2,892 sq ft (268,6 m²), (-320B, -320C) 3,050 sq ft (283,4 m²).

Accommodation: Flight crew of three or four; typical mixed-class seating for 14 plus 135 passengers, and maximum seating for (-320B) 195 or (-320C) 219.

Status: First intercontinental model 707-320 flown on 11 January 1959; first -420 flown on 19 May 1959; first -320B flown on 31 January 1962; first -320C flown on 19 February 1963. Production totals, -320, 69; -420, 37; -320B (to April 1974) 176; -320C (to end 1973) 308 (including military examples).

Notes: The 707-320 was the first intercontinental model of the Boeing 707 jetliner, and the -420 was similar apart from the engines. The -320B introduced turbofan engines and has wing improvements, and the -320C has a side-loading freight door.

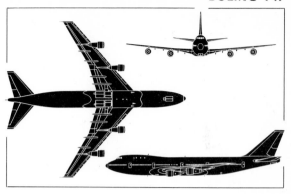

The photograph and silhouette depict the Boeing 747, the former illustrating a 747-257B variant in the markings of the Swiss national airline Swissair

Country of Origin: USA.

Type: Long-range airliner.

Power Plant: Four (-100, -200) 43,500 lb st (19 730 kgp) Pratt & Whitney JT9D-3, 45,000 lb st (20 410 kgp) JT9D-3W, 45,500 lb st (20 635 kgp) JT9D-7 or 47,000 lb st (21 320 kgp) JT9D-7W; (-300) 51,000 lb st (32 135 kgp) General Electric CF6-50D; (-400) 52,000 lb st (23 586 kgp) JT9D-70; (-200 and 747SP) 46,150 lb st (20 950 kgp) JT9D-7A turbofans.

Performance: Max speed (-100), 595 mph (958 km/h) at 30,000 ft (9 150 m), (-200), 608 mph (978 km/h) at 30,000 ft (9 150 m); best economy cruise (-100, -200), 580 mph (935 km/h); cruise ceiling, 45,000 ft (13 705 m); no reserves range with max payload (-100), 3,730 mls (6 000 km), (-200), 4,985 mls (8 023 km), (747SP), over 7,000 mls (11 100 km); range with max fuel, FAR reserves, (-200), 7,090 mls (11 410 km).

Weights: Basic operating (-100), 359,100 lb (162 885 kg), (-200), 367,900 lb (166 876 kg), (747SP), 345,000 lb (156 489 kg), (747SP), 321,000 lb (146 603 kg); max payload (-100), 167,400 lb (75 931 kg), (-200), 158,600 lb (71 940 kg), (747SP), 130,000 lb (58 967 kg); max take-off, (-100), 735,000 lb (333 390 kg),

(-200), 785,000 lb (356 070 kg), (-300, -400), 800,000 lb (362 874 kg), (747SP), 520,000 lb (235 868 kg), (747SP), 650,000 lb (294 835 kg).

Dimensions: Span, 195 ft 8 in (59.64 m), length (all but 747SP), 231 ft 4 in (70,51 m), (747SP), 183 ft (55,78 m); height (all but 747SP), 63 ft 5 in (19,33 m), (747SP), 68 ft 5 in (20,85 m); wing area, 5,500 sq ft (511 m²).

Accommodation: Flight crew of three. Typical mixed-class accommodation (-100, -200, -300, -400), 48 plus 337 passengers, max one-class seating 500 or (747SR) 537 or (747SP) 412.

Status: Prototype (-100) first flown 9 February 1969; first improved -100 flown 24 July 1970; first -200 flown 11 October 1970; first 747F flown 30 November 1971; first 747C flown 23 March 1973; first -300 flown 26 June 1973. First service flown 22 January 1970. Total built and on order (mid-1974), 264.

Notes: The 747-100 and 747-200 differ primarily in weight and power. The 747F is a pure freighter and the 747C is a convertible passenger/freighter, both with upwards-hinged nose. The 747SR has reduced weights for short-haul operation and the 747SP has a shortened fuselage for low-density long-haul operations.

LOCKHEED L-1011 TRISTAR

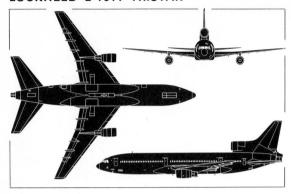

The Lockheed L-1011-1 is shown in the photograph (above) in the colours of Eastern Air Lines, and the silhouette also shows the initial service variant

Country of Origin: USA.

Type: Medium-range airliner.

Power Plant: Three 42,000 lb st (19 050 kgp) Rolls-Royce RB.211-22B turbofans.

Performance: Max cruising speed, 575 mph (925 km/h) = Mach 0·85 at 35,000 ft (10 670 m); best range cruise, 544 mph (875 km/h) = Mach 0·82 at 35,000 ft (10 670 m); initial rate of climb, 2,800 ft/min (14,3 m/sec); service ceiling, 42,000 ft (12 800 m); range with max payload, 2,878 mls (4 629 km); range with max fuel, 4,467 mls (7 189 km) with payload of 40,000 lb (18 145 kg).

Weights: Operating empty, 234,275 lb (106 265 kg); max payload, 90,725 lb (41 150 kg); max take-off, 430,000 lb (195 045 kg).

Dimensions: Span, 155 ft 4 in (47,34 m); length, 178 ft 8 in (54,35 m); height, 55 ft 4 in (16,87 m); wing area, 3,456 sq ft (320,0 m²).

Accommodation: Flight crew of two to four; typical mixed-class accommodation for 256 passengers with maximum high-density one class layout for 400.

Status: First aircraft (no prototype built) flown on 17 November 1970; second in December 1970; third on 17 May 1971, fourth in September 1971 and fifth on 2 December 1971. First flight with engines at 42,000 lb (19 050 kg) thrust rating, 8 September 1971; first flight with initial-standard RB.211-22C engines, 13 March 1972. Full US certification on 14 April 1972; first airline services 26 April 1972 (by Eastern) and 25 June 1972 (by TWA). Total orders (May 1974) 133 plus 71 options.

Notes: The Lockheed TriStar was one of two closely similar aircraft developed during 1966 and 1967 (the other being the McDonnell Douglas DC-10, see page 12) primarily to meet the needs of the US domestic airlines for a large-capacity short- to medium-range airliner, bringing the kind of advanced technology and comfort of the Boeing 747 (page 9) down the scale to shorter routes. With orders from Eastern and TWA, Lockheed launched the TriStar in March 1968, selecting as power plant the new Rolls-Royce RB.211 engine. Other major airlines that ordered the Lockheed tri-jet in the first phase of its development included Delta, Air Canada, Pacific Southwest, All Nippon Airways, LTU, Court Line and British Airways. The L.1011-100 version, with more fuel and higher gross weight, has been ordered by Cathay Pacific and Saudia.

Extra-Large capacity transport

McDONNELL DOUGLAS DC-8 SERIES 60

The silhouette (right) shows the DC-8 Srs 63 and the photograph shows one of these aircraft in service with Saturn Airways, a US supplemental airline

Country of Origin: USA.

Type: Long-range airliner.

Power Plant: Four 17,000 lb st (7 945 kgp) Pratt & Whitney JT3D-1 or 18,000 lb st (8 172 kgp) JT3D-3 or -3B or 19,000 lb (8 618 kgp) JT3D-7 turbofans.

Performance: Max cruising speed (Srs 61), 580 mph (933 km/h); (Srs 62), 586 mph (943 km/h), (Srs 63), 583 mph (938 km/h); best economy cruise (Srs 61), 529 mph (851 km/h), (Srs 62), 523 mph (842 km/h), (Srs 63), 523 mph (842 km/h); initial rate of climb (Srs 61), 2,270 ft/min (11,5 m/sec), (Srs 62), 2,240 ft/min (11,4 m/sec), (Scrs 63), 2,165 ft/min (11,0 m/sec); range with max payload (Srs 61), 3,750 mls (6 035 km), (Srs 62), 6,000 mls (9 640 km), (Srs 63), 4,500 mls (7 240 km).

Weights: Basic operating (Srs 61), 148,897 lb (67 538 kg), (Srs 62), 141,903 lb (64 366 kg), (Srs 63), 153 749 lb (69 739 kg); max payload (Srs 61), 66,665 lb (30 240 kg), (Srs 62), 47,335 lb (21 470 kg), (Srs 63), 67,735 lb (30 719 kg); max take-off, (Srs 61), 325,000 lb (147 415 kg), (Srs 62), 335,000 lb (151 950 kg), (Srs 63), 350,000 lb (158 760 kg).

Dimensions: Span (Srs 61), 142 ft 5 in (53,41 m), (Srs 62, 63),

148 ft 5 in (45,23 m); length (Srs 61, 63), 187 ft 4 in (57,12 m), (Srs 62), 157 ft 5 in (47,98 m); height, 42 ft 5 in (12,92 m); wing area, (Srs 61), 2,884 sq ft (267,9 m²), (Srs 62, 63), 2,927 sq ft (271,9 m²).

Accommodation: Flight crew of three plus two supernumerary seats on flight deck; max seating for up to (Srs 61, 63) 259 passengers or (Srs 62) 189 passengers.

Status: First Srs 61 flown 14 March 1966; first Srs 62 flown 29 August 1966; first Srs 63 flown 10 April 1967. Entered airline service (Srs 61) 25 February 1967, (Srs 62) 22 May 1967, (Srs 63) 27 July 1967. Production totals, Srs 61, 78; Srs 61CF, 10; Srs 62, 52; Srs 62C, F and AF, 16; Srs 63, 41; Srs 63CF, AF and PF, 66. Production ended May 1972.

Notes: The Series 60 DC-8 was introduced in April 1965 in three alternative stretched versions, with different payload/range trade-offs. Convertible passenger/freight versions (CF) of all three, and non-convertible all-freight versions (AF) of the Srs 62 and 63 were also produced. Some Srs 63s were built with structural provision of the 63CF but without the freight door or floor, and designated Srs 63PF.

11

McDONNELL DOUGLAS DC-10

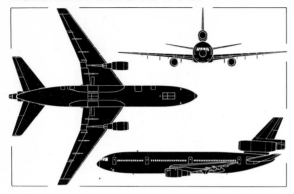

The Series 30 variant of the DC-10 is shown in the silhouette (left) and the photograph (above) illustrates a 30CF operated by the Belgian airline Sabena

Country of Origin: USA.

Type: Long-range airliner.

Power Plant: Three (-10) 40,000 lb st (18 144 kgp) General Electric CF6-6D or (-30) 51,000 lb st (23 134 kgp) CF6-50C or (-40) 48,500 lb st (22 000 kgp) Pratt & Whitney JT9D-20 or 53,000 lb st (24 040 kgp) JT9D-59A turbofans.

Performance: Max cruising speed at 31,000 ft (9 450 m) (-10), 579 mph (932 km/h), (-30), 570 mph (917 km/h), (-40) 561 mph (903 km/h); initial rate of climb (-10), 2,750 ft/min (13,9 m/sec), (-30), 2,320 ft/min (11,8 m/sec), (-40), 2,100 ft/min (10,7 m/sec); service ceiling (-10), 35,000 ft (10 670 m), (-30), 32,700 ft (9 965 m), (-40), 31,200 ft (9 510 m); range with max payload (-10), 2,430 mls (3,910 km), (-30), 4,272 mls (6 875 km); (-40) 4,200 mls (6 600 km); range with max fuel (-10), 5,180 mls (8 335 km), (-30), 6,910 mls (11 118 km), (-40), 6,678 mls (10 747 km).

Weights: Basic operating (-10), 231,779 lb (105 142 kg), (-30), 263,087 lb (119 334 kg), (-40), 267,650 lb (121 403 kg); max payload (-10), 103,221 lb (46 820 kg), (-30), 104 913 lb (47 587 kg), (-40), 100,350 lb (45 518 kg), (CF), 147,000 lb (66 678 kg);

max take-off (-10) 430,000 lb (195 045 kg), (-30, -40), 555,000 lb (251 744 kg).

Dimensions: Span (-10), 155 ft 4 in (47,37 m), (-30, -40), 165 ft 4 in (40,42 m); length (-10) 181 ft 5 in (55,3 m), (-30), 181 ft 7 in (55,35 m), (-40), 182 ft 3 in (55,55 m); height 58 ft 1 in (17,7 m); wing area (-10), 3,861 sq ft (358,7 m²), (-30, -40), 3,921 sq ft (364,3 m²).

Accommodation: Flight crew of three and standard mixed-class layout for 48 plus 222 six- and eight-abreast or up to a maximum of 380 in one-class high density layout.

Status: First DC-10 (-10) flown on 29 August 1970; second and third examples flown on 24 October and 23 December 1970; first -40 flown on 28 February 1972; first -30 flown 21 June 1972; first 30CF flown 28 February 1973. Total orders by spring 1974 -10, 95; -10CF, 8; -30, 74; -30CF, 8; -40, 29.

Notes: The DC-10 was launched in 1968 with the backing of orders from American and United Airlines and entered service with both these companies in August 1971. The CF convertible passenger/ freight versions have a side-loading cargo door, a freight floor and cargo handling system.

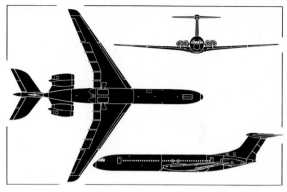

The photograph depicts a Standard VC10 in the livery of Gulfair, the airline of the Arab Emirates in the Gulf area, the silhouette showing the Super VC10

Country of Origin: United Kingdom.

Type: Long haul airliner.

Power Plant: Four 20,370 lb st (9 240 kgp) Rolls-Royce Conway RCo 42 (VC10) or 21,800 lb st (9 888 kgp) RCo 43D Mk 550 (Super VC10) turbofans.

Performance (VC10): High speed cruise, 568 mph (914 km/h) at 25,000 ft (7 620 m) long range cruise, 550 mph (886 km/h) at 38,000 ft (11 600 m); range with max payload, 5,040 mls (8 115 km); range with max fuel, 6,070 mls (9 765 km).

Performance (Super VC10): High speed cruise, 581 mph (935 km/h) at 31,000 ft (9 450 m); long range cruise, 550 mph (886 km/h) at 38,000 ft (11 600 m); range with max payload, 4,720 mls (7 600 km); range with max fuel, 7,128 mls (11 470 km).

Weights (VC10): Operating weight empty, 146,979 lb (66 675 kg); max take-off, 314,000 lb (142 430 kg); max payload, 38,532 lb (17 480 kg); max landing, 216,000 lb (97 976 kg).

Weights (Super VC10): Operating weight empty, 158,594 lb (71 940 kg); max take-off, 335,000 lb (151 950 kg); max payload, 60,321 lb (27 360 kg); max landing, 237,000 lb (107 500 kg).

Dimensions: Span, 146 ft 2 in (44,55 m); length (VC10), 158 ft 8 in (48,36 m); length (Super VC10), 171 ft 8 in (52,32 m); height 39 ft 6 in (12,04 m); wing area (VC10), 2,851 sq ft (264,9 m²), wing area (Super VC10), 2,932 sq ft (272,4 m²).

Accommodation: Basic flight crew of three, with provision for navigator, and seating for maximum of 151 (VC10) or 174 (Super VC10) passengers.

Status: VC10 prototype flown on 29 June 1962. First production VC10 flew 8 November 1962. First Super VC10 flew 7 May 1964. Production completed in 1970, 54 built including prototype.

Notes: Initial production version of Standard VC10 for BOAC (now British Airways) was Model 1101, of which 12 were delivered. Ghana Airways bought two Model 1102 and BUA (now British Caledonian) bought three Model 1103, with large freight loading door, in addition to the original prototype converted to Model 1109 and first used by Laker Airways. BOAC acquired 17 Super VC10s as Model 1151s and East African Airways bought five Model 1153s. During 1974, British Airways Overseas Division disposed of its 11 Standard VC10s, selling four to Gulf Air and transferring others to the European Division. Fourteen Model 1106s for the RAF combined features of the VC10 and Super VC10.

BAC/AEROSPATIALE CONCORDE

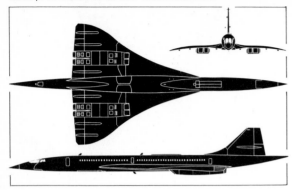

The production standard of Concorde is shown in the silhouette and the photograph shows the first production model, Concorde 201, in the markings of Air France

Country of Origin: Britain and France.

Type: Medium range supersonic airliner.

Power Plant: Four 38,050 lb st (17 260 kgp) Rolls-Royce/SNECMA Olympus 593 Mk 610 turbojets with silencers and reversers.

Performance: Max cruising speed, 1,450 mph (2 333 km/h) at 54,500 ft (16 600 m); best range cruise, Mach 2·05; service ceiling about 60,000 ft (18 288 m); range with max payload, 3,050 mls (4 900 km); range with max fuel 4,490 mls (7 215 km).

Weights: Basic operating, 170,000 lb (77 110 kg); typical payload, 26,500 lb (12 000 kg); max take-off, 400,000 lb (181 400 kg); max landing, 240,000 lb (108 860 kg).

Dimensions: Span, 84 ft 0 in (25,60 m); length, 203 ft 11½ in (62,17 m); height, 40 ft 0 in (12,19 m); wing area 3,856 sq ft (358,25 m²).

Accommodation: Flight crew of three (two pilots and an engineer) plus one supernumerary; standard cabin arrangements for up to 128 three-abreast, or up to 144 in high density layout.

Status: First prototype (001) flown on 2 March 1969; second prototype (002) flown on 9 April 1969; first preproduction (01)

flown on 17 December 1971; second preproduction (02) flown on 10 January 1973; first production (201) flown on 6 December 1973; second production (202) flown on 13 February 1974.

Notes: Concorde development as a joint Anglo-French venture is based on an agreement dated 29 November 1962, which covered the development and construction of the first six airframes (including two for static testing). Subsequent inter-government agreements have funded 16 production aircraft and the purchase of long-lead time materials for another six. First firm orders were placed in late 1972, by British Airways (BOAC) for five and by Air France for four. In addition, CAAC of China has a preliminary purchase agreement for three and Iranair a similar agreement to buy two. Production aircraft, expected to enter service in 1976, have the characteristics given above, and Concorde 02 is similar although flown at the lower weight of 324,000 lb (146 964 kg). The two prototypes had an overall length of 184 ft 6 in (56,24 m), design gross weight of 326,000 lb (148 000 kg) and lower rated engines. The first preproduction example had the fuselage lengthened by 8 ft 6½ in (2,60 m), revised wing configuration and other changes but lacked the long rear fuselage extension of the production model.

Large capacity transport

BOEING 707-120 AND 720

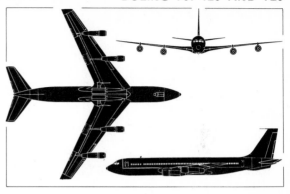

Shown in the silhouette is the Boeing 707-120B while the photograph shows the Boeing 720B (707-047B) with a slightly shorter fuselage

Country of Origin: USA.

Type: Medium-range jet airliner.

Power Plant: Four (-120) 13,500 lb st (6 123 kgp) Pratt & Whitney JT3C-6 or (-220) 15,800 lb st (7 167 kgp) JT4A-3 or (-720) 12,000 lb st (5 448 kgp) JT3C-7 or 13,000 lb st (5 902 kgp) JT3C-12 turbojets or (-120B, 720B) 17,000 lb st (7 718 kgp) JT3D-1 or 18,000 lb st (8 165 kgp) JT3D-3 turbofans.

Performance: Max cruising speed at 25,000 ft (7 620 m), (-120), 571 mph (919 km/h), (-720) 587 mph (945 km/h), (-120B) 618 mph (995 km/h); best economy cruise (-120) 549 mph (884 km/h), (-720, -120B), 557 mph (897 km/h); initial rate of climb, (-120, -720), 2,400 ft/min (12,2 m/sec), (-120B), 5,050 ft/min (25,6 m/sec); service ceiling (-120), 37,500 ft (11 430 m), (120B), 42,000 ft (12 800 m), (-720) 40,000 ft (12 200 m); no reserves range with max payload, (-120), 3,217 mls (5 177 km), (-720), 4,235 mls (6 820 km), (-120B), 4,235 mls (6 820 km); no reserves range with max fuel, (-120), 4,650 mls (7 485 km), (-720) 5,240 mls (8 430 km), (-120B), 6,215 mls (10 000 km).

Weights: Basic operating, (-120), 118,000 lb (53 520 kg), (-720) 110,800 lb (50 260 kg), (-120B) 124,585 lb (56 511 kg); max pay-

load (-120), 52,000 lb (23 590 kg), (-720), 28,200 lb (12 790 kg), (-120B), 45,515 lb (20 600 kg); max take-off (-120), 257,000 lb (116 575 kg), (-720), 229,000 lb (103 870 kg), (-120B), 258,000 lb (117 027 kg).

Dimensions: Span, 130 ft 10 in (39,87 m); length, (120, 220), 144 ft 6 in (44,04 m), (-720B), 136 ft 9 in (41,68 m); height (-120, -220, -120B), 42 ft (12,80 m), (-720, -720B), 41 ft 7 in. (12,67 m); wing area (-120, -220, -720), 2,433 sq ft (226,04 m²), (-120B, -720B), 2,521 sq ft (234,2 m²).

Accommodation: Flight screw of three or four; typical mixed-class accommodation for (-120, -220, -120B) 30 plus 95 or maximum one-class of 181, (-720, -720B) 26 plus 98.

Status: Model 367-80 prototype first flown on 15 July 1954; first -120 flown on 20 December 1957; first -220 flown on 11 June 1959; first 720 flown on 23 November 1959; first -120B flown on 22 June 1960; first 720B flown on 6 October 1960. Production, -120, 63; -220, 5; -120B, 78; -720, 65; -720B, 89.

Notes: The 707-120 was intended primarily for US domestic operation. The 720 was a shorter-fuselage "lightweight" version (sometimes known as 707-020).

15

BOEING 727

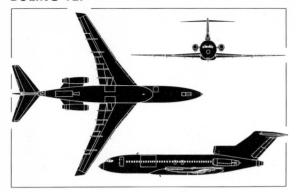

The photograph (above) depicts a Boeing 727-235 in National Airways colours while the silhouette (left) shows the short-fuselage 727-100C

Country of Origin: USA.

Type: Medium-range airliner.

Power Plant: Three (-100) 14,000 lb st (6 350 kg) Pratt & Whitney JT8D-1 or -7 or 14,500 lb st (6 577 kgp) JT8D-9 or (-200, Advanced -200) JT8D-9 or 15,000 lb st (6 804 kgp) JT8D-11 or 15,500 lb st (7 030 kgp) JT8D-15 or 16,000 lb st (7 257 kgp) JT8D-17 turbofans.

Performance: Max cruising speed (-100), 607 mph (977 km/h) at 21,000 ft (6 400 m), (-200), 599 mph (964 km/h) at 24,700 ft (7 530 m); economy cruise, 570 mph (917 km/h) at 30,000 ft (9 145 m), initial rate of climb (-100), 2,900 ft/min (14,7 m/sec), (-200), 2,600 ft/min (13,2 m/sec); service ceiling (-100), 36,500 ft (11 125 m), (-200) 33,500 ft (10 210 m); range with max payload (-100), 2,025 mls (3 260 km); (-200), 1,845 mls (2 970 km), (Advanced -200), over 2,800 mls (4 500 km).

Weights: Operating weight empty (-100), 89,000 lb (40 370 kg) (-100C), 92,500 lb (41 957 kg), (Advanced -200), 100,000 lb (45 360 kg); max payload (-100), 35,900 lb (16 284 kg), (-100C) 43,800 lb (19 867 kg), (Advanced -200), 42,800 lb (19 414 kg); max take-off (-100), 169,000 lb (76 655 kg), (-200), 184,200 lb (83 550 kg), (Advanced -200), 207,500 lb (94 120 kg).

Dimensions: Span, 108 ft 0 in (32,92 m); length (-100), 133 ft 2 in (40,59 m), (-200, Advanced), 153 ft 2 in (46,69 m); height, 34 ft 0 in (10,36 m); wing area, 1,700 sq ft (157,9 m²).

Accommodation: Flight crew of three; typical mixed-class accommodation for (-100) 28 plus 66 passengers, (-200) 20 plus 114; max one-class seating for (-100) 125 or (-200) 189.

Status: Prototype 727-100 first flown on 9 February 1963; first 727C/QC flown on 30 December 1965; first 727-200 flown on 27 July 1967; first Advanced -200 flown on 3 March 1972. Entered airline service 2 January 1964. Total on order (May 1974); Srs 100. 571; Srs 200, 577.

Notes: Model 100 and Model 200 differ primarily in fuselage length, both being available with side-loading freight doors and convertible (C) or quick-change (QC) interiors. The Advanced -200 was announced in May 1971 with a gross weight of 190,500 lb (86 410 kg), noise reduction features and other improvements. A 207,500 lb (94 120 kg) version made its first flight on 26 July 1973 with JT8D-15 engines and the first example with JT8D-17 engines was to fly in March 1974.

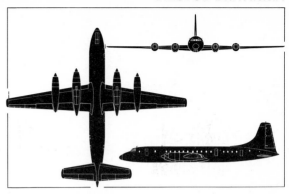

The photograph (above) illustrates a Britannia 312 in service with Monarch Airlines and the silhouette (right) also shows the long-fuselage Srs 300 version

Country of Origin: United Kingdom.
Type: Medium- to long-range passenger airliner.
Power Plant: Four (Srs 100) 3,780 shp Bristol Proteus 705 or (Srs 310) 4,450 shp Proteus 765 turboprops.
Performance: Max cruising speed (Srs 100), 363 mph (584 km/h), (Srs 310), 397 mph (639 km/h); best economy cruise (Srs 100), 329 mph (529 km/h), (Srs 310), 357 mph (575 km/h); range with max payload (Srs 100), 1,970 mls (3 170 km), (Srs 310), 3,100 st mls (4 990 km); range with max fuel (Srs 100), 2,710 mls (4 360 km), (Srs 310), 3,310 st mls (5 327 km).
Weights: Empty equipped (Srs 100), 88,300 lb (40 050 kg), (Srs 310), 93,500 lb (42 410 kg); max payload (Srs 100), 24,700 lb (11 200 kg), (Srs 310), 34,500 lb (15 650 kg); max take-off (Srs 100), 155,000 lb (70 306 kg), (Srs 310), 185,000 lb (83 915 kg).
Dimensions: Span, 142 ft 3 in (43,36 m); length, (Srs 100), 114 ft 0 in (31,69 m), (Srs 310), 124 ft 3 in (37,87 m); height (Srs 100), 36 ft 9 in (11,20 m), (Srs 310), 37 ft 6 in (11,43 m); wing area, 2,075 sq ft (192,76 m²).
Accommodation: Typical layouts for (Srs 100) 90–115 or (Srs 310) 110–139 passengers in one-class layouts.

Status: Prototypes first flown on (Srs 100) 16 August 1952 and (Srs 310) 31 December 1956. Production comprised 15 Series 102 and 45 Srs 300/310, plus 23 Srs 250 for military use, assembled in Belfast by Shorts.
Notes: The Bristol Britannia was evolved to a BOAC specification for a Medium Range Empire (MRE) passenger transport, outlined soon after the end of the war. The initial production version was superseded by the long-fuselage Srs 300, and the similar Srs 310 which had additional fuel tankage. After service with BOAC and a few other major operators, Britannias passed into the hands of the charter airlines and gave long and useful service in this rôle, but by 1974 they had been almost totally replaced by jet transports and only a handful remained in airline use, primarily in the UK. The RAF, however, continues to operate its fleet of Britannia 250s, these being in effect Srs 100s with special provision for freight carrying, and about 20 are operated by Nos 99 and 511 Squadrons based at RAF Brize Norton. Two versions are in use, with only minor differences, designated Britannia C Mk 1 and C Mk 2. Among the final commercial users of the Britannia were Aer Turas, Monarch and Cubana.

CANADAIR CL-44

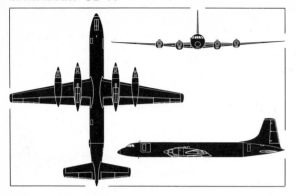

Both photograph and silhouette show the Canadair CL-44, the former showing the unusual swing-tail feature of this cargo and passenger transport

Country of Origin: Canada.

Type: Long-range cargo and passenger airliner.

Power Plant: Four 5,730 hp Rolls-Royce Tyne 515/10 turboprops.

Performance (CL-44D): Cruising speed, 386 mph (621 km/h) at 20,000 ft (6 100 m) at a weight of 190,000 lb (86 180 kg); range with max payload, 3,260 mls (5 245 km); range with max fuel, 5,587 mls (8 990 km) with payload of 35,564 lb (16 132 kg).

Weights (CL-44D): Operating weight empty, 88,952 lb (40 348 kg) max payload, 63,272 lb (28 725 kg); max take-off, 210,000 lb (95 250 kg); max landing, 165,000 lb (74 843 kg).

Dimensions: Span, 142 ft 3½ in (43,37 m); length (CL-44D) 136 ft 10¾ in (41,73 m); length (CL-44J) 151 ft 10 in (46,28 m); height, 38 ft 8 in (11,80 m); wing area, 2,075 sq ft (192,76 m²).

Accommodation: Flight crew of three. Accommodation for up to 214 passengers in CL-44J and up to 178 in CL-44D, or freight on pallets or individual loads.

Status: First flight of CL-44D-4 (derived from military CL-44D) on 16 November 1960. Airline deliveries began May 1961 and completed January 1965. First flight of CL-44J (Canadair 400) 8 November 1965. First flight of CL-44-O, 26 November 1969. Total production (including military versions, some of which have later entered commercial service) 39.

Notes: The CL-44D was developed in Canada from the Bristol Britannia, using basically the same wing and tail unit with a modified fuselage and different engines. Twelve were built for the RCAF as CC-106 Yukons, followed by the CL-44D-4 commercial version with a swing-tail to permit straight-in freight loading. Initial customers were Flying Tiger, Slick, Seaboard and Loftleidir. The last production aircraft was a CL-44J with fuselage extended by 15 ft (4,57 m), and three others were converted to this standard, sometimes called Canadair 400. One CL-44-O (converted by Conroy Aircraft) has an oversize fuselage cross-section and is used to carry outsize loads. Principal users in 1974 were Transmeridian, Trans Mediterranean, British Air Ferries and National Air Charters of Zambia (using two examples leased from Bahamas International). The CL-44s and Canadair 400s previously used by Loftleidir had been acquired by Cargolux and were being used exclusively for freighting. A few CC-106 Yukons, upon being phased out of service by the Canadian Armed Forces, have also been purchased for airline use, primarily in South America.

Large capacity transport

DASSAULT-BREGUET MERCURE

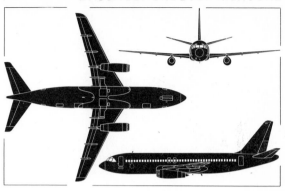

The photograph and silhouette both depict the Dassault-Breguet Mecure in its only production configuration, as operated by the French airline Air Inter

Country of Origin: France.

Type: Short-range airliner.

Power Plant: Two 15,500 lb st (7 030 kgp) Pratt & Whitney JT8D-15 turbofans.

Performance: Max cruising speed, 579 mph (932 km/h at 20,000 ft (6 100 m); best economy cruise, 533 mph (858 km/h) at 30,000 ft (9 145 m); initial rate of climb, 3,300 ft/min (16,76 m/sec) at 100,000 lb (45 359 kg) weight; range with max payload, 466 mls (750 km); range with max fuel, 1,025 mls (1 650 km).

Weights: Basic operating: 68,563 lb (31 000 kg); max payload, 35,274 lb (16 000 kg), max take-off, 119,227 lb (54 500 kg).

Dimensions: Span 100 ft 3 in (30,55 m); length 114 ft 3½ in (34,84 m); height, 37 ft 3¼ in (11,36 m); wing area 1,249 sq ft (116,0 m²).

Accommodation: Flight crew of two and typical mixed-class accommodation for 155.

Status: Prototypes 01 and 02 flown on 28 May 1971 and 7 September 1972 respectively. First production aircraft flown on 17 July 1973. Certification on 12 February 1974, first deliveries March 1974, first service 4 June 1974 (on French domestic routes from Paris, by Air Inter).

Notes: The Mercure was developed as a Dassault-Breguet private venture and the company's largest civil aircraft project, with the French government making a contribution to the launching costs. Other contributions, representing about 30 per cent of the total, came from Italy (Aeritalia), Spain (CASA), Belgium (SABCA), Switzerland (F+W) and Canada (Canadair), each of these companies participating in manufacture in proportion to their investment. The first prototype flew with JT8D-11 engines, a shorter fuselage and flat tailplane, being updated to the production standard in September 1971. Initial orders for this variant came from Air Inter; for 10, this being the only customer up to early 1974. Deliveries had been scheduled to begin in January 1974 following certification in November 1973, but this objective was not achieved, and full clearance of the Mercure to permit operation in Cat III weather conditions was delayed until September 1974. Dassault has also studied, primarily for Air France, a Mercure 200 with 16,000 lb st (7 250 kgp) JT8D-17 engines and higher gross weight, and a Super Mercure with SNECMA/GE CFM-56 engines but these appear unlikely to go ahead.

HAWKER SIDDELEY TRIDENT

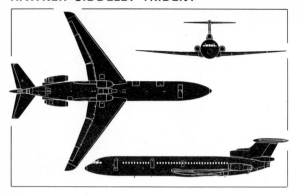

Shown in the photograph (above) is a Trident 2E in Chinese colours, while the silhouette shows the Trident 3B with its additional engine in the rear fuselage

Country of Origin: United Kingdom.

Type: Short- and medium-range airliner.

Power Plant: Three (1) 9,850 lb st (4 468 kgp Rolls-Royce Spey 505-5 or (1E) 11,400 lb st (5 170 kgp) Spey 511-5 or (2E, 3) 11,960 lb st (5 425 kgp) Spey 512-5W turbofans plus (3 only) one 5,250 lb st (2 381 kgp) RB.162-86 turbojet.

Performance: Max cruising speed (1), 606 mph (975 km/h), (2E), 596 mph (960 km/h), (3), 568 mph (913 km/h), (Super 3), 562 mph (904 km/h); long-range cruise (1), 540 mph (869 km/h), (2E), 505 mph (812 km/h), (3), 535 mph (862 km/h), (Super 3), 541 mph (870 km/h); no-reserves range with max payload (1), 2,040 mls (3 283 km), (2E), 3,155 mls (5 078 km), (3), 2,060 mls (3 320 km), (Super 3), 2,290 mls (3 687 km); no reserves range with max fuel (1), 2,405 mls (3 870 km), (2E), 3,558 mls (5 726 km), (3), 2 870 mls (4 615 km), (Super 3), 2,735 mls (4 400 km).

Weights: Basic operating (1), 67,500 lb (30,617 kg), (2E), 73,250 lb (33 250 kg), (3), 82,250 lb (37 310 kg), (Super), 82,420 lb (37 385 kg); max payload (1), 22,400 lb (10 160 kg), (2E), 29,600 lb (13 426 kg), (3), 35,250 lb (15 990 kg), (Super), 35,350 lb (16 034 kg); max take-off (1), 115,000 lb (52 163 kg),

143,500 lb (65 090 kg), (3 and Super), 158,000 lb (71 670 kg).

Dimensions: Span (1), 89 ft 11 in (27,41 m), (1E), 95 ft (28,95 m), (2, 3 and Super), 98 ft 0 in (29,9 m); (1, 2), 114 ft 9 in (34,98 m), (3 and Super), 131 ft 2 in (40 m); height (1, 2), 27 ft 0 in (8,23 m), (3 and Super), 28 ft 3 in (8,6 m); wing area (1), 1,358 sq ft (126,2 m²), (2, 3 and Super), 1,461 sq ft (135,7 m²).

Accommodation: Flight crew of three and maximum seating for (1) 103 or (2) 149 or (3 and Super) 180.

Status: First Trident 1 (no prototypes built) flown on 9 January 1962; first 2E flown on 27 July 1967; first 3 flown on 11 December 1969 (first flight with RB.162 booster in operation, 22 March 1970). Production and sales (to early 1974), Trident 1C, 24; 1E, 15; 2E, 50; 3B, 26; Super 3B, 2.

Notes: The (originally DH121) Trident won a BEA design competition for a short-haul jet in 1958, and the three principal versions built for BEA (now British Airways) were the Trident 1C, the 2E or Trident Two and 3B or Trident Three. The 2E was selected by the Chinese Government as new equipment for CAAC, which has ordered 33 up to 1974, plus two Super 3Bs, the latter being longer-range versions of the basic 3B.

The photograph shows a standard Ilyushin Il-62 as operated by CSA Czechoslovak Airlines, and the silhouette depicts the more recent Il-62M-200 version

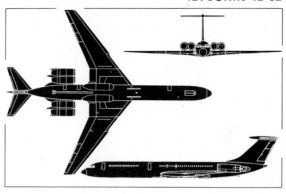

Country of Origin: Soviet Union.
NATO Code Name: *Classic.*
Type: Long-range jet airliner.
Power Plant: Four 23,150 lb st (10 500 kgp) Kuznetsov NK-8-4 or (Il-62M-200) 25,350 lb. st (11 500 kgp) Soloviev D-30KU turbofans.
Performance: Cruising speed (Il-62), 510–560 mph (820–900 km/h), (-200), 528–560 mph (850–900 km/h) at 33,000–39,400 ft (10 000–12 000 m); initial rate of climb (Il-62), 3,540 ft/min (18,0 m/sec); range with max payload (Il-62), 4,160 mls (6 700 km), (-200), 4,970 mls (8 000 km).
Weights: Basic operating (Il-62), 153,000 lb (69 400 kg); max payload (Il-62 and -200), 50,700 lb (23 000 kg); max take-off, (Il-62) 357,000 lb (162 000 kg), (-200) 363,760 lb (165 000 kg).
Dimensions: (Il-62 and -200), span, 141 ft 9 in (43,20 m); length 174 ft 3½ in (53,12 m); height 40 ft 6¼ in (12,35 m); wing area, 3,010 sq ft (279,6 m²).
Accommodation: Flight crew of five (two pilots, navigator, radio operator and flight engineer, plus provision for two supernumerary crew. Typical one-class accommodation for 168 or 186 passengers

six-abreast or (-200) up to 198 passengers six-abreast.
Status: Prototype first flown January 1963; airline service with Aeroflot began 15 September 1967. Production total (estimated) 200–300 by 1973.
Notes: The Ilyushin Il-62 was the Soviet Union's first long-range jet airliner developed specifically for commercial use, and is the only aircraft other than the British VC-10 to feature four rear-mounted engines. In the prototype, these engines were 16,535 lb st (7 500 kgp) Lyulka AL-7 turbojets, fitted pending availability of the NK-8 turbofans required for the production aircraft. Five aircraft were used in the lengthy development programme, which occupied over four years and resulted in considerable modification to the wing profile to achieve satisfactory stalling characteristics. The Il-62 entered service on Aeroflot's transatlantic routes and is used on other long-range routes inside and outside the Soviet Union. Examples have also been supplied to CSA (4), Interflug (3), LOT (2), CAAC (5), and Egypt Air (3). The Il-62M-200 appeared in 1971 and has more powerful engines and a high-density layout within the same overall dimensions. This version is expected to become Aeroflot's standard long-range airliner in the later 'seventies.

McDONNELL DOUGLAS DC-8 SERIES 10-50

Large capacity transport

Shown in the photograph is a DC-8 Srs 55 in service with SAS, while the silhouette also shows the Srs 50 version, the first of the DC-8s to have turbofan engines

Country of Origin: USA.

Type: Long-range airliner.

Power Plant: Four (Srs 20, 30) 15,500 lb st (7 167 kgp) Pratt & Whitney JT4A-3 or -5 or 16,500 lb st (7 620 kgp) JT4A-9 or -10 or 17,500 lb st (7 945 kgp) JT4A-11 or -12 or (Srs 40) 17,500 lb st (7 945 kgp) Rolls-Royce Conway 509 turbojets; (Srs 50) 17,000 lb st (7 945 kgp) Pratt & Whitney JT3D-1 or 18,000 lb st (8 172 kgp) JT3D-3 or -38 turbofans.

Performance: Max cruising speed (Srs 20), 579 mph (932 km/h), (Srs 30), 592 mph (952 km/h), (Srs 40), 586 mph (943 km/h), (Srs 50), 580 mph (933 km/h); initial rate of climb (Srs 20), 2,650 ft/min (13,4 m/sec); no-reserves range with max payload (Srs 20), 4,655 mls (7 490 km), (Srs 30), 5,405 mls (8 690 km), (Srs 40), 5,590 mls (9 000 km), (Srs 50), 6,185 mls (9 950 km).

Weights: Basic operating (Srs 20), 127,056 lb (57 632 kg), (Srs 30), 133,803 lb (60 692 kg), (Srs 40), 132,425 lb (60 068 kg), (Srs 50), 132,325 lb (60 020 kg); max weight limited payload (Srs 20), 34,500 lb (15 650 kg), (Srs 30), 43,800 lb (19 867 kg), (Srs 40), 41,000 lb (18 597 kg), (Srs 50), 46,500 lb (21 092 kg) (Srs 50F), 95,300 lb (43 227 kg); max take-off (Srs 20), 276,000 lb (125 190 kg), (Srs 30, 40), 315,000 lb (142 880 kg); (Srs 50, 50F), 325,000 lb (147 415 kg).

Dimensions: Span 142 ft 5 in (43,41 m); length 150 ft 6 in (45,87 m); height 42 ft 4 in (12,91 m); wing area (early) 2,773 sq ft (257,6 m²), (extended leading edge) 2,868 sq ft (266,5 m²).

Accommodation: Flight crew of three plus two supernumerary seats on flight deck; typical mixed class accommodation for 132 and up to 179 seats in one-class layouts.

Status: First DC-8 (Srs 10) flown on 30 May 1958; first Srs 20 flown 29 November 1958; first Srs 30 flown 21 February 1959; first Srs 40 flown 23 July 1959; first Srs 50 flown 20 December 1960. Entered airline service 18 September 1959. Production quantities: prototype (later Srs 50) 1; Srs 10, 28 (21 later converted to Srs 20 and 11 to Srs 50); Srs 20, 34; Srs 30, 57 (3 later converted to Srs 50), Srs 40, 32; Srs 50, 87; Srs 50F, 54 (ended 1972).

Notes: The DC-8 was the Douglas competitor for the Boeing 707 (see page 8) launched in 1955. A 3-ft (0,91-m) span increase was introduced on the 30th DC-8 and later retrofitted to all early models, and a 4 per cent increase in wing chord at the leading edge came in on the 148th DC-8 and was retrofitted to some.

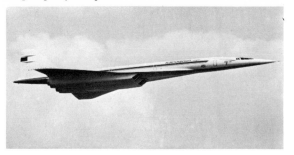

Both the photograph and the silhouette depict the production version of the Tupolev Tu-144, representing a major design change from the prototype

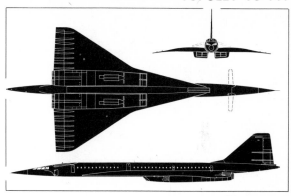

Country of Origin: Soviet Union.
NATO Code Name: *Charger.*
Type: Supersonic airliner.
Power Plant: Four 44,000 lb st (20 000 kgp) Kuznetsov NK-144 turbofans with reheat.
Performance: Max operating speed, up to 1,550 mph (2 500 km/h), 2·35 at altitudes up to 62,300 ft (19 000 m); normal cruising speed, 1,430 mph (2 300 km/h); operational ceiling, 62,300 ft (19 000 m); range, 3,245–3,510 mls (6 000–6 500 km).
Weights: Basic operating: 187,000 lb (85 000 kg); max payload, 30,800 lb (14 000 kg); max fuel load, 176,370 lb (80 000 kg); max take-off, 396,820 lb (180 000 kg).
Dimensions: Span, 94 ft 6 in (28,8 m); length, 211 ft 5 in (64,45 m); height, 42 ft 0 in (12,8 m); wing area, 4,720 sq ft (438 m²).
Accommodation: Flight crew of three (two pilots and a flight engineer); basic layout in cabin provides 140 passenger seats in three sections including 11 three-abreast and the remainder five-abreast.
Status: First prototype flown on 31 December 1968, followed by two other prototypes in the same configuration. First production

example flown in 1972.
Notes: The Tu-144 was the world's first supersonic transport to fly, some two months ahead of the Concorde (see page 14) which it closely resembled in general configuration. The first supersonic flight was made on 5 June 1969. The prototypes were smaller than the production model for which data are given above, having a span of 90 ft 8½ in (27,65 m) and length of 196 ft 10 in (60,0 m), a weight of 395,000 lb (179 150 kg) and engines rated at 38,580 lb (17 500 kg) thrust each. The production model showed many new features including a heavily-modified wing planform and profile, paired instead of individual engine nacelles, a completely new undercarriage and the installation of retractable canard surfaces or foreplanes just behind the cockpit. During test flying, the Tu-144 is reported to have achieved a speed of Mach 2·4. Introduction into Aeroflot service, on domestic and international routes, is expected in 1975. Up to 140 passengers can be carried, although the example exhibited at Paris had less than 100 seats, which may represent the initial service standard. Containerised baggage and freight are accommodated in a compartment behind the passenger seating, there being no underfloor holds.

TUPOLEV TU-154

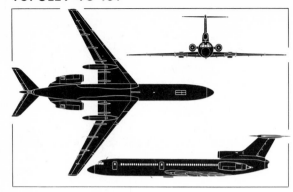

The photograph and silhouette show the standard Tupolev Tu-154, the former showing one of eight acquired by Egyptair at the end of 1973

Country of Origin: Soviet Union.
NATO Code Name: *Careless.*
Type: Medium-range turbofan airliner.
Power Plant: Three 20,950 lb st (9 500 kgp) Kuznetsov NK-8-2 turbofans.
Performance: Max cruising speed, 605 mph (975 km/h) at 31,150 ft (9 500 m); best economy cruise, 560 mph (900 km/h) at 36,000 ft (11 000 m); long-range cruise, 528 mph (850 km/h) at 36,000 ft; operating ceiling, 40,000 ft (12 000 m); range with max payload, 2,360 mls (3 800 km); range with max fuel, 4,287 mls (6 900 km) (with optional centre-wing tanks) with 70 passengers.
Weights: Operating empty, 95,900 lb (43 500 kg); max payload, 44,090 lb (20 000 kg); max take-off, 198,416 lb (90 000 kg).
Dimensions: Span, 123 ft 2½ in (37,55 m); length, 157 ft 1¾ in (47,90 m); height, 37 ft 4¾ in (11,40 m); wing area, 2,169 sq ft (201,45 m²).
Accommodation: Flight crew of three (two pilots and flight engineer) with optional provision for navigator, and typical mixed-class accommodation for 24 plus 104 passengers or typical all-tourist class accommodation for 158 passengers or max high-density accommodation for 164 passengers.
Status: First of six prototype and pre-production aircraft flown on 4 October 1968. Initial delivery (seventh aircraft) August 1970; route-proving began in August 1971; regular scheduled passenger services began on 9 February 1972.
Notes: The Tu-154 was developed as a successor for the Tu-104, Il-18 and An-10 on Aeroflot routes and followed the successful configuration of the Tu-134 (see page 41). Comparable in size and capacity with the Boeing 727-200 (see page 16), the Tu-154 is considerably more powerful, indicating the emphasis placed by Aeroflot on good field performance; in common with most Soviet commercial types, it can operate safely from airfields with category B surfaces, including packed earth and gravel. A stretched version, the Tu-154M, with uprated NK-8 turbofans and up to 240 seats, was reported under development in 1973. In addition to about 80 in service with Aeroflot by the end of that year. CSA had ordered seven, Balkan Bulgarian had four, Malev had three, Egyptair had ordered eight and Aviogenex of Yugoslavia planned to acquire two. Further export sales were being discouraged in 1974 to give priority to Aeroflot's needs.

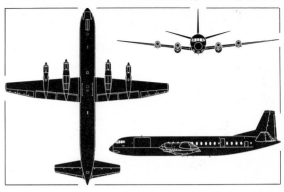

An ex-Air Canada Vanguard is shown in the photograph and the silhouette shows the Merchantman freighting version used by British Airways

Country of Origin: United Kingdom.

Type: Medium range turboprop airliner.

Power Plant: Four Rolls-Royce Tyne (V.951 and V.953) 506 turboprops of 4,985 ehp each, or (V.952) 512 turboprops of 5,545 ehp each.

Performance: (V.952), High speed cruise, 425 mph (684 km/h) at 20,000 ft (6 100 m) ; long-range cruise, 420 mph (676 km/h) at 25,000 ft (7 620 m) ; initial rate of climb, 2,700 ft/min (13,7 m/sec) ; service ceiling, 30,000 ft (9 145 m) ; range with max payload (no reserves), 1,830 mls (2 945 km) at 25,000 ft (7 620 m) ; range with max fuel, 3,100 mls (4 990 km) at 25,000 ft (7 620 m).

Weights: (V.952). Empty equipped, 82,500 lb (37 422 kg) ; max payload, 37,000 lb (16 785 kg) ; max take-off, 146,500 lb (66 448 kg) ; max landing, 130,500 lb (61 238 kg).

Dimensions: Wing span, 118 ft 7 in (36,15 m) ; length, 122 ft 10½ in (37,45 m) ; height, 34 ft 11 in (10,64 m) ; wing area, 1,529 sq ft (142,0 m²).

Accommodation: Three-man flight deck and up to 139 passengers, depending on layout.

Status: Prototype (V.950) flown on 20 January 1959. First V.951 flown on 22 April 1959, certificated on 2 December 1960 and entered service with BEA on 1 March 1961. First V.952 flown on 21 May 1960 and first V.953 flown on 1 May 1961. Total of 43 built.

Notes: The Vanguard was designed primarily to meet BEA (now British Airways European Division) requirements for a "big Viscount" but was overtaken by the advent of jet propelled airliners and sales were made only to BEA and to TCA (now Air Canada). The BEA fleet comprised six V.951s with Tyne 506 engines and 135,000 lb (61 235 kg) gross weight and 14 V.953s with the same engines but strengthened structure for the weights quoted above. The same structure and weights were initially developed for the 22 V.952s ordered by TCA, these also having the uprated Tyne 512 engines. BEA converted nine Vanguards to Merchantman standard with large cargo loading door and freight floor and was planning to convert four or five more in 1974, when the last passenger-carrying Vanguards were retired by British Airways European Division. Plans were also being made to convert one to have a swing tail, permitting it to load and carry spare Rolls-Royce RB.211 turbofan engines. Aircraft retired by Air Canada and BEA have entered service with various smaller operators.

AEROSPATIALE (SUD) SE 210 CARAVELLE

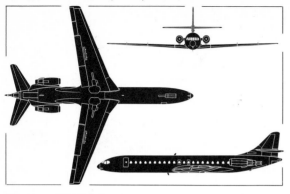

The silhouette shows the Caravelle 12, the final production variant, while the photograph shows a Caravelle 10R in the colours of the German charter specialist LTU.

Country of Origin: France.

Type: Short- to medium-range airliner.

Power Plant: Two (III) 11,400 lb st (5 170 kgp) Rolls-Royce Avon 527 or (VI-N) 12,200 lb st (5 535 kgp) Avon 531 or (VI-R) 12,600 lb st (5 725 kgp) Avon 532R or 533R turbojets or (10B, 10R, 11R) 14,000 lb st (6 350 kgp) Pratt & Whitney JT8D-7 or (12) 14,500 st (6 577 kgp) JT8D-9 turbofans.

Performance: Max cruising speed at 25,000 ft (7 620 m) (III), 500 mph (805 km/h), (VI-N and VI-R), 525 mph (845 km/h), (12), 512 mph (825 km/h); best economy cruise (III), 450 mph (725 km/h), (VI-N), 490 mph (790 km/h), (VI-R), 488 mph (785 km/h); range with max payload, typical reserves, (III), 1,056 mls (1 700 km), (VI-N), 1,460 mls (2 350 km), (VI-R), 1,430 mls (2 300 km), (12), 1,580 mls (2 540 km).

Weights: Basic operating (III), 59,985 lb (27 210 kg), (VI-N), 60,250 lb (27 330 kg), (VI-R), 63,175 lb (28 655 kg), (12), 70,100 lb (31 800 kg); max payload (III), 18,520 lb (8 400 kg), (VI-N), 17,415 lb (7 900 kg), (VI-R), 18,080 lb (8 200 kg), (12), 29,100 lb (13 200 kg); max take-off (III), 101,413 lb (46 000 kg), (VI-N), 105,822 lb (48 000 kg), (VI-R), 110,230 lb (50 000 kg), (12), 127,870 lb (58 000 kg).

Dimensions: Span, 112 ft 6 in (34,30 m); length (III, VI-R, VI-N, 10R), 105 ft 0 in (32,01 m), (10B), 108 ft 3½ in (33,01 m), (11R), 107 ft 4 in (32,71 m), (12), 118 ft 10½ in (36,24 m); height (III, VI-N, VI-R, 10R, 11R), 28 ft 7 in (8,72 m), (10B, 12), 29 ft 7 in (9,01 m); wing area, 1,579 sq ft (146,7 m²).

Accommodation: Flight crew of two or three and up to (III, VI-R, VI-N, 10R) 80 passengers, (10B) 104 passengers, (11R) 99 passengers or (12) 128 passengers.

Status: Prototypes first flown on 27 May 1955 and 6 May 1956. First production Srs I flown 18 May 1958; 19 built (and 13 Srs 1A). First Srs III flown 30 December 1959; 78 built. First Srs VI-N flown 10 September 1960; 53 built. First Srs VI-R flown 6 February 1961, 56 built. Srs VII flown 29 December 1960, one only. First Srs 10B flown 3 March 1964; 22 built. First Srs 10R flown 18 January 1965; 20 built. First Srs 11R flown 21 April 1967; 6 built. First Srs 12 flown 29 October 1970; 12 built.

Notes: Production of the Caravelle ended late in 1972 with 282 built. Variants differ in power plant, fuselage length and gross weights, as indicated in the data quoted here.

An Antonov An-12 is shown in Algerian civil markings in the photograph, while the silhouette shows the fully-civilianized An-12V

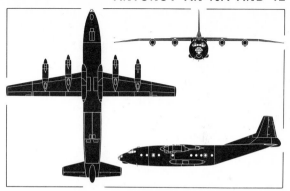

Country of Origin: USSR.
NATO Code Name: *Cat.*
Type: Medium-range airliner.
Power Plant: Four Ivchenko AI-20K turboprops of 4,000 ehp each.
Performance: Max speed, 444 mph (715 km/h); high speed cruise, 422 mph (680 km/h) at 32,800 ft (10 000 m); long range cruise, 391 mph (630 km/h); service ceiling, 33,500 ft (10 200 m); range with max payload, 745 mls (1 200 km) with 1-hr fuel reserve; range with max fuel, 2,530 mls (4 075 km) with payload of 18,600 lb (8 440 kg) and no reserves.
Weights: Max payload, 32,000 lb (14 500 kg); max fuel load, 22,600 lb (10 250 kg); max take-off, 121,500 lb (55 100 kg).
Dimensions: Wing span, 124 ft 8 in (38,0 m); length, 111 ft 6½ in (34,0 m); height, 32 ft 3 in (9,83 m); wing area, 1,292 sq ft (120 m²).
Accommodation: Flight crew of four (two pilots, radio operator and navigator) and standard seating for 100 passengers, with alternative layouts for up to 130.
Status: First flown March 1957. Production believed to exceed 500 and to be now complete.

Notes: Development of the An-10 began in Oleg K Antonov's design bureau at Kiev in the Ukraine in 1955 as one of the first generation of turbine-engined Soviet airliners. Prototypes flew with Kuznetsov NK-4 turboprops but after this engine had been evaluated in service against the Ivchenko AI-20, the latter was selected to power the production versions of the An-10, which entered service with an 84-passenger layout in July 1959. A developed version, the An-10A, appeared in service in February 1960, with the fuselage lengthened by 6 ft 7 in (2,0 m) and basic accommodation increased to 100 (data above). The An-10A became the workhorse of Aeroflot's second-level routes during the 'sixties, sometimes operating on skis in the far North, and joined by a freighter version, the An-12, which had been developed primarily for military use (see *Military* volume, page 104). No use has been made of An-10s by any operators outside the Soviet Union, and Aeroflot was reported to be retiring its entire fleet of this type in 1974. A few An-12s have operated in the civil markings of Algeria, Poland, Bulgaria, Egypt, Ghana, Iraq and Cuba. Some of these were converted military examples, retaining the rear turret installation but others were the fully-civilianised An-12V variant with a fairing replacing the turret.

BAC ONE-ELEVEN

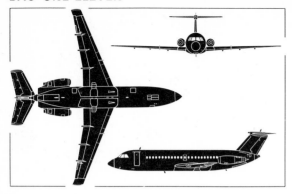

The photograph shows the extended-fuselage BAC One-Eleven 500 in Philippine Airlines livery, the silhouette showing the One-Eleven 475 variant

Country of Origin: United Kingdom.

Type: Short-range airliner.

Power Plant: Two (Srs 200) 10,330 lb st (4 686 kgp) Rolls-Royce Spey 506 or (Srs 300, 400) 11,400 lb st (5 171 kgp) Spey 511 or (Srs 475, 500) 12,550 lb st (5 692 kgp) Spey 512-DW turbofans.

Performance: Max cruising speed (all Srs), 541 mph (871 km/h) at 21,000 ft (6 400 m); best economy cruise (all Srs), 461 mph (742 km/h) at 25,000 ft (7 620 m); initial rate of climb (Srs 200), 2,500 ft/min (12,7 m/sec), (Srs 475), 2,600 ft/min (13,2 m/sec), (Srs 500), 2,400 ft/min (12,2 m/sec); range with typical capacity payload (Srs 200) 875 mls (1 410 km), (Srs 475), 1,865 mls (3 000 km), (Srs 500), 1,480 mls (2 380 km); range with max fuel (Srs 200), 2,130 mls (3 430 km), (Srs 475), 2,285 mls (3 677 km), (Srs 500), 2,149 mls (3 458 km).

Weights: Basic operating (Srs 200) 46,405 lb (21 049 kg), (Srs 475), 51,731 lb (23 464 kg), (Srs 500), 54,582 lb (24 758 kg); max payload (Srs 200), 19 095 lb (8 661 kg), (Srs 475), 21,269 lb (9 647 kg), (Srs 500), 26,418 lb (11 983 kg); max take-off (Srs 200) 79,000 lb (35 833 kg), (Srs 475), 98,500 lb (44 678 kg), (Srs 500), 104,500 lb (47 400 kg).

Dimensions: Span (Srs 200, 300, 400), 88 ft 6 in (26,97 m), (Srs 475, 500), 92 ft 6 in (28,50 m); length, (Srs 200, 300, 400, 475), 93 ft 6 in (28,50 m), (Srs 500), 107 ft (32,61 m); height, 24 ft 6 in (7,47 m); wing area (Srs 200, 300, 400), 1,003 sq ft (93,18 m²), (Srs 475, 500), 1,031 sq ft (95,78 m²).

Accommodation: Flight crew of two (with one supernumerary seat) and typical mixed class layout (except Srs 500) for 16 plus 49 passengers or (except Srs 500) maximum one-class layout, for 89 or (Srs 500 only) 119 passengers.

Status: Prototype first flown 20 August 1963; first production Srs 200 flown on 19 December 1963; first Srs 300/400 development aircraft flown 13 July 1965. Srs 500 development aircraft flown 7 February 1968; first Srs 475 development aircraft flown on 27 August 1970; first production aircraft flown 5 April 1971. Production quantities: Prototypes, 3; Srs 200, 56; Srs 300, 8; Srs 400, 70; Srs 475, 5; Srs 500, 71.

Notes: BAC One-Eleven evolved from original Hunting Aircraft project (H.107) as a Viscount successor. Srs 500 is only major "stretch" of original version.

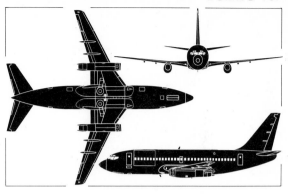

The photograph depicts a Boeing 737-2A3 in PLUNA's colourful markings, the silhouette also showing the 727-200 variant in convertible (C) configuration

Country of Origin: USA.

Type: Short- and medium-range airliner.

Power Plant: Two (-100, -200) 14,000 lb st (6 350 kgp) Pratt & Whitney JT8D-7 or 14,500 lb st (6 577 kgp) JT8D-9 or (-200 only) 15,500 lb st (7 030 kgp) JT8D-15 turbofans.

Performance: Max cruising speed (-100), 605 mph (974 km/h), (-200), 576 mph (927 km/h) at 22,600 ft (6 890 m); best economy cruise (-100), 570 mph (917 km/h), (-200), 553 mph (890 km/h); initial rate of climb (-100), 3,500 ft/min (17,8 m/sec), (-200), 3,760 ft/min (19,1 m/sec); range with max payload (-100), 1,840 mls (2 960 km), (-200), 2,370 mls (3 815 km); range with max fuel (-100), 2,240 mls (3 605 km), (-200), 2,530 mls (4 075 km).

Weights: Operating weight empty (-100), 52,607 lb (23 862 kg) (-200), 59,300 lb (26 898 kg); max payload (-100), 29,093 lb (13 196 kg), (-200), 35,700 lb (16 193 kg); max take-off (-100), 97,000 lb (44 000 kg), (-200), 115,500 lb (52 390 kg).

Dimensions: Span 93 ft 0 in (28,35 m); length (-100), 94 ft 0 in (28,65 m), (-200), 100 ft 0 in (30,48 m); height, 37 ft 0 in (11,28 m); wing area, 980 sq ft (91,05 m²).

Accommodation: Flight crew of two or three; typical one-class accommodation for up to (-100) 115 or (-200) 130 passengers.

Status: First 737-100 flown on 9 April 1967; first 737-200 flown on 8 August 1967; first 737-200C flown in August 1968; first Advanced 737-200 flown on 15 April 1971. Entered airline service 10 February 1968. Total ordered (to May 1974): Srs 100, 30; Srs 200, 382.

Notes: Smallest of the family of Boeing jet transports, the 737 retains the same fuselage cross-section as the 707 and 727, thus achieving commonality of many components. This allowed Boeing to achieve a very rapid development cycle, the 737 entering service only four years after design work began. The -100 and -200 differ primarily in fuselage length and both can be supplied in convertible (C) or quick-change (QC) configuration with side-loading freight door. The Advanced 737, introduced in 1971, has uprated engines, higher weights, increased fuel provision and other improvements. Modifications are also available to permit operation of the Boeing 737 from rough-field surfaces, and special interior layouts have been developed to give a "wide-body" look. An executive transport version is available and the USAF has 19 as navigation trainers, designated T-43A.

CONVAIR (GENERAL DYNAMICS) 880

The photograph and silhouette show the Convair 880-M, the former depicting an aircraft of Cathay Pacific Airlines based in Hong Kong

Country of Origin: USA.

Type: Medium-range airliner.

Power Plant: Four (880) 11,200 lb st (5 080 kgp) General Electric CJ805-3 or (880-M) 11,650 lb st (5 285 kgp) CJ805-3B turbojets.

Performance: Max cruising speed (880), 605 mph (974 km/h), (880-M), 587 mph (945 km/h); best economy cruise, 541 mph (871 km/h); operational ceiling, 41,000 ft (12 500 m); range with max payload (880), 2,845 mls (4 575 km), (880-M), 2,880 mls (4 630 km); range with max fuel (880), 3,130 mls (5 040 km), (880-M), 3,385 mls (5 450 km).

Weights: Basic operating (880), 89,000 lb (40 370 kg), (880-M), 94,600 lb (42 910 kg); max payload, (880), 22,500 lb (10 205 kg), (880-M), 24,000 lb (10 885 kg); max take-off (880), 184,500 lb (83 690 kg), (880-M), 193,000 lb (87 540 kg).

Dimensions: Span 120 ft 0 in (36,58 m); length, 129 ft 4 in (39,42 m); height, 36 ft 4 in (11,0 m); wing area, 2,000 sq ft (185,8 m²).

Accommodation: Flight crew of three (two pilots and an engineer); typical mixed-class seating for 16 plus 74 or maximum of up to 124 in one-class high-density layout.

Status: Prototype first flown on 27 January 1959, followed by second and third aircraft on 31 March and 10 August 1959. Certification on 1 May 1960 and first commercial service in May 1960. First 880-M flown on 3 October 1960, certification on 24 July 1961. Production total, 65.

Notes: The Convair 880 was launched in 1954 following the Boeing 707 and DC-8 and was intended to operate over shorter ranges at higher speeds than the earlier types. The original 880 was purchased by TWA, Delta and Northeast, the 880-M being a range-extended version with higher weights and leading-edge flaps which was ordered by a few overseas operators. Cathay Pacific, based in Hong Kong, became the largest 880 operator outside the USA by 1972 by purchasing several from Japan Air Lines and VIASA, but these were being replaced in 1973 and 1974 and the Convair 880 then remained in use in only small numbers, the TWA and Delta fleets being retired in 1974. The Model number 880 represented the design cruising speed of 600 mph expressed in ft per sec, and it replaced the original designation of Convair 600. The aircraft was also known for a time as the Golden Arrow.

CONVAIR (GENERAL DYNAMICS) 990

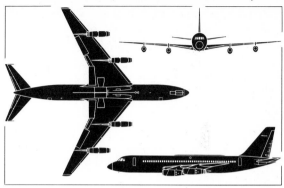

The Convair 990 is shown in the silhoutte and the photograph, which depicts one of the aircraft operated on IT charters by Spantax of Spain

Country of Origin: USA.

Type: Long-haul airliner.

Power Plant: Four 16,050 lb st (7 280 kgp) General Electric CJ805-23B turbofans.

Performance: Max level speed (M = 0·871), 615 mph (990 km/h) at 20,000 ft (6,100 m) at a weight of 200,000 lb (90 720 kg); long-range cruising speed (Mach 0·84), 556 mph (895 km/h) at 35,000 ft (10 670 m); service ceiling, 41,000 ft (12 500 m); range with max payload, 3,800 mls (6 115 km); range with max fuel, 5,446 mls (8 770 km).

Weights: Basic operating, 120,900 lb (54 840 kg); max payload, 26,440 lb (11 992 kg); max take-off, 253,000 lb (114 760 kg); max landing, 202,000 lb (91 625 kg).

Dimensions: Span, 120 ft 0 in (36,58 m); length, 139 ft 2½ in (42,43 m); height, 39 ft 6 in (12,04 m); wing area, 2,250 sq ft (209 m²).

Accommodation: Flight crew of three or four. Cabin provides accommodation for up to 106 passengers.

Status: First flown 24 January 1961. FAA Type Approval on 15 December 1961 and first airline delivery 8 January 1962. Deliveries completed September 1963, 37 built.

Notes: The original Convair Model 990 (also known in the early days as Convair 600) was evolved from the Model 880 (see page 30) primarily to meet the requirements of American Airlines, its new features being a longer fuselage, uprated engines and "speed fairings" on the wing trailing edge. Early flight testing revealed excessive drag and a series of modifications was introduced, primarily affecting the engine pod and pylon configuration, and resulting in a change of designation to Model 990A. The delays in delivery caused by the investigation of the drag problem and subsequent modifications of the aircraft already built, restricted the market for the Convair 990, which also proved smaller than required by most airlines by the early 'sixties. Original customers were American Airlines, which had a fleet of 20, Swissair, Varig, APSA and Garuda. Principal users in 1974 were Modern Air Transport, Spantax and Swissair, the last-named still using its 990s for scheduled services but the other users specialising in inclusive tour and charter flights. One specially modified example was also specially modified for use as a flying laboratory by the National Aeronautics and Space Agency.

DOUGLAS DC-6, DC-6A, DC-6B

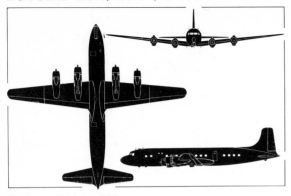

The photograph shows a Douglas DC-6A as operated formerly by Martinair Holland, while the silhouette depicts the externally-similar Douglas DC-6B

Country of Origin: USA.

Type: Medium-range airliner.

Power Plant: Four (DC-6) 2,400 hp Pratt & Whitney R-2800-CA15 or CB16 or (DC-6A, B), 2,500 hp R-2800-CB17 piston radial engines.

Performance: Typical cruising speed (DC-6), 328 mph (528 km/h), (DC-6A, B), 316 mph (509 km/h); initial rate of climb (DC-6), 1,070 ft/min (5,45 m/sec), (DC-6A, B), 1,120 ft/min (6,2 m/sec); no reserves range with max payload (DC-6), 3,340 mls (5 375 km); (DC-6A), 2,925 mls (4 700 km), (DC-6B) 3,000 mls (4 828 km); no reserves range with max fuel (DC-6), 3,940 mls (6 340 km), (DC-6A, B), 4,720 mls (7 596 km).

Weights: Basic operating (DC-6), 52,700 lb (23 905 kg), (DC-6A), 57,000 lb (25 855 kg), (DC-6B) 58,635 lb (26 595 kg); max payload (DC-6), 21,300 lb (9 662 kg), (DC-6A), 28,188 lb (12 780 kg), (DC-6B), 24,565 lb (11 143 kg); max take-off (DC-6) 97,200 lb (44 130 kg), (DC-6A, B), 107,000 lb (48 534 kg).

Dimensions: Span 117 ft 6 in (35,81 m); length (DC-6), 100 ft 7 in (30,66 m), (DC-6A, B), 105 ft 7 in (32,2 m); height (DC-6), 29 ft 1 in (8,86 m), (DC-6A, B), 29 ft 3 in (8,92 m); wing area,

1,463 sq ft (135,9 m²).

Accommodation: Flight crew of three or four. Typical mixed-class seating for (DC-6) 80 or (DC-6B) 102 passengers, or maximum seating for (DC-6) 83 or (DC-6B) 180 passengers.

Status: Prototype (XC-112) first flown 15 February 1946; first commercial deliveries 1947. First DC-6A flown 29 September 1949. First DC-6B flown 10 February 1951. Total production 704, including 175 DC-6, 77 DC-6A, 286 DC-6B and 166 military.

Notes: The DC-6 was evolved during World War II as a larger successor to the DC-4/C-54 (see *Military* volume, page 114), the prototype being built under USAAF contract as the XC-112. In production, the DC-6 became the first post-war Douglas airliner and in its three versions was the most numerous of the piston-engined types that preceded the jet transports. The DC-6A and B had lengthened fuselages and higher weights, the A being an all-freight version with two large side-loading freight doors and the B being the passenger-carrying version. No longer in major service in 1974, examples of the DC-6 family are still flying in many parts of the world on low-cost charter and cargo operations and a few still serve as military transports.

Medium capacity transport

The photograph depicts a privately-operated Douglas DC-7B and the silhouette shows the DC-7C which was the last of the piston-engined Douglas commercial transports

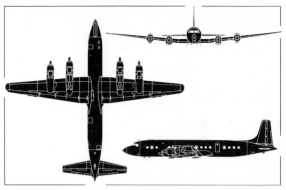

Country of Origin: USA.

Type: Medium long-range airliner.

Power Plant: Four (DC-7, 7B) 3,250 hp Wright R-3350-DA4 or (7B, 7C, 7F) 3,400 hp R-3350-EA1 or EA4 piston radial engines.

Performance: Typical cruising speed (DC-7), 359 mph (578 km/h), (DC-7B), 357 mph (574 km/h), (DC-7C, F) 345 mph (555 km/h); initial rate of climb (DC-7), 1,520 ft/min (7,7 m/sec); service ceiling (DC-7), 25,900 ft (7 894 m), (DC-7C), 21,700 ft (6 615 m); range with max payload (DC-7B), 2,760 mls (4 440 km), (DC-7C), 3,610 mls (5 810 km); no-reserves range with max fuel (DC-7), 4,340 mls (6 985 km), (DC-7B), 4,915 mls (7 900 km), (DC-7C), 5,642 mls (9 077 km), (DC-7F), 4,433 mls (7 130 km).

Weights: Empty (DC-7), 66,300 lb (30 075 kg); basic operating (DC-7B), 74,690 lb (33 880 kg), (DC-7C), 80,000 lb (36 287 kg), (DC-7F), 66,200 lb (30 030 kg); max payload (DC-7), 20,000 lb (9 070 kg), (DC-7B), 21,311 lb (9 665 kg), (DC-7C), 21,500 lb (9 752 kg), (DC-7F), 34,600 lb (15 700 kg); max take-off (DC-6), 122,200 lb (55 429 kg), (DC-7B, 7F), 126,000 lb (57 153 kg), (DC-7C), 143,000 lb (64 865 kg).

Dimensions: Span (DC-7, 7B, 7F), 117 ft 6 in (35,81 m), (DC-7C), 127 ft 6 in (38,8 m); length, (DC-7, 7B, 7F), 108 ft 11 in (33,24 m), (DC-7C), 112 ft 3 in (34,23 m); height, (DC-7, 7B, 7F), 29 ft 3 in (8,9 m), (DC-7C), 31 ft 8 in (9,65 m); wing area, (DC-7, 7B, 7F), 1,463 sq ft (136,0 m²), (DC-7C), 1,637 sq ft (152,0 m²).

Accommodation: Flight crew of three-five and provision in cabin for typical mixed-class accommodation of (DC-7, 7B) 91 or (DC-7C) 89, and maximum accommodation in one-class high-density layout for (DC-7, 7B), 99 (DC-7C) 105 passengers.

Status: DC-7 prototype first flown on 18 May 1953; DC-7B on 25 April 1955 and DC-7C on 20 December 1955. Production totals, DC-7, 120; DC-7B, 97; DC-7C, 121.

Notes: The DC-7 evolved as a "stretch" of the DC-6 family, based initially on the same wing with a longer fuselage and a switch to the more powerful Wright Turbo Compound engines. The DC-7B was a longer-range version of the initial DC-7, with the same overall dimensions, while the DC-7C Seven Seas was the ultimate stretch of the basic design, with increased span and more fuselage length. Some DC-7s and DC-7Bs were converted for use as specialised freighters after being withdrawn from passenger service, as DC-7Fs.

C

HAWKER SIDDELEY COMET

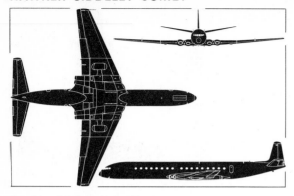

The photograph shows a Comet 4 in the markings of Dan Air for use on IT charters and the silhouette depicts the Comet Srs 4B with a longer fuselage and shorter span

Country of Origin: United Kingdom.
Type: Medium-range airliner.
Power Plant: Four 10,500 lb st (4 763 kgp) Rolls-Royce Avon (Comet 4) 524 (Comet 4B) 525B (Comet 4C) 525 turbojets.
Performance: Max cruising speed (4), 518 mph (833 km/h), (4B, 4C), 535 mph (861 km/h); best economy cruise (4), 504 mph (811 km/h) (4B, 4C), 526 mph (847 km/h); no-reserves range with max payload (4), 4,030 mls (24 500 km), (4B), 3,450 mls (5 552 km), (4C), 3,540 mls (5 697 km); range with max fuel (4), 4,400 mls (7 081 km), (4B), 3,800 mls (6 115 km), (4C), 4,310 mls (6 936 km).
Weights: Basic operating (4), 74,500 lb (33 790 kg), (4B), 78,300 lb (35 516 kg), (4C), 78,500 lb (35 610 kg); max payload (4), 22,040 lb (10 000 kg), (4B), 24,950 lb (11 310 kg), (4C), 28,950 lb (13 130 kg); max take-off (4, 4C), 162,000 lb (73 482 kg), (4B), 158,000 lb (71 668 kg).
Dimensions: Span (4, 4C), 115 ft 0 in (35,05 m), (4B), 107 ft 10 in (32,87 m); length, (4), 111 ft 6 in (33,98 m), (4B, 4C), 118 ft 0 in (35,97 m); height, 29 ft 5 in (8,97 m); wing area, (4, 4C), 2,121 sq ft (197,0 m²), (4B), 2,059 sq ft (191,3 m²).

Accommodation: Flight crew of four and typical mixed-class seating for (4) 67 or (4B, 4C) 89 passengers or maximum high density for (4) 97 or (4B, 4C) 102 passengers.
Status: Long fuselage prototype Comet 3 first flown on 19 July 1954, and as Comet 3B on 21 August 1958. First production Comet 4 flown on 27 April 1958, first 4B flown on 27 June 1959; first 4C flown in October 1959. Production totals, Comet 4, 28; 4B, 18; 4C, 28 (including six military) completed 1964.
Notes: The Comet 4 series was evolved from experience gained by BOAC with the Comet 1, the world's first jet airliner to enter commercial service (in 1952). It featured a lengthened fuselage, extensively revised structure, more fuel capacity and new engines, and in the hands of BOAC two Comet 4s operated the first-ever transatlantic jet services in October 1958. The Comet 4B, evolved for BEA, had a shorter span, longer fuselage and less fuel, for shorter-range operations, and the Comet 4C, purchased by several foreign airlines, had the 4B's long fuselage with the original wing span and fuel. By 1974, most Comet operators had phased the type out of service but Dan Air had built up a fleet of about 20 through second-hand purchases for its IT charter programme.

Both silhouette and photograph show the standard Ilyushin IL-18, the latter depicting an aircraft in service with the Hungarian airline Malev

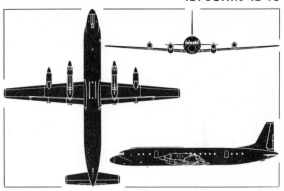

Country of Origin: Soviet Union.
NATO Code Name: *Coot.*
Type: Medium-range airliner.
Power Plant: Four (II-18V) 4,000 eshp Ivchenko AI-20K or (II-18D, E) 4,250 eshp AI-20M turboprops.
Performance: Max cruising speed (II-18V), 404 mph (650 km/h), (II-18D, E), 419 mph (675 km/h); best economy cruise (II-18V), 373 mph (600 km/h), (II-18D, E), 388 mph (625 km/h); operating altitude, 26,250–32,800 ft (8 000–10 000 m); range with max payload (II-18E), 1,990 mls (3 200 km), (II-18D), 2,300 mls (3 700 km); range with max fuel (II-18E), 3,230 mls (5 200 km), (II-18D), 4,040 mls (6 500 km).
Weights: Empty equipped, (II-18E), 76,350 lb (34 630 kg), (II-18D), 77,160 lb (35 000 kg); max payload, 29,750 lb (13 500 kg); max take-off (II-18V, E), 134,925 lb (61 200 kg), (II-18D), 141,100 lb (64 000 kg).
Dimensions: Span, 122 ft 8½ in (37,4 m); length, 117 ft 9 in (35,9 m); height, 33 ft 4 in (10,17 m); wing area, 1,507 sq ft (140 m²).
Accommodation: Flight crew of five (two pilots, navigator,

engineer, radio operator) and typical layout for 65 or 90 passengers with maximum high-density accommodation for 110 (winter) and 122 (summer).
Status: Prototype first flown in July 1957; initial service with Aeroflot on 20 April 1959. Production total believed to exceed 700, including 94 exported to 16 customers.
Notes: The II-18 was the first Soviet airliner to approximate to Western design and performance standards, being comparable in many respects to the Lockheed Electra and Vickers Vanguard. An initial batch of 20 was built, in which the AI-20 engines alternated with the Kuznetsov NK-4 but after this full-scale evaluation the latter engine was dropped. The standard production version then became the II-18V, but this was later superseded by the II-18E with uprated engines and revised accommodation providing for high-density layouts. The II-18D is a long-range version of the II-18E, with more fuel and higher weights. II-18s have been supplied to most East European airlines, and a few are used as VIP transports by countries other than the Soviet Union; a version has also been developed for maritime reconnaissance (see *Military* volume, page 79).

LOCKHEED L-1049 CONSTELLATION

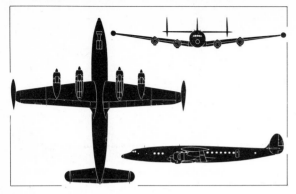

The photograph (above) shows a privately-owned Lockheed L-1049G Constellation, the same variant being depicted in the silhouette (left)

Country of Origin: USA.

Type: Medium- to long-range airliner.

Power Plant: Four (L-1049) 2,700 hp Wright R-3350-CA1 or (L-1049G and H) 3,400 hp Wright R-3350-DA3, EA3 or EA-6 Turbo Compound piston engines.

Performance: Typical cruising speed (L-1049), 255 mph (410 km/h) at 15,000 ft (4 572 m), (L-1049G and H), 305 mph (491 km/h) at 20,000 ft (6 096 m); initial rate of climb (L-1049G), 1,140 ft/min (5,8 m/sec); range with max payload (L-1049), 1,980 mls (3 186 km), (L-1049G), 3,070 mls (4 940 km), (L-1049H), 1,640 mls (2 640 km); range with max fuel (L-1049), 3,100 mls (4 988 km) (L-1049G), 4,020 mls (6 469 km).

Weights: Basic operating (L-1049), 74,700 lb (33 883 kg), (L-1049G), 79,237 lb (35 950 kg), (L-1049H), 71,614 lb (32 485 kg); max payload (L-1049), 18,800 lb (85 275 kg), (L-1049G and H), 24,300 lb (11 022 kg); max take-off (L-1049), 120,000 lb (54 431 kg) (L-1049G and H), 137,500 lb (62 368 kg).

Dimensions: Span, 123 ft 0 in (37,49 m); length, 113 ft 7 in (34,62 m); height, 24 ft 9 in (7,54 m); wing area, 1,650 sq ft (153,3 m²).

Accommodation: Flight crew of four or five; typical mixed-class accommodation for 89 passengers with maximum high-density one-class layout for 106.

Status: Prototype Model 49 Constellation (XC-69) first flown on 9 January 1943; first L-649 flown 18 October 1946; first L-1049 flown on 13 October 1950; first L-1049C flown 17 February 1953; first L-1049G flown 7 December 1954; first L-1049H flown 20 September 1956. Production totals, Model 49, 88; L-649 and L-749, 133; L-1049, 24; L-1049C/D/E/F, 115; L-1049G, 130; L-1049H, 54 (plus military versions).

Notes: The Constellation shared honours with the DC-6/DC-7 family (see page 33) as the backbone of international air transport in the first post-war decade, and like the Douglas types it survives into 1974 as a freighter and for low-cost operations away from the main trunk routes. Conceived in 1939 to meet a TWA requirement, it was first produced in military guise, but all 22 C-69s built were later converted for airline use. The L-649 followed as the first true commercial version, the L-749 being similar with more range and the L-1049 being the first fuselage-stretched version, built in variants up to L-1049H.

The Lockheed Electra is shown in the photograph and the silhouette, the former depicting an example converted for all-cargo service with Ansett Airlines of Australia

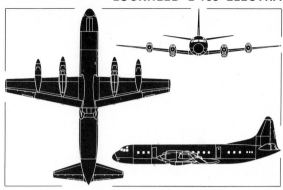

Country of Origin: USA.

Type: Short- to medium-range airliner.

Power Plant: Four 3,750 ehp Allison 501-D13A turboprops.

Performance: Max cruising speed, 405 mph (652 km/h) at 22,000 ft (6 700 m); best economy cruise, 374 mph (602 km/h); initial rate of climb, 1,670 ft/min (8,5 m/sec); service ceiling, 27,000 ft (8 230 m); range with max payload, 2,200 mls (3 540 km); range with max fuel, (L-188A), 2,500 mls (4 023 km), (L-188C), 3,020 mls (4 860 km).

Weights: Basic operating: 61,500 lb (27 895 kg); max payload, 22,825 lb (10 350 kg); max take-off, 116,000 lb (52,664 kg).

Dimensions: Span, 99 ft 0 in (30,18 m); length, 104 ft 6 in (31,81 m); height, 32 ft 10 in (10,0 m); wing area, 1,300 sq ft (120,8 m²).

Accommodation: Flight crew of two or three and typical mixed-class accommodation for 67 passengers or maximum high-density one-class layout for 99.

Status: Prototype first flown on 13 February 1958; fourth flown on 10 April 1958 and fifth (first customer aircraft) flown on 19 May 1958. Certification on 22 August 1958, first airline services by Eastern (12 January 1959) and American (23 January 1959). Production totals, L-188A, 115; L-188C, 55.

Notes: The Electra was designed by Lockheed as the company's first post-war commercial airliner. Aimed at the short to medium-range routes, the Electra was first ordered in June 1955 becoming the only US airliner with turboprop engines. Production of the Electra ended in 1960, the programme having proved less successful than expected because the pure jet types proved to be economic when operating on the shorter routes for which the Electra had been designed. Original production Electras were delivered at a gross weight of 113,000 lb (51 260 kg) but the higher weights indicated above were introduced for the L-188C overwater version and were later applicable to all models. Electras had been retired by most major airlines by the early 'seventies but many had been acquired second-hand by other operators especially in South America, where they are still in service; others are used as executive transports and by specialist air transport organisations. The P-3 Orion maritime reconnaissance aircraft (see *Military* volume, page 82) was derived from the Electra design, using the same basic wing and powerplant, with revised fuselage.

McDONNELL DOUGLAS DC-9

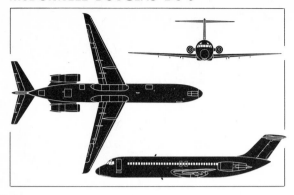

The Series 30 version of the DC-9 is shown in both the silhouette and the photograph, the latter showing an aircraft in service with Swissair

Country of Origin: USA.

Type: Short-range airliner.

Power Plant: Two (Srs 10) 12,500 lb st (5 670 kgp) Pratt & Whitney JT8D-5 or 14,000 lb st (6 350 kgp) JT8D-1 or -7 or (Srs 20 and 30) 14,500 lb st (6 580 kgp) JT8D-9 or 15,000 lb st (6 800 kgp) JT8D-11 or (Srs 30, 40, 50) 15,500 lb st (7 030 kgp) JT8D-15 or (Srs 50) 16,000 lb st (7 257 kgp) JT8D-17 turbofans.

Performance: Max cruising speed (Srs 10), 561 mph (903 km/h), (Srs 30), 572 mph (918 km/h), (Srs 40), 562 mph (903 km/h), long range cruise (Srs 30), 496 mph (796 km/h), (Srs 40), 503 mph (806 km/h); range with max payload (Srs 10), 656 mls (1 055 km), (Srs 30), 1,100 mls (1 770 km), (Srs 40), 820 mls (1 320 km).

Weights: Operating empty (Srs 10), 49,900 lb (22 634 kg), (Srs 30), 58,500 lb (26 535 kg), (Srs 40), 60,300 lb (27 350 kg); max weight-limited payload (Srs 10), 23,850 lb (10 800 kg), (Srs 30), 29,860 lb (13 550 kg), (Srs 40), 33,718 lb (15 300 kg); max take-off (Srs 10), 90,700 lb (41 140 kg), (Srs 30), 108,000 lb (49 000 kg), (Srs 40), 114,000 lb (51 800 kg).

Dimensions: Span (Srs 10), 89 ft 5 in (27,25 m), (Srs 20–50), 93 ft 5 in (28,5 m); length (Srs 10, 20), 104 ft 5 in (31,82 m), (Srs 30), 119 ft 4 in (36,37 m), (Srs 40), 125 ft 7 in (38,3 m), (Srs 50), 132 ft (40,3 m); height (Srs 10–30), 27 ft 6 in (8,38 m), (Srs 40, 50), 28 ft (8,53 m); wing area (Srs 10), 934 sq ft (86,77 m²), (Srs 20–50), 1,001 sq ft (92,97 m²).

Accommodation: Flight crew of two or three; typical mixed-class seating for (Srs 10 and 20) 12 plus 60 (Srs 30) 12 plus 85 (Srs 40) 12 plus 95 and (Srs 50) 12 plus 110 or maximum high-density seating for (Srs 10 and 20) 90, (Srs 30) 115 (Srs 40) 125 and (Srs 50) 139 passengers.

Status: First DC-9 (Srs 10) flown on 25 February 1965; certificated 22 November 1965 and entered commercial service (Delta) on 29 November. First Srs 30 flown 1 August 1966, first Srs 40 flown on 28 November 1967, first Srs 20 flown on 18 September 1968; first Srs 50 to fly and enter service in 1975. Total production and orders (March 1974), 800 including Srs 10, 137; Srs 20, 10; Srs 30, 538; Srs 40, 48; Srs 50, 18; (military, 29).

Notes: The DC-9 was launched in 1955 and is now the world's second most successful jet airliner (after the Boeing 727). Original Srs 10 had a "plain" wing; all later versions have leading edge slats and extended tips.

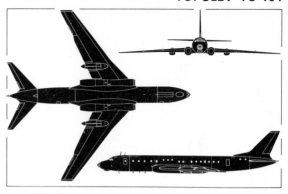

The photograph shows a Tupolev Tu-104 in the markings of the Soviet airline Aeroflot and the silhouette shows the extended-fuselage Tu-104B version

Country of Origin: Soviet Union.

NATO Code Name: *Camel.*

Type: Medium-range airliner.

Power Plant: Two (Tu-104) 14,880 lb st (6 750 kgp) Mikulin AM-3 or (Tu-104A, B) 21,385 lb st (9 700 kgp) AM-3M-500 turbojets.

Performance: Max cruising speed, 560 mph (900 km/h) ; best economy cruise, 497 mph (800 km/h) ; service ceiling, 37,750 ft (11 500 m) ; range with max payload at 33,000 ft (10 000 m), (Tu-104A), 1,645 mls (2 650 km), (Tu-104B), 1,305 mls (2 100 km) ; range with max fuel, 1,925 mls (3 100 km).

Weights: Empty (Tu-104A), 91,710 lb (41 600 kg), (Tu-104B), 93,700 lb (42 500 kg) ; max payload (Tu-104A), 19,840 lb (9 000 kg), (Tu-104B), 26,455 lb (12 000 kg) ; max take-off, 167,550 lb (76 000 kg).

Dimensions: Span, 113 ft 4 in (34,54 m) ; length (Tu-104A), 127 ft 5½ in (38,85 m), (Tu-104B), 131 ft 5 in (40,06 m) ; height, 39 ft 0 in (11,90 m) ; wing area (Tu-104A), 1,877 sq ft (174,4 m²), (Tu-104B), 1,975 sq ft (183,5 m²).

Accommodation: Flight crew of five (two pilots, navigator, engineer and radio operator) ; typical mixed-class accommodation for 16 plus 54 passengers or up to 100 in one-class high-density arrangement.

Status: Prototype Tu-104 first flown early 1955 ; first of pre-production batch flown on 17 June 1955 ; first Tu-104A flown in 1957 ; first Tu-104B flown in 1958. Total production believed to exceed 200.

Notes: A simple adaptation of the Tu-16 bomber (see *Military* volume, page 69), the Tu-104 was the Soviet Union's first commercial jet airliner and the second in the world to enter regular service, after the Comet (see page 34). The first small batch of 50-seat Tu-104s was in service from 15 September 1956 onwards. In 1958, Aeroflot introduced a new version, the Tu-104A, with the interior redesigned to accommodate 70 passengers in a mixed-class layout, and improved engines. A small stretch of the fuselage allowed a further increase to be made in the passenger capacity, and this version was introduced in 1959 as the Tu-104B. A similar interior was subsequently fitted in the original Tu-104As, in which guise they were known as Tu-104V, with increased gross weight. Six Tu-104As were acquired by Czech Airlines CSA.

TUPOLEV TU-124

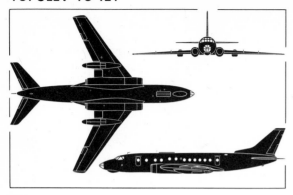

Both the photograph and the silhouette show the Tupolev Tu-124, the former depicting an aircraft in the markings of CSA Czech Air Lines

Country of Origin: Soviet Union.
NATO Code Name: *Cookpot.*
Type: Short-haul airliner.
Power Plant: Two 11,905 lb st (5 400 kgp) Soloviev D-20P turbofans.
Performance: Max cruising speed, 540 mph (870 km/h); best economy cruise, 497 mph (800 km/h) at 33,000 ft (10 000 m); range with max payload, 760 mls (1 220 km); range with max fuel, 1 305 mls (2 100 km).
Weights: Empty. 49,600 lb (22 500 kg); max payload, 13,228 lb (6 000 kg); max take-off, 83,775 lb (38 000 kg).
Dimensions: Span, 83 ft 9½ in (25,55 m); length, 100 ft 4 in (30,58 m); weight, 26 ft 6 in (8,08 m); wing area, 1,281 sq ft (119 m²).
Accommodation: Flight crew of four (two pilots, navigator and stewardess); typical one-class accommodation for 56 passengers in three separate cabins, with alternative *de luxe* layouts for 22 or 36 occupants.
Status: Prototype first flown June 1960. Production deliveries initiated mid-1962. Production total, several hundred.

Notes: Closely following the Tu-104 (see page 39) in overall configuration, the Tu-124 was smaller by some 25 per cent overall and was therefore a completely new design. It was intended to replace the Ilyushin Il-14 on Aeroflot's shorter routes, in the overall scheme to modernise commercial aviation in the Soviet Union, and special attention was paid in the design to features facilitating operation of the Tu-124 from short, unprepared landing strips. These features included double-slotted flaps and combined spoiler/lift dumper/air brakes on the wing. The Tu-124 was first projected with a 44-passenger layout but the standard version, designated Tu-124V, had seats for 56 in three cabins with 12, 12 and 32 seats respectively. When the Tu-124 entered service with Aeroflot on 2 October 1962, it was the first turbofan-engined airliner used on a regular basis. Two special versions, with a higher standard of accommodation for fewer passengers, were subsequently designated—the Tu-124K with 36 seats and the Tu-124K2 with only 22 seats. These versions may have been for use as VIP transports in the Soviet Union. Three Tu-124s were operated by Czech Airlines CSA and one by Interflug in East Germany. Three others were supplied in military guise to the Indian Air Force.

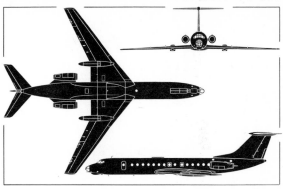

The photograph shows a Tupolev Tu-134 in the markings of Balkan Bulgarian Airlines, and the silhouette depicts the Tu-134A variant

Country of Origin: Soviet Union.

NATO Code Name: *Crusty.*

Type: Short-haul airliner.

Power Plant: Two 14,990 lb st (6 800 kgp) Soloviev D-30 turbofans.

Performance: Max cruising speed, 559 mph (900 km/h) at 28,000 ft (8 500 m); long-range cruise, 466 mph (750 km/h); initial rate of climb, 2,910 ft/min (14,8 m/sec); service ceiling, 39,370 ft (12 000 m); range with max payload (Tu-134), 1,490 mls (2 400 km), (Tu-134A), 1,243 mls (2 000 km); range with max fuel (Tu-134, Tu-134A), 2,175 mls (3 500 km).

Weights: Basic operating (Tu-134), 60,627 lb (27 500 kg), (Tu-134A), 63,950 lb (29 000 kg); max payload (Tu-134), 16,975 lb (7 700 kg), (Tu-134A), 18,000 lb (8 200 kg); max take-off (Tu-134), 98,105 lb (44 500 kg), (Tu-134A), 103,600 lb (47 000 kg).

Dimensions: Span, 95 ft 1¾ in (29,00 m); length (Tu-134), 112 ft 8¼ in (34,35 m), (Tu-134A), 122 ft 0 in (37,10 m); height, 29 ft 7 in (9,02 m); wing area, 1,370·3 sq ft (127,3 m²).

Accommodation: Flight crew of three (two pilots and navigator);

typical mixed-class seating (Tu-134) for 16 plus 48 passengers or one-class high-density accommodation for up to 72 or (Tu-134A) 80.

Status: Prototype first flown late 1962. Five pre-production aircraft produced 1963–64. Production deliveries began 1966.

Notes: Originally developed as the Tu-124A, the Tu-134 was based on a similar fuselage to that of its progenitor, but featured a rear-engined layout. The Tu-134 replaced the Tu-104 in production at a factory in Kharkov, and after a period of proving flights over Aeroflot routes within the Soviet Union in 1967, it went into international service in September of that year. Although most Tu-134s have the familiar Tupolev glazed nose containing the navigation station, a few have a conical "solid" nose, probably containing weather and mapping radar. A second version of the design introduced in 1970 was the Tu-134A, with the fuselage lengthened by 6 ft 10½ in (2,10 m), thrust reversers on the engines and a new standard of radio and navigation equipment. The Tu-134 was the first Soviet jet airliner to see widespread service with airlines other than Aeroflot, users including CSA, Interflug, Balkan Bulgarian, LOT, Malev, Aviogenex, Iraqi Airways and Egypt Air.

ANTONOV AN-24

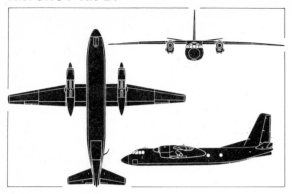

Shown in the photograph is an Antonov An-24V operated by Polish Air Lines LOT, and the silhouette depicts the freight-carrying An-24T variant

Country of Origin: Soviet Union.
NATO Code Name: *Coke* and (An-30) *Clunk*
Type: Short-range airliner/feederliner.
Power Plant: Two 2,550 ehp Ivchenko (An-24V Srs I) AI-24 or (An-24V Srs II, An-24RV, An-24T, An-24RT) AI-24A turboprops plus (AI-24RV, RT only) one 1,985 lb st (900 kg) Type RU-19-300 turbojet in starboard nacelle.
Performance: Max cruising speed, 310 mph (498 km/h); best range cruise, 280 mph (450 km/h); initial rate of climb (An-24V), 1,515 ft/min (7,7 m/sec); service ceiling (An-24V), 27,560 ft (8 400 m); range with max payload, (An-24V, RV), 340 mls (550 km) (An-24T, RT), 397 mls (640 km); range with max fuel, (An-24V), 1,490 mls (2 400 km), (An-24T), 1,864 mls (3 000 km).
Weights: Empty (An-24V), 29,320 lb (13 300 kg); basic operating, (An-24T), 32,404 lb (14 698 kg); max payload (An-24V, RV), 12,125 lb (5 500 kg), (An-24T), 10,168 lb (4 612 kg); max take-off, (An-24V, T), 46,300 lb (21 000 kg), (An-24 RV, RT), 48,060 lb (21 800 kg).
Dimensions: Span, 95 ft 9½ in (29,20 m); length, 77 ft 2½ in (23,53 m); height, 27 ft 3½ in (8,32 m); wing area, 807·1 sq ft

(74,98 m²).
Accommodation: (An-24V) Flight crew of three (two pilots and radio operator/navigator), and normal accommodation for 50 passengers in one-class four-abreast seating, with optional mixed passenger/freight layouts.
Status: First prototype flown in April 1960; commercial service began September 1963. Several hundred in service in 1973, with production of special-purpose versions continuing.
Notes: Development of the An-24 began in 1958, as the first turboprop airliner by the Antonov design bureau, to provide a replacement for the Il-12/14 and Li-2 on Aeroflot routes inside the Soviet Union. The original An-24 was a 44–48 seater, followed by the standard An-24V with increased capacity. For short-field operation, the An-24RV has a turbojet boost engine in one nacelle. Specialised freight carrying versions are the An-24T and An-24RT, for military as well as civil use; these and the military An-26 (NATO Code-name *Curl*) are described in the *Military* volume. A version specially equipped for aerial survey, with a revised front fuselage and raised cockpit, is designated An-30. About 70 An-24s have been exported for airline use outside the USSR.

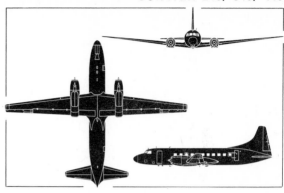

The photograph shows an ex-airline Convair 340 operated as an executive transport by Union Oil Company and the silhouette shows the Convair 440 Metropolitan

Country of Origin: USA.

Type: Short-haul airliner/feederliner.

Power Plant: Two 2,400 hp Pratt & Whitney (240) R2800-CA3, CA15, CA18, CB3 or CB16, (340, 440) 2,500 hp R-2800-CB16 or CB17 piston radials.

Performance: Max cruising speed (240), 270 mph (435 km/h), (440), 300 mph (483 km/h) at 13,000 ft (3 962 m) ; best economy cruise (240), 245 mph (394 km/h), (440), 289 mph (465 km/h) at 20,000 ft (6 100 m) ; initial rate of climb (440), 1,260 ft/min (6,4 m/sec) service ceiling (440), 24,900 ft (7 590 m) ; range with max payload (240), 400 mls (644 km) (340), 100 mls (161 km), (440), 285 mls (459 km) ; range with max fuel (240), 1,030 mls (1 658 km), (340 and 440), 1,930 mls (3 106 km).

Weights: Basic operating (240), 29,526 lb (13 413 kg), (340), 31,609 lb (14 335 kg), (440), 33,314 lb (15 110 kg) ; max payload (240), 9,561 lb (4 336 kg), (340), 13,391 lb (6 075 kg), (440), 12,836 lb (5 820 kg) ; max take-off (240), 42,500 lb (19 277 kg), (340), 47,000 lb (21 318 kg), (440), 49,700 lb (22 544 kg).

Dimensions: Span (240), 91 ft 9 in (27,96 m), (340, 440), 105 ft 4 in (32,12 m) ; length (240), 74 ft 8 in (22,76 m), (340), 79 ft 2 in (24,14 m), (440 with nose radar), 81 ft 6 in (24,84 m) ; height (240), 26 ft 11 in (8,20 m) (340, 440), 28 ft 2 in (8,59 m) ; wing area (240) 817 sq ft (75,9 m²), (340, 440), 920 sq ft (85,5 m²).

Accommodation: Flight crew of two and (240) 40, (340) 44 or (440) 52 passengers.

Status: First Model 240 flown 16 March 1947 ; first 340 flown 5 October 1951 ; first 440 (prototype) flown 6 October 1955 (production) 15 December 1955. First commercial service (240) 1 June 1948 (340) 1952 (440) February 1956. Production totals 240, 176 (plus 393 non-airline), 340, 212 (plus 99 non-airline), 440 (plus non-airline), production completed 1958.

Notes: The Convairliner family evolved from the Convair Model 110, first flown on 9 July 1946 to satisfy an American Airlines requirement. The Model 240 was the production version, ordered by American, with which it entered service in June 1948, and many other airlines. The Model 340 was a "stretch" with increased span and length and higher weights and the Model 440 Metropolitan had further refinements. The 340 and 440 remain in airline service in 1974, together with many turboprop conversions of the Convairliner series (see page 44).

CONVAIR 580, 600, 640

Depicted by the silhouette is the Convair 580 with Allison turbo-props, while the photograph shows a Dart-engined Convair 600 (with nose radar)

Country of Origin: USA.

Type: Short-haul airliner.

Power Plant: Two (580) 3,750 shp Allison 501-D13H turbo-props or (600, 640) 3,025 eshp Rolls-Royce Dart 542-4 turboprops.

Performance: Cruising speed (580), 342 mph (550 km/h), (600), 309 mph (497 km/h) (640), 300 mph (482 km/h); range with max fuel (580), 2,866 mls (4 611 km), (600), 1,900 mls (3 060 km), (640), 1,230 mls (1 975 km).

Weights: Basic operating (600), 28,380 lb (12 872 kg), (640), 30,275 lb (13 732 kg); max payload (580), 8,870 lb (4 023 kg), (600), 9,700 lb (4 400 kg), (640), 15,800 lb (7 167 kg); max take-off (580), 58,140 lb (26 371 kg), (600), 46,200 lb (20 955 kg), (640), 55,000 lb (24 950 kg).

Dimensions: Span (540, 640), 105 ft 4 in (32,12 m), (600), 91 ft 9 in (27,98 m); length (540, 640), 81 ft 6 in (24,84 m); height, (580), 29 ft 2 in (8,89 m), (600), 26 ft 11 in (8,22 m), (640), 28 ft 2 in (8,59 m); wing area, (580, 640), 920 sq ft (85,5 m²), (600), 817 sq ft (75,8 m²).

Accommodation: Flight crew of two and up to (580, 640) 56 or (600) 52 passengers in one-class high-density seating.

Status: First Convair Turboliner (Allison 501-A2) flown 29 December 1950; first YC-131C (Allison 501-D13) flown 29 June 1954; first Super Convair 580 flown 19 January 1960; first Eland-Convair flown 4 February 1958; first Convair 540 flown 11 October 1958; first Canadair CL-66 flown 2 February 1959; first Convair 600 flown 20 May 1965.

Notes: Of more than 500 Convair 240/340/440s built for airline use, (see page 43) over 200 were subsequently converted to have turboprop engines. The earliest programme was installation of Allison T38s for makers' trials, followed by two YC-131Cs for USAF evaluation. A Napier-sponsored programme led to the Eland-powered Model 540; seven Model 340s were converted, and then Canadair built ten new airframes as CL-66 Cosmopolitans for the RCAF and converted three more. Allison modified 170 Convairs to Model 580s, ending in 1969. Rolls-Royce Dart engined models were the 600 if based on the Convair 240 and 640 if based on the 340 or 440. Some 580s and 600/640s remained in airline service in 1974, plus numerous others which, after initial airline use, had been fitted with modified interiors for use as executive transports, primarily in the USA.

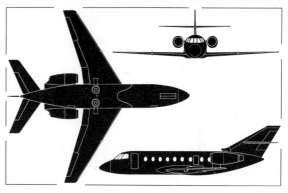

The prototype Dassault-Breguet Falcon 30 is shown in the photograph (above), while the silhouette depicts the initial production standard

Country of Origin: France.
Type: Short-range transport.
Power Plant: Two 6,060 lb st (2 750 kgp) Avco-Lycoming ALF 502D turbofans.
Performance: Max cruising speed, 512 mph (825 km/h) at 25,000 ft (7 620 m); best economy cruise, 441 mph (710 km/h) at 35,000 ft (10 670 m); range with 8,000 lb (3 628 kg) payload, 575 mls (925 km) at max cruise, 750 mls (1 200 km) at economical cruise; range with 40 passengers and typical reserves, 840 mls (1 357 km), range with max fuel, 2,530 mls (4 070 km).
Weights: Basic operating, 21,825 lb (9 900 kg); max payload, 8,000 lb (3,625 kg); max take-off, 35,275 lb (16 000 kg); max landing, 32,190 lb (14 600 kg).
Dimensions: Span, 59 ft 1½ in (18,03 m); length, 64 ft 11 in (19,77 m); height, 19 ft 10 in (6,05 m); wing area, 530 sq ft (49,0 m²).
Accommodation: Normal flight crew of two and standard accommodation for (Falcon 30) 30 passengers three-abreast or (Falcon 40) 40 passengers four-abreast.
Status: First prototype (small diameter fuselage) first flown 11 May

1973 and flown with lengthened fuselage on 23 November 1973. Second prototype (production standard) first flown mid-1974. Production deliveries to begin early 1976.
Notes: The Mystère/Falcon 30 is an outgrowth of the Mystère/Falcon 20 (see page 103) intended to provide a short-range small-capacity jet transport primarily for the third-level airlines. Initially projected as the Falcon 20T, it was based on the Falcon 20 wings and tail unit with a new fuselage but after production of a prototype was put in hand, a change in the US regulations relating to third-level airline operations permitted an increase in capacity, weight and power. Consequently, the fuselage diameter was increased for the proposed production version and applies from the second prototype onwards. The fuselage of the first prototype was lengthened by 1 ft 4 in (42 cm) and the tailplane was enlarged subsequent to the first stage of flight testing. The Falcon 30 has 30 passenger seats to comply with US regulations, but the same fuselage can have a high-density layout for 40 passengers for operators outside the US, and in this guise is known as the Mystère 40-100. The first announced order was from the French domestic airline Touraine Air Transport, for four Mystère 40s.

DE HAVILLAND CANADA DHC-7 DASH-7

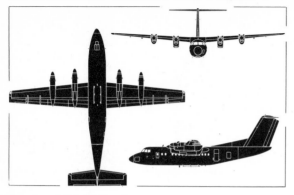

The silhouette (left) and illustration (above) depict the de Havilland Canada DHC-7, the latter showing the markings of the first customer, Widerøe

Country of Origin: Canada.

Type: STOL short-range airliner.

Power Plant: Four 1,120 shp Pratt & Whitney (UACL) PT6A-50 turboprops.

Performance (Estimated): Max cruising sped, 274 mph (441 km/h) at 7,500 ft (2 286 m); best range cruise, 230 mph (370 km/h) at 20,000 ft (6 096 m); initial rate of climb, 1,470 ft/min (7,48 m/sec); service ceiling, 24,000 ft (7 315 m); range with max payload, 733 mls (1 180 km), range with max fuel, 2,000 mls (3 220 km).

Weights: Operating empty, 24,440 lb (11 130 kg); max payload, 11 060 lb (4 017 kg); max take-off, 41 000 lb (18 597 kg).

Dimensions: Span, 93 ft 0 in (28,35 m); length, 80 ft 4 in (24,50 m); height, 26 ft 3 in (8,00 m); wing area, 860 sq ft (79,9 m²).

Accommodation: Flight crew of two and basic accommodation for 48 passengers with optional arrangement for 54 passengers, four-abreast.

Status: Two pre-production prototypes under construction for first flight in late 1974. Production planning provides for first production aircraft to fly in 1975, with initial production rate of two a month

rising to four a month by 1977.

Notes: The Dash-7 is the latest and largest in a series of specialised STOL aircraft originated by the de Havilland Canada company, earlier types including the Beaver, Otter, Caribou, Buffalo and Twin Otter. Launched later in 1972 with the financial backing of the Canadian government, the Dash-7 is intended to make airline-standard flying possible from airfields with runways little more than 2,000 ft (610 m) in length. Like the earlier DHC types, it derives its STOL capability from an aerodynamic lift system using double slotted flaps operating in the slipstream from four large-diameter slow-running propellers. These propellers, and the PT6A-50 turbo-prop engines, are also designed to provide low noise levels, both inside the cabin and externally during take-off and landing. Marketing support for the Dash-7 is provided by the Boeing Commercial Airplane Co following technical evaluations made in 1971 and conclusion of a new joint marketing agreement in 1972. The first firm order for the Dash-7 was placed early in 1974 by Widerøe's Flyveselskap A/S of Norway, for two to be delivered in 1977 and Rocky Mountain Airlines also ordered two, although no firm commitment to produce the Dash-7 had been made by DHC.

The Douglas DC-3 shown in the photograph above is operated as a business transport by the Storer Broadcasting Company, the silhouette showing the standard aircraft

Country of Origin: USA.

Type: Short-haul airliner.

Power Plant: Two 1,200 hp Pratt & Whitney R-1830-92 Twin Wasp piston engines.

Performance (typical post-war conversion of C-47): Max speed, 215 mph (346 km/h); high speed cruise 194 mph (312 km/h); economical cruise, 165 mph (266 km/h) at 6,000 ft (1 829 m); initial climb, 1,070 ft/min (5,4 m/sec); service ceiling, 21,900 ft (6 675 m); range with max payload, 350 mls (563 km); range with max fuel, 1,510 mls (2 430 km).

Weights: Operating weight empty, 17,720 lb (8 030 kg); max payload, 6,600 lb (3 000 kg); max take-off (US, passenger) 25,200 lb (11 430 kg); max take-off (British C of A, freight), 28,000 lb (12 700 kg).

Dimensions: Span, 95 ft 0 in (28,96 m); length, 64 ft 6 in (19,66 m); height, 16 ft 11½ in (5,16 m); wing area, 987 sq ft (91,7 m²).

Accommodation: Flight crew of two or three and up to 27 passengers.

Status: First flown (as DST-Douglas Sleeper Transport) on 17 December 1935, certificated on 21 May 1936 and entered airline service on 25 June 1936. Production totalled 10,655, of which 430 were delivered initially as civil aircraft and the remainder were initially delivered for military use, many later being civilianised.

Notes: Developed from the DC-1 and DC-2, the DC-3 in its many variants became one of the most-known and most widely-used of military and civil transports, and well over 500 were still in active airline service throughout the world in 1973. Versions built for civil use were 21 DST (Wright Cyclone engines) and 19 DST-A (Twin Wasp engines); 265 DC-3s (Cyclone) with up to 18 seats for day-time operations; 115 similar DC-3A (Twin Wasp) and 10 DC-3B (Cyclone) with interiors convertible for day or night use. Post-war, Douglas converted 21 military C-47s to DC-3C and completed parts of 28 military C-117As as DC-3Ds; five DC-3s were Cyclone-powered Super DC-3 conversions. Other ex-military DC-3s were often known by the RAF name Dakota. (See also page 113, *Military* volume.) The majority of airlines using DC-3s in 1974 are those in North and South America, primarily the smaller operators serving short routes, frequently involving minimum airfield facilities. Considerable numbers of DC-3s also still serve in Asia and Australasia, although few operators have more than four or five in service.

FAIRCHILD FH-227

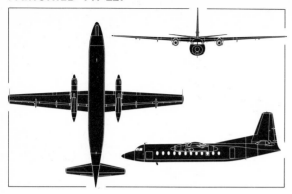

Both photograph and drawing show the Fairchild FH-227, developed by Fairchild from the Fokker F.27 and having increased passenger capacity

Country of Origin: USA.

Type: Feederliner.

Power Plant: Two (FH-227, B, C) 2,250 shp Rolls-Royce Dart 532-7 or (FH-227 D, E) 2,300 shp Dart 532-7L turboprops.

Performance: Max cruising speed, 294 mph (473 km/h) at 15,000 ft (4 570 m); best economy cruise, 270 mph (435 km/h) at 25,000 ft (7 620 m); initial rate of climb, 1,560 ft/min (7,9 m/sec); service ceiling, 28,000 ft (8 535 m); range with max payload (FH-227B), 606 mls (975 km), (FH-227E), 656 mls (1 055 km); range with max fuel (FH-227B), 1,580 mls (2 540 km), (FH-227E), 1,655 mls (2 660 km).

Weights: Empty (FH-227B), 23,200 lb (10 523 kg), (FH-227E), 22,923 lb (10 398 kg); max payload, (FH-227B), 12,600 lb (5 715 kg), (FH-227E), 11,200 lb (5 080 kg); max take-off, (FH-227B, FH-227D), 45,500 lb (20 640 kg), (FH-227B, FH-227C, FH-227E), 43,500 lb (19 730 kg).

Dimensions: Span, 95 ft 2 in (29,0 m); length, 83 ft 8 in (25,50 m); height, 27 ft 7 in (8,41 m); wing area, 754 sq ft (70,0 m²).

Accommodation: Flight crew of two and up to 56 passengers four-abreast in one-class high-density layout.

Status: First FH-227 flown on 27 January 1966; FAA Type Approval, 24 June 1966 airline deliveries began June 1966. Production quantities, FH-227, 12; FH-227B, 67; (other variants by conversion).

Notes: The FH-227 was evolved by Fairchild during 1965 as a stretched version of the Fokker F.27 (see page 49) which the US company was building under licence. The fuselage was lengthened by 6 ft (1,83 m) compared with the 4 ft 11 in (1,5 m) stretch offered by Fokker-VFW in the F.27 Mk 500, and other special features were introduced to make the aircraft more specifically suited to the US market. The 12 FH-227s included two prototype/demonstrators and 10 for Mohawk later exchanged one-for-one for FH-227Bs which introduced higher weights and revised structure. Some FH-227s were later converted to FH-227C with some features of the B model but the original weights, or to FH-227E with uprated engines. The FH-227Bs became FH-227Ds if fitted with the uprated engines and other improvements. Principal users of the FH-227B in addition to Mohawk were Ozark and Piedmont in the US and Paraense in Brazil, plus a few business users; second-hand sales added a few other airlines to the list of operators.

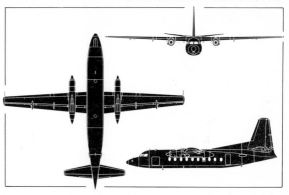

The silhouette (right) depicts a Fokker F.27 Mk 200 and the photograph (above) depicts a Friendship in the markings of Garuda Indonesian Airways

Country of Origin: Netherlands.

Type: Feederliner.

Power Plant: Two (Mk 100, F-27) 1,720 eshp Rolls-Royce Dart 511 or 511-7E or (Mk 100, F-27A) 1,850 eshp Dart 514-7 or (Mk 200, 300, 400, 500, 600, F-27A) 2,105 eshp Dart 528 or 528-7E or (Mk 200–600, F-27J) 2,230 eshp Dart 532-7 or (F-27F) 2,180 ehp Dart 529-7E.

Performance: Cruising speed (Mk 100), 266 mph (428 km/h), (Mk 200), 302 mph (486 km/h), (Mk 500), 298 mph (480 km/h) ; (Mk 100), 1,070 ft/min (5,4 m/sec), (Mk 200), 1,475 ft/min (7,5 m/sec), (Mk 500), 1,450 ft/min (7,4 m/sec) ; service ceiling (Mk 100), 29,000 ft (8 840 m), (Mk 200, 500), 29,500 ft (9 000 m) ; range with max payload, (Mk 100), 775 mls (1 250 km), (Mk 200), 1,285 mls (2 070 km), (Mk 500), 992 mls (1 596 km) ; range with max fuel (Mk 100), 1,255 mls (2 020 km), (Mk 200), 1,374 mls (2 211 km), (Mk 500), 1,170 mls (1 883 km).

Weights: Empty, 22,696 lb (10 295 kg), operating empty, 24,600 lb (11 159 kg), (Mk 500), 25,950 lb (11 771 kg) ; max payload, (Mk 100), 10,320 lb (4 681 kg), (Mk 200), 10,340 lb (4 690 kg), (Mk 500), 12,320 lb (5 588 kg) ; max take-off (Mk 100, 300),

40,500 lb (18 370 kg), (Mk 200, 400, 500, 600), 45,000 lb (20 410 kg).

Dimensions: Span 95 ft 2 in (29,00 m) ; length, (Mk 100, 400, 600), 77 ft 3½ in (23,56 m), (Mk 500), 82 ft 2½ in (25,06 m) ; height (Mk 100–400, 600), 27 ft 11 in, (Mk 500), 28 ft 7¼ in (8,71 m) ; wing area, 753·5 sq ft (70,0 m²).

Accommodation: Flight crew of two (with provision for one supernumerary crew) and (Mk 100, 200, F.27, F.27A, F.27J) typical layouts for 40 passengers four-abreast or up to 52 in high density layouts ; (Mk 300, 400, 600, F.27B) mixed passenger/cargo loads.

Status: Prototypes first flown on 24 November 1955 (with Dart 507s and short fuselage) and 29 January 1957 respectively ; first production Mk 100 flown on 23 March 1958. Fairchild prototypes first flown on 12 April and 23 May 1958 respectively. First deliveries in June 1958 (Fairchild F.27 to Piedmont) ; November 1958 (Fokker F.27 to Aer Lingus) ; January 1959 (F.27A to Bonanza) ; October 1958 (F.27B to Northern Consolidated). First Mk 500 flown 15 November 1967 ; first deliveries (to ALM) June 1968. Production totals (including orders to end 1973), 409 by Fokker-VFW, 128 by Fairchild (F.27 variants).

FOKKER F.28 FELLOWSHIP

The photograph shows a Fokker F.28 Fellowship Mk 1000 supplied to the Government of Nigeria, and the silhouette depicts the Mk 6000 version

Country of Origin: Netherlands.

Type: Short-range airliner.

Power Plant: Two (Mk 1000, 2000) 9,850 lb st (4 468 kgp) Rolls-Royce Spey 555-15 or (Mk 5000, 6000) 9,675 lb st (4 390 kgp) Spey 555-15H turbofans.

Performance: Max cruising speed, 528 mph (849 km/h) at 21,000 ft (6 400 m); best economy cruise, 519 mph (836 km/h) at 25,000 ft (7 620 m); long-range cruise, 420 mph (676 km/h) at 30,000 ft (9 150 m); max operating ceiling, 35,000 ft (10 675 m); range with max payload (Mk 1000), 956 mls (1 538 km), (Mk 2000), 540 mls (870 km), (Mk 5000), 1,115 mls (1 797 km), (Mk 6000), 1,025 mls (1 650 km); range with max fuel, (Mk 1000), 1,208 mls (1 945 km), (Mk 2000), 1,215 mls (1 955 km).

Weights: Operating empty (Mk 1000), 35,517 lb (16 144 kg), (Mk 2000), 36,953 lb (16 707 kg), (Mk 5000), 36,250 lb (16 432 kg), (Mk 6000), 37,760 lb (17 127 kg); max payload, (Mk 1000), 19,700 lb (8 936 kg), (Mk 2000), 18,024 lb (8 200 kg), (Mk 5000, 6000), approx 18,250 lb (8 278 kg); max take-off (Mk 1000, 2000), 65,000 lb (29 480 kg), (Mk 5000, 6000), 70,000 lb (31 752 kg).

Dimensions: Span (Mk 1000, 2000), 77 ft 4¼ in (23,58 m), (Mk 5000, 6000), 82 ft 3¾ in (25,09 m); length, (Mk 1000, 5000), 89 ft 10¾ in (27,40 m), (Mk 2000, 6000), 97 ft 1¾ in (29,61 m); weight, 27 ft 9½ in (8,47 m); wing area (Mk 1000, 2000), 822 sq ft (76,4 m²), (Mk 5000, 6000), 850 sq ft (78,97 m²).

Accommodation: Flight crew of two (with one supernumerary seat); typical one-class accommodation for (Mk 1000, 5000) 60 or (Mk 2000, 6000) 75 passengers five-abreast or maximum high-density of 65 and 79 respectively or (Mk 1000-C) mixed loads.

Status: First flights of three prototypes (Mk 1000) on 9 May, 3 August and 20 October, 1967 respectively; Dutch certification and first delivery (to LTU) on 24 February 1969. First Mk 2000 flown on 28 April 1971; certification August 1972, first delivery (to Nigeria Airways) October 1972. First Mk 6000 flown 27 September 1973. Total sales (to early 1974), 86.

Notes: The Fellowship was developed as a successor to the F.27 Friendship (see page 48). The initial basic model is the Mk 1000, joined in 1973 by the first of the longer-fuselage Mk 2000s to enter service. The Mk 5000 and 6000, for service in 1975, are as Mk 1000 and 2000 respectively with leading-edge slats, extended wing tips, improved and quieter engines and higher weights.

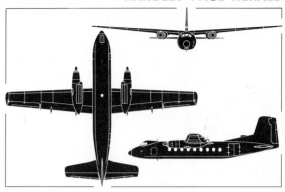

Shown in the photograph is a Handley Page Herald 200 as operated by British Island Airways, the silhouette (right) also showing the Series 200

Country of Origin: United Kingdom.

Type: Short-range feederliner.

Power Plant: Two 2,105 ehp Rolls-Royce Dart 527 turboprops.

Performance: Max cruising speed (Mk 100), 273 mph (439 km/h), (Mk 100), 274 mph (441 km/h) at 15,000 ft (4 572 m); best economy cruise, 265 mph (426 km/h) at 23,000 ft (7 010 m); initial rate of climb, (Srs 100), 2,000 ft/min (10,1 m/sec), (Srs 200), 1,805 ft/min (9,1 m/sec); service ceiling, (Srs 100), 33,000 ft (10 050 m), (Srs 200), 27,900 ft (8 504 m); no-reserves range with max payload (Mk 100), 708 mls (1 140 km), (Mk 200), 1,110 mls (1 786 km); no-reserves range with max fuel (Mk 100), 1,640 mls (2 640 km), (Mk 200), 1,620 mls (2 607 km).

Weights: Operating empty (Mk 100), 25,300 lb (11 480 kg), (Mk 200), 25,800 lb (11 700 kg); max payload, (Srs 100), 10,290 lb (4 668 kg), (Srs 200), 11,242 lb (5 100 kg); max take-off (Mk 100), 41,000 lb (18 597 kg), (Mk 200), 43,000 lb (19 505 kg).

Dimensions: Span, 94 ft 9 in (28,88 m); length, (Mk 100), 71 ft 11 in (21,92 m), (Mk 200), 75 ft 6 in (23,01 m); height, 24 ft 1 in (7,34 m); wing area, 886 sq ft (82,3 m²).

Accommodation: Flight crew of two and typical mixed-class seating for (Mk 100) 40 or (Mk 200) 44 passengers four-abreast and max high-density seating for (Mk 100) 47 or (Mk 200) 56 passengers.

Status: First of two prototypes (with Leonides engines) first flown 25 August 1955 and second (also with Leonides) on 3 August 1956. Both prototypes converted to Dart-engined Herald Srs 100 and flown on 11 March 1958 and 17 December 1958 respectively; second prototype converted to Srs 200 and flown on 8 April 1961. First commercial services (Srs 100) May 1961. Production totals: prototypes, 2; Srs 100, 4; Srs 200, 36; Srs 400, 8.

Notes: The Herald was conceived in the early 'fifties as a feeder-liner powered by four Alvis Leonides Major piston engines but after two prototypes had been built a revised market assessment led to substitution of Dart turboprops for the production version. Nevertheless, the type achieved little commercial success, as the production figures above indicate. The Series 100 and 200 differed primarily in fuselage length and Srs 400 was a military version of the latter, purchased only by Royal Malaysian Air Force. Principal commercial users in 1974 were British Island Airways and British Midland Airways.

HAWKER SIDDELEY HS.748

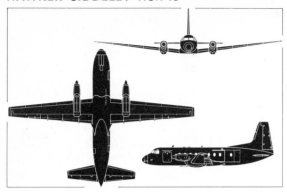

The Hawker Siddeley HS.748 Srs 2A is shown in both the photograph and the silhouette, the former depicting an aircraft operated by Air Malawi

Country of Origin: United Kingdom.

Type: Short-range transport.

Power Plant: Two (Srs 1) 1,880 ehp Rolls-Royce Dart 514 or (Srs 2) 2,105 ehp Dart 531 or (Srs 2A, 2C) 2,280 ehp Dart 532-2L or 2S turboprops.

Performance: Max cruising speed (Srs 1), 265 mph (426 km/h), (Srs 2A), 278 mph (448 km/h) at 10,000 ft (3 050 m) ; initial rate of climb (Srs 1), 810 ft/min (4,1 m/sec), (Srs 2A), 1,320 ft/min (6,7 m/sec) ; service ceiling, (Srs 1), 20,000 ft (6 100 m), (Srs 2A), 25,000 ft (7 600 m) ; range with max payload, (Srs 1), 105 mls (167 km), (Srs 2A), 530 mls (852 km) ; range with max fuel (Srs 1), 1,590 mls (2 560 km), (Srs 2, 2A), 1,987 mls (3 150 km).

Weights: Basic operating (Srs 1), 24,000 lb (10 885 kg), (Srs 2A), 26,700 lb (12 110 kg) ; max payload (Srs 1), 13,000 lb (5 900 kg), (Srs 2A), 11,800 lb (5 350 kg) ; max take-off, (Srs 1), 39,500 lb (17 915 kg), (Srs 2, 2A), 44,495 lb (20 182 kg).

Dimensions: Span, 98 ft 6 in (30,02 m) ; length, 67 ft 0 in (20,42 m) ; height, 24 ft 10 in (7,57 m) ; wing area, 810·75 sq ft (73,35 m²).

Accommodation: Flight crew of two and typical one-class accommodation for 40 or maximum high-density layouts for 58 passengers.

Status: Two prototypes flown on 24 June 1960 and 10 April 1961 respectively. First production Srs 1 flown on 30 August 1961 ; British C of A issued January 1962 ; first airline service (Skyways) Spring 1962. Prototype Srs 2 flown 6 November 1961, first production Srs 2 flown August 1962 ; British C of A October 1962. Srs 2C first flown on 31 December 1971. Production totals : Prototypes, 2 ; Srs 1, 18 ; Srs 2, 88 ; Srs 2A, 82 ; assembled by HAL in India, Srs 1, 4 ; and 2, 65 ; Srs 2C, 4.

Notes: The HS (originally Avro) 748 was given a go-ahead in January 1959 as a private-venture feederliner in the category of a "DC-3 replacement". The original Srs 1 was quickly replaced by the Srs 2 with uprated engines, a further improvement being made in mid-1967 with introduction of the Srs 2A. The standard 748 has a wide forward loading door to facilitate its use as a convertible passenger/freighter ; the Srs 2C in addition has a large door in the rear fuselage port side that can be opened in flight for air-dropping of paratroops and supplies. The HS.748 is also assembled by HAL at Bangalore, India, from British components, for Indian Airlines and the Indian Air Force.

The Martin 4-0-4 is still in small scale airline service in the USA, as for example by Marco Island Airways shown above, and a few are operated as company transports

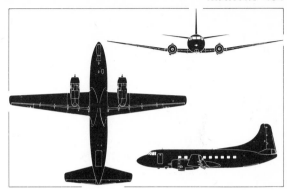

Country of Origin: USA.

Type: Short-range feederliner.

Power Plant: Two 2,400 hp Pratt & Whitney R-2800-CB-16 Double Wasp piston engines.

Performance: Max speed 312 mph (500 km/h) at 14,500 ft (4 420 m); typical cruise, 276 mph (442 km/h) at 18,000 ft (5 486 m); initial rate of climb, 1,905 ft/min (9,6 m/sec); service ceiling, 29,000 ft (8 845 m); range with payload of 10,205 lb (4 633 kg), 310 miles (500 km); range with maximum fuel, 1,070 miles (1 715 km).

Weights: Empty equipped, 29,126 lb (13 223 kg); max payload, 11,692 lb (5 263 kg); max take-off, 44,900 lb (20 385 kg); max landing, 43,000 lb (19 522 kg).

Dimensions: Span, 93 ft 3½ in (28,44 m); length, 74 ft 7 in (22,75 m); height, 28 ft 2 in (8,61 m); wing area, 864 sq ft (79,89 m²).

Accommodation: Typical layouts provide 48 or 52 passenger seats in one-class accommodation.

Status: Martin 202 first flown 22 November 1946; Martin 303 first flown 20 June 1947; Martin 404 prototype first flown 21 October 1950; Martin 404 first production flown 27 July 1951, entered airline service 5 October 1951 (TWA). Production totals, 31 Martin 202; 12 202A; one 303 and 101 Martin 404 (plus two military RM-1s for US Coast Guard).

Notes: The Martin 202 was evolved in the early post-war era as a potential replacement for the DC-3, competing in this market with the Convair 240/340/440 family, which achieved greater success than the Martin product. The 202 and 202A, respectively powered by 2,400 hp R-2800-CA-18 and CB-16 engines, are now out of service, and were unpressurised, but the Martin 303 prototype was pressurised and this feature plus further improvements were incorporated in the Martin 404. The latter type served for many years with two major US airlines, TWA and Eastern, and although it had been largely phased out of service by the mid-'sixties, one airline—Southern Airways of Atlanta, Georgia—still had a fleet of eight in service in 1974 and a few other examples were operating in South America. A small number of Martin 404s was also acquired for use as business transports after their airline service was completed, almost entirely for operation by US corporations, and were still operating in this rôle in 1974.

NAMC YS-11

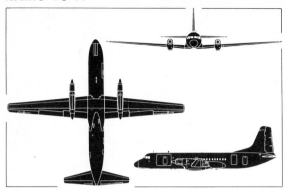

The photograph shows a NAMC YS-11 Srs 200 in service with the Brazilian air line VASP, and the silhouette illustrates the Srs 300 version

Country of Origin: Japan.

Type: Short- medium-range transport.

Power Plant: Two 3,060 hp Rolls-Royce Dart 542-10K turbo-props.

Performance: Max cruising speed at 15,000 ft (4 575 m) (200/300/400), 291 mph (469 km/h), (500/600/700), 290 mph (466 km/h); best economy cruise at 20,000 ft (6 100 m), (200/300/400), 281 mph (452 km/h), (500/600/700), 278 mph (447 km/h); initial rate of climb (200/300/400), 1,220 ft/min (6,2 m/sec); service ceiling (200/300/400), 22,900 ft (6 980 m); no-reserves range with max payload, 680 mls (1 090 km); no-reserves range with max fuel, 2,000 mls (3 215 km).

Weights: Operating empty (200, 500), 33,993 lb (15 419 kg), (300/600), 34,899 lb (15 830 kg), (400/700), 32,639 lb (14 805 kg); max payload (200), 14,508 lb (6 581 kg), (300), 13,602 lb (6 170 kg), (400), 15,862 lb (7 195 kg), (500), 15,610 lb (7 081 kg); max take-off (200/300/400), 54,010 lb (24 500 kg), (500/600/700), 55,115 lb (25 000 kg).

Dimensions: Span, 104 ft 11¾ in (32,00 m); length, 86 ft 3½ in (26,30 m); height, 29 ft 5½ in (8,98 m); wing area, 1,020·4 sq ft (94,8 m²).

Accommodation: Flight crew of two; typical one-class accommodation (200, 500) for 60 passengers four-abreast, or (300, 600) mixed passenger/cargo loads, with side-loading freight door or (400, 700) cargo only, with optional provision for troop seats.

Status: Two prototypes first flown on 30 August and 28 December 1962 respectively. First production aircraft flown on 23 October 1964; Japanese certification on 25 August 1964, FAA certification on 18 October 1965; airline deliveries began March 1965. Production totals, prototypes, 2; YS-11 (Srs 100), 47; YS-11A (Srs 200/300/400/500), 133, completed 1972.

Notes: Design of the YS-11 began in 1957 and its development and production became a joint industry undertaking, directed by a specially-formed organisation, NAMC. The first production batch of 47 aircraft were Series 100, with gross weight of 51,808 lb (23 500 kg) and payload of 11,538 lb (5 235 kg). Major production version was the YS-11A with higher weights, in three configurations; all-passenger Srs 200, mixed passenger/freighter 300 and all-cargo 400. The 500, 600 and 700 had the same configurations respectively with increased payload, but few were included in the final sales total.

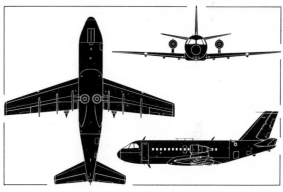

The photograph and silhouette illustrate the VFW614 with its unique overwing engine pods; the aircraft depicted (above) is the second prototype

Country of Origin: Federal Germany.

Type: Short-range transport.

Power Plant: Two 7,473 lb st (3 392 kgp) Rolls-Royce/ SNECMA M45H Mk 501 turbofans.

Performance: Max cruising speed, 457 mph (735 km/h) at 21,000 ft (6 400 m); long-range cruise, 390 mph (627 km/h) at 25,000 ft (7 620 m); initial rate of climb, 3,360 ft/min (17,1 m/sec); service ceiling, 25,000 ft (7 600 m); range with max payload, 700 mls (1 126 km); range with max fuel, 1,553 mls (2 500 km).

Weights: Operating empty, 26,900 lb (12 200 kg); max payload, 8,600 lb (3 900 kg); max take-off, 44,000 lb (19 950 kg).

Dimensions: Span, 70 ft 6 in (21,50 m); length, 67 ft 6 in (20,60 m); height, 25 ft 8 in (7,84 m); wing area, 688·9 sq ft (64,00 m²).

Accommodation: Flight crew of two; alternative cabin layouts for 36, 40 or 44 passengers four-abreast in one-class arrangement.

Status: Three prototypes first flown on 14 July 1971, 14 January 1972 and 10 October 1972 respectively. German and US certification scheduled for May and July 1974 respectively, with production deliveries starting early 1975. First contract placed May 1974, by Cimber Air for two.

Notes: Initial design work on the aircraft now in production as the VFW 614 began in 1962 under the designation E 614 by the working partnership of Weser, Focke Wulf and HFB (ERNO). Early studies were based on using Lycoming PLF 1 turbofans, but the Anglo-French M45H was picked in 1965 and the following year the German government gave its support for a limited go-ahead, extended in July 1968 to approval for three prototypes and two static test vehicles. The production go-ahead was given in mid-1970, with 24 airline purchase options in hand, but the programme twice suffered temporary termination, due to the Rolls-Royce bankruptcy and an accident suffered by the first prototype on 1 February 1972. Full series production was finally resumed on 13 December 1972, with 26 options in hand from nine customers. Production is a collaborative effort embracing, in addition to VFW-Fokker, MBB in Germany, SABCA and Fairey in Belgium and Fokker-VFW in the Netherlands. The first firm order for the VFW 614 was placed by Cimber Air in 1974; other companies holding options at that time included Sterling Airways, Bavaria Fluggesellschaft, General Air, TABA, Yemen Airlines, SATA of Algeria and the Spanish Ministry of Aviation.

VICKERS VISCOUNT

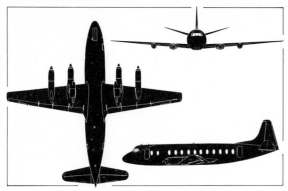

Shown in the photograph (above) is a Vickers Viscount 806 in the latest markings of British Airways, the silhouette also showing the Srs 800 version

Country of Origin: United Kingdom.

Type: Short-range turboprop transport.

Power Plant: Four (V700) 1,635 ehp Rolls-Royce Dart 506 or (V700D, V800) 1,740 ehp Dart 510 or (V806) 1,890 ehp Dart 520 or (V810) 1,990 ehp Dart 525 turboprops.

Performance: Cruising speed (V700), 315 mph (507 km/h) at 22,500 ft (6 858 m), (V810), 350 mph (563 km/h) at 20,000 ft (6 100 m) ; service ceiling (V700, V810), 25,000 ft (7 620 m) ; no-reserves range with max payload (V700), 1,750 mls (2 815 km), (V810), 1,725 mls (2 775 km) ; no-reserves range with max fuel, (V700), 2,080 mls (3 345 km), (V810), 1,760 mls (2 830 km).

Weights: Basic operating (V700), 38,100 lb (17 280 kg), (V810), 41,565 lb (18 753 kg) ; max payload (V700), 11,100 lb (5 035 kg), (V810), 14,500 lb (6 577 kg) ; max take-off (V700), 61,500 lb (27 895 kg), (V700D), 64,500 lb (29 260 kg), (V810), 72,500 lb (32 886 kg).

Dimensions: Span, 93 ft 8½ in (28,5 m) ; length (V700, 700D), 81 ft 9 in (24,93 m), (V800), 85 ft 8 in (26,11 m) ; height, 26 ft 9 in (8,16 m) ; wing area, 963 sq ft (89,46 m²).

Accommodation: Flight crew of two or three and typical layouts for (V700) 40 first-class or 47–63 tourist/economy class five-abreast or (V800) typical mixed-class layout for 12 plus 47 passengers or a maximum of 71 five-abreast in high-density layout.

Status: Prototype (V630) first flown 16 July 1948 ; prototype (V700) first flown on 28 August 1950 ; entered service (BEA) 18 April 1953 ; first production V802 flown on 27 July 1956 ; first V806 flown on 9 August 1957 ; first V810 flown on 23 December 1957. Production totals : prototypes 4 ; V700 series, 287 ; V800 series, 47 ; V806, 20 ; V810 series, 86 ; grand total 444.

Notes: The Viscount was the world's first turboprop transport to enter service and numerically was the most successful of the first generation of turbine airliners. The main production version was the V700, with the V700D being a more powerful version with higher gross weight. The 800 series introduced a lengthened fuselage and was produced in two principal forms with different versions of the Dart engine ; the V806, exclusive to BEA, was an interim model with less power than the fully developed V810. Over 200 Viscounts of all types remained in service in various parts of the world in 1974 for both scheduled and charter flights, and a few were also operating as military and VIP transports.

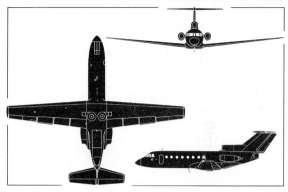

A standard production Yak-40 is depicted in Aeroflot colours (above), while the silhouette (right) shows the early version with small "acorn" fairing at the tailplane fin junction

Country of Origin: Soviet Union.

NATO Code Name: *Codling.*

Type: Short-range airliner.

Power Plant: Three 3,307 lb st (1 500 kgp) Ivchenko AI-25 turbofans.

Performance: Max speed, 373 mph (600 km/h) at sea level and 466 mph (750 km/h) at 17,000 ft (5 180 m); max cruise, 342 mph (550 km/h) at 19,685 ft (6 000 m); economy cruise, 310 mph (500 km/h) at 32,810 ft (10 000 m); initial rate of climb, 2,000 ft/min (10,16 m/sec); service ceiling, 38,715 ft (11 800 m); range with max payload, 807 mls (1 300 km); range with max fuel, 920 mls (1 480 km).

Weights: Empty (27-seat version) 20,725 lb (9 400 kg), (executive version) 21,715 lb (9 850 kg); max payload (40-seat version) 7,320 lb (3 320 kg), (executive version) 1,765 lb (800 kg) max take-off, 36,375 lb (16 500 kg).

Dimensions: Span, 82 ft 0¼ in (25,00 m); length, 66 ft 9½ in (20,36 m); height, 21 ft 4 in (6,50 m); wing area, 753·5 sq ft (70 m²).

Accommodation: Flight crew of two, and alternative arrange-ments for 27 or 34 passengers, three-abreast, or 40 in high-density four-abreast layout; or 8–10 passengers in business executive configuration.

Status: First of five prototypes flown 21 October 1966 and first production deliveries to Aeroflot made in 1966, with first com-mercial service flown on 30 September. Production total by early 1974, about 450.

Notes: In the category of a "DC-3 replacement", the Yak-40 is the smallest of the present generation of Soviet jet transports. The three-engined configuration indicates that good field performance took preference over operating economics in the design, and the Yak-40 is approved for operation from Class 5 (grass) airfields. Another feature intended to improve the short landing performance is the introduction of a clam-shell thrust reverser on the centre engine, on later production models. Deliveries were to begin in 1974 of a Yak-40V, with increased fuel capacity and 3,858 lb st (1 750 kgp) AI-25T engines. The Yak-40 is the subject of a major sales export campaign, among early customers outside the Soviet Union being Balkan Bulgarian Airline, CSA, Olympic Airways, Aertirrena of Italy, General Air of Germany and Bakhtar Afghan Airlines.

AEROSPATIALE (NORD) 262 AND FREGATE

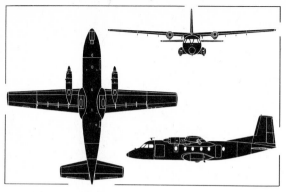

The Aérospatiale N.262A is shown in the silhouette (left) and the photograph (above) depicts an example of the Fregate in use as a demonstrator by Aérospatiale

Country of Origin: France.

Type: Third-level airliner.

Power Plant: Two 1,145 ehp Turboméca Bastan VII turboprops.

Performance (N 262A): Max speed, 239 mph (385 km/h); typical cruising speed, 233 mph (375 km/h); initial rate of climb, 1,200 ft/min (6,1 m/sec); service ceiling, 23,500 ft (7 160 m); range with max payload, 605 mls (975 km); range with max fuel, 1,095 mls (1 760 km).

Weights (N 262A): Basic operating weight, 15,496 lb (7 029 kg); max payload, 7,209 lb (3 270 kg); max take-off, 23,370 lb (10 600 kg); max landing, 22,710 lb (10 300 kg).

Dimensions: Span (N 262A), 71 ft 10 in (21,90 m), (Fregate), 74 ft 1¾ in (22,60 m); length, 63 ft 3 in (19,28 m); height, 20 ft 4 in (6,2 m); wing area (N 262A), 592 sq ft (55,0 m²), (Fregate), 601 sq ft (55,79 m²).

Accommodation: Flight crew of two; standard airline version seats 26 passengers; maximum, 29.

Status: Prototype Nord 262 first flown on 24 December 1962; first production Nord 262B flown on 8 June 1964, certificated and entered service July 1964; first Nord 262A flown early 1965, cer-

tificated March 1965, entered service August 1965; prototype N262C Fregate (new engines and wing-tips) flown July 1968; Fregate certificated December 1970. Production totals, one prototype, three pre-production, Nord 262A, 67; Nord 262B, four; N 262C, four; N 262D, 18.

Notes: Origin of this French feederliner was the MH-260, developed by Avions Max Holste as a turboprop derivative of the MH-250 Super Broussard which had Wasp piston engines. Ten pre-production MH-260s were operated by Air Inter and Widerøe's Flyveselskap while Nord developed the design with a circular-section pressurized fuselage, this being the Nord 262. Air Inter received the first four, designated Nord 262B, the main production version being the Nord 262A, the principal operators of which are Rousseau Aviation, Linjeflug, Cimber Air, Interregionalflug, STA (Algeria), Tunis Air and the Aéronavale. The Nord 262A had 1,080 ehp Bastan VIC engines and was followed, after Nord became part of Aérospatiale, by the Nord 262C and D, respectively civil and military versions with uprated Bastan VIIA engines and extended wing-tips. Nord 262s re-fitted with Pratt & Whitney PT6A-45 engines in 1975 are renamed Mohawk 298s.

The Antonov An-14 light transport, shown in Aeroflot colours (above). Serves in several utility rôles in the Soviet Union. The silhouette depicts the standard version

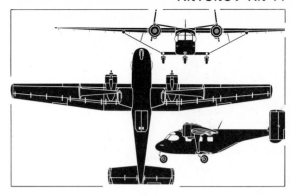

Country of Origin: USSR.
NATO Code Name: *Clod.*
Type: General purpose light transport and (An-14M) feederliner.
Power Plant: Two (An-14) 300 hp Ivchenko AI-14RF radial piston engines or (An-14M) 810 shp Isotov TVD-850 turboprops.
Performance: Max cruising speed (An-14), 118 mph (190 km/h), (An-14M), 189 mph (305 km/h); best economy cruise (An-14), 109 mph (175 km/h); service ceiling (An-14), 19,685 ft (6 000 m); range with max payload (An-14), 292 mls (470 km); max range (An-14), 423 mls (680 km), (An-14M), 714 mls (1 150 km).
Weights: Empty (An-14), 5,500 lb (2 495 kg), (An-14M), 7,715 lb (3 500 kg); max payload (An-14), 1,590 lb (720 kg), (An-14M), 2,865 lb (1 300 kg); max take-off (An-14), 7,935 lb (3 600 kg), (An-14M), 12,345 lb (5 600 kg).
Dimensions: Span, 72 ft 2 in (21,99 m); length (An-14), 37 ft 1½ in (11,31 m), (An-14M), 42 ft 7 in (12,98 m), height (An-14), 15 ft 2½ in (4,63 m), (An-14M), 15 ft 1 in (4,60 m); wing area, 441 sq ft (41,0 m²).
Accommodation: Flight crew of one or two and provision in cabin for (An-14) six or seven passengers or (An-14M) 15 passen-

gers three-abreast (two plus one).
Status: Prototype An-14 first flown 15 March 1958. Further prototypes and pre-production aircraft flown during 1959–1964. Quantity production initiated in 1965.
Notes: The An-14 was developed to meet Aeroflot requirements for a small utility transport with a better performance and greater comfort than the general-purpose An-2 (see page 74) which it was designed to succeed in some rôles. The prototypes underwent a protracted development process and the production model, when it eventually appeared, introduced a new wing with tapered outer panels, a new tail unit and uprated engines. Several hundred An-14s were built, primarily for Aeroflot but also for military duties, and some were adapted for agricultural, ambulance and cargo duties. A few were exported, in both civil and military guise, to Soviet Bloc nations in Europe. In 1969, a prototype of the An-14M was first flown, this having the basic An-14 wing but a new enlarged fuselage and turboprop engines. Production was expected to begin in 1973, with the designation changed to An-28, and like the An-14 this new variant was intended to serve with Aeroflot in a variety of rôles.

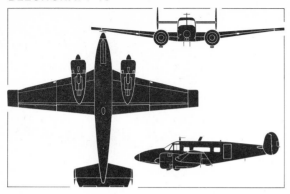

A late-production variant of the Beech 18 is shown in the photograph (above) in service in Colombia and in the silhouette, the extended wingtips being a prominent feature

Country of Origin: USA.

Type: Light general purpose transport.

Power Plant: Two 450 hp Pratt & Whitney R-985AN-14B Wasp Jr piston radial engines.

Performance: (Super H18) Max cruising speed, 220 mph (354 km/h) at 10,000 ft (3 050 m); best economy cruise, 185 mph (298 km/h) at 10,000 ft (3 050 m); initial rate of climb 1,400 ft/min (7,1 m/sec); service ceiling, 21,400 ft (6 520 m); range with max fuel, 1,530 mls (2 460 km).

Weights: (Super H18) Basic operating, 5,845 lb (2 651 kg); max take-off, 9,900 lb (4 490 kg).

Dimensions: (Super) 49 ft 8 in (15,14 m); length, 35 ft 2½ in (10,70 m); height, 9 ft 4 in (2,84 m); wing area, 360·7 sq ft (33,54 m²).

Accommodation: Flight crew of two and typical accommodation for 7–9 passengers in cabin.

Status: Prototype Model 18 first flown on 15 January 1937. First FAA Type approval 15 June 1938; first post-war model (D18S) approved 26 April 1946; H18 approved 11 July 1962. Production total, over 9,000, including 5,204 military versions, 1,030 post-war

Model C18 and D18, and 756 H18; completed 1969.

Notes: The Beech 18 enjoyed 32 years of continuous production, believed to be a world record. Original models had 300 hp Jacobs L-6 or 350 hp Wright R-760E engines but the Wasp Jr became standard in the pre-war C18S and in the range of military variants including the C-45, JRB and SNB. Production of the C18S was resumed after the war, and progressive improvements were introduced in the D18S of 1946, the D18C of 1947 with Continental R9-A engines, the E18S of 1954, the G18S of 1959 and the H18 of 1962. Many ex-military models also passed into commercial use. The Beech 18 also became the basis for several conversion schemes to make it more attractive in the third-level airline and business rôles. An optional nosewheel undercarriage was developed by Volpar and marketed in kit form, this being fitted from scratch on many of the Beech-built H18s; Volpar also developed its own turboprop conversion of the Beech 18 (see page 72). Other derivatives of the Beech 18 were the Dumodliner with fuselage lengthened to carry 14 passengers, and the PAC Tradewind with a single fin and rudder, and the Hamilton Westwind II (PT6A-34) and Westwind III (PT6A-20 or -27).

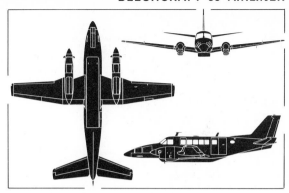

Shown in the photograph is a Beech 99 operated as an airliner by Air-Alpes and carrying a baggage pannier beneath the fuselage, also shown in the silhouette

Country of Origin: USA.

Type: Commuter transport.

Power Plant: Two (Model 99 and A99) 550 shp Pratt & Whitney PT6A-20 or (99A, A99A, B99) 680 shp PT6A-27 turboprops.

Performance: Max cruising speed (99), 254 mph (409 km/h) at 8,000 ft (2 440 m), (B99), 283 mph (455 km/h) at 8,000 ft (2 440 m); initial rate of climb (99), 1,700 ft/min (8,6 m/sec), (B99), 2,090 ft/min (10,6 m/sec); service ceiling (99), 23,650 ft (7 210 m), (B99), 26,313 ft (8 020 m); range with max payload, (99), 422 mls (679 km), (B99), 530 mls (853 km); range with max fuel, (99), 907 mls (1 459 km), (B99), 838 mls (1 348 km).

Weights: Empty equipped, (99), 5,722 lb (2 595 kg), (B99), 5,872 lb (2 663 kg); max take-off (99), 10,400 lb (4 717 kg), (B99), 10,900 lb (4 944 kg).

Dimensions: Span, 45 ft 10½ in (14,00 m); length, 44 ft 6¾ in (13,58 m); height, 14 ft 4¼ in (4,38 m); wing area, 279·7 sq ft (25,98 m²).

Accommodation: Flight crew of two and standard accommodation in airline version for 15 passengers two-abreast or six in executive layouts.

Status: Long-fuselage Queen Air prototype first flown in December 1965, and with turboprop engines in July 1966. FAA Type certification and first production delivery, 2 May 1968. Total production to March 1974, 153.

Notes: The Beech 99, largest of the company's range of twin-engined aircraft, was evolved from the original piston-engined Queen Air during 1965. Preliminary tests were conducted with a long-fuselage Queen Air before Pratt & Whitney PT6A turboprops were first installed, using the nacelles that meanwhile had been evolved for the King Air (see page 96). The Beech 99 is intended primarily for commuter airline use and most of those built to date are used in this rôle by US operators. An optional extra is a wide cargo-loading door ahead of the standard passenger door (which incorporates an air-stair) and this facilitates use of the Beech 99 in mixed passenger-cargo operations. An executive layout has also been designed, providing roomy accommodation for six passengers. The Model 99A had PT6A-27 engines derated to 550 shp, and nine of these aircraft supplied to the Chilean Air Force in 1969 were designated Model 99A (FACH). A ventral pannier is available to increase the baggage capacity.

BRITTEN-NORMAN ISLANDER

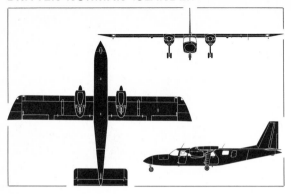

The photograph shows an Islander in original standard configuration operated as a light transport for company use and the silhouette depicts the newer BN-2A-8S version

Country of Origin: United Kingdom.

Type: General purpose light transport.

Power Plant: Two (BN-2A, A1, A6, A7, A8, A9) 260 hp Avco Lycoming O-540-E4C5 or (BN-2A, A2, A3) 300 hp Avco Lycoming IO-540-K or (BN-2A10, A11) 270 hp Avco Lycoming TIO-540-H piston engines.

Performance: Max speed (A8), 170 mph (273 km/h), (A2), 180 mph (290 km/h); typical cruise at 9,000 ft (2 750 m), (A8), 158 mph (254 km/h), (A2), 168 mph (270 km/h); initial rate of climb (A8), 1,050 ft/min (5,3 m/sec), (A2), 1,250 ft/min (6,35 m/sec); service ceiling (A8), 14,600 ft (4 450 m), (A2), 19,400 ft (5 913 m); range at typical cruise speed (A8), 822 mls (1 322 km), (A2), 800 mls (1 287 km); range with max fuel (A9), 1,193 mls (1 920 km).

Weights: Basic operating (A8), 3,588 lb (1 627 kg), (A2), 3,738 lb (1 695 kg); max take-off (A to A11), 6,300 lb (2 857 kg), (BN-2A-D), 6,600 lb (2 993 kg).

Dimensions: Span (A, A2, A6, A8, A10), 49 ft 0 in (14,94 m), (A1, A3, A7, A9, A11), 53 ft 0 in (16,15 m); length (A to A11), 35 ft 7¾ in (10,86 m), (BN.2A-S), 39 ft 5¼ in (12,02 m); height, (all) 13 ft 8¾ in (4,18 m); wing area (A, A2, A6, A8, A10), 325 sq ft (30,19 m²), (A1, A3, A7, A9, A11), 337 sq ft (31,25 m²).

Accommodation: Pilot and standard accommodation for nine or (BN.2A-S) 11 passengers two abreast with no aisle in fuselage.

Status: First prototype flown (with 210 hp R-R Continental IO-360 engines) on 13 June 1965 and (with Lycoming O-540 engines) on 17 December 1965. Second prototype flown on 20 August 1966; first production BN-2 flown on 24 April 1967. Prototype BN-2S (R-R Continental TSIO-520) flown on 6 September 1968. First by IRMA (Rumania) flown 4 August 1969. First BN-2A2 flown on 30 April 1970. First BN-2A10 flown on 30 April 1971. First Defender flown on 20 May 1971. First BN-2A8S flown on 22 August 1972. Production total to mid-1974, over 500.

Notes: The Islander was conceived in 1963 as a light transport in the category of a Rapide replacement. Originally powered by 210 hp engines, it has subsequently evolved through the versions indicated above; long-range models have extra fuel in extended wing tips and the A6, 7, 8 and 9 subvariants introduce various refinements. The D suffix indicates increased gross weight and S indicates a longer nose and extra cabin accommodation. Also available is a version with Rajay superchargers on the O-540 engines, indicated by an R suffix.

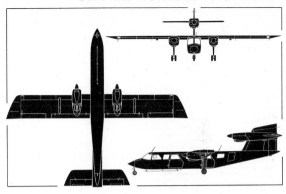

The photograph and silhouette show the initial production standard Trislander, the former depicting an aircraft in the markings of JF Airlines

Country of Origin: United Kingdom.

Type: Commuter and third-level airliner.

Power Plant: Three 260 hp Lycoming O-540-E4C5 piston engines.

Performance: Max speed, 183 mph (294 km/h) at sea level; max cruising speed (75 per cent engine power), 176 mph (283 km/h) at 6,500 ft (1 988 m); typical cruise (67 per cent engine power), 174 mph (280 km/h) at 9,000 ft (2 750 m); best economy cruise (59 per cent engine power), 168 mph (270 km/h) at 13,000 ft (3 960 m); initial rate of climb, 980 ft/min (4,98 m/sec); service ceiling, 13,150 ft (4 010 m); range with max payload (VFR reserves) 210 mls (338 km); range with max fuel, 860 mls (1 384 km).

Weights: Basic operating, 6,178 lb (2 800 kg); max payload, 3,550 lb (1 610 kg); max take-off, 10,000 lb (4 536 kg).

Dimensions: Span, 53 ft 0 in (16,15 m); length, 43 ft 9 in (13,34 m); height, 13 ft 5¾ in (4,11 m); gross wing area, 337 sq ft (31,25 m²).

Accommodation: Pilot and up to 18 passenger seats, two abreast with no aisle in cabin.

Status: Long-fuselage Islander prototype first flown on 14 July 1968. Prototype Trislander (same airframe) first flown 11 September 1970. First production Trislander flown 6 March 1971. British certification 14 May 1971; FAA Type approval 4 August 1971. Initial delivery (to Aurigny) 29 June 1971. Production/order total to end-1973, about 20.

Notes: The BN-2A Mk III Trislander is an outgrowth of the Islander, evolved by way of a "long-fuselage" Islander flown in 1968, and using the same wing and powerplant with a lengthened fuselage of the same cross section, with the addition of a third engine located on the enlarged fin. Initial aircraft were delivered with a gross weight of 9,350 lb (4 241 kg) but this was later increased to 10,000 lb (4 536 kg) as indicated above. Production began at the Britten-Norman factory at Bembridge on the Isle of Wight, using components produced under contract by BHC, but following acquisition of Britten-Norman by the Fairey Group in 1972, the Trislander production line was transferred to Gosselies in Belgium, deliveries from the new location starting early in 1974. New Trislander variants include a version with the extended nose of the BN-2A8S variant of the Islander (see page 62), increasing the overall length to 47 ft 6 in (14,48 m).

DE HAVILLAND DHC-6 TWIN OTTER

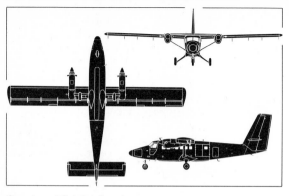

The photograph shows a de Havilland Twin Otter 200 serving with Southwest Air Lines in Japan and the silhouette depicts the Srs 300 version

Country of Origin: Canada.

Type: Commuter and third-level airliner.

Power Plant: Two (Srs 100, 200) 579 eshp Pratt & Whitney PT6A-20 or (Srs 300, 300S) 652 eshp PT6A-27 turboprops.

Performance: Max cruising speed (Srs 100), 184 mph (297 km/h), (Srs 300), 210 mph (338 km/h); best economy cruise (Srs 100), 156 mph (251 km/h); initial rate of climb (Srs 100), 1,550 ft/min (7,9 m/sec), (Srs 300), 1,600 ft/min (8,1 m/sec); service ceiling (Srs 100), 25,500 ft (7 770 m), (Srs 300), 26,700 ft (8 140 m); range with max payload, 115 mls (160 km); range with max fuel (Srs 100), 920 mls (1 480 km), (Srs 300), 1,103 mls (1 775 km).

Weights: Basic operating (Srs 100), 6,170 lb (2 800 kg), (Srs 300), 7,320 lb (3 320 kg); max payload, 4,430 lb (2 010 kg); max take-off (Srs 100), 11,579 lb (5 252 kg), (Srs 300), 12,500 lb (5 670 kg).

Dimensions: Span, 65 ft 0 in (19,81 m); length (Srs 100), 49 ft 6 in (15,09 m), (Srs 300), 51 ft 9 in (15,77 m); height, 18 ft 7 in (5,66 m); wing area, 420 sq ft (39,02 m²).

Accommodation: Pilot and second seat on flight deck and up to 20 seats in cabin with central aisle.

Status: Prototype first flown on 20 May 1965; type approval and first deliveries May 1966. Series 200 deliveries began April 1968. Series 300 deliveries began Spring 1969. Production totals, Srs 100, 115; Srs 200, 115; Srs 300, over 190, with production continuing.

Notes: The Twin Otter originated, as the name indicates, as a twin-engined version of the Otter (see page 82) with many of the same fuselage and wing components. The first three examples had 579 eshp PT6A-6 engines. Initial production batch of Srs 100s was followed by an equal quantity of Srs 200s, with lengthened nose and internal changes to increase the baggage space. The Srs 300, in production in 1974, introduced uprated engines and higher operating weights. In 1973, the Canadian Government ordered six Twin Otters for the Airtransit experiment by Air Canada, intended to gather data on a short-range scheduled STOL service, and these were of a new Srs 300S type with special instrumentation and other features for specific STOL operation, including spoilers in the upper wing surfaces. They went into service in July 1974. A seaplane version of the Twin Otter is also available, with twin floats, and nearly 50 of this version have been delivered.

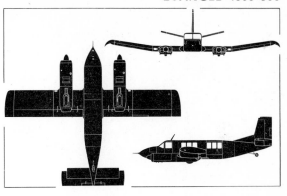

The photograph and silhouette depict the Evangel 4500 general purpose light transport, the former showing an early production model in the markings of the Colombian air line RANSA

Country of Origin: USA.

Type: Light general purpose transport.

Power Plant: Two 300 hp Lycoming IO-540-K1B5 flat-six piston engines.

Performance: Max speed, 230 mph (370 km/h); max cruising speed, 182 mph (293 km/h) at 6,000 ft (1 830 m); economical cruise, 175 mph (282 km/h) at 10,000 ft (3 050 m); initial rate of climb, 1,500 ft/min (7,6 m/sec); service ceiling, 21,030 ft (6 410 m); range with max fuel, 700 mls (1 126 km) at 175 mph (282 km/h) at 10,000 ft (3 050 m) and 637 mls (1 025 km) at 182 mph (293 km/h) at 6,000 ft (1 830 m).

Weights: Empty, 3,530 lb (1 600 kg); max take-off and landing, 5,500 lb (2 495 kg).

Dimensions: Span, 41 ft 3 in (12,52 m); length, 31 ft 6 in (9,60 m); height, 9 ft 6 in (2,90 m); wing area, 251 sq ft (23,32 m²).

Accommodation: Pilot and eight passengers.

Status: Prototype first flown June 1964; first production aircraft flown January 1969; FAA Type Approval 21 July 1970. Production, eight to spring of 1974 with production continuing.

Notes: Design of the Evangel 4500 was undertaken to produce a light general purpose transport with a STOL performance and with characteristics suiting it for operation in "out-back" conditions with the minimum of ground support services. The structure is designed to withstand rough usage and light alloy skins are used throughout to permit easy repair of minor damage in the field. A box-like fuselage structure and untapered wings facilitate production, maintenance and repair. Access to the cabin is gained through large doors, one in each side of the fuselage, to permit easy loading of freight, and the simple cabin furnishing includes inward-facing seats for all but two of the passengers. Although there are no special aero-dynamic devices to achieve STOL performance, other than conventional single-slotted flaps on the trailing edge, the Evangel 4500 has a take-off run of only 500 ft (152 m) and clears 50 ft (15,2 m) in a distance of 1,125 ft (343 m), thanks primarily to the very low wing loading. After successful testing of the prototype, the Evangel entered production in 1970 and among the South American customers for the aircraft are RANSA in Colombia and LORASA of Peru. Also under development in 1973 was a version with turbo-supercharged engines and max take-off weight increased to 5,800 lb (2 630 kg).

GRUMMAN (McKINNON) GOOSE

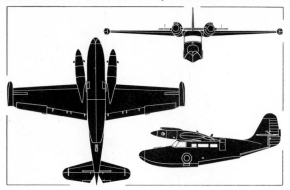

Both the photograph and the silhouette depict the Grumman Goose as converted by McKinnon to have turboprops, retractable wing-tip floats and an extended bow

Country of Origin: USA.

Type: Commuter third-level and business transport amphibian.

Power Plant: Two (G-21, G-21A) 450 hp Pratt & Whitney R-985-SB-2 piston engines or (G-21D, E) 579 eshp Pratt & Whitney PT6A-20 or (G-21G) 715 eshp PT6A-27 turboprops.

Performance: Max speed (G-21A), 201 mph (323 km/h), (G-21G), 236 mph (380 km/h); cruising speed (G-21A), 191 mph (307 km/h); initial rate of climb (G-21A), 1,300 ft/min (6,6 m/sec); service ceiling (G-21A), 22,000 ft (6 706 m), (G-21G) 20,000 ft (6 096 m); range with max fuel (G-21A), 800 mls (1 287 km), (G-21G), 1,600 mls (2 575 km).

Weights: Empty (G-21A), 5,425 lb (2 461 kg), (G-21G), 6,700 lb (3 040 kg); max take-off (G-21A), 8,000 lb (3 629 kg), (G-21G) 12,500 lb (5 670 kg).

Dimensions: Span (G-21A), 49 ft 0 in (14,95 m), (G-21G), 50 ft 10 in (15,49 m); length (G-21A), 38 ft 4 in (11,7 m), (G-21G), 39 ft 7 in (12,07 m); height (G-21A) 12 ft 0 in (3,66 m); wing area (G-21A), 375 sq ft (34,8 m²), (G-21G), 377·64 sq ft (35,07 m²).

Accommodation: (G-21A) Pilot and up to seven passengers or (G-21G) pilot and up to 11 passengers.

Status: G-21 first flown June 1937; Type Approval 29 September 1937; G-21A Type Approval 5 February 1938. G-21C first flown 25 January 1958, Type Approval 7 November 1958 and first production model flown 30 December 1958. First G-21E flown 1966, Type Approval February 1967; G-21G Type Approval 29 August 1969. Total G-21 production, about 350.

Notes: A few examples of the original G-21A Goose amphibian survive in airline service, primarily in Alaska, where their amphibious capability makes them hard to replace, despite their age. The G-21B was a pure flying-boat version of the design. Since 1958, McKinnon Enterprises has offered a series of conversion and modernization schemes, and various examples are in business and airline use. The G-21C and G-21D had four 340 hp Lycoming piston engines, the latter with a lengthened bow. The G-21E introduced two PT6A-20 turboprops and the G-21G has the uprated PT6A-27s; retractable wing-tip floats are a feature of these conversions. A major increase in gross weight, accommodation and range has been achieved, as the data above show. The G-21F designation applied to a projected McKinnon conversion that was to have AiResearch TPE-331 turboprops.

HAWKER SIDDELEY (DH) DOVE

The Hawker Siddeley (originally de Havilland) Dove is shown in its Srs 8 executive transport variant in both the photograph and the silhouette

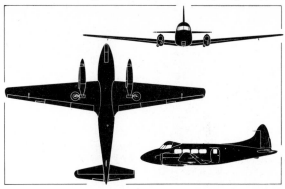

Country of Origin: United Kingdom.
Type: Feederline and executive transport.
Power Plant: Two 400 hp de Havilland Gipsy Queen 70 Mk 3 in-line six-cylinder engines.
Performance: (Dove 8), Max speed, 230 mph (370 km/h), cruising speeds, 187–210 mph (301–338 km/h) at 8,000 ft (2 440 m); range with max payload, 385 mls (620 km); range with max fuel, 880 mls (1 415 km).
Weights: Empty, 6,325 lb (2 869 kg); max take-off, 8,950 lb (4 060 kg); payload, 1,477 lb (670 kg).
Dimensions: Span, 57 ft (17,40 m); length, 39 ft 3 in (11,96 m); height, 13 ft 4 in (4,06 m); wing area, 335 sq ft (31,1 m²).
Accommodation: Two pilots and various seating arrangements for up to 11 passengers.
Status: First prototype flew on 25 September 1945, as Britain's first post-war civil product. Production totalled 540, being completed in 1968.
Notes: Initial production versions were Dove 1 and Dove 2, respectively passenger transport and executive models, with 330 hp Gipsy Queen 70–3 engines and 8,000 lb (3 629 kg) gross weight.

Dove 1B and 2B were similar with 240 hp Gipsy Queen 70–4s. The Dove 5 and 6, respectively airliner and executive versions, had 380 hp Gipsy Queen 70–2 engines and 8,800 lb (3 992 kg) gross weight. The Dove 7 (airliner) and 8 (executive) introduced the Gipsy Queen 70 Mk 3 with ejector exhausts, and a larger Heron-type cockpit canopy. The Dove 8A or Custom 600 was specially equipped for the North American market. Several Dove conversion schemes have been developed in the USA, including the Riley Turbo-Executive 400, which has 400 hp Lycoming IO-720 flat-eight engines with Riley Turbo 300 turbosuperchargers. Associated with this modification is a swept-back fin and rudder, and several other options are offered, including a remanufactured flight deck, flush-rivetting of the entire wing, addition of airstairs, re-styled cabin interior and a high grade exterior finish. Another modification programme based on the Dove produced the Carstedt Jet Liner 600, this having a lengthened fuselage, gross weight of 9,150 lb (4 150 kg) and two 605 ehp Garrett AiResearch TPE 331 turboprops. Two of these conversions were acquired early in 1974 by International Air Cargo of Washington DC. Many original Doves remain in use as business transports and for third-level airline and commuter use.

HAWKER SIDDELEY (DH) HERON (AND SAUNDERS ST-27)

Commuter/Light transport

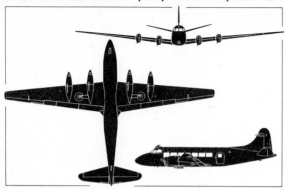

While the silhouette (left) shows the Hawker Siddeley Heron in its standard version, the photograph (above) depicts the Saunders ST-27 with turboprops and longer fuselage

Country of Origin: United Kingdom (and Canada).
Type: Third-level airline and business transport.
Power Plant: Four (D.H. 114) 250 hp de Havilland Gipsy Queen 30 Mk 2 piston engines or (ST-27) two 783 eshp Pratt & Whitney (VACL) PT6A-34 turboprops.
Performance: Max cruising speed (Heron 2B), 191 mph (307 km/h), (ST-27), 230 mph (370 km/h); best economy cruise (Heron 2B), 183 mph (294 km/h), (ST-27), 210 mph (338 km/h); initial rate of climb (Heron 2B), 1,075 ft/min (5,5 m/sec), (ST-27), 1,600 ft/min (8,1 m/sec); service ceiling (Heron 2B), 17,200 ft (5 242 m), (ST-27), 25,000 ft (7 620 m); range with max payload (Heron 2B), 1,163 mls (1 867 km), (ST-27), 115 mls (185 km); range with max fuel (Heron 2B), 1,800 mls (2 896 km), (ST-27), 817 mls (1 315 km).
Weights: Empty equipped (Heron 2B), 9,200 lb (4 173 kg), (ST-27), 7,900 lb (3 583 kg); max payload (Heron 2B), 2,600 lb (1 180 kg), (ST-27), 4,950 lb (2 245 kg); max take-off (Heron 2B, ST-27), 13,500 lb (6 123 kg).
Dimensions: Span, 71 ft 6 in (21,79 m); length (Heron 2B), 48 ft 6 in (14,78 m), (ST-27), 59 ft 0 in (17,98 m); height, 15 ft 7 in

(4,75 m); wing area, 499 sq ft (46,36 m²).
Accommodation: Flight crew of two and (Heron) up to 17 or (ST-27) 20–23 passengers.
Status: Prototype D.H. 114 first flown on 10 May 1950; first Srs 2 flown on 14 December 1952. Production total, 148. Prototype ST-27 first flown on 28 May 1969; UK certification 16 September 1970, Canadian certification 14 May 1971. Production total, 13.
Notes: The Heron was developed as a "big brother" to the D.H. 104 Dove (see page 67) with four engines and longer fuselage. The initial Srs 1 had fixed nosewheel landing gear, that on the Srs 2 being retractable; the Srs 2D introduced DH fully-feathering propellers, and other suffixes indicated special interiors. One Super Heron was a conversion in Mexico with 340 hp Lycoming engines, and Shin Meiwa in Japan modified five Heron 1s to have 260 hp Continentals. The Saunders ST-27 is a re-manufactured Heron with turboprop engines and lengthened fuselage, the first two entering service in Columbia in 1971 and others operating in Canada. For deliveries starting in 1975, the ST-27B will have more fuel and will comply with FAR Part 25; the prototype is a converted ST-27 and is designated ST-27A.

68

LET L-410 TURBOLET

The LET L-410 Turbolet light transport has entered local service in Czechoslovakia and is in production for Aeroflot in the Soviet Union. The photograph shows an early example

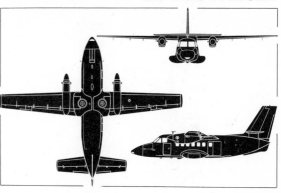

Country of Origin: Czechoslovakia.
Type: Commuter and third-level airliner.
Power Plant: Two 736 eshp M-601 or 715 eshp Pratt & Whitney (UACL) PT6A-27 turboprops.
Performance: Max cruising speed, 236 mph (380 km/h) at 9,840 ft (3 000 m), best economy cruise, 227 mph (365 km/h); initial rate of climb, 1,810 ft/min (9,2 m/sec); service ceiling, 26,575 ft (8 100 m); range with max payload, 124 mls (200 km); range with max fuel, 807 mls (1 300 km).
Weights: Basic weight empty, 6,834 lb (3 100 kg); operating weight empty (cargo version), 7,275 lb (3 300 kg); max cargo payload, 4,078 lb (1 850 kg); max take-off, 11,905 lb (5 400 kg); max landing, 11,465 lb (5 200 kg).
Dimensions: Span, 57 ft 4¼ in (17,48 m); length, 44 ft 7¾ in (13,61 m); height, 18 ft 6½ in (5,65 m); wing area, 353·7 sq ft (32,86 m²).
Accommodation: Flight crew of one or two; accommodation in cabin for 15–19 passengers three-abreast (2+1).
Status: Prototype first flown on 16 April 1969; production deliveries began in 1971.

Notes: The Turbolet was developed at the Kunovice works of the Czech National Aircraft Industry, being the first indigenous design to emerge from this factory. Design work began in 1966 and although it was always intended that the L-410 should be powered by locally-developed turboprops, Canadian Pratt & Whitney PT6A-27s were utilised in the four prototypes used for certification and are available as a production option. As first flown the prototype L-410 was a little smaller than production aircraft, the fuselage being subsequently lengthened by 1 ft (0,30 m) and the span increased by 1 ft 6 in (0,46 m). The basic Turbolet is intended as a commuter or third-level airliner, and the first production models (all with PT6A engines) were delivered to a new Czech domestic airline, Slov-Air, which had four in regular service by 1972. The type was also selected by Aeroflot in the Soviet Union, apparently after a competitive evaluation involving also the An-14M (see page 59) and the Beriev Be-30. Other Turbolet versions are an eight-seat executive model and an all cargo variant. Deliveries of the version of the L-410 powered by the M-601 engine with Avia three-blade, reversible-pitch propellers, were expected to begin in 1975. The engine had previously been flight-tested in an Avia-14.

SHORT SD3-30

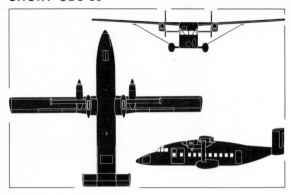

Scheduled to fly in the summer of 1974, the Short SD3-30, depicted by the silhouette and (above) by an artist's impression, is an enlarged version of the Skyvan

Country of Origin: United Kingdom.

Type: Third-level airliner.

Power Plant: Two 1,120 shp Pratt & Whitney (UACL) PT6A-45 turboprops.

Performance (Estimated): Max cruising speed, 228 mph (367 km/h) at 10,000 ft (3 280 m); long-range cruise, 184 mph (296 km/h); initial rate of climb, 1,280 ft/min (6,5 m/sec); range with max payload, 276 mls (444 km) with 30 passengers at long-range cruise speed, 870 mls with 20 passengers at long-range cruise speed.

Weights: Empty equipped weight, 13,890 lb (6 300 kg); design max payload, 7,500 lb (3 400 kg); max take-off, 21,700 lb (9 840 kg).

Dimensions: Span, 74 ft 9 in (22,78 m); length, 58 ft 0½ in (17,69 m); height, 15 ft 8 in (4,78 m); wing area, 453 sq ft (42,1 m²).

Accommodation: Flight crew of two (with functional provision for one-pilot operation) and standard accommodation for 30 passengers in three-abreast (two plus one) layout. Baggage compartments in nose and at rear of cabin, on main floor level, with external access to each.

Status: Prototype first flight scheduled for August 1974. Two prototypes and three pre-production models for certification, leading to British C of A in September 1975. Production rate rising to four a month by end of 1976.

Notes: The SD3-30 is an outgrowth of the Skyvan (see page 89) optimised for the commuter and regional air transport rôle. A major objective was to achieve a selling price of $1m (£400,000) in 1973 values, a go-ahead for the project being given on 23 May 1973 with a UK government loan of £4·25m towards the launching costs. The fuselage cross section and basic structure is the same as that of the Skyvan and the wing design is similar although of greater span. Operations from semi-prepared surfaces are possible and special attention is given to low noise levels, a contribution to which is made by the use of large-diameter, slow running five-bladed propellers. Shorts also propose to develop a military version of the design as the SD3-M, with special interior arrangements to permit a wide range of military loads to be carried, such as 34 equipped troops or 26 armed paratroops, 15 stretcher casualties, Land Rovers or similar vehicles or 8,000 lb (3 630 kg) of cargo.

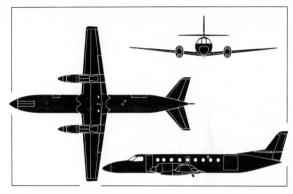

The Swearingen Metro is shown in the photograph above in the markings of Air Wisconsin. When operated as a business transport, the same type of aircraft is known as the Merlin IV

Country of Origin: USA.

Type: Commuter and third-level airliner and (Merlin 4) business transport.

Power Plant: Two 940 shp Garrett-AiResearch TPE 331-3UW-303G turboprops.

Performance: Max cruising speed, 294 mph (473 km/h) at 10,000 ft (3 050 m); best range cruise, 279 mph (449 km/h) at 20,000 ft (6 100 m); initial rate of climb, 2,400 ft/min (12.2 m/sec); maximum certificated altitude, 31,000 ft (9 450 m); range with max payload (Metro), 100 mls (161 km), (Merlin 4), 473 mls (761 km); range with max fuel (Metro), 500 mls (804 km), (Merlin 4), 1,775–2,300 mls (2 855–3 700 km); max ferry range, 2,464 mls (3 965 km).

Weights: (Metro) Empty, less avionics, 7,400 lb (3 356 kg); (Merlin 4); empty, including avionics 8,370 lb (3 796 kg); max payload, 3,920 lb (1 778 kg); max take-off, 12,500 lb (5 670 kg).

Dimensions: Span, 46 ft 3 in (14.10 m); length, 59 ft 4¼ in (18,09 m); height, 16 ft 8 in (5,08 m); wing area, 277·5 sq ft (25,78 m²).

Accommodation: Flight crew of two and (Metro) up to 22 passengers two abreast in cabin, with central aisle or (Merlin 4) up to 12 passengers in cabin.

Status: Prototype first flown on 26 August 1969; FAA type approval (Metro) 11 June 1970, (Merlin 4) 22 September 1970. Deliveries began 28 December 1970. Production total (Metro and Merlin 4) about 15 by end-1973.

Notes: The Metro, and its business and executive versions known as the Merlin 4, was the first wholly new design by the original Swearingen Aircraft Company, which had previously specialised in conversions of other makers' types for business users (see Merlin II and III, page 125). Construction of the prototype Metro began in August 1968; one or two were delivered by Swearingen, but production plans were interrupted when Swearingen encountered financial difficulties in 1971. These were resolved by acquisition of the company by Fairchild Industries in November of that year. Active marketing of the Metro was resumed after an 18-month interval in 1972 and regular airline operations began in mid-1973. By mid-1974, Commuter Airlines had ordered four, Mississippi Valley Airlines had one and Air Wisconsin had five with two more on order.

VOLPAR TURBO 18 AND TURBOLINER

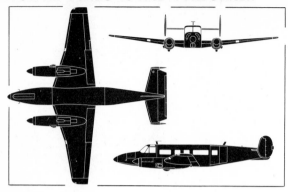

The Volpar Turboliner is a heavily modified conversion of the Beech 18, new features visible in the photograph above including turbo-prop engines, wide loading door and ventral fin

Country of Origin: USA.

Type: General purpose light transport and commuter.

Power Plant: Two 705 eshp Garrett-AiResearch TPE 331-1-101B turboprops.

Performance: Max cruising speed, 280 mph (451 km/h); best economy cruise, 256 mph (412 km/h); initial rate of climb (Turbo 18), 1,710 ft/min (8,7 m/sec), (Turboliner), 1,520 ft/min (7,7 m/sec); service ceiling (Turbo 18), 26,000 ft (7 925 m), (Turboliner), 24,000 ft (7 315 m); range with max payload (Turbo 18), 461 mls (741 km), (Turboliner), 346 mls (556 km); range with max fuel, (Turbo 18), 2,170 mls (3 492 km), (Turboliner), 2,076 mls (3 340 km).

Weights: Basic operating (Turbo 18), 5,500 lb (2 495 kg), (Turboliner cargo), 5,900 lb (2 676 kg), (Turboliner airliner), 6,600 lb (2 993 kg); max payload (Turbo 18), 4,786 lb (2 171 kg); max take-off (Turbo 18), 10,286 lb (4 666 kg), (Turboliner), 11,500 lb (5 216 kg).

Dimensions: Span, 46 ft 0 in (14,02 m); length (Turbo 18), 37 ft 5 in (11,40 m), (Turboliner), 44 ft 2½ in (13,47 m); height, 9 ft 7 in (2,92 m); wing area, 374 sq ft (34,75 m²).

Accommodation: Flight crew of two and (Turbo 18) up to 10 passengers or (Turboliner) up to 15 passengers or 400 cu ft (11,33 m²) of cargo.

Status: First Turbo 18 conversion, 1965; FAA Type approval 17 February 1966. First Turboliner conversion flown 12 April 1967; FAA Type approval 29 March 1968. Production totals, Turbo 18 over 24; Turboliner, over 20.

Notes: Volpar Inc was formed in 1960 to market a nosewheel undercarriage conversion kit for the Beech 18 (see page 59) and in 1964 the company began work on a more extensive conversion scheme for the Beech 18 including installation of TPE331 turbo-props. This was certificated as the Turbo 18 and conversion kits have been supplied to several operators, including Air Asia which had a fleet of 15 Turbo 18s. A further development in 1967 was the Turbo-liner with a stretched fuselage and other features to suit third-level airline operations. The Turboliner II had new features to allow it to comply with the requirements for air taxi operations. Another variant is the Mini Tanker with a 400-US gal (1 513-l) tank in the fuselage and facilities for in-flight refuelling of light attack aircraft and helicopters.

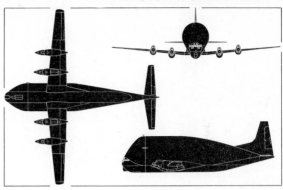

The ungainly Super Guppy (photograph) is based on the Boeing Stratocruiser. Two of the "production" Model 201s are used by Aeromaritime in Europe

Country of Origin: USA.

Type: Outsize cargo transport.

Power Plant: Four (Mini Guppy) 3,500 hp Pratt & Whitney R-4360-B6 piston engines or (Guppy-201) 4,912 shp Allison 501-D22C turboprops.

Performance (Guppy-201): Max speed, Mach = 0·413 IAS above 14,800 ft (4 510 m); max cruising speed, 288 mph (463 km/h) at 20,000 ft (6 100 m); economical cruising speed, 253 mph (407 km/h) at 20,000 ft (6 100 m); initial rate of climb, 1,500 ft/min (7,6 m/sec); service ceiling, 25,000 ft (7 620 m); range with max payload, 505 mls (813 km); range with max fuel, 2,920 mls (4 700 km).

Weights (Guppy-201): Empty, 100,000 lb (45 359 kg); max payload, 54,000 lb (24 494 kg); max take-off, 170,000 lb (77 110 kg); max landing, 160,000 lb (72 570 kg).

Dimensions: Span (B-377MG and Guppy-201), 156 ft 3 in (47,62 m); length (B-377MG), 132 ft 10 in (40,49 m), (Guppy-201), 143 ft 10 in (43,84 m); height (B-377MG), 38 ft 3 in, (Guppy-201), 48 ft 6 in (14,78 m) wing area, 1,965 sq ft (182,52 m²).

Accommodation: Flight crew of four (two pilots, navigator, flight engineer); no passenger provision.

Status: Prototype B-377PG Pregnant Guppy first flown 19 September 1962; prototype B-377SG Super Guppy flown 31 August 1965; prototype B-377MG Mini-Guppy flown on 24 May 1967; prototype Guppy-101 flown on 13 March 1970; first Guppy-201 flown on 24 August 1970 and second on 24 August 1972.

Notes: Basis of the distinctive Guppy series of outsize transports is the Boeing Stratocruiser, the original Pregnant Guppy being a Stratocruiser with a lengthened fuselage having a new upper lobe of large diameter. It was developed to transport the large booster rockets used in the US space programme and was later joined by the even larger Super Guppy, based on the C-97J version of the Stratocruiser with Pratt & Whitney T34 turboprops. The Mini-Guppy has piston engines and a longer and wider fuselage than the basic Stratocruiser on which it is based, while the Guppy 201 is a "production" version of the Super Guppy with Allison 501 turboprops substituted. The single Guppy 101, like the Mini-Guppy but with Allison 501's, crashed soon after its first flight. Two Guppy 201s have been bought by Aérospatiale and are operated in Europe.

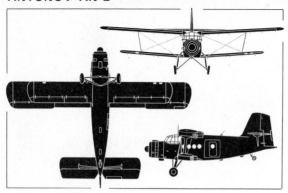

The Antonov An-2 utility transport was one of the largest single-engined biplanes produced, several thousand being built in the Soviet Union and Poland

Country of Origin: USSR.
NATO Code Name: *Colt.*
Type: General-purpose and utility.
Power Plant: One 1,000 hp Shvetsov ASh-621R piston radial engine.
Performance: Max speed, 160 mph (258 km/h) at 5,740 ft (1 750 m); best economy cruise, 115 mph (185 km/h); initial rate of climb, 689 ft/min (3,5 m/sec); service ceiling, 14,425 ft (4 400 m); typical range 560 mls (900 km).
Weights: Empty, 7,605 lb (3 450 kg); max payload (agricultural) 3,300 lb (1 500 kg); max take-off, 12,125 lb (5 500 kg).
Dimensions: Span, 59 ft 8½ in (18,18 m); length, 40 ft 8¼ in (12,40 m); height, 13 ft 1½ in (4,0 m); wing area, 770 sq ft (71,6 m²).
Accommodation: Flight crew of two with provision for third seat on flight deck. Basic layout for 12 passengers three-abreast, or six stretchers or special arrangements for agricultural or water-bombing use.
Status: Prototype (ASh-21 engine) first flown in 1947. Production totals, over 5,000 in USSR by 1960, over 5,000 in Poland 1960 to

date, plus an unspecified quantity produced under licence in Peoples Republic of China.
Notes: The An-2 was designed to the requirements of the Soviet Ministry of Agriculture and Forestry and was first known as the SKh-1, indicating its agricultural rôle. It proved to have much wider applications than originally envisaged, however, and enjoyed a 12-year production life in the USSR, production then being transferred to Poland where it was expected to continue at the WSK-Mielec factory until the mid-'seventies. Some were also built in China with the local name Fong Chou. Soviet-built variants included the An-2P (Polish An-2T) basic version; An-2S (Polish An-2R) agricultural version with diffuser under the fuselage; An-2M, improved agricultural version, with larger tail unit and many detailed refinements; An-2V (design bureau An-4, Polish An-2M) floatplane; An-2L water-bomber floatplane and An-2ZA (design bureau An-6) for high-altitude meteorological research. Polish versions carried different designations, including the An-2T, An-2R and An-2M, the An-2TP with improved passenger comfort; An-2P passenger variant introduced in 1968; An-2TD paradrop version and An-2S ambulance.

AVIATION TRADERS ATL-98 CARVAIR (AND DOUGLAS DC-4)

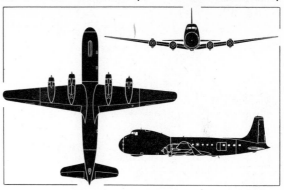

The photograph shows an Aviation Traders Carvair in the colours of British Air Ferries, the principal user in 1974 of this type derived from the DC-4

Country of Origin: United Kingdom.

Type: Specialised short-haul vehicle ferry.

Power Plant: Four Pratt & Whitney R-2000-7M2 Twin Wasp radial engines of 1,450 hp.

Performance: Max speed, 250 mph (402 km/h) ; max cruise, 213 mph (342 km/h) ; economical cruise, 207 mph (334 km/h) ; initial rate of climb, 650 ft/min (3,3 m/sec) ; service ceiling, 18,700 ft (5 700 m) ; range with max payload, 2,300 mls (3 700 km) ; range with max fuel, 3,445 mls (5 560 km).

Weights: Empty equipped, 41,365 lb (18 762 kg) ; max payload, 19,335 lb (8 770 kg) ; max take-off, 73,800 lb (33 475 kg) ; max landing, 64,170 lb (29 100 kg).

Dimensions: Span, 117 ft 6 in (35,82 m) ; length, 102 ft 7 in (31,27 m) ; height, 29 ft 10 in (9,09 m) ; wing area, 1,462 sq ft (135,8 m²).

Accommodation: Flight crew of two or three and provision for up to 85 passengers ; vehicle ferry version usually accommodates 22 passengers in rear cabin and up to five cars.

Status: First flown 21 June 1961 ; entered airline service March 1962. Total of 21 aircraft converted.

Notes: Developed by Aviation Traders to meet the needs of its sister company Channel Air Bridge, the Carvair was an ingenious conversion of the Douglas DC-4 for vehicle ferry, general freight and mixed traffic operations. It embodied an entirely new forward fuselage incorporating an hydraulically-operated sideways-opening nose door and a raised flight deck over the forward part of the cargo hold. The remainder of the DC-4 airframe was unchanged apart from increases in height and area of the vertical tail surfaces. The first operator was Channel Air Bridge (later merged into BUA, which set up British Air Ferries to run its vehicle ferry services). Airlines in Luxembourg, Eire, Canada, France, Spain, Dominica and Australia have used Carvairs but by 1973 BAF was the principal and almost only user with a fleet of nine in service and others in store. The original DC-4 also remained in service in some numbers early in 1974, primarily in South America, Africa and Asia, where about 70 were being used for low-cost charters, freight services and other miscellaneous transport duties. The DC-4 had originated pre-war but no commercial production took place until after the war ended, when the last 79 of a total of 1,242 built were delivered for airline use.

BRISTOL 170 FREIGHTER

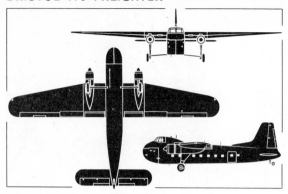

The Bristol 170 Freighter 31 is shown in the photograph and the silhouette, the former depicting an aircraft in service with Safe Air, the last major user of the type in 1974

Country of Origin: United Kingdom.

Type: Short-range specialised freight transport.

Power Plant: Two (Mk 31, 32) 1,950 hp Bristol Hercules 734 piston radial engines.

Performance (Mk 31, 32): Max cruising speed, 193 mph (311 km/h); best economy cruise, 163 mph (262 km/h); initial rate of climb, 1,380 ft/min (7,0 m/sec); service ceiling, 24,500 ft (7 467 m); range with max payload, 820 mls (1 320 km); range with max fuel, 1,730 mls (2 784 km).

Weights: Basic operating (Mk 31), 27,229 lb (12 380 kg), (Mk 32), 29,554 lb (13 400 kg); max payload: 12,500 lb (5 670 kg); max take-off (Mk 31, 32), 44,000 lb (19 958 kg).

Dimensions: (Mk 31, 32), span 108 ft 0 in (32,92 m); length (Mk 31), 68 ft 4 in (20,83 m), (Mk 32), 73 ft 8 in (22,45 m); height, (Mk 31), 21 ft 6 in (6,56 m), (Mk 32), 23 ft 9 in (7,24 m); wing area, 1,487 sq ft (138,0 m²).

Accommodation: Flight crew of two or three with (Mk 31) 15 passengers and two cars or (Mk 32) 23 passengers and 3 cars, or 60 passengers.

Status: Prototype Type 170 first flown on 2 December 1945; second prototype flown on 30 April 1946; third prototype flown on 23 June 1946; fourth prototype flown on 15 September 1946. British C of A granted on 7 June 1946. Total production 214, completed in March 1958.

Notes: The Bristol 170 was evolved during 1944 from the company's experience with the pre-war Bombay, as a utilitarian passenger and cargo transport. Initial development was directed towards military needs, but the 170 became Bristol's first post-war product and was put into production for civil use. Most were built as Freighters, with opening nose doors and the emphasis on freight carrying; some with fixed nose doors and all-passenger accommodation were named Wayfarer. Principal production series, were the Mk I (Freighter), Mk II (Wayfarer), Mk XI with increased span, fuel and gross weight; Mk 21 with Hercules 672 and further weight increase, Mk 31 with Hercules 734, dorsal fin and higher weight, and Mk 32 with lengthened nose to accommodate one more car in the vehicle-ferry rôle. In 1974, the only major commercial user was Safe Air Ltd of New Zealand, specialising in freight carrying between the islands, using 11 Mk 31s. A few Bristol 170s also remain in military use, primarily with the RNZAF.

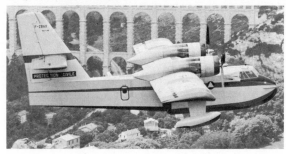

The Canadair CL-215 amphibian is depicted in the silhouette and an example operated by the French Protection Civile *as a water bomber is shown in the photograph*

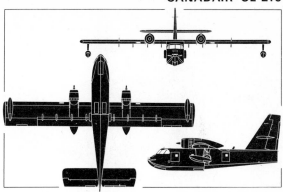

Country of Origin: Canada.

Type: Water-bomber and utility amphibian.

Power Plant: Two 2,100 hp Pratt & Whitney R-2800-83AM-2AH or -12AD/CA3 piston radial engines.

Performance: Max cruising speed, 181 mph (291 km/h) at 10,000 ft (3 048 m); initial rate of climb, 1,000 ft/min (5,08 m/sec); range with 6,750 lb (3 060 kg) payload, 610 mls (982 km); range with 4,500 lb (2 040 kg) payload, 1,117 mls (1 797 km).

Weights: Basic operating (tanker), 27,740 lb (12 585 kg), (utility), 27,540 lb (12 490 kg); max payload (tanker), 12,000 lb (5 442 kg), (utility), 6,800 lb (3 085 kg); max take-off (tanker), 43,500 lb (19 728 kg), (utility), 37,700 lb (17 100 kg).

Dimensions: Span, 93 ft 10 in (28,60 m); length, 65 ft 0¼ in (19,82 m); height, 29 ft 5½ in (8,92 m); wing area, 1,080 sq ft (100 m²).

Accommodation: Flight crew of two and folding seats for eight passengers; utility version can carry up to 29 passengers or 12 stretchers in rescue rôle or 6,800 lb (3 085 kg) of cargo.

Stratus: Prototype first flown on 23 October 1967. First deliveries (to French *Protection Civile*) in June 1969. Production/orders: Province of Quebec, 15; *Protection Civile*, 12; Spanish government, 10; Greek government, 2.

Notes: The CL-215 was developed to meet the need for a specialised aerial tanker for fire-fighting duties in Canada and other heavily-forested areas. Its entire load of 1,200 Imp gal (5 455 l) of water or fire retardent can be dropped in one second and its tanks can be refilled in 12 seconds as the aircraft taxies across a lake. An initial production batch of 30 CL-215s was built in 1968–71, of which 15 went to the Quebec government, 12 to France, two to Spain and one to Greece. During 1973, a second batch of 20 was put into production, of which eight were for Spain, one for Greece and the remainder for future sale. The new-batch CL-215s for delivery from April 1974 onwards had several new features, including the R-2800-83AM-12AD/CA3 engines, provision for AVQ-21 radar or a camera and infra-red sensor pod in the nose, an extra 312-Imp gal (1 500-l) of fuel and an optional loud hailer in the port nacelle, to allow the crew to pass messages to fire-fighters on the ground. The CL-215 can also be used to spray pesticides and insecticides, with a spray bar fitted beneath the wings and an air-sea rescue variant has also been designed.

CESSNA 180, 185 SKYWAGON

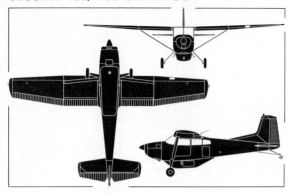

Shown in the photograph is the 1974 model of the Skywagon 185, while the silhouette depicts a Model 185 with ventral cargo pack to extend its versatility

Country of Origin: USA.

Type: Light utility transport.

Power Plant: One (180) 225 hp Continental O-470-A or -J or 230 hp O-470-K, -L or -R or (185) 260 hp Continental IO-470-F or (A185) 300 hp Continental IO-520-D piston engine.

Performance: Max cruising speed (180), 162 mph (261 km/h), (185), 169 mph (272 km/h), (A185E) 141 mph (227 km/h); best economy cruise, (180), 121 mph (195 km/h), (A185), 129 mph (208 km/h); initial rate of climb (180), 1,090 ft/min (5,5 m/sec), (185), 1,010 ft/min (5,1 m/sec); (A185E), 845 ft/min (4,3 m/sec); service ceiling (180), 19,600 ft (5 975 m), (185), 17,150 ft (5 229 m), (A185E), 13,400 ft (4 085 m); range with standard fuel, (180), 695 mls (1 118 km), (185), 660 mls (1 062 km), (A185E), 525 mls (845 km); range with max fuel (180), 1,215 mls (1 955 km), (185), 1,075 mls (1 730 km), (A185E), 685 mls (1 102 km).

Weights: Empty equipped (180), 1,545 lb (700 kg), (185), 1,585 lb (719 kg), (A185E), 1,835 lb (832 kg); max take-off (180), 2,800 lb (1 270 kg), (185 and A185), 3,350 lb (1 519 kg).

Dimensions: Span, 35 ft 10 in (10,92 m); length, 25 ft 9 in (7,85 m); height, 7 ft 9 in (2,36 m); wing area, 174 sq ft (16,16 m²).

Accommodation: Pilot plus optional provision in cabin for up to five passengers in three pairs.

Status: First Model 180 Type Approval 23 December 1952; first Model 185 Type Approval 31 January 1961; first A185E Type Approval 24 September 1965. Production totals to early 1974, Model 180, 5,424; Model 185 and A185, 2,339; production continuing.

Notes: The Model 180 and 185 are members of the Cessna Utiline range of light aircraft (together with the Model 207, see page 79). The first to be developed was the Model 180, which appeared originally as a four-seater similar to the Model 170, and was gradually evolved into the present utility model which can seat six and has special features for quick-loading of freight. The Model 185, named Skywagon like the Model 180, differs from the earlier model primarily in having a more powerful engine. A version suitable for agricultural duties, with still more power, was introduced in 1965 as the A185, and the name AGcarryall was adopted for this variant in 1971. It can carry a 157-US gal (571-l) chemical tank under the fuselage and spray bars under the wings, the data quoted (A185E) being for this configuration.

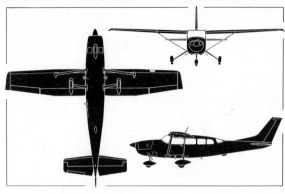

The largest of the Cessna range of single-engined utility aircraft is the Skywagon 207, the 1974 model of which is illustrated in the photograph and silhouette

Country of Origin: USA.

Type: Light utility transport.

Power Plant: One (206) 285 hp Continental IO-520-A or (U206B, 207) 300 hp IO-520-F (T206) 285 hp Continental TSIO-520-C or (T207) 285 hp TSIO-520-G piston engine.

Performance: Max cruising speed (206), 164 mph (264 km/h). (T206), 184 mph (296 km/h), (207), 159 mph (256 km/h), (T207), 163 mph (262 km/h); best economy cruise (206, 207), 131 mph (211 km/h), (T206), 139 mph (224 km/h), (T207), 156 mph (251 km/h); initial rate of climb (206), 920 ft/min (4,7 m/sec), (T206), 1,030 ft/min (5,2 m/sec); (207), 810 ft/min (4,1 m/sec), (T207), 885 ft/min (4,5 m/sec); service ceiling (206), 14,800 ft (4 511 m). (T206), 26,300 ft (8 020 m), (207), 13,300 ft (4 054 m), (T207), 24,200 ft (7 376 m); range with normal fuel (206), 650 mls (1 045 km), (T206), 700 mls (1 127 km), (207), 585 mls (941 km), (T207), 610 mls (982 km); range with max fuel, (206), 1,020 mls (1 640 km), (T206), 1,050 mls (1 690 km), (207), 925 mls (1 490 km), (T207), 910 mls (1 445 km).

Weights: Empty (206), 1,750 lb (793 kg), (T206), 1,950 lb (884 kg), (207), 1,890 lb (857 kg), (T207), 1,990 lb (903 kg); max

take-off (206, T206), 3,600 lb (1 633 kg), (207, T207), 3,800 lb (1 724 kg).

Dimensions: Span, 35 ft 10 in (10,92 m); length (206, T206), 28 ft 0 in (8,53 m), (207, T207), 31 ft 9 in (9,68 m); height, 9 ft 7½ in (2,93 m); wing area, 174·0 sq ft (16,17 m²).

Accommodation: Pilot and provision for (206, T206) up to five or (207, T207) six additional occupants.

Status: Model 206 first type-approved on 19 July 1963; T206 first approved on 20 December 1965. First Model 207 flown on 11 May 1968 and first production model flown on 3 January 1969. First T207 flown on 6 January 1969. Type approval, Model 206 and T206, 31 December 1968. Production quantities (to early 1974): Model 206 and T206, 2,894; Model 207 and T207, 236.

Notes: To extend its range of "flying station wagons", Cessna introduced the Model 205 in 1962; a *de luxe* model was also marketed as the Super Skylane; production totalled 1,217 between 1962 and 1971. Similar in most respects to the Model 205, the Model 206 was initially marketed as the Skywagon and Turbo-Skywagon, but subsequently these names were transferred to the larger Model 207, and the 206 became the Stationair.

CURTISS C-46

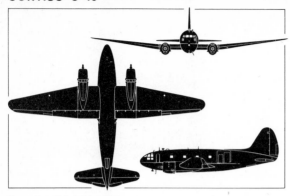

Shown in the photograph are ex-military Curtiss C-46s converted for use as cargo carriers by the Shamrock company in the USA, typical of the continuing operation of this type in 1974

Country of Origin: USA.

Type: Cargo aircraft.

Power Plant: Two 2,000 shp Pratt & Whitney R-2800-34 piston engines.

Performance: Max speed, 269 mph (433 km/h); max cruising speed, 187 mph (301 km/h) at 7,000 ft (2 133 m); initial rate of climb, 1,300 ft/min (6,6 m/sec); service ceiling, 27,600 ft (8 412 m); range with max payload, 110 mls (117 km); range with max fuel, 1,170 mls (1 880 km) with 5,700 lb (2 585 kg) payload.

Weights: Empty equipped, 33,000 lb (14 970 kg); max payload, 11,630 lb (5 265 kg); max take-off (passenger) 47,100 lb (21 364 kg), (freighter), 48,000 lb (21 772 kg).

Dimensions: Span, 108 ft 0 in (32,92 m); length, 76 ft 4 in (23,27 m); height, 21 ft 8 in (6,60 m); wing area, 1,358 sq ft (126 m²).

Accommodation: Typical seating accommodation for 52–62 passengers in high density layouts.

Status: Prototype (CW-20) first flown 26 March 1940. Production (military C-46), 3,141, completed in 1945. No production of commercial models as such.

Notes: The Curtiss CW-20 was launched as a private venture in 1938 to compete with the Douglas DC-3 in the US market. With a similar configuration, it differed in having larger fuselage capacity and a shorter range. No production for the civil market occurred, because of the intervention of the war, but large-scale manufacture was undertaken for the US Army Air Force and the C-46 Commando gave particularly valuable service in the Pacific theatre. Post-war, many were acquired by civilian operators, initially for passenger flying but subsequently being used almost exclusively as freighters, for which their large fuselage capacity made them especially suitable. At the end of 1973, over 100 were still reported in airline operation, almost wholly on the North and South American continent, with a small number in Asia. During the early 'fifties, several programmes were launched to up-date the ex-military C-46s and to allow them to comply with more stringent airworthiness requirements then being introduced. Some of the surviving examples incorporate the results of these modification programmes, which led to the introduction of such designations as Super 46C and C-46R. One improved version had two Marboré boost turbojets mounted beneath the fuselage.

DE HAVILLAND DHC-2 BEAVER

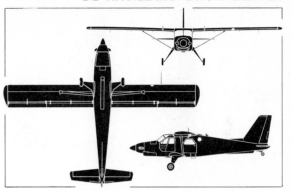

The standard version of the de Havilland Canada DHC-2 Beaver is shown in the photograph and the silhouette depicts the Mk III Turbo-Beaver

Country of Origin: Canada.

Type: Light utility transport.

Power Plant: One 450 hp Pratt & Whitney R-985-SB3 piston radial engine or (Turbo Beaver) 578 shp Pratt & Whitney (UACL) PT6A-20 turboprop.

Performance: Max cruising speed (Mk I), 135 mph (217 km/h) at sea level, (Turbo), 157 mph (252 km/h); best economy cruise, (Mk I), 125 mph (201 km/h), (Turbo), 140 mph (225 km/h); initial rate of climb, (Mk I), 1,020 ft/min (5,2 m/sec), (Turbo), 1,185 ft/min (6,0 m/sec); service ceiling (Mk I), 18,000 ft (5 490 m), (Turbo), 20,500 ft (6 250 m); range with max payload (Mk I), 483 mls (777 km), (Turbo), 260 mls (418 km); range with max fuel (Mk 2), 778 mls (1 252 km), (Turbo), 677 mls (1 090 km).

Weights: Basic operating (Mk I), 3,000 lb (1 361 kg); (Turbo), 2,760 lb (1 252 kg); max take-off, (Mk I), 5,100 lb (2 313 kg), (Turbo), 5,370 lb (2 435 kg).

Dimensions: Span, 48 ft 0 in (14,64 m); length (Mk I), 30 ft 4 in (9,24 m), (Turbo), 35 ft 3 in (10,75 m); height (Mk I), 9 ft 0 in (2,75 m), (Turbo), 11 ft 0 in (3,35 m); wing area, 250 sq ft (23,2 m²).

Accommodation: Pilot and (Mk I) up to seven passengers including one adjacent to pilot, or (Turbo) up to 10 passengers including one adjacent to pilot.

Status: Prototype DHC-2 first flown August 1947; type certification on 12 March 1948, Mk II prototype first flown 1953; Mk III Turbo Beaver first flown 30 December 1963. Production total, Mk I, 1,657 including 968 L-20A/U-6A for US Army and 46 Beaver AL Mk I for British Army; one Mk II.

Notes: The Beaver was the first of the range of specialised "bush" aircraft developed and produced by de Havilland Canada. A single Mk II prototype was built with Alvis Leonides 504 engine, and the last few production aircraft from the line at Downsview near Toronto were to Mk III Turbo-Beaver standard. In Australia, SWP Aircraft Engineering converted a Beaver for agricultural duties in 1969 with a Garrett-AiResearch TPE 331 turboprop and revised tail unit; this aircraft was known as the Wallaroo 605. A TPE 331-2U-203 rated at 715 eshp is also the power plant in the Volpar Model 4000, an ex-Army U-6A, first flown in April 1972 and subsequently delivered to the US Department of the Interior, with performance similar to that of the Turbo-Beaver.

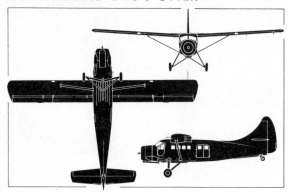

The de Havilland Canada DHC-3 Otter, shown in the photograph and silhouette, is operated as a utility transport and freighter in many under-developed areas

Country of Origin: Canada
Type: Light utility transport.
Power Plant: One 600 hp Pratt & Whitney R-1340-S1H1-G or S3H1-G piston radial engine.
Performance: Max cruising speed, 132 mph (212 km/h) at sea level; best economy cruise, 121 mph (195 km/h) at sea level; initial rate of climb, 850 ft/min (4,3 m/sec); service ceiling (S1H1-G), 18,800 ft (5 730 m), (S3H1-G), 17,400 ft (5 300 m); range with max payload, 875 mls (1 410 km); range with max fuel, 945 mls (1 520 km).
Weights: Basic operating (landplane), 4,431 lb (2 010 kg), (seaplane), 4,892 lb (2 219 kg), (skiplane), 4,652 lb (2 147 kg), (amphibian), 5,412 lb (2 455 kg); max payload, 2,100 lb (953 kg); max take-off, (landplane, skiplane, amphibian), 8,000 lb (3 629 kg), (seaplane), 7,967 lb (3 614 kg).
Dimensions: Span, 58 ft 0 in (17,69 m); length, 41 ft 10 in (12,80 m); height, (landplane), 12 ft 7 in (3,83 m), (seaplane), 15 ft 0 in (4,57 m); wing area, 375 sq ft (34,84 m²).
Accommodation: Pilot and co-pilot or passenger side-by-side and nine passengers in main cabin with optional seat for tenth passenger; optional layouts for carriage of six stretchers or assorted freight loads.
Status: Prototype first flown on 12 December 1951. Type certification as landplane and seaplane in November 1952. Production total 460, including 223 for US Army and US Navy and 66 for RCAF. Production completed in 1966.
Notes: The Otter evolved from de Havilland experience with the Beaver (page 81) with the same primary rôle of a general utility passenger and freight transport to operate in "bush" conditions. From the outset, provision was made for operation of the Otter as a floatplane (in which case a small ventral fin is fitted) and it was the first single-engined aircraft certificated in accordance with the ICAO category D airworthiness requirements. Others often operate as skiplanes, particularly in Canada, Alaska and Scandinavia, and a later development was an amphibious version, using specially modified Edo floats accommodating retractable main and nose wheels. The installation reduced the cruising speed of the standard Otter floatplane by about 4 mph (6,4 km/h). Derived from the Otter, the larger, twin-engined Twin Otter, with turboprop powerplant, is described on page 64.

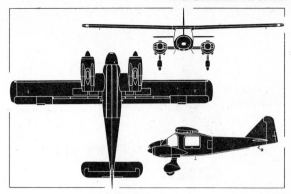

Illustrated by the photo (above) is a Dornier Do 28D Skyservant while the silhouette (right) shows the earlier Do 28 light utility transport

Country of Origin: Federal Germany.

Type: Light utility transport.

Power Plant: Two (Do 28A) 250 hp Lycoming O-540-A1D or (Do 288) 290 hp Lycoming O-540-A piston engines.

Performance: Max cruising speed (Do 28B), 170 mph (274 km/h), (Do 288-1-S), 138 mph (222 km/h) ; best economy cruise, 150 mph (242 km/h) ; initial rate of climb, 1,400 ft/min (7,1 m/sec) ; service ceiling, 19,400 ft (5 900 m) ; range with max payload, 768 mls (1 235 km) ; range with max fuel, 1,100 mls (1 680 km).

Weights: Basic operating (Do 28B), 3,960 lb (1 800 kg), (Do 28B-1-S), 4,415 lb (2 003 kg) ; max take-off, 6,000 lb (2 720 kg).

Dimensions: Span, 45 ft 3½ in (13,80 m) ; length, 29 ft 6 in (9,0 m) ; height, 9 ft 2 in (2,80 m) ; wing area, 241 sq ft (22,4 m²).

Accommodation: Pilot and provision for one passenger on flight deck ; up to six passengers in cabin.

Status: Prototype first flown on 29 April 1959. Deliveries began 1961. First Do 28B flown in April 1963, production deliveries began 1964. Prototype Do 28A-1-S flown in 1964. Production : two prototypes, 60 Do 28A-1, 60 Do 28B-1, completed 1971.

Notes: The Do 28 was developed to be in essence a twin-engined

version of the Do 27 (see *Military* volume, page 143), and the initial prototype had the same fuselage with a revised nose, and an extended-span wing of the same structure. To avoid major redesign of the wing, the engines were located on stub wings cantilevered off the fuselage sides ; in the prototype, these were 180 hp Lycoming O-360-A1As but a switch was made to the more powerful O-540s in the second prototype and these were the standard engine in the initial production batch of 60 Do 28A-1s. One of these was converted to a Do 28A-1-S floatplane by the Jobmaster Company in Seattle. The Do 28B-1 introduced uprated engines, higher gross weight, an enlarged tailplane, provision for auxiliary fuel tanks in the wings and other minor improvements. Of 60 Do 28B-1s built, six were converted to Do 28B-1-S seaplanes by Jobmaster. The Do 28D Skyservant was derived from the Do 28B and is described in the *Military* volume, page 144. First flown on 23 February 1966 and certificated one year later, the Do 28D has a longer fuselage of larger cross section, and in the main production form Do 28D-1, a slightly increased wing span. About half of the total sales of 220 Skyservants to date are for civil use most of the remainder having been delivered to the Luftwaffe.

HAWKER SIDDELEY ARGOSY

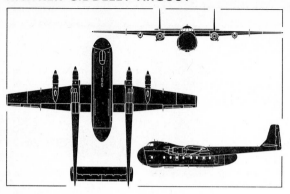

The photograph and silhouette both depict the Series 200 version of the Hawker Siddeley Argosy. The similar Srs 100 is also still in limited commercial service

Country of Origin: United Kingdom.
Type: Cargo aircraft.
Power Plant: Four (100) 2,100 Rolls-Royce Dart 526 or (220) 2,230 shp Dart 532/1 turboprops.
Performance: Max cruising speed (220), 282 mph (455 km/h); best economy cruise (Srs 100), 276 mph (444 km/h), (Srs 220), 280 mph (451 km/h); initial rate of climb (Srs 220), 900 ft/min (4,6 m/sec); service ceiling (Srs 220), 21,000 ft (6 400 m); range with max payload (Srs 100), 330 mls (530 km); (Srs 220), 485 mls (780 km); range with max fuel (Srs 100), 1,780 mls (2 865 km), (Srs 220), 1,760 mls (2 835 km).
Weights: Empty equipped (Srs 100), 50,000 lb (22 680 kg); (Srs 220), 48,920 lb (22 186 kg); max payload (Srs 100), 28,000 lb (12 700 kg); (Srs 220), 32,000 lb (14 515 kg); max take-off (Srs 100), 88,000 lb (39 915 kg), (Srs 220), 93,000 lb (42 185 kg).
Dimensions: Span, 115 ft 0 in (35,05 m); length, 86 ft 9 in (26,44 m); height, 29 ft 3 in (8,91 m); wing area, 1,458 sq ft (135,45 m²).
Accommodation: Flight crew of two and provision for up to 89 passengers in high-density layout.

Status: Prototype first flown on 8 January 1959; first Srs 200 flown on 11 March 1964. Production totals, Srs 100, 10; Srs 200, 1; Srs 220, 6. First AW660 Argosy C Mark 1 flown on 4 March 1961; production total 56.
Notes: The Argosy was the final production of the Armstrong Whitworth subsidiary of Hawker Siddeley before it was completely absorbed into the parent HSA. It was developed as a private venture primarily for airline cargo service but production was limited to 17 for the civil market, plus 56 of a specialised transport version for the RAF. In 1974, a small fleet of Argosy 100s was in service in the UK with Air Bridge Carriers and another was being used in Australia, while Safe Air in New Zealand was evaluating a Srs 220 and three others of this type were in service in Canada. The RAF had retired the bulk of its Argosy transports but retained a few in Cyprus, plus a squadron based in the UK with its aircraft modified for calibration duties, and a batch modified as navigation trainers. The Srs 200/220 differed from the Srs 100 in having a refined structure with lower bare weight and uprated engines. The Srs 220s originally went into service as cargo carriers with BEA and have subsequently changed hands several times.

HELIO H-250 AND H-295 COURIER

Special high-lift features give the Helio H-250 Courier, which was re-instated in production in 1974, unusually good low-speed flying characteristics

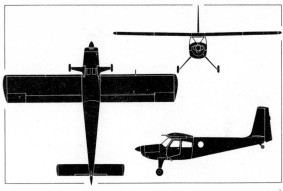

Country of Origin: USA.

Type: Light utility transport.

Power Plant: One (H-250) 250 hp Lycoming O-540-A1A5 or (H-295) 295 hp Lycoming GO-480-G1D6 piston engine.

Performance: Max cruising speed (H-250), 152 mph (245 km/h), (H-295), 165 mph (265 km/h); best economy cruise (H-250), 133 mph (214 km/h), (H-295), 150 mph (241 km/h); initial rate of climb, (H-250), 830 ft/min (4,2 m/sec), (H-295), 1,150 ft/min (5,8 m/sec); service ceiling (H-250), 15,200 ft (4 633 m), (H-295), 20,500 ft (6 250 m); range with standard fuel (H-250), 644 mls (1 036 km), (H-295), 660 mls (1 062 km); range with max fuel (H-250), 1,288 mls (2 073 km), (H-295), 1,380 mls (2 220 km).

Weights: Empty (H-250), 1,960 lb (889 kg). (H-295) 2,080 lb (943 kg); max take-off, (H-250, H-295), 3,400 lb (1 542 kg).

Dimensions: Span (H-250, H-295), 39 ft 0 in (11,89 m); length (H-250), 31 ft 6 in (9,60 m), (H-295), 31 ft 0 in (9,45 m); height (H-250, H-295), 8 ft 10 in (2,69 m); wing area (H-250, H-295), 231 sq ft (21,46 m²).

Accommodation: Pilot and five passengers, in three pairs of seats.

Status: Original Koppen-Bollinger Helioplane flown on 8 April 1949. First Courier H-390 flown 1953; first production Courier H-391 flown and certificated in 1954. First Courier H-250 flown in May 1964; type approval November 1964. First Super Courier H-295 flown on 24 February 1965. Production, more than 450 (all Courier variants) including over 130 L-28/U-10 for USAF and foreign governments.

Notes: The original Helioplane was a modified Piper Vagabond with special full-span automatic leading-edge slats and high-lift flaps to provide safe flight at very low speeds and a good STOL performance. Initial production models had four seats and were known as the Helio Four or Courier H-390. Successive models of the same basic design added one or two seats and introduced more power. Much of the company's output was absorbed by the USAF, which used Super Couriers with the designation U-10A, U-10B and U-10D in the Vietnam campaign and supplied others through MAP to various nations. Two Couriers were fitted experimentally with an Allison 250-B15 turboprop as the H-370; the larger Stallion, with Garrett AiResearch or Pratt & Whitney turboprops, is described in the *Military* volume, page 148. The HT-295 Super Courier, introduced in 1974, has a nosewheel undercarriage.

LOCKHEED L-100 HERCULES

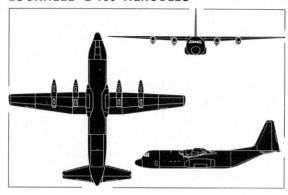

The photograph depicts the L-382B version of the Lockheed Hercules civil freighter while the silhouette depicts the long-fuselage 382G

Country of Origin: USA.

Type: Medium-range freighter.

Power Plant: Four (L-100) 4,050 eshp Allison 501-D22 or (L-100-20, -30) 4,508 eshp 501-D22A turboprops.

Performance: Max cruising speed (L-100), 357 mph (575 km/h); (-20, -30), 377 mph (607 km/h); initial rate of climb (L-100), 1,830 ft/min (9,3 m/sec), (-20, -30), 1,900 ft/min (9,65 m/sec); range with max payload (L-100), 2,230 mls (3 588 km); (-20), 2,560 mls (4 120 km), (-30), 2,130 mls (3 425 km); range with max fuel (L-100), 3,220 mls (5 182 km), (-20), 4,840 mls (7 789 km), (-30), 4,740 mls (7 630 km).

Weights: Operating empty (-100), 67,336 lb (30 543 kg), (-20), 70,837 lb (32 131 kg), (-30), 71,400 lb (32 386 kg); max payload, (L-100), 48,758 lb (22 116 kg), (-20), 49,163 lb (22 300 kg), (-30), 125,000 lb (56 700 kg); max take-off, 155,000 lb (70 308 kg).

Dimensions: Span, 132 ft 7 in (40,41 m); length (L-100), 97 ft 9 in (29,79 m), (-20), 106 ft 0½ in (32,32 m), (-30), 112 ft 8½ in (34,35 m); height, 38 ft 3 in (11,66 m); wing area, 1,745 sq ft (162,12 m²).

Accommodation: Flight crew of three or four. Certificated as a freighter, with mechanised freight-handling system and straight-in rear loading. No provision for passenger-carrying.

Status: First certificated for commercial use (Model 382) on 16 February 1965. First L-100-20 flown on 19 April 1968 and certificated on 4 October 1968. First L-100-30 flown on 14 August 1970 and entered service in December 1970. Production (all commercial versions), approximately 50 by 1974.

Notes: One C-130E was converted as a civil demonstrator in 1965 and about 16 examples were delivered as Model 382B or L-100 to operators in the US, Canada, Pakistan and Zambia. In 1968 the demonstrator was converted to L-100-20 standard with a 100-in (2,54-m) fuselage extension ahead of the wing and an extra 40-in (1,02-m) section aft of the wing. Several operators had their original Hercules modified to this configuration (also known as Model 382E) and others were delivered new. Developed primarily for Saturn Airways and subsequently adopted by some other operators, the L-100-30 (Model 382G) had another 80-in (2,03-m) of fuselage length and some previous military features deleted. Its initial application by Saturn was to ferry Rolls-Royce RB.211 engines from the UK to the USA for the TriStar programme.

PILATUS PC-6 PORTER AND TURBO PORTER

The photograph illustrates a standard Pilatus Porter with Lycoming engine, while the silhouette shows the Turbo-Porter with Astazou turboprop engine

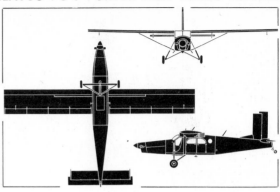

Country of Origin: Switzerland.
Type: Light utility transport.
Power Plant: One (PC-6) 340 hp Lycoming GSO-480-B1A6 or (PC-6/350) 350 hp IGO-540-AIA or (Turbo-Porter A1) 573 shp Turbomeca Astazou XII or (A2) Astazou XIVE or (B) 550 shp Pratt & Whitney (UACL) PT6A-6A or (B1) PT6A-20 or (B2) PT6A-27, or (Turbo Porter C) 575 shp AiResearch TPE 331-25D or (C/1) TPE 331-1-100 turboprop.
Performance: Max cruising speed (H2), 134 mph (216 km/h), (B2), 161 mph (259 km/h), (C1), 164 mph (264 km/h); best economy cruise (H2), 118 mph (190 km/h), (B2), 150 mph (240 km/h), (C1), 144 mph (231 km/h); initial rate of climb (H-2), 550 ft/min (2,8 m/sec), (B2), 1,580 ft/min (8,0 m/sec), (C1), 1,607 ft/min (8,1 m/sec); service ceiling (H2), 17,400 ft (5 300 m), (B2), 30,025 ft (9 150 m), (C1) 27,875 ft (8 500 m); range with normal fuel (H2), 932 mls (1 500 km); range with max fuel (B2), 634 mls (1 020 km), (C1), 683 mls (1 100 km).
Weights: Empty equipped (H2), 2,755 lb (1 250 kg), (B2) 2,601 lb (1 180 kg), (C1), 2,612 lb (1 185 kg); max take-off (all), 4,850 lb (2 200 kg).

Dimensions: Span, 49 ft 8 in (15,13 m); length (H2), 33 ft 5$\frac{1}{2}$ in (10,20 m), (B), 36 ft 1 in (11,00 m), (C), 35 ft 9 in (10,90 m); height, 10 ft 6 in (3,20 m); wing area, 310 sq ft (28,80 m²).
Accommodation: Pilot and one passenger seat at front of cabin and six or up to eight other passenger seats in pairs.
Status: First of five prototypes flown on 4 May 1959; certification (340 hp Lycoming) 1 December 1959, deliveries began 1960. First PC-6A flown 2 May 1961; certification 26 November 1962. First PC-6B flown 1 May 1964; certificated 8 June 1965. First PC-6C flown in October 1965; certification 1 December 1966. Prototype PC-6D flown 2 April 1970. Production totals, over 250 in Switzerland, 100 by Fairchild in USA.
Notes: Design of the STOL PC-6 Porter began in 1957 and the type has evolved through numerous versions as indicated above. Basic H1 versions, regardless of power plant, have a gross weight of 4,444 lb (2 015 kg), the H2 versions having the higher weights quoted here. The A, B and C suffixes indicate different turboprop versions of the Turbo Porter; the PC-6D was a prototype only with a 500 hp Lycoming TIO-720. Fairchild versions, with AiResearch or Pratt & Whitney turboprops, are known simply as Porters.

PZL-104 WILGA

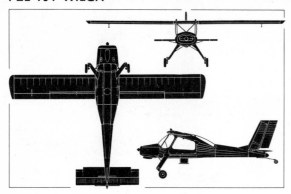

Depicted in the photograph (above) is the PZL 104 Wilga 3 general purpose light aircraft and the silhouette (left) shows the Wilga 32 version

Country of Origin: Poland.

Type: Light utility aircraft.

Power Plant: One (32) 230 hp Continental O-470-L or O-470-R or (35 and 40) 260 hp Ivchenko AI-14R or (43) 225 hp Continental O-470-K engine.

Performance: Max cruising speed (32), 93 mph (150 km/h), (35), 120 mph (193 km/h); best economy cruise (32), 84 mph (135 km/h), (35), 79 mph (127 km/h); initial rate of climb (32), 865 ft/min (4,4 m/sec), (35), 1,245 ft/min (6,3 m/sec); service ceiling (32), 12,075 ft (3 680 m), (35), 15,025 ft (4 580 m); range with maximum fuel (32), 390 miles (630 km), (35), 410 miles (660 km).

Weights: Empty equipped (32), 1,624 lb (737 kg), (35), 1,829 lb (830 kg); max take-off (all) 2,711 lb (1 230 kg).

Dimensions: Span, 36 ft 4⅞ in (11,14 m); length, 26 ft 6¾ in (8,10 m); height (32), 8 ft 2½ in (2,50 m), (35), 9 ft 7¾ in (2,94 m); wing area, 166·8 sq ft (15,50 m²).

Accommodation: Pilot and up to three passengers or two stretchers and attendant.

Status: Prototype Wilga 1 first flown on 24 April 1962; prototype

Wilga 2 flown on 1 August 1963; prototype Wilga C flown on 30 December 1963; prototype Wilga 3 flown on 31 December 1965; first Wilga 35 flown on 28 July 1967; first Wilga 32 flown on 12 September 1967; prototype Wilga 40 flown on 17 July 1969. Production total, all models, over 150.

Notes: The Wilga (Thrush) series of utility aircraft serve in various rôles, mostly within Poland, including club flying, light transport, ambulance, glider towing and paradropping. Variants produced since 1962 differ primarily in type of engine fitted. Wilga 1 and 2 had a 180 hp WN-6B, the latter having a redesigned fuselage and tail unit. Wilga C had a 225 hp Continental O-470 and Wilga 3 had a 260 hp AI-14R, production models being the 3A for club use and 3S ambulance. The Wilga 32 and 35 (details above) had improved cabin features and the 32 had a shorter undercarriage. Suffix letters indicate club (A), ambulance (S) and passenger/liaison (P) versions. The Wilga 40 had a locally-produced AI-14 engine, leading-edge auto-slots, all-moving tail and extra fuel, and Wilga 43 was similar, with the Continental engine. A version of the Wilga 32 went into production as the Lipnur Gelatik 32 in Indonesia, where about 56 had been built by 1974.

Cargo and utility aircraft

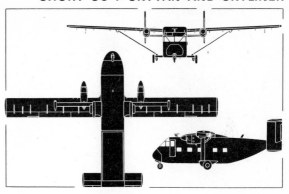

A Short Skyvan Srs 3 is shown in the photograph in operation with Olympic Airways and the silhouette also depicts the Srs 3 version of this light transport

Country of Origin: United Kingdom.

Type: Utility transport and third-level airliner.

Power Plant: Two (Srs 2) 730 eshp Turboméca Astazou XII or (Srs 3) 715 shp Garrett AiResearch TPE 331-201 turboprops.

Performance: Max cruising speed, 203 mph (327 km/h) at 10,000 ft (3 050 m); best economy cruise, 173 mph (278 km/h) at 10,000 ft (3 050 m); initial rate of climb, 1,640 ft/min (8.3 m/sec); service ceiling, 22,500 ft (6 858 m); range with max payload, 265 mls (426 km); range with max fuel, 694 mls (1 115 km).

Weights: Basic operating (Skyvan), 7,314 lb (3 318 kg), (Skyliner), 8,940 lb (4 055 kg); max payload, 4,600 lb (2 086 kg); max take-off (Skyvan), 12,500 lb (5 670 kg), (Skyliner), 13,700 lb (6 210 kg), (Skyvan 3M overload), 14,500 lb (6 577 kg).

Dimensions: Span, 64 ft 11 in (19,79 m); length, 40 ft 1 in (12,21 m); height, 15 ft 1 in (4,60 m); wing area, 373 sq ft (34,65 m²).

Accommodation: Flight crew of one or two and (Skyvan) up to 19 passengers three abreast (2+1) or 12 stretcher patients and attendants and (Skyliner) up to 22 passengers.

Status: Prototype SC.7 (Continental engines) first flown 17 January 1963; (Astazou engines) first flown 2 October 1963; first development Srs 2 flown 29 October 1965; first Srs 3 flown 15 December 1967. Total deliveries/orders (to mid-1974) 100 including more than 30 for military use.

Notes: The Skyvan design originated in 1959, the object being to produce a small utility aircraft with the maximum capacity for ungainly loads. Results of F. G. Miles' research into the Hurel Dubois high-aspect ratio wing fitted to an Aerovan were acquired and incorporated in the design of the prototype, which was first flown with 390 hp Continental GTSIO-520 engines. Before production began, the design was modernised by substitution of Astazou II turboprops rated at 520 shp and the prototype was re-engined, being designated Skyvan Srs 1 and 1A respectively with the different engine types. The initial production deliveries were Srs 2 Skyvans with Astazou XIIs but an early switch was made to TPE 331 engines in the Srs 3 and most Srs 2s were converted. The Srs 3A, introduced in September 1970, had gross weight increased from 12,500 lb (5 670 kg) to 13,700 lb (6 215 kg). Srs 3M is a military variant, and Skyliner is an all-passenger version with improved standard of cabin furnishing.

AEROSPATIALE CORVETTE 100

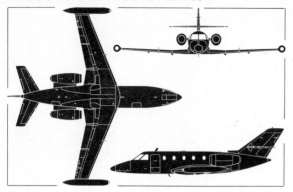

Two pre-production Aérospatiale Corvette 100s are shown in the photograph, one carrying wing-tip fuel tanks, and the silhouette also shows the Corvette 100

Country of Origin: France.

Type: Light business transport and commuter.

Power Plant: Two 2,310 lb st (1 048 kgp) Pratt & Whitney (UACL) JT15D-4 turbofans.

Performance: Max cruising speed, 495 mph (796 km/h) at 30,000 ft (9 144 m); best economy cruise, 391 mph (630 km/h) at 36,100 ft (11 000 m); initial rate of climb, 3,000 ft/min (15,25 m/sec); service ceiling, 38,000 ft (11 580 m); range with max payload, 1,022 mls (1 645 km); range with max fuel (including tip tanks) 1,670 mls (2 690 km).

Weights: Empty equipped, 7,985 lb (3 622 kg); max payload, 2,248 lb (1 020 kg); max take-off, 13,450 lb (6 100 kg).

Dimensions: Span, 42 ft 0 in (12,80 m), (over tip tanks) 43 ft 5¼ in (13,24 m); length, 45 ft 4 in (13,82 m); height, 13 ft 10 in (4,23 m); wing area, 236·8 sq ft (22,00 m²).

Accommodation: Flight crew of one or two and 6 to 12 passenger seats in cabin according to version, or three stretchers and two attendants.

Status: Prototype (SN 600) first flown on 16 July 1970. First pre-production (SN 601) flown on 20 December 1972 and second on 7 March 1973. First full production Corvette 100 flown on 9 November 1973. Certification in May 1974 followed by production deliveries starting in July.

Notes: The Corvette 100 is the first Aérospatiale entry in the biz-jet field, the aircraft having originally been evolved as a joint Sud-Nord project shortly before their merger led to creation of the Aérospatiale company. Initial deliveries were to be made in 1974 to Air Alpes, which had ordered four, Air Alsace, the *Protection Civile* in France (as an air ambulance), Africair, Thenair, Air Sud and to Air Center, the US distributors of the Corvette, in Oklahoma. Development of a "stretched" version was under way in 1974, this being the Corvette 200 with the fuselage lengthened by 6 ft 7 in (2,0 m), increasing maximum accommodation to 18 passengers; Air Alpes has an option on eight of this version, which will have a gross weight of about 15,430 lb (7 000 kg) and uprated engines. An option on one Srs 200 is also held by Air Alpes associate Air Champagne, plus a contract for one Srs 100. Also under study by Aérospatiale was the Corvette 300 which would have enlarged fuselage diameter, 30 seats and three engines, for operation in the rôle of commuter/third-level airliner.

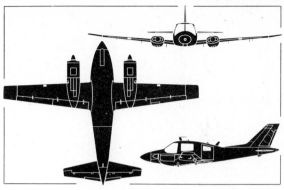

Both the silhouette (right) and the photograph (above) show the B206-S turbo-supercharged version of the Beagle twin-engined business transport

Country of Origin: United Kingdom.

Type: Light business twin.

Power Plant: Two (B.206C) 310 hp R-R/Continental GIO-470A or (B.206B) 340 hp GTSIO-520 piston engines.

Performance: Max cruising speed (B.206C), 207 mph (333 km/h), (B.206S), 220 mph (354 km/h); best economy cruise (B.206C), 185 mph (298 km/h), (B.206B), 187 mph (301 km/h); initial rate of climb (B.206C), 1,170 ft/min (5,9 m/sec), (B.206S), 1,590 ft/min (8,1 m/sec); service ceiling (B.206C), 17,500 ft (5 330 m), (B.206S), 25,400 ft (7 750 m); range with max fuel (B.206C), 1,805 mls (2 900 km), (B.206B), 1,600 mls (2 570 km).

Weights: Empty equipped (B.206C), 4,620 lb (2 095 kg), (B.206S) 4,762 lb (2 159 kg); max payload (B.206C), 1,800 lb (816 kg); max take-off (all), 7,500 lb (3 401 kg).

Dimensions: Span, 45 ft 9½ in (13,96 m); length, 33 ft 8 in (10,26 m); height, 11 ft 3 in (3,43 m); wing area, 212·9 sq ft (19,78 m²).

Accommodation: Typical layouts provide for pilot and four to seven passengers.

Status: Prototype (B.206X) first flown 15 August 1961; second prototype (B.206Y) flown 12 August 1962; pre-production aircraft flown on 24 January and 20 February 1964; first production B.206C flown 17 July 1964; first B.206S flown 23 June 1965; first military B.206R flown on 24 December 1964. Production total 85, completed in 1970.

Notes: The Beagle 206 was the first original design of the Beagle Aircraft Ltd, which was established in 1960 to foster the development of light aircraft in the UK. The first prototype was smaller than subsequent production aircraft, deliveries of which began in May 1965. Supercharged engines gave the B.206S, or Series 2, improved performance, and this variant also incorporated a large loading door in the port fuselage side. Three Srs 3s were also built, with deepened rear fuselage and accommodation for up to 10 passengers but this variant had not completed the flight test stage by the time the Beagle company was forced to go out of business after the British government had withdrawn its support in 1970. Included in the production total were 20 of the military B.206R versions, which were used for communications duties by the RAF with the name Basset CC Mk 1. These aircraft were phased out of service in 1974 and offered for sale to civilian users.

BEECHCRAFT 50 TWIN BONANZA

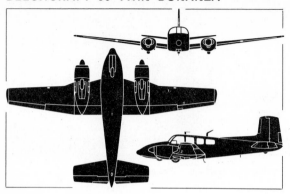

The Beechcraft Twin-Bonanza was an outgrowth of the original single-engined Bonanza and was one of the first of the Beech business twins

Country of Origin: USA.

Type: Light private and business twin.

Power Plant: Two (50, A50, B50) 260 hp Lycoming GO-435-C2 or (C50) 275 hp GO-480-F6 or (D50) 295 hp GO-480-C2C6 or (E50, F50) 340 hp GO-480-AIA6 or (G50, H50, J50) 340 hp IGSO-480-AIA6 piston engines.

Performance: Max speed (D50B), 214 mph (344 km/h), (J50), 235 mph (378 km/h); cruising speed (D50B), 203 mph (327 km/h), (J50), 223 mph (359 km/h); initial rate of climb (D50B), 1,450 ft/min (7,4 m/sec), (J50), 1,270 ft/min (6,45 m/sec); service ceiling (D50B), 20,000 ft (6 100 m), (J50), 29,150 ft (8 885 m); range with max fuel (D50B, J50), 1,650 mls (2 655 km).

Weights: Empty (D50B), 4,090 lb (1 855 kg), (J50), 4,460 lb (2 023 kg); max take-off (D50B), 6,300 lb (2 858 kg), (J50), 7,300 lb (3 310 kg).

Dimensions: Span (D50B), 45 ft 3½ in (13,80 m), (J50), 45 ft 11½ in (14,00 m); length, 31 ft 6½ in (9,61 m); height, 11 ft 4 in (3,45 m); wing area, 277 sq ft (25,83 m²).

Accommodation: Pilot and five or (J50) up to six passengers.

Status: Prototype Model 50 first flown on 15 November 1949;

FAA Type Approval on 25 May 1951. Production total, 974 all models.

Notes: The Twin Bonanza evolved, as the name suggests, as a twin-engined derivative of the Bonanza (see page 134), from which it differed in having a conventional tail as well as two engines. In production for more than 10 years, it was the first of the post-war light twins to gain acceptance and helped to create the business aircraft market which now accounts for a large share of the production of aircraft in the general aviation category. Successive versions differed primarily in power plant, as indicated above; the D50 was also produced in several sub-variants with only minor differences, designated the D50A, D50B, D50C and D50E. In addition to its production by Beech, the Twin Bonanza provided the basis for various conversion schemes, including the Swearingen Excalibur 800 which was a D50 airframe with 400 hp IO-720 engines and other improvements. The Bay Aviation Super-V was another twin engined conversion of the original single-engined Bonanza, but in this case retained the latter's V-tail. As explained on page 134, later models of the single-engined Bonanza were also produced with a conventional tail unit, as used on the Twin Bonanza.

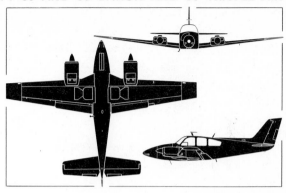

The photograph shows the Beechcraft Baron 58 while the silhouette depicts the Baron D55, a derivative of the Twin Bonanza by way of the Travel Air

Country of Origin: USA.

Type: Light private and business twin.

Power Plant: Two (95) 180 hp Lycoming O-360-A1A or (B55) 260 hp Continental IO-470-L or (58) 285 hp Continental IO-520-C piston engines.

Performance: Max cruising speed (95), 200 mph (322 km/h), (B55), 225 mph (362 km/h), (58), 230 mph (370 km/h); best economy cruise (B55), 195 mph (314 km/h), (58), 186 mph (299 km/h); initial rate of climb (95), 1,360 ft/min (6,9 m/sec), (B55), 1,670 ft/min (8,5 m/sec), (58), 1,694 ft/min (8,6 m/sec); service ceiling (95), 19,300 ft (5 885 m), (B55), 19,700 ft (6 000 m), (58), 17,800 ft (5 425 m); range with max fuel (95), 1,410 mls (2 270 km), (B55), 1,218 mls (1 960 km), (58), 1,368 mls (2 200 km).

Weights: Basic operating (95), 2,570 lb (1 165 kg), (B55), 3,082 lb (1 398 kg), (58), 3,238 lb (1 468 kg); max take-off (95), 4,000 lb (1 815 kg), (B55), 5,100 lb (2 313 kg), (58), 5,400 lb (2 449 kg).

Dimensions: Span (all), 37 ft 10 in (11,53 m); length (95), 25 ft 4 in (7,72 m), (B55), 27 ft 0 in (8,23 m), (58), 29 ft 10 in (9,09 m); height (all), 9 ft 6 in (2,90 m); wing area (95), 193·8 sq ft (18,00 m²), (B55, 58), 199·2 sq ft (18,50 m²).

Accommodation: Pilot and (95) up to four and (B55 and 58) up to five passengers.

Status: Prototype Model 95 first flown on 6 August 1956; FAA Type Approval 18 June 1957. First Model 95-55 Baron flown on 29 February 1960; Type Approval on 3 November 1960. Prototype Model 58 flown June 1969; Type Approval on 19 November 1969. Production totals (to March 1974), Model 55 series, 2,650; Model 58, 455.

Notes: This series of light twins began as the Model 95, essentially a scaled-down Twin Bonanza (see page 92). Originally to be known as the Badger, it was marketed as the Travel Air and 719 were built. It was followed in 1960 by the Model 95-55 Baron with more power and swept-back fin. There have been several variants in the Baron range with various engines and other changes, including the Model 56TC turbosupercharged models, now discontinued. Current in 1974 were the Model B55 (described above), the E55 with 285 hp IO-520-C engines and the Model 58 of which the principal distinguishing feature is its lengthened fuselage (as described above), this being powered by the same engines as the E55 version of the Baron.

BEECHCRAFT 60 DUKE

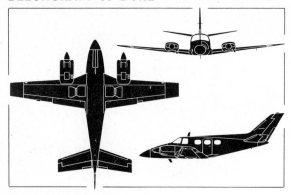

The silhouette and photograph depict the Beechcraft Duke A60, an attractive member of the Beech range of business twins in production in 1974

Country of Origin: USA.

Type: Light business and executive transport.

Power Plant: Two 380 hp Lycoming TIO-541-E1A4 or E1C4 piston engines.

Performance: Max cruising speed, 278 mph (447 km/h) at 25,000 ft (7 620 m) and 252 mph (406 km/h) at 15,000 ft (4 570 m); best economy cruise, 210 mph (338 km/h) at 25,000 ft (7 620 m) and 197 mph (317 km/h) at 15,000 ft (4 570 m); initial rate of climb, 1,600 ft/min (8,1 m/sec); service ceiling, 30,800 ft (9 390 m); range with max fuel, 973 mls (1 566 km) at 271 mph (436 km/h) at 25,000 ft (7 620 m), 1,161 mls (1,868 km) at 197 mph (317 km/h) at 15,000 ft (4 570 m).

Weights: Empty, 4,195 lb (1 902 kg); max take-off, 6 775 lb (3 073 kg).

Dimensions: Span, 39 ft 3 in (11,96 m); length, 33 ft 10 in (10,31 m); height, 12 ft 4 in (3,76 m); wing area, 212·9 sq ft (19,78 m²).

Accommodation: Normal layout provides four individual seats (including pilot); optional provision can be made for two additional seats.

Status: Prototype first flown on 29 December 1966. FAA Type Approval (Model 60) on 1 February 1968, (Model A60) 30 January 1970. Production total (to March 1974), Model 60, 123; Model A60, 353.

Notes: The Duke was added to the range of Beech business aircraft in 1968 to provide the advantages of pressurisation and turbo-supercharging in a smaller-sized business aircraft. The cabin, which can seat up to six, is pressurised at a differential of 4·6 lb/sq in (0·32 kg/cm²) by means of air from the engine turbo-superchargers, and provides sea level conditions at altitudes of 10,000 ft (3 050 m) and the equivalent of 10,000 ft (3 050 m) at a cruising altitude of 24,800 ft (7 559 m). Standard fuel capacity is 118 Imp gal (538 l) but provision is made for extra long-range tanks in the wings, bringing the capacity to 170 Imp gal (772 l) and the ranges quoted here are for the Duke with this maximum fuel capacity. The initial production version of the Duke was the Model 60, superseded in 1971 by the A60 with a series of improvements including lighter-weight turbosuperchargers of superior performance, increasing the altitude at which full engine power could be achieved and thus improving the overall performance.

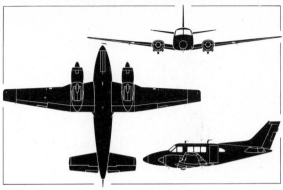

The photograph depicts a Beechcraft Queen Air B80 and the same version of this piston-engined business transport and light airliner is shown in the silhouette

Country of Origin: USA.

Type: Business and executive transport.

Power Plant: Two (65, 70) 340 hp Lycoming IGSO-480-AIA6, AIB6 or AIE6 or (880) 380 hp IGSO-540-AIA or AID piston engines.

Performance: Max cruising speed (65, 70), 214 mph (344 km/h), (80), 224 mph (360 km/h); best economy cruise (65, 70), 171 mph (275 km/h), (80), 183 mph (294 km/h); initial rate of climb (65), 1,300 ft/min (6,6 m/sec), (70), 1,375 ft/min (6,9 m/sec), (80), 1,275 ft/min (6,45 m/sec); service ceiling (65), 27,000 ft (8 230 m), (70, 80), 26,800 ft (8 170 m); range with max fuel (65, 70), 1,660 mls (2 671 km), (80), 1,550 mls (2 494 km).

Weights: Empty, (65) 4,990 lb (2 263 kg), (70) 5,010 lb (2 272 kg), (80), 5,060 lb (2 295 kg); max take-off (65), 7,700 lb (3 493 kg), (70), 8,200 lb (3 720 kg), (80), 8,800 lb (3 992 kg).

Dimensions: Span (65), 45 ft 10½ in (13,98 m), (70, 80), 50 ft 3 in (15,32 m); length (all), 35 ft 6 in (10,82 m); height (all), 14 ft 2½ in (4,33 m); wing area (65), 277·06 sq ft (25,73 m²), (70, 80), 293·9 sq ft (27,3 m²).

Accommodation: Pilot and second pilot or passenger on flight deck, and four to nine passengers in the cabin.

Status: Prototype Queen Air first flown on 28 August 1958, FAA Type Approval (65) 4 February 1959 and (A65) 3 November 1966. Queen Air 70 first flown in 1968, Type Approval 27 November 1968. Prototype Queen Air 80 flown on 22 June 1961; Type Approval 20 February 1962, (A80) 26 March 1964, (B80) 22 October 1965. Production totals, 65 and A65, 333 (plus 71 military U-8F) completed in 1971; Model 70, 42, completed in 1971; Model 80, A80, B80, 476 to March 1974.

Notes: The Queen Air was added to the Beech range as the largest of its twins in 1958, although later types now in production have extended the size range upwards. The original Queen Air 65 had an unswept vertical tail and was followed by the A65 with swept-back fin-and-rudder and more fuel. The Queen Air 80 introduced more powerful engines and the A80 and B80 versions had increased span and higher gross weight. The longer span wing was then offered with the smaller engines to achieve greater economy with the same useful load, this being the Queen Air 70. Commuter versions are known as Queen Airliners; only the Model 80s remained in production in 1974 but many Model 65s and 70s were still in operation.

BEECHCRAFT 90, 100 KING AIR

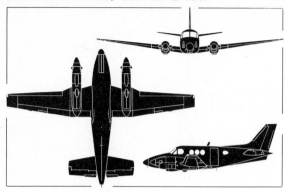

Shown in the photograph is a Beechcraft King Air A100 while the silhouette shows the E90 version of this turboprop-engined business transport

Country of Origin: USA.

Type: Business and executive transport.

Power Plant: Two (90) 525 eshp Pratt & Whitney (UACL) PT6A-6 or (90, A90, B90, C90) 527 eshp PT6A-20 or (E90, 100, A100) 715 eshp PT6A-28 turboprops.

Performance: Max cruising speed (C90), 253 mph (407 km/h) at 16,000 ft (4 880 m), (E90), 285 mph (459 km/h) at 16,000 ft (4 880 m), (A100), 271 mph (436 km/h) at 21,000 ft (6 400 m); best economy cruise (100), 260 mph (418 km/h) at 21,000 ft (6 400 m), (A100), 272 mph (438 km/h) at 10,000 ft (3 050 m); initial rate of climb (C90), 2,000 ft/min (10.1 m/sec), (A100), 1,963 ft/min (9.9 m/sec); service ceiling (C90), 25,600 ft (7 800 m), (E90), 27,620 ft (8 419 m), (A100), 24,850 ft (7 575 m); range at max cruise (C90), 1,321 mls (2 126 km), (E90), 1,507 mls (2 425 km), (A100), 1,395 mls (2 245 km); range with max fuel (C90), 1,446 mls (2 327 km), (E90), 1,870 mls (3 009 km), (A100), 1,482 mls (2 385 km).

Weights: Empty (C90), 5,680 lb (2 576 kg), (E90), 5,876 lb (2 665 kg), (A100), 6,728 lb (3 051 kg); max take-off (C90), 9,650 lb (4 377 kg), (E90), 10,100 lb (4 581 kg), (A100), 11,500 lb

(5 216 kg).

Dimensions: Span (C90, E90), 50 ft 3 in (15,32 m), (A100), 45 ft $10\frac{1}{2}$ in (13,98 m); length (C90, E90), 35 ft 6 in (10,82 m), (A100), 39 ft $11\frac{1}{4}$ in (12,17 m); height (C90, E90), 14 ft $2\frac{1}{2}$ in (4,33 m), (A100), 15 ft $4\frac{1}{4}$ in (4,68 m); wing area (C90, E90), 293·9 sq ft (27,30 m²), (A100), 279·7 sq ft (26,0 m²).

Accommodation: Pilot and second pilot or passenger in cockpit and up to six passengers in cabin, (A100) Flight crew of two and up to 13 seats in the cabin.

Status: King Air prototype first flown on 20 January 1964; FAA Type Approval (90) 19 May 1964, (A90) 7 March 1966 (B90) 14 November 1967, (C90) 23 October 1970, (E90) 1972, (100) 24 July 1969, (A100) 7 May 1971. Production totals, Model 90, 729 (including about 160 military U-21 variants); Model 100, 191 (plus five military U-21F).

Notes: The original King Air 90 was basically a Queen Air 65 (see page 95) fitted with PT6A-6 turboprops and a pressurized cabin. The King Air 100, on the other hand, has the powerplant and wings of the Beech 99 (see page 61) married to a new fuselage which has the same cross section as the Model 90 but is longer.

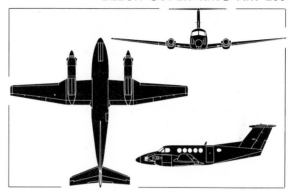

The Beechcraft Super King Air, shown in the photograph and silhouette, was introduced in 1974 as the largest and most powerful of the Beech range of business twins

Country of Origin: USA.

Type: Business and general purpose transport.

Power Plant: Two 850 shp Pratt & Whitney (UACL) PT6A-41 turboprops.

Performance: Max cruising speed, 333 mph (536 km/h) at 12,000 ft (3 658 m) typical cruise, 320 mph (515 km/h) at 25,000 ft (7 620 m); initial rate of climb, 2,520 ft/min (12,8 m/sec); service ceiling, 32,300 ft (9 845 m); range at max cruise, 1,840 mls (2 961 km); range at best range speed, 2,045 mls (3 290 km).

Weights: Typical empty equipped, 7,650 lb (3 470 kg); typical useful load, 4,940 lb (2 240 kg); maximum take-off weight, 12,500 lb (5 670 kg).

Dimensions: Span, 54 ft 6 in (16,6 m); length, 43 ft 9 in (13,16 m); height, 14 ft 11½ in (4,54 m); wing area, 303 sq ft (28,1 m²).

Accommodation: Two seats on flight deck; typical layouts in cabin provide for six, or a maximum of eight, seats.

Status: First prototype flown (as Beech Model 101) on 27 October 1972; second prototype flown on 15 December 1972. FAA Type Approval, December 1973. Commercial deliveries began February 1974.

Notes: The Super King Air (originally developed as the Beech Model 101) is the largest of the company's business twins, and has a number of features that distinguish it from the other King Airs (see page 95). These new features include the T-tail, increased wing span and length, uprated engines, greater fuel capacity, increased cabin pressurization differential, and higher operating weights. Concept studies began in mid-1969, with wind-tunnel testing of the T-tail configuration, and initial development began in October 1970. Tunnel testing of the actual Model 101 design began in December 1970, followed by construction of a prototype incorporating a stall-recovery parachute and special emergency-escape provision for the pilot. Certification testing was completed by November 1963. A new, longer-span, centre section results in the engines of the Super King Air being farther from the fuselage than on earlier King Air models and this, combined with the use of slow-turning propellers and special sound proofing panels, achieves a low sound level throughout the cabin. Early deliveries of the Super King Air included three for the US Army. During 1974, Beech Aircraft was also studying a stretched version of the Super King Air, with a lengthened fuselage incorporating 21 seats.

CESSNA 310, 320 SKYKNIGHT, 340

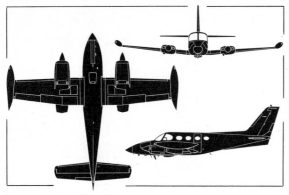

Depicted in the photograph is the Cessna Model 310P (1969 Model), one of the company's most successful business twins, and the silhouette shows a Model 340

Country of Origin: USA.

Type: Business and executive transport.

Power Plant: Two (310, A, B) 240 hp Continental O-470-B or -M or (310C to H) 260 hp IO-470-D or (310I, J) IO-470-U or (310K to Q) IO-470-V or -VO or (320, A, B, C) 260 hp TSIO-470-B or (T310, 320D, E, F) 285 hp TSIO-520-B or (340) 285 hp TSIO-520-K.

Performance: Max cruising speed (310Q), 221 mph (356 km/h), (T310Q), 259 mph (417 km/h), (320), 245 mph (394 km/h), (340), 241 mph (388 km/h); best economy cruise (310Q), 183 mph (295 km/h), (T310Q), 231 mph (372 km/h), (320), 222 mph (357 km/h), (340), 202 mph (325 km/h); initial rate of climb (310Q), 1,495 ft/min (7,6 m/sec), (T310Q), 1,790 ft/min (9,1 m/sec), (320), 1,820 ft/min (9,25 m/sec), (340), 1,500 ft/min (7,6 m/sec); service ceiling (310Q), 19,500 ft (5 943 m), (T310Q), 28,200 ft (8 595 m), (320), 28,100 ft (8 565 m), (340), 26,500 ft (8 075 m); range with max payload (340), 680 mls (1 094 km); range with max fuel (310Q), 1,729 mls (2 782 km), (T310Q), 1,929 mls (3 104 km), (320), 1,326 mls (2 134 km).

Weights: Empty, (310Q), 3,223 lb (1 462 kg), (T310Q), 3,302 lb (1 497 kg), (320), 3,260 lb (1 497 kg), (340), 3,700 lb (1 678 kg); max take-off (310Q, 320), 5,300 lb (2 404 kg), (T310Q), 5,500 lb (2 494 kg), (340), 5,975 lb (2 710 kg).

Dimensions: Span (310, T310, 320), 36 ft 11 in (11,25 m), (340), 38 ft 1¼ in (11,62 m); length (310, T310, 320), 29 ft 3 in (8,92 m), (340), 34 ft 4 in (10,46 m); height, (310, T310, 320), 10 ft 6 in (3,20 m), (340), 12 ft 6¾ in (3,82 m); wing area (310, T310, 320), 179 sq ft (16,63 m²), (340), 184·7 sq ft (17,16 m²).

Accommodation: Normal accommodation (310, T310, 320) for four or five occupants (including pilot) or (340) two pilots and four passengers in individual seats.

Status: Prototype Model 310 first flown 3 January 1953. First FAA Type Approval (310) 22 March 1954, (T310) 30 August 1968, (320) 24 May 1961, (340) 15 October 1971. Production totals, 310 and T310 (to early 1974), 3,737; 320 (completed 1968) 575; Model 340 (to early 1974), 233.

Notes: The Model 310 was the first post-war Cessna twin. The Model 320 Skyknight with turbo-supercharged engines was in production from 1961 to 1968. The Model 340 has the wing and landing gear of the Model 414 and a pressurized cabin.

The distinctive Cessna Model 337 Skymaster, with its twin-boom tail unit and tandem engines, is shown in the silhouette (T-337G) and photograph (1974 model)

Country of Origin: USA.
Type: Business and executive transport.
Power Plant: Two (336) 210 hp Continental IO-360-A or (337) 210 hp IO-360-C or -D or (T337) 210 hp TSIO-360-A or -B (P337) 225 hp TSIO-360.
Performance: Max cruising speed (336), 173 mph (278 km/h), (337F), 190 mph (306 km/h), (P337), 230 mph (370 km/h) ; best economy cruise (336), 123 mph (198 km/h), (337F), 150 mph (241 km/h) ; initial rate of climb (336), 1,340 ft/min (6,8 m/sec), (337F), 1,100 ft/min (5,6 m/sec), (P337), 1,250 ft/min (6,3 m/sec) ; service ceiling (336), 19,000 ft (5 800 m), (337F), 18,000 ft (5 490 m), (P337), 30,300 ft (9 235 m) ; range with standard fuel (336), 945 mls (1 520 km), (337F), 925 mls (1 488 km), (P337), 1,070 mls (1 722 km) ; range with max fuel (336), 1,315 mls (2 115 km), (337F), 1,285 mls (2 068 km), (P337), 1,505 mls (2 422 km).
Weights: Empty equipped (336), 2,322 lb (1 061 kg), (337F), 2,695 lb (1 222 kg), (P337), 2,900 lb (1 315 kg) ; max take-off (336), 3,900 lb (1 770 kg), (337F), 4,630 lb (2 100 kg), (P337), 4,700 lb (2 132 kg).
Dimensions: Span (336), 38 ft 0 in (11,58 m), (337 all variants),

CESSNA 336 AND 337 SUPER SKYMASTER

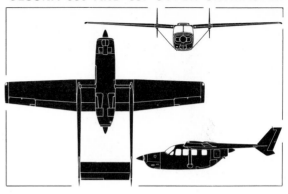

37 ft 2 in (11,63 m) ; length (336), 29 ft 7 in (9,02 m), (337 all variants), 29 ft 9 in (9,07 m) ; height (all), 9 ft 4 in (2,84 m) ; wing area (336), 201 sq ft (18,67 m²), (337 all variants), 202·5 sq ft (18,81 m²).
Accommodation: Normal layout for four including pilot with optional provision for two additional seats.
Status: Prototype Model 336 first flown on 28 February 1961 ; first production model flown in August 1962 ; FAA Type Approval 22 May 1962 ; first deliveries May 1963. Model 337 Type Approval 8 October 1964, first deliveries February 1965 Model T337 Type Approval 25 October 1966. Production (to early 1974), Model 336, 195 ; Model 337 and T337, 1,485 ; Model P337, 124 ; F337, 42 ; FP337, 4.
Notes: The Cessna Model 336 Skymaster introduced the company's CLT (Centre Line Thrust) configuration for twin-engined aircraft. The first batch of 195 Skymasters had fixed landing gear and this type was followed by the retractable-gear Model 337 Super Skymaster in February 1965. Other variants are the Turbo-System (T337) with turbo-superchargers, the Pressurised Skymaster (P337) and the F337 and FT337 built by Reims Aviation in France.

CESSNA 401, 402, 411, 414, 421

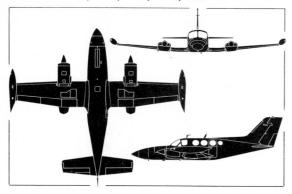

Shown in the photograph (above) is the 1974 model Cessna 402 Businessliner, while the silhouette (left) shows the similar but pressurized Model 421

Country of Origin: USA.

Type: Business and executive transport and third-level airliner.

Power Plant: Two (401, 402) 300 hp Continental TSIO-520-E, (414) 310 hp TSIO-520-J or (421) 375 hp GTSIO-520-H piston engines.

Performance: Max cruising speed (401, 402), 240 mph (386 km/h), (414), 252 mph (405 km/h), (421), 270 mph (435 km/h); best economy cruise (401, 402), 215 mph (346 km/h), (414), 225 mph (362 km/h); initial rate of climb (401, 402), 1,610 ft/min (8,2 m/sec), (414), 1,580 ft/min (8,03 m/sec) (421), 1,850 ft/min (9,4 m/sec); service ceiling (401, 402), 26,180 ft (7 980 m), (414), 30,100 ft (9 175 m), (421), 31,000 ft (9 480 m); range with max fuel (401, 402), 1,454 mls (2 339 km), (414), 1,432 mls (2 304 km), (421), 1,716 mls (2 761 km).

Weights: Empty (401), 3,665 lb (1 662 kg), (402), 3,719 lb (1 662 kg), (402), 3,719 lb (1 686 kg), (414), 4,039 lb (1 832 kg), (421), 4,410 lb (2 000 kg); max take-off (401, 402), 6,300 lb (2 858 kg), (414), 6,350 lb (2 880 kg), (421), 7,450 lb (3 379 kg).

Dimensions: Span over tip tanks (401, 402, 414), 39 ft 10¼ in (12,15 m), (421), 41 ft 10¼ in (12,76 m); length (401, 414), 33 ft 9 in (10,29 m), (402, 421), 36 ft 1 in (11,00 m); height (401, 402), 11 ft 8 in (3,56 m), (414, 421), 11 ft 10 in (3,61 m); wing area (401, 402, 414), 195·72 sq ft (18,18 m²), (421), 211·65 sq ft (19,66 m²).

Accommodation: Two seats in the cockpit and (401, 402, 421) up to six or (414) five passenger seats in the cabin.

Status: Model 401 first flown on 26 August 1965; Model 421 first flown on 14 October 1965; Model 414 first flown 1 November 1968. FAA Type Approval, Model 401, 20 September 1966; Model 402, 20 September 1966; Model 421, 1 May 1967; Model 414, 24 September 1969. Production totals (to early 1974), Model 401, 404; Model 402, 560; Model 411, 301; Model 414, 261; Model 421, 762.

Notes: First of the Cessna "400-series" twins was the Model 411, first flown on 18 July 1962 and powered by 340 hp GTSIO-520 engines. Production totalled 301, ending in 1968. The Model 401 was a cheaper, lower-powered version and Model 402 for the air taxi/commuter market. The Model 421 introduced a pressurized cabin and this same fuselage was then combined with Model 401 wings and engines in the Model 414.

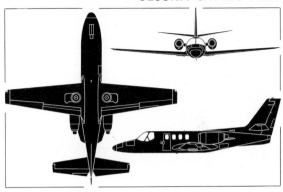

The Cessna 500 Citation, shown in the photograph and silhouette, is one of the smallest and fastest-selling business jets on the market in 1974

Country of Origin: USA.

Type: Executive twinjet.

Power Plant: Two 2,200 lb st (998 kgp) Pratt & Whitney (UACL) JT15D-1 turbofans.

Performance: Max cruising speed, 400 mph (644 km/h) at 24,800 ft (7 560 m); initial rate of climb, 3,350 ft/min (17,0 m/sec); service ceiling, 35,000 ft (10 668 m); range with maximum payload, 1,080 mls (1 738 km); range with maximum fuel, 1,540 mls (2 478 km).

Weights: Basic operating, 6,390 lb (2 898 kg); max payload, 2,010 lb (911 kg); max take-off, 11,500 lb (5 216 kg).

Dimensions: Span, 43 ft 9 in (13,33 m); length, 43 ft 6 in (13,26 m); height, 14 ft 4 in (4,37 m); wing area, 260 sq ft (24,2 m²).

Accommodation: Flight crew of two and normal provision for five or a maximum of six passengers in the cabin.

Status: Two prototypes first flown on 15 September 1969 and 23 January 1970 respectively. First production model flown mid-1971. First Type Approval 9 September 1971. Production total, 136 by January 1974, with production then continuing at a rate of 9 a month.

Notes: The Citation was launched in 1968 (originally with the name Fanjet 500) as the first Cessna jet type for the commercial market and one that was rather smaller than the typical biz-jets already in service with the larger business corporations. The first prototype had a gross weight of 9,500 lb (4 310 kg), shorter fuselage, flat tailplane, smaller vertical tail surfaces and engine nacelles farther forward, by comparison with the second prototype and production configuration. Initial certification was at a gross weight of 10,350 lb (4 695 kg) for the first 70 aircraft and to 11,000 lb (4 990 kg) for the first 70 aircraft and to 11,500 lb (5 216 kg) with effect from the 71st Citation. Successful marketing of the Citation also led to progressive increases in the production rate, to a planned 12 a month in 1974—a rate which would put the Citation firmly at the top of the biz-jet sales league. The production rate was held at nine per month, however, pending resolution of the fuel crisis early in 1974. During 1972, Cessna announced it was developing a Model 600 as a "step-up" aircraft for Citation owners, with more power, larger cabin and greater range, but this project was abandoned late in 1973 because of the uncertain future market attributable to fuel shortages.

DASSAULT-BREGUET FALCON 10

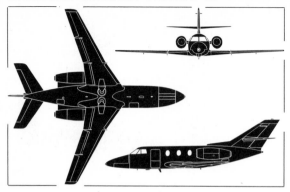

The Dassault-Breguet Falcon 10, shown in the photograph and silhouette, entered service in 1974 having been developed as a scaled-down version of the Mystere 20

Country of Origin: France.

Type: Light business transport and commuter.

Power Plant: Two 3,230 lb st (1 465 kgp) Garrett-AiResearch TFE 731-2 turbofans.

Performance: Max cruising speed, 567 mph (912 km/h) at 30,000 ft (9 145 m) and 495 mph (796 km/h) or Mach 0·75 at 45,000 ft (13 716 m); range with four passengers, 2,075 mls (3 330 km) at 45,000 ft (13 716 m) at max cruise.

Weights: Empty equipped, 10,417 lb (4 725 kg); max take-off, 18,298 lb (8 300 kg).

Dimensions: Span, 42 ft 11 in (13,08 m); length, 45 ft 5¾ in (13,86 m); height, 14 ft 6 in (4,41 m); wing area, 259·4 sq ft (24,1 m²).

Accommodation: Flight crew of two with provision for third crew member on jump seat. Executive version provides for four passengers, or up to seven in commuter versions.

Status: First prototype flown on 1 December 1970. Pre-production prototypes flown on 15 October 1971 and 16 October 1972 respectively. First production Falcon 10 flown on 30 April 1973. French certification, 11 September 1973; US certification, 20 September 1973. Orders (mid-1974), 61 plus 109 on option.

Notes: The Mystère/Falcon 10 evolved during 1969 as a scaled-down version of the Mystère/Falcon 20 (see page 103), having the same overall configuration with two turbofan engines. The first prototype was fitted with 2,950 lb st (1 340 kgp) General Electric CJ 610 engines and underwent considerable development before it was lost in an accident on 31 October 1973. The second aircraft was flown with the TFE 731-2 engines selected for the initial production standard, and after being used, with Falcon 10-03, to complete certification flying, it was fitted with a SNECMA-Turboméca Larzac 02 in the starboard nacelle, for engine development flying. Following the accident to Falcon 10-01, the third aircraft was modified in various respects, and a ventral fin was fitted for completion of the flight test programme, but this feature was not adopted for the production aircraft, deliveries of which began in September 1973, 14 aircraft being completed by the middle of 1974. The Falcon 10 is marketed in North America by Falcon Jet Corporation, a joint Pan American/Dassault-Breguet company that was originally set up to promote the sale of the larger Mystère/Falcon 20 in the USA (see page 103).

One of the first of the business jets to enter production, the Dassault-Breguet Mystère 20 was subsequently renamed Fan Jet Falcon for the US market

Country of Origin: France.
Type: Business and executive transport and commuter.
Power Plant: Two (Standard and C) 4,125 lb st (1 870 kgp) General Electric CF700-2C or (D) 4,250 lb st (1 930 kgp) CF700-2D or (E, F) 4,315 lb st (1 960 kgp) CF700-2D-2 turbofans.
Performance: Max cruising speed (Standard), 534 mph (860 km/h), (F), 536 mph (862 km/h); best economy cruise, 466 mph (750 km/h); absolute ceiling, 42,000 ft (12 800 m); range with max fuel (Standard), 2,038 mls (3 280 km), (C), 2,165 mls (3 484 km), (D), 2,200 mls (3 540 km), (E), 2,187 mls (3 520 km), (F), 2,222 mls (3 580 km).
Weights: Empty (Standard), 15,430 lb (7 000 kg), (C), 15,560 lb (7 060 kg), (D), 15,600 lb (7 075 kg), (E), 15,690 lb (7 160 kg), (F), 15,970 lb (7 245 kg); max payload (Standard), 3,220 lb (1 460 kg), (C), 3,090 lb (1 401 kg), (D), 3,050 lb (1 363 kg), (E), 3,600 lb (1 632 kg), (F), 3,320 lb (1 505 kg); max take-off (Standard, C), 26,450 lb (12 000 kg), (D), 27,340 lb (12 400 kg), (E, F), 28,660 lb (13 000 kg).
Dimensions: Span, 53 ft 6 in (16,30 m); length, 56 ft 3 in (17,15 m); height, 17 ft 5 in (5,32 m); wing area, 440 sq ft (41,00 m²).

Accommodation: Crew of two on flight deck and typical executive layouts for eight-ten passengers or up to 14 in high-density commuter-type layouts.
Status: Prototype first flown (with JT12A-8 engines) on 4 May 1963 and (with CF 700 engines) on 10 July 1964. First production Mystère 20 flown on 1 January 1965. French and U.S. certification on 9 June 1965. Total sales (to November 1973), 298 in 31 countries.
Notes: The Mystère/Falcon 20 was originally developed on a joint basis by Dassault and Sud, and Aérospatiale continues to participate in its manufacture. For the US market, the name Fan Jet Falcon was adopted, now usually contracted to Falcon. The initial production variant is identified as the Standard Falcon; the C and D introduced uprated engines, with the D (starting at aircraft No 172) having more fuel also. The E is as the D with a further engine uprate and the F is an improved model with leading-edge slats, improved trailing edge flaps, more fuel, better electrical system and other changes. A long-range derivative of the Falcon 20 was under development in 1974 as the Falcon 50, with a lengthened fuselage and three Garrett-AiResearch TFE-331 turbojets.

GRUMMAN (AND McKINNON) G.44A WIDGEON/SUPER WIDGEON

Business aircraft

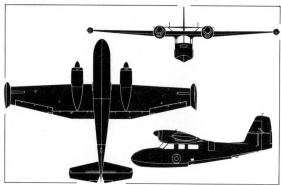

The Grumman Widgeon amphibian, shown in original Ranger-engined form in the photograph and silhouette, continues to serve as a business transport and light aircraft

Country of Origin: USA.

Type: Business amphibian.

Power Plant: Two 200 hp Ranger 6-440C-5 or (Super), 270 hp Lycoming GO-480-B1D piston engines.

Performance: Max speed (G-44A), 160 mph (257 km/h), (Super), 190 mph (306 km/h); typical cruise (G-44A), 130 mph (209 km/h), (Super), 175 mph (282 km/h); initial rate of climb (G-44A), 1,000 ft/min (5,1 m/sec), (Super), 1,750 ft/min (8,9 m/sec); service ceiling (Super), 18,000 ft (5 490 m); range with max fuel (Super), 1,000 mls (1 600 km).

Weights: Empty (G-44A), 3,240 lb (1 470 kg), (Super), 3,800 lb (1 724 kg); max take-off (G-44A), 4,525 lb (2 052 kg), (Super), 5,500 lb (2 500 kg).

Dimensions: Span (all), 40 ft 0 in (12,19 m); length (all), 31 ft 1 in (9,47 m), height (all), 11 ft 5 in (3,48 m); wing area (all), 245 sq ft (22,76 m²).

Accommodation: Maximum seating for six including one or two pilots.

Status: Grumman G-44 first flown July 1940. Production totals include 176 for military use built during World War II, 50 commercial

G-44A and 40 SCAN-30 built in France.

Notes: The original G-44 design was an attempt by Grumman to provide a small sporting amphibian for the commercial market, following the success of the larger Goose (see page 66). The outbreak of World War II prevented immediate production being undertaken for civil use but the US Navy and Army Air Force bought substantial numbers of the design and others were used by the US Coast Guard. Post-war, the type found a limited market as a business transport and in third-level airline service, and the lack of newer amphibians of equivalent performance has kept the Widgeon in use into the 'seventies. Most of the batch of 40 built in France were later sold in the USA and many of these, as well as original Grumman G-44As, have been converted to Super Widgeon standard by McKinnon Enterprises. The conversion includes a change of power plant, structural changes for higher gross weight, additional fuel capacity in the outer wings, larger windows, improved sound-proofing, modernized instrumentation, and (optionally) retractable wing-tip floats. More than 70 Widgeons have been converted to this standard by McKinnon, and many of these remain in airline and executive use in 1974.

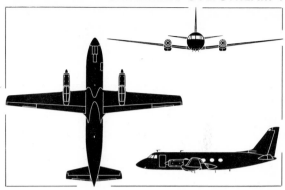

The photograph and silhouette show the Grumman Gulfstream I, the former depicting the first production aircraft that was acquired by National Distillers

Country of Origin: USA.

Type: Turboprop business transport.

Power Plant: Two 2,210 eshp Rolls-Royce Dart 529-8X or 529-8E (R Da 7/2) turboprops.

Performance: Max cruising speed, 348 mph (560 km/h) at 25,000 ft (7 625 m); best economy cruise, 288 mph (463 km/h) at 25,000 ft (7 625 m); initial rate of climb, 1,900 ft/min (9,6 m/sec); service ceiling, 33,600 ft (10 240 m); range with max (high density) payload, 900 mls (1 450 km); range with max fuel, 2,540 mls (4 088 km) with 2 740 lb (1 243 kg) payload.

Weights: Empty equipped, 21,900 lb (9 933 kg); max (executive) payload, 4,270 lb (1 937 kg); max (high density) payload, 6,292 lb (2 853 kg); max take-off, 35,100 lb (15 920 kg).

Dimensions: Span, 78 ft 6 in (23,92 m); length, 63 ft 9 in (19,43 m); height, 22 ft 9 in (6.94 m); wing area, 610·3 sq ft (56,7 m²).

Accommodation: Flight crew of two and typical executive layouts for about 10, with provision for high density layouts seating up to 24 passengers.

Status: First three aircraft (to production standard) flown on 14 August and 11 November 1958 and 17 February 1959 respectively.

US Certification obtained on 21 May 1959 and deliveries began at once. Production totalled 200, ending in February 1969.

Notes: Grumman began design of a turbine-powered business aircraft under the company designation G-159 in 1956, the first projects being based on the TF-1 Trader (a transport version of the S-2 Tracker anti-submarine aircraft—see *Military* volume, page 77) adapted to use Dart engines. These studies were followed by a series of completely original preliminary designs, out of which the Gulfstream I evolved. Based on extensive market studies, Grumman set out to produce a large, long-range transport capable of operating to airline standards, to replace large numbers of DC-3s and similarly elderly piston-engined types then in use, primarily in the USA. Designed to operate wholly independently of external services and equipment, the Gulfstream I is in use with numerous business corporations; in addition the US Navy bought nine for use as navigator/bombardier trainers (designated TC-4C) and the US Coast Guard bought two (as VC-4A) for VIP transport duties. A 24-seat version of the Gulfstream I was certificated in 1962, for airline use, but was not produced. One Gulfstream I with 19 seats operated a third-level airline service in 1973.

GRUMMAN GULFSTREAM II

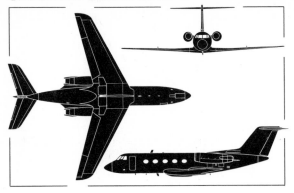

The Grumman Gulfstream II (photograph and silhouette) was derived from the Gulfstream I, having the same fuselage cross section and similar cabin

Country of Origin: USA.
Type: Turbofan business transport.
Power Plant: Two 11,400 lb st (5 171 kgp) Rolls-Royce Spey 511-8 (RB.163-25) turbofans.
Performance: Max cruising speed, 588 mph (946 km/h); typical cruise, 515 mph (829 km/h) at 38,000 ft (11 582 m); initial rate of climb, 4,350 ft/min (22,1 m/sec); service ceiling, 43,000 ft (13,100 m); range with max payload, 2,855 mls (4 590 km); range with max fuel, 3,886 mls (6 254 km).
Weights: Basic operating: 35,200 lb (15 966 kg); max payload, 3,800 lb (1 723 kg); max internal fuel load, 23,300 lb (10,570 kg); max take-off, 62,000 lb (28 122 kg).
Dimensions: Span, 68 ft 10 in (20,98 m); length, 79 ft 11 in (24,36 m); weight, 24 ft 6 in (7,47 m); wing area, 793·5 sq ft (73,72 m²).
Accommodation: Flight crew of three; typical executive layouts for about 10 passengers; max certificated accommodation for 19 passengers.
Status: First flight of production model (no prototypes built) on 2 October 1966; US certification on 19 October 1967; first com-

mercial delivery on 6 December 1967. Total orders and deliveries up to late 1973, 145, with production continuing at 1·5 per month.
Notes: The Gulfstream II was launched by the Grumman Aerospace Corporation in May 1965 as a follow-on for the turboprop-powered Gulfstream I (page 105). Its size is similar, with a maximum of 19 passengers, and it is aimed specifically at the top end of the executive market, providing facilities and comforts comparable with full international airline standards. Its long range puts it in a class of its own, and makes it particularly attractive to large international corporations, as shown by the fact that 97 per cent of Gulfstream II operators in 1973 had an annual turnover of more than $100 m (£40m) each. Some companies operate several Gulfstream IIs, the largest single operator being the 3M concern, which had eight in service in 1973. The type has also been adopted as a VIP transport by several governments, including those of Cameroon, the Ivory Coast, Gabon, Uganda and Malaysia; in addition, the US Coast Guard uses one as a staff transport, designated VC-11A. The Grumman American Aviation Corporation became responsible for Gulfstream II marketing in 1973 and production was transferred from Bethpage to Savannah, Ga.

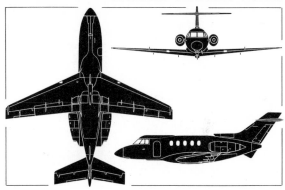

Shown in the silhouette (right) is the Hawker Siddeley HS.125 in its Series 400 version, while the photograph (above) depicts the slightly larger Series 600 variant

Country of Origin: United Kingdom.

Type: Executive jet.

Power Plant: Two (Srs 1A and 1B) 3,120 lb st (1 415 kgp) Rolls-Royce Viper 521 or (Srs 1A/522, 1B/522, 3A, 3B and 400) 3,360 lb st (1 525 kgp) Viper 22 or (Srs 600A and 600B) 3,750 lb st (1 700 kgp) Viper 601 turbojets.

Performance (Srs 400) : Max operating speed (Mach 0·755 TAS) 508 mph (818 km/h) at 31,000 ft (9 450 m) ; long range cruise, 450 mph (724 km/h) at 37,000 ft (11 300 m) ; initial rate of climb, 4,800 ft/min (24,4 m/sec) ; range with 1,000 lb (454 kg) payload and 45-min reserve, 1,762 mls (2 835 km).

Performance (Srs 600) : Max operating speed (Mach 0·780 TAS) 526 mph (847 km/h) at 31,000 ft (9 450 m) ; long range cruise, 503 mph (810 km/h) at 40,000 ft (12 192 m) ; initial rate of climb, 4,900 ft/min (27,3 m/sec) ; range with full tanks, 45 min reserve, 1,875 mls (3 020 km).

Weights: Typical operating weight empty (Srs 400), 12,260 lb (5 557 kg) ; max take-off (Srs 400), 23,300 lb (10 569 kg), (Srs 600), 25,000 lb (11 340 kg) ; max landing (Srs 400), 20,000 lb (9 072 kg), (Srs 600), 22,000 lb (9 979 kg).

Dimensions: Span, 47 ft 0 in (14,32 m) ; length (Srs 400), 47 ft 5 in (14,42 m), (Srs 600), 50 ft 5¾ in (15,37 m) ; overall height, 17 ft 3 in (5,26 m) ; gross wing area, 353 sq ft (32,8 m²).

Accommodation: Two man flight deck with dual control ; accommodation to customer requirement, up to 12 passengers in Srs 400 or 14 in Srs 600.

Status: Prototype HS. 125 flew (as DH125) on 13 August 1962, second prototype on 12 December 1962 and first production Srs 1 on 12 February 1963. First Srs 600 flew on 21 January 1971. Over 300 sold ; in production, 1974.

Notes: First eight aircraft were Srs 1 with Viper 520s and 20,000 lb (9 070 kg) gross weight. Srs 1A (for USA market) and Srs 1B had uprated engines and increased gross weights ; 77 were built. Twenty Srs 20 were Dominie T Mk 1 navigation trainers for RAF. Srs 3A (USA) and 3B (UK) had 21,700 lb (9 843 kg) gross weight and various refinements, while the 3A-R and 3B-R had a ventral long-range tank and 22,800 lb (10 342 kg) weight ; 65 were built. Srs 400 had further improvements and higher weights and more than 100 were built before the Srs 600, with lengthened fuselage, became the sole production version in 1973.

IAI WESTWIND 1123 (AND JET COMMANDER)

Business aircraft

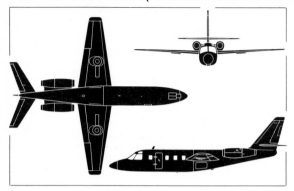

The silhouette (left) shows the Jet Commander 1121, subsequently marketed by IAI as the Westwind, and the photograph depicts the Eleven-23 variant

Country of Origin: Israel (and USA).

Type: Business and executive transport.

Power Plant: Two (1121, 1121A) 2,850 lb st (1 293 kgp) General Electric CJ610-1 or (1121B, 1122) 2,950 lb st (1 340 kgp) CJ610-5 or (1123) 3,100 lb st (1 406 kgp) CJ610-9 turbojets.

Performance: Max cruising speed (1121), 500 mph (805 km/h), (1123), 541 mph (871 km/h) at 19,400 ft (5 913 m) ; best economy cruise, (1121), 470 mph (756 km/h), (1123), 420 mph (676 km/h) ; initial rate of climb (1121), 5,000 ft/min (25,4 m/sec), (1123), 4,040 ft/min (20,5 m/sec) ; operating ceiling, 45,000 ft (13 716 m) ; range with max payload (1123), 1,600 mls (2 575 km) ; max range (1121), 1,840 mls (2 965 km), (1123), 2,120 mls (3 410 km).

Weights: Basic operating (1121), 10,075 lb (4 570 kg), (1123), 11,750 lb (5 330 kg) ; max payload (1121), 2,200 lb (1 000 kg) ; max take-off (1121), 16,800 lb (7 620 kg), (1121A), 17,500 lb (7 938 kg), (1123), 20,700 lb (9 390 kg).

Dimensions: Span (1121), 43 ft 3½ in (13,20 m), (1123), 44 ft 9½ in (13,65 m) ; length (1121), 50 ft 5 in (15,37 m), (1123), 52 ft 3 in (15,93 m) ; height, 15 ft 9½ in (4,81 m) ; wing area (1121), 303·3 sq ft (28,18 m²), (1123), 308·3 sq ft (28,64 m²).

Accommodation: Two seats on flight deck and up to (1121) seven or (1123) 10 passengers in cabin.

Status: Two prototypes (1121) first flown on 27 January 1963 and 14 April 1964 respectively. First production (1121) flown 5 October 1964 and first delivery 11 January 1965. Prototype 1123 first flown 28 September 1970, FAA Type Approvals, (1121) 4 November 1964, (1121A) 19 September 1967, (1121B) 23 April 1968, (1122) 30 December 1968, (1123) 8 December 1971. Production totals, 1121, 120 ; 1121A, 11 ; 1121B, 19 ; 1122, 2 ; 1123, about 20 to end-1973.

Notes: The Model 1121 was the original Aero Commander Jet Commander. After the Aero Commander operation was acquired by Rockwell and merged with North American in 1967, the entire Jet Commander programme was sold to Israel Aircraft Industry. IAI assumed responsibility for the sale of the last 49 Jet Commanders manufactured by Aero Commander, including the 1121A and 1121B with, respectively, higher gross weight and uprated engines. The "stretched" Model 1123 entered production at Lod in Israel in 1972 and the name was changed in 1973 from Commodore Jet to Westwind Eleven 23.

108

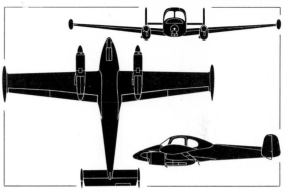

Both the photograph and the silhouette show the standard L-200 Morava, a light twin built in considerable numbers for use in Czechoslovakia and the Soviet Union

Country of Origin: Czechoslovakia.

Type: Private touring and light business twin.

Power Plant: Two (L-200) 160 hp Walter Minor 6-III or (L-200A and D) 210 hp M337 piston engines

Performance: Max cruising speed (L-200A), 182 mph (293 km/h), (L-200D), 175 mph (290 km/h); best economy cruise, 159 mph (256 km/h); initial rate of climb (L-200A), 1,150 ft/min (5,8 m/sec), (L-200D), 1,260 ft/min (6,4 m/sec), service ceiling, 18,700 ft (5 700 m); range with max fuel (L-200A), 1,100 mls (1 770 km) at 10,000 ft (3 050 m), (L-200D), 1,063 mls (1 710 km).

Weights: Empty (L-200A), 2,810 lb (1 275 kg), (L-200D), 2,932 lb (1 330 kg); max take-off, 4,300 lb (1 950 kg).

Dimensions: Span, 40 ft 4½ in (12,31 m); length, 28 ft 3 in (8,61 m); height, 7 ft 4 in (2,25 m); wing area, 186 sq ft (17,28 m²).

Accommodation: Two individual seats for pilot and one passenger, with single rear seat for two or three more passengers, or pilot, attendant and two stretchers.

Status: Prototype XL-200 first flown on 8 April 1957. Production

began in 1958. Production total over 1,000 including 160 L-200A.

Notes: The Morava was designed by Ladislav Smrcek and prototypes were built at the Moravan works at Otrokovice. Production was centred at the former LET works at Kunovice, the L-200A initial production version being preceded by the pre-production L-200 series with lower-powered engines. The L-200A and L-200D were basically similar, the former having Type V410 electrically-operated two-bladed propellers and the latter having Type V506 hydraulically-operated three-bladed constant speed propellers and other improvements including a strengthened undercarriage, improved hydraulics with a duplicate engine-driven pump, better electronics and revised equipment. Production of the L-200D was also undertaken in Yugoslavia by the Letalski Institut "Branko Ivanus" Slovenija (LIBIS). The Morava achieved only limited acceptance outside the Soviet Bloc countries in Europe and the Middle East. The major user of the type was Aeroflot in the Soviet Union, which acquired several hundred for operation as air ambulances and communications aircraft for government officials; the Czech airline CSA also used a considerable number of L-200 Moravas as air taxis.

LEARJET 24 AND 25

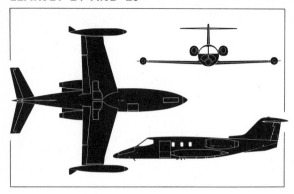

The silhouette (left) depicts the Model 24D version of the Gates Learjet, whereas the photograph (above) shows the lengthened Model 25B

Country of Origin: USA.

Type: Turbojet business transport.

Power Plant: Two 2,950 lb st (1 340 kgp) General Electric CJ610-6 turbojets.

Performance: Max cruising speed, 534 mph (859 km/h) at 45,000 ft (13 720 m); best economy cruise (24D), 481 mph (774 km/h), best range cruise (25B, C), 508 mph (818 km/h), initial rate of climb (24), 6,800 ft/min (34,7 m/sec) (25B, C), 6,050 ft/min (30,7 m/sec); service ceiling (24), 45,000 ft (13 720 m); max range with 45 min reserve (24D, four passengers), 1,886 mls (3 030 km), (25B, seven passengers), 1,800 mls (2 896 km), (25C, two passengers), 2,438 mls (3 927 km).

Weights: Typical empty, (24D), 7,150 lb (3 243 kg), (25B), 7,650 lb (3 470 kg), (25C), 7,600 lb (3 447 kg); max payload (24D), 2,738 lb (1 241 kg), (25B), 2,336 lb (1 059 kg), (25C), 2,446 lb (1 109 kg); max take-off (24D), 13,500 lb (6 124 kg), (25B, C), 15,000 lb (6 803 kg).

Dimensions: Span, 35 ft 7 in (10,84 m); length (24D), 43 ft 3 in (13,18 m), (25B, C), 47 ft 7 in (14,50 m); height, 12 ft 7 in (3,84 m); wing area 231,8 sq ft (21,53 m²).

Accommodation: Two seats on flight deck and up to (24D) six or (25B, C) eight passengers in cabin.

Status: Prototype (23) first flown 7 October 1963; Model 23 certificated 31 July 1964, first delivery 13 October 1964. First Model 24 flown 24 February 1966; certificated 17 March 1966; 24B certificated 17 December 1968. Model 25 first flown 12 August 1966, certificated 10 October 1967. Production total all models, 447 by 30 April 1974, including 104 Learjet 23 and 80 Learjet 24 and 24A.

Notes: Original Learjet design was by William P Lear as the SAAC-23, completed in Switzerland by Swiss American Aviation Corporation and built in Wichita, with 2,850 lb st (1 290 kgp) CJ610-1 engines and 12,500 lb (5 670 kg) gross weight. Model 24 was improved model with 13,000 lb (5 900 kg) weight and CJ610-4 engines, while the 24B had a further increase in weight and uprated engines. The 24D, still in production in 1974, has general engineering improvements. Model 25 introduced a fuselage stretch and was followed by the 25B with the same improvements as the 24D, and the 25C which traded passenger payload for fuel to achieve greater range.

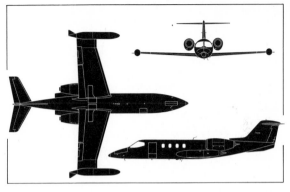

The Learjet 35, shown in both the photograph and silhouette, differs from the Models 24 and 25 (previous page) primarily in having turbofan engines

Country of Origin: USA.

Type: Turbofan business transport.

Power Plant: Two 3,500 lb st (1 588 kgp) Garrett AiResearch TFE 731-2 turbofans.

Performance: Max operating speed, 548 mph (882 km/h) at 38,000 ft (11 582 m), equivalent to an MMO of 0·83; initial rate of climb, 5,150 ft/min (2,6 m/sec); service ceiling, 42,500 ft (12 950 m); range with max payload, 2,572 mls (4 140 km); range with max fuel (35), 3,028 mls (4 875 km), (36), 3,620 mls (5 826 km).

Weights: Operating weight empty (35), 9,142 lb (4 146 kg), (36), 9,102 lb (4 130 kg); max payload (35), 1,914 lb (868 kg), (36), 1,954 lb (886 kg); max take-off, 17,000 lb (7 711 kg).

Dimensions: Span, 39 ft 8 in (12,09 m); length, 48 ft 8 in (14,83 m); height, 12 ft 3 in (3,73 m); wing area, 253·3 sq ft (23,5 m²).

Accommodation: Two seats on flight deck and provision for up to (Model 35) seven or (Model 36) five passengers in cabin.

Status: Prototype (Learjet 26) first flown 4 January 1973; prototype Model 35 flown 22 August 1973. FAA Type Approval granted in June, 1974.

Notes: Gates Learjet initiated a programme to introduce turbofans

on its basic business transport in 1971, but development was slowed by a recession in the market. The Garrett AiResearch TFE 731 engine was selected and with a Learjet 25 airframe as the basis (see page 110) a prototype with these engines was flown (as the Learjet 26) early in 1973. For marketing purposes, the designation of this new version was changed to Model 36, and the Learjet 35 was introduced at the same time with reduced fuel but greater payload. Compared with the Model 25, both types have a slightly longer fuselage with an extra cabin window, and increased wing span through an extension at the tips. An executive-size door is standard, with a large cargo door available on option. With its fuel capacity of 767 Imp gal (3 487 l) the Model 35 has a true US transcontinental non-stop range, or can fly San Francisco–Honolulu and similar stages non-stop. The greater range of the Model 36, which has a fuel capacity of 924 Imp gal (4 200 l), allows it to fly non-stop transatlantic stages between the east coast of the USA and major cities in Europe. Two development aircraft, representing the Model 35 and 36 respectively, were undergoing flight testing with a view to obtaining certification by the late summer, 1974, when deliveries were to begin against a backlog of 32 orders.

LOCKHEED JETSTAR

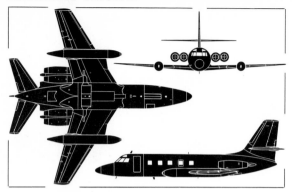

Both the photograph and silhouette show the standard model of the Lockheed JetStar, production of which ended in 1973 in favour of the JetStar II

Country of Origin: USA.

Type: Business and executive transport.

Power Plant: Four (Mk I) 2,400 lb st (1 090 kgp) Pratt & Whitney JT12A-6 or 2,570 lb st (1 166 kgp) JT12A-6A or 3,300 lb st (1 497 kgp) JT12A-8 turbojets or (Mk II) 3,700 lb st (1 678 kgp) Garrett AiResearch TFE 731-1 turbofans.

Performance: Max cruising speed (I), 570 mph (917 km/h), (II), 564 mph (908 km/h); best economy cruise (I), 507 mph (816 km/h), (II), 504 mph (811 km/h); initial rate of climb (I), 5,200 ft/min (26,4 m/sec) at 38,000-lb (17 235-kg) wt, (II), 4,200 ft/min (21,3 m/sec) at max wt; service ceiling (I), 37,400 ft (11 400 m); certificated ceiling (II), 43,000 ft (13 106 m); range with max payload, (I), 2,120 mls (3 410 km); range with 10 passengers (II), 3,185 mls (5 126 km); range with max fuel (I), 2,235 mls (3 595 km).

Weights: Basic operating (I), 22,074 lb (10 012 kg), (II), 23,578 lb (10 694 kg); max payload (I), 2,926 lb (1 327 kg), (II), 2,422 lb (1 100 kg), max take-off (I), 42,000 lb (19 051 kg), (II), 43,250 lb (19 618 kg).

Dimensions: Span, 54 ft 5 in (16,60 m); length, 60 ft 5 in (18,42 m); height, 20 ft 5 in (6,23 m); wing area, 542·5 sq ft (50,40 m²).

Accommodation: Flight crew of two and layouts for up to 10 passengers in typical executive layouts.

Status: Two prototypes, first flown on 4 September 1957 and in April 1958; first production JetStar flown on 2 July 1960. First Mk II flown 10 July 1974. Production total, Mk I, 162 (including military deliveries).

Notes: The JetStar originated at the Lockheed California Division in Burbank in 1956. Two prototypes were built and flown with two 4,850 lb st (2 200 kgp) Bristol Siddeley Orpheus turbojets each but four Pratt & Whitney JT12A-6s were chosen as the production power plant, and the first prototype flew in the new configuration in January 1960. The JetStar was put into production at the Lockheed Georgia Division in Marietta and production continued from 1960 to 1973. Successive production batches introduced uprated engines, the Mk I data quoted here being for the "Dash 8" version with JT12A-8s. Lockheed plans to market the re-engined JetStar II in 1975 and Garrett AiResearch was to offer conversion kits for JetStar Is, subject to the results of flight tests of a prototype conversion in the second half of 1974.

The silhouette (right) shows the MBB Hansa and the photograph (above) depicts an example operated by the Ruksluchtvaarstschool in Holland

Country of Origin: Federal Germany.

Type: Business and executive transport and commuter.

Power Plant: Two 2,850 lb st (1 293 kgp) General Electric CJ610-1 or 2,950 lb st (1 340 kgp) CJ610-5 or 3,100 lb st (1 406 kgp) CJ610-9 turbojets.

Performance (with CJ610-9 engines): Max cruising speed, 513 mph (825 km/h) at 25,000 ft (7 620 m); best economy cruise, 420 mph (675 km/h) at 35,000 ft (10 670 m); initial rate of climb, 4,250 ft/min (21,6 m/sec); operational ceiling, 40,000 ft (12 200 m); range with max fuel, 1,472 mls (2 370 km).

Weights: Basic operating (passenger): 11,960 lb (5 425 kg), (cargo) 11,874 lb (5 386 kg); max payload (passenger) 3,913 lb (1 775 kg), (cargo) 4,000 lb (1 814 kg); max take-off, 20,280 lb (9 200 kg).

Dimensions: Span, 47 ft 6 in (14,49 m); length, 54 ft 6 in (16,61 m); height, 16 ft 2 in (4,94 m); wing area, 324·4 sq ft (30,14 m²).

Accommodation: Flight crew of two and typical arrangements for up to seven passengers in executive version and up to 12 passengers and a stewardess in commuter airline versions.

Status: Two prototypes, first flown on 21 April and 19 October

1964 respectively. First production model flown on 2 February 1966. Production total, 50 (including military examples).

Notes: A product of the Hamburger Flugzeugbau (itself a successor of the famous Blohm und Voss company) before its merger into MBB, the Hansa is notable for its configuration, with the wing swept forward. This layout has several claimed advantages, notably the long, uninterrupted cabin space ahead of the wing and a large permissible range of CG travel. Intended primarily for the business/executive market, the Hansa sold only in limited numbers, and several special-purpose versions were evolved, such as an airline pilot/navigator trainer used at the Dutch Civil Training School. Other rôles include airways checking, air survey and target towing. Several of the production batch of Hansas entered service with the Luftwaffe as special purpose trainers, radar trainers and communications aircraft. The first 15 Hansas had the CJ610-1 engine, followed by 20 with the -5; the -9 engine was introduced with the 31st aircraft. Optional modifications on the final production batch permitted an increased gross weight of 21,160 lb (9 600 kg) accompanied by an increase of 880 lb (400 kg) in the maximum payload that could be carried.

MITSUBISHI MU-2

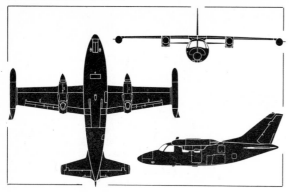

Depicted by the silhouette (left) is the Mitsubishi MU-2F business transport and the photograph (above) shows the uprated and lengthened MU-2J version

Country of Origin: Japan.

Type: Business transport.

Power Plant: Two (MU-2B, D) 605 eshp Garrett AiResearch TPE331-25A or (MU-2F, G) 705 eshp TPE 331-1-151A or (MU-2J, K) 724 eshp TPE 331-6-251M turboprops.

Performance: Max cruising speed at 15,000 ft (4 572 m) (MU-2F), 340 mph (547 km/h), (MU-2J), 345 mph (555 km/h), (MU-2K), 365 mph (587 km/h); best economy cruise (MU-2F), 310 mph (499 km/h), (MU-2J), 305 mph (490 km/h), (MU-2K), 310 mph (499 km/h); initial rate of climb (MU-2F), 2,875 ft/min (14,6 m/sec), (MU-2J), 2,690 ft/min (13,6 m/sec), (MU-2K), 3,100 ft/min (15,7 m/sec); service ceiling (MU-2F), 30,400 ft (9 265 m), (MU-2J), 30,800 ft (9 388 m), (MU-2K), 33,200 ft (10 120 m); max range (MU-2F), 1,640 mls (2 640 km), (MU-2J), 1,462 mls (2 350 km), (MU-2K), 1,600 mls (2 575 km).

Weights: Empty equipped (MU-2J), 6,800 lb (3 084 kg), (MU-2K), 5,920 lb (2 685 kg); max take-off (MU-2B), 8,930 lb (4 050 kg), (MU-2D), 9,350 lb (4 240 kg), (MU-2F, K), 9,920 lb (4 500 kg), (MU-2G, J), 10,800 lb (4 900 kg).

Dimensions: Span (MU-2A), 35 ft 11 in (10,95 m), (MU-2B later), 39 ft 2 in (11,95 m); length (MU-2B, D, F, K), 33 ft 3 in (10,13 m), (MU-2G, J), 39 ft 5 in (12,01 m); height (MU-2B, D, F, K), 12 ft 11 in (3,94 m), (MU-2G, J), 13 ft 8 in (4,17 m); wing area (MU-2B and later), 178 sq ft (16,54 m²).

Accommodation: Two side by side on flight deck and up to a maximum of (MU-2B, D, F, K) seven or (MU-2G, J) nine in cabin.

Status: Prototype MU-2A first flown on 14 September 1963; MU-2B flown on 11 March 1965; MU-2D flown on 5 March 1966; MU-2F flown on 6 October 1967; MU-2G flown on 10 January 1969; MU-2J flown in August 1970; MU-2K flown in 1971. Production totals, MU-2A, 3; MU-2B, 34; MU-2D, 18; MU-2F, 94 by mid-1973; MU-2G, 41 by mid-1973; MU-2J, 54 by mid-1973; MU-2K, 42 by mid-1973. Grand total (including military) to March 1974, 344.

Notes: The MU-2 was the first original post-war Mitsubishi Aircraft design to enter production. Final assembly is handled primarily by Mitsubishi Aircraft International at San Angelo, Texas. The initial MU-2A prototypes had Turboméca Astazou IIK turboprops, Garrett AiResearch units being substituted for production. MU-2G and MU-2J have longer fuselages.

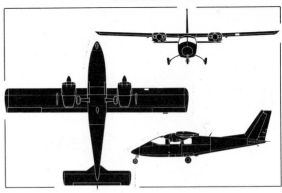

The Partenavia P.68 Victor, shown in the photograph and the silhouette, is one of the few light business twins featuring a high-wing layout

Country of Origin: Italy.

Type: Light business and touring twin.

Power Plant: Two 200 hp Lycoming IO-360-A1B piston engines.

Performance: Max speed, 208 mph (334 km/h); cruising speed, 194 mph (312 km/h) at 6,000 ft (1 828 m); best economy cruise, 186 mph (299 km/h) at 9,000 ft (2 473 m); initial rate of climb, 1,700 ft/min (8,6 m/sec); service ceiling, 21,500 ft (6 550 m); range at max cruise speed, 882 mls (1 420 km); range with max fuel, 1,045 mls (1 681 km) at 186 mph (299 km/h).

Weights: Empty, 2,425 lb (1 100 kg); max take-off, 4,100 lb (1 860 kg).

Dimensions: Span, 39 ft 4½ in (12,00 m); length, 30 ft 2 in (9,19 m); height, 11 ft 1¾ in (3,40 m); wing area, 200·2 sq ft (18,60 m²).

Accommodation: Six seats in pairs in cabin, with dual controls standard.

Status: Prototype first flown on 25 May 1970. Italian and US Type Approval, December 1971. First delivery January 1972. Production, 14 built up to early 1974, projected future production rate three a month.

Notes: The P.68 Victor was designed, like the P.64/P.66 Oscar (see page 164) by Prof Ing Luigi Pascale and is the first twin-engined type built by Partenavia. It is aimed at the same market as the Piper PA-34 Seneca (see page 119) and has a very similar specification, although it is of totally different configuration with a high wing and fixed landing gear. Considerable use is made of glass fibre mouldings in the structure of the Victor, including the whole of the wing leading edge, and special attention is given to the finish of the aircraft. After construction and flight testing of two prototypes, Partenavia put in hand a pre-production batch of 10 aircraft, all of which had been completed by mid-1973; further production was put in hand at a new factory in Southern Italy and the company was also seeking overseas licensees for the design. Future production models were to be offered with the option of a retractable under-carriage. Among the first operators of the Victor was the Alifoto company of Turin, using it for aerial photogrammetric duties, and another of the first batch of aircraft was sold to Società Ricerche Esperienze Meteorologiche (SOREM) for special meteorological research duties with sensors under each wing tip. The principal production version is designated P.68B, with 6-in (15-cm) longer fuselage and 4,320-lb (1 960-kg) gross weight.

PIPER PA-23 AZTEC AND APACHE

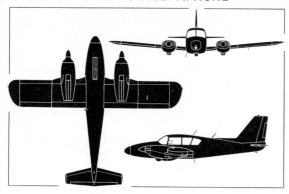

The photograph shows a Piper Aztec C and the silhouette depicts the similar Aztec D, these being the higher-performance derivatives of the original Apache

Country of Origin: USA.

Type: Business and executive transport.

Power Plant: Two (Apache) 150 hp Lycoming O-320 or 160 hp O-320-B or 235 hp O-540 or (Aztec) 250 hp Lycoming O-540 or IO-540 or TIO-540 series of piston engines.

Performance: Max cruising speed (23-150), 170 mph (272 km/h), (E23-250), 210 mph (338 km/h), (Turbo), 245 mph (394 km/h) ; best economy cruise (E23-250), 204 mph (328 km/h), (Turbo), 218 mph (351 km/h) ; initial rate of climb (23-150), 1,350 ft/min (6,9 m/sec), (E23-250), 1,490 ft/min (7,6 m/sec), (Turbo), 1,530 ft/min (7,8 m/sec) ; absolute ceiling (23-150), 20,000 ft (6 100 m), (E23-250), 21,100 ft (6 430 m), (Turbo), over 30,000 ft (9 145 m) ; range with max fuel (23-150), 1,260 mls (2 016 km), (E23-250), 1,210 mls (1 947 km), (Turbo), 1,310 mls (2 108 km).

Weights: Empty, 2,215 lb (1 006 kg), (E23-250), 3,042 lb (1 397 kg), (Turbo), 3,229 lb (1 464 kg) ; max take-off (23-150) 3,500 lb (1 590 kg), (E23-250 and Turbo), 5,200 lb (2 360 kg).

Dimensions: Span (23-150), 37 ft 1¾ in (11,32 m), (E23-250 and Turbo), 37 ft 2½ in (11,34 m) ; length (23-150), 27 ft 4¼ in (8,34 m), (E23-250 and Turbo), 31 ft 2¾ in (9,52 m) ; height (23-150), 9 ft 6 in (2,87 m), (E23-250 and Turbo), 10 ft 4 in (3,15 m) ; wing area (23-150), 204 sq ft (18,95 m²), (E23-250 and Turbo), 207·6 sq ft (19,28 m²).

Accommodation: Basic layouts provide for (Apache) four or five occupants or (Aztec) six occupants, including pilot.

Status: Prototype (Twin Stinson) first flown on 2 March 1952. Production deliveries began in March 1954. FAA Type Approvals (PA-23-150) 29 January 1954, (PA-23-160) 14 October 1957 (PA-23-250) 18 September 1959, (PA-23-235) 22 January 1962, (PA-E23-250) 21 June 1965. Production (to end-1973), over 3,000.

Notes: The PA-23 was the first Piper twin-engined light aircraft, being known as the Twin Stinson when the prototype first flew. The name was changed to Apache, in the company's series of Indian tribe names, before production deliveries began. Original Apaches had 150 hp engines and a characteristic rounded fin and rudder. Introduction of 250 hp engines, a lengthened nose and swept-back fin in the 1959 model were accompanied by a change of name to Aztec, although the PA-23 designation was retained. The PA-23-235 Apache has Aztec-style rear fuselage and swept-back fin.

PIPER PA-30 AND PA-39 TWIN COMANCHE

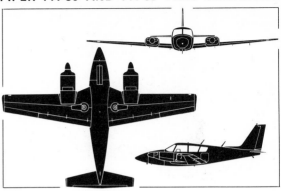

Essentially a twin-engined version of the Piper Comanche (page 168), the Twin Comanche C is shown in both the silhouette (right) and the photograph (above)

Country of Origin: USA.
Type: Light business and private twin.
Power Plant: Two (PA-30, PA-39) 160 hp Lycoming IO-320-B1A or (PA-30T, PA-39T) 160 hp Lycoming IO-320-C1A piston engines.
Performance: Max cruising speed (-30, -39), 198 mph (319 km/h), (-30T, -39T), 240 mph (386 km/h) at 24,000 ft (7 300 m); best economy cruise (-30, -39), 188 mph (303 km/h), (-30T, -39T), 207 mph (333 km/h) at 24,000 ft (7 300 m); initial rate of climb (-30, -39), 1,460 ft/min (7,4 m/sec), (-30T, -39T), 1,290 ft/min (6,5 m/sec); service ceiling (-30, -39), 20,000 ft (6 100 m), (-30T, -39T), 25,000 ft (7 620 m); range with max fuel (-30, -39), 1,200 mls (1 930 km), (-30T, -39T), 1,710 mls (2 750 km).
Weights: Empty (-30, -39), 2,270 lb (1 029 kg), (-30T, 39T), 2,416 lb (1 095 kg); max take-off (-30, -39), 3,600 lb (1 633 kg), (-30, -39 when fitted with wing-tip tanks, -30T, -39T), 3,725 lb (1 690 kg).
Dimensions: Span, 36 ft 0 in (10,97 m); span over tip tanks, 36 ft 9½ in (11,22 m); length, 25 ft 2 in (7,67 m); height, 8 ft 2⅞ in (2,51 m); wing area, 178 sq ft (16,54 m²).

Accommodation: Two pairs of seats for pilot and three passengers; optional provision for third pair of seats.
Status: Prototype PA-30 first flown on 7 November 1962; first production aircraft on 3 May 1963. FAA Type Approval, PA-30, 5 February 1963, PA-39, 3 December 1969.
Notes: The Twin Comanche was developed to supersede the Apache (see page 116) in the Piper range as the smallest of its twins. Successive models were designated Twin Comanche A, B and C, all with the same power plant but with detail refinements. They were paralleled by Turbo Twin Comanche models, differing in having Rajay turbosuperchargers. Wing-tip tanks were optional. Early in 1970 Piper introduced the PA-39 Twin Comanche C/R, differing from the Twin Comanche C only in having "handed" engines with the propellers rotating in opposite directions. A Turbo version of the PA-39 was also marketed, and the PA-30 was discontinued in favour of the PA-39 in 1971. All Twin Comanche production ended late in 1972 following major flood damage to the Piper factories. During 1974, the PA-40 Arapaho was under development as a successor to the Twin Comanche, from which it was reported to differ in relatively minor respects.

PIPER PA-31 NAVAJO AND NAVAJO CHIEFTAIN

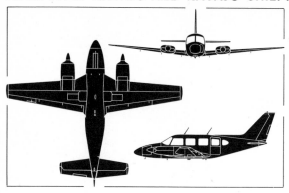

Shown in the silhouette is the standard PA-31 Navajo while the photograph depicts the enlarged Navajo Chieftain. The PA-31T Cheyenne is similar with turboprop engines

Country of Origin: USA.

Type: Business and executive transport.

Power Plant: Two (PA-31-300) 300 hp Lycoming IO-540-M1A5 or (Turbo) 310 hp TIO-540-A1A, A1B, -A2A, -A2B or -A2C or (PA-31P) 425 hp TIGO-541-E or (Chieftain) 350 hp TIO-540-J2BD engines.

Performance: Max cruising speed (-300), 213 mph (343 km/h), (PA-31P), 266 mph (428 km/h), (Chieftain), 260 mph (420 km/h) ; best economy cruise (-300), 178 mph (286 km/h), (PA-31P), 222 mph (357 km/h) ; initial rate of climb (-300), 1,670 ft/min (8,5 m/sec), (PA-31P), 1,740 ft/min (8,8 m/sec), (Chieftain), 1,390 ft/min (7,0 m/sec) ; service ceiling (-300), 16,000 ft (5 060 m), (Chieftain), 27,200 ft (8 291 m) ; maximum operating ceiling (PA-31P), 29,000 ft (8 840 m) ; range with max fuel (-300), 1,590 mls (2 555 km), (PA-31P), 1,335 mls (2 148 km), (Chieftain), 1,100 mls (1 770 km).

Weights: Empty, 3,849 lb (1 745 kg), (PA-31P), 4,842 lb (2 196 kg), (Chieftain), 3,991 lb (1 808 kg) ; max take-off (-300), 6,500 lb (2 948 kg), (PA-31P), 7,800 lb (3 538 kg), (Chieftain), 7,000 lb (3 171 kg).

Dimensions: Span, 40 ft 8 in (12,40 m) ; length (-300 and Turbo), 32 ft 7½ in (9,94 m), (PA-31P), 34 ft 6 in (10,52 m), (Chieftain), 34 ft 8 in (10,6 m) ; height (-300 and Turbo and Chieftain), 13 ft 0 in (3,96 m), (PA-31P), 13 ft 3 in (4,04 m) ; wing area, 229 sq ft (21,3 m²).

Accommodation: Basic layout for (-300, Turbo and PA-31P) six or up to maximum of eight or (Chieftain) eight or up to maximum of ten occupants including pilot.

Status: Prototype Navajo first flown on 30 September 1964 ; deliveries (Turbo Navajo) began 17 April 1967 ; PA-31P first flown March 1968. FAA Type Approvals, (Turbo) 24 February 1966, (PA-31-300) 12 June 1967, (PA-31P) 26 November 1969. Production total, over 1,000 of all variants by early 1974.

Notes: The PA-31 Navajo joined the Piper range of business twins in 1967 and four versions were in production by 1974. The basic model was the PA-31-300, and the Turbo Navajo differed from it in having more powerful turbo-supercharged engines. The PA-31P Pressurized Navajo introduced a pressurized cabin and had a reconfigured fuselage. The PA-31-350 Navajo Chieftain, introduced in 1973, has the fuselage lengthened by 2 ft (0,61 m).

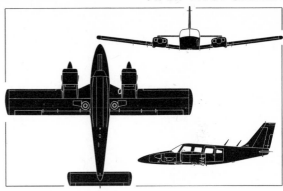

The Piper PA-34 Seneca, depicted in the photograph (above) and silhouette (right) was derived from the single-engined Cherokee Six (page 170)

Country of Origin: USA.

Type: Light business and touring twin.

Power Plant: One 200 hp Lycoming LIO-360-C1E6 (starboard) and one 200 hp IO-360-C1E6 (port) piston engine.

Performance: Max speed, 195 mph (314 km/h); cruising speeds, 186 mph (299 km/h) at 6,000 ft (1 830 m), 178 mph (286 km/h) at 13,300 ft (4 055 m) and 166 mph (267 km/h) at 18,300 ft (5 580 m); initial rate of climb, 1,360 ft/min (6,9 m/sec); service ceiling, 19,400 ft (5 915 m); range at max cruising speed, 856 mls (1 377 km); range with max fuel, 1,130 mls (1 818 km) at 166 mph (267 km/h).

Weights: Empty, 2,599 lb (1 178 kg); max take-off, 4,200 lb (1 905 kg).

Dimensions: Span, 38 ft 10¾ in (11,85 m); length, 28 ft 6 in (8,69 m); height, 9 ft 10¾ in (3,02 m); wing area, 206·5 sq ft (19,18 m²).

Accommodation: Six seats in pairs in cabin, with optional provision for seventh occupant between two centre seats. Alternative layouts provide for cargo-carrying.

Status: Prototype flown in 1970. FAA Type Approval (PA-34-200) on 7 May 1971. Production deliveries began late 1971.

Notes: The PA-34 was derived from the PA-32 Cherokee Six (see page 170) in the same way that the Twin Comanche was developed from the Comanche. Thus, the tail unit, rear fuselage and cabin area of the two types are substantially identical, but the wing incorporates a new centre section on which the two engines are mounted, and a new nose cone is provided, incorporating a baggage compartment for 100 lb (45 kg). Like the PA-39 versions of the Twin Comanche (see page 117), the Seneca has "handed" engines, the direction of rotation of the basic Lycoming IO-360 being changed—for the starboard installation—by some relatively small modifications to the engine and retiming of the cylinder firing sequence. The Seneca was originally certificated at a gross weight of 4,000 lb (1 815 kg), an increase of 200 lb (90 kg) being approved for the 1973 model, which also introduced aerodynamically-refined wing tips and several modifications to improve passenger comfort and safety. The passenger seats are easily removable and a large loading door adjacent to the standard rear loading door in the port side of the fuselage is optional, providing for large cargo items to be loaded.

ROCKWELL COMMANDER 685 AND SHRIKE COMMANDER

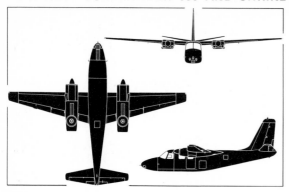

The original Aero Commander high-wing twin has carried several different names and designations including Shrike Commander as depicted in the photograph and silhouette

Country of Origin: USA.

Type: Business and executive transport.

Power Plant: Two (Shrike) 290 hp Lycoming IO-540-E1B5 or (685) 435 hp Continental GTSIO-520-F piston engines.

Performance: Max cruising speed (Shrike), 203 mph (326 km/h) at 9,000 ft (2 745 m), (685), 255 mph (410 km/h) at 24,000 ft (7 315 m) ; initial rate of climb (Shrike), 1,340 ft/min (6,8 m/sec), (685), 1,490 ft/min (7,6 m/sec) ; service ceiling (Shrike), 19,400 ft (5 913 m), (685), 27,500 ft (8 382 m) ; range with standard fuel (Shrike), 750 mls (1 207 km), (685), 1,274 mls (2 050 km) ; range with max fuel (Shrike), 920 mls (1 480 km), (685), 1,730 mls (2 784 km).

Weights: Empty (Shrike), 4,635 lb (2 102 kg), (685), 6,021 lb (2,731 kg) ; max take-off (Shrike), 6,750 lb (3 062 kg), (685), 9,000 lb (4 082 kg).

Dimensions: Span (Shrike), 49 ft 0½ in (14,95 m), (685), 46 ft 6½ in (14,18 m) ; length (Shrike), 36 ft 7 in (11,15 m), (685), 42 ft 11¾ in (13,10 m) ; height (Shrike), 14 ft 6 in (4,42 m), (685), 14 ft 11½ in (4,55 m), wing area (Shrike), 255 sq ft (23,69 m²).

Accommodation: Two seats on flight deck and typical layout (Shrike) for up to five or (685) up to seven passengers in cabin.

Status: Prototype Commander L-3805 first flown 23 April 1948. Model 520 certificated 31 January 1952 ; Model 560 on 28 May 1954 ; Model 500 on 24 July 1958 ; Model 680 on 14 October 1955 ; Model 720 on 5 December 1958 ; Model 685 on 17 September 1971.

Notes: The range of Commander piston-engined twins is derived from the original Aero Commander L-3805, which went into production as the Commander 520, a six/seven seater with 240 hp Lycoming GO-435-C2 engines and gross weight of 5,500 lb (2 495 kg). The Model 560 followed with 260 hp GO-480 engines, swept tail and 6,000 lb (2 720 kg) weight and Model 500 had 250 hp O-540-A2B engines. Some Model 500 variants had 260 hp Continental IO-470-M engines and later models had higher weights. Progressive development led to introduction of more powerful engines, higher weights and pressurisation in various combinations in the model 680 and 720 variants, and the Grand Commander had a longer fuselage. The latter subsequently became the Courser Commander and the Model 500 became the Shrike Commander, joined in 1971 by the pressurised Commander 685.

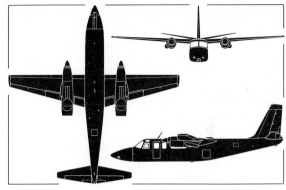

Turboprop versions of the basic Commander series have included the Turbo II shown in the photograph (above) and the similar Hawk Commander depicted by the silhouette (right)

Country of Origin: USA.

Type: Business and executive transport.

Power Plant: Two (680T) 605 hp Garrett AiResearch TPE-331-43 or (680W) 605 eshp TPE-331-43BL or (690) 717 eshp TPE-331-5-251K turboprops.

Performance: Max cruising speed (680T), 285 mph (459 km/h), (681B), 278 mph (447 km/h), (690), 322 mph (518 km/h); best economy cruise (690), 266 mph (428 km/h) at 25,000 ft (7 620 m); initial rate of climb (680T), 2,120 ft/min (10,75 m/sec), (681B), 2,007 ft/min (10,2 m/sec); (690), 2,849 ft/min (14,5 m/sec); service ceiling (680T), 28,000 ft (8 530 m), (681B), 25,600 ft (7 800 m), (690), 32,900 ft (10 030 m); range with max payload (690), 808 mls (1 300 km); range with max fuel (680T), 1,000 mls (1 610 km), (681B), 1,491 mls (2 400 km), (690), 1,567 mls (2 522 km).

Weights: Empty (680T), 5,450 lb (2 472 kg), (681B), 5,647 lb (2 561 kg), (690), 5,910 lb (2 680 kg); empty equipped (690A), 6,870 lb (3 116 kg); max take-off (680T), 8,950 lb (4 060 kg); (681B), 9,400 lb (4 265 kg), (690), 10,250 lb (4 649 kg).

Dimensions: Span (680T, 681B), 44 ft $0\frac{3}{4}$ in (13,43 m), (690),

46 ft $6\frac{1}{2}$ in (14,19 m); length (680T), 41 ft $3\frac{1}{4}$ in (12,58 m), (681B, 690), 42 ft $11\frac{3}{4}$ in (13,10 m); (690A), 44 ft 3 in (13,49 m); height (680T, 681B), 14 ft 6 in (4,42 m), (690), 14 ft $11\frac{1}{2}$ in (4,56 m); wing area (680T, 681B), 242·5 sq ft (22,53 m²), (690), 266 sq ft (24,7 m²).

Accommodation: Two individual seats on flight deck and up to (680T, 681B) seven or (690) nine seats in cabin.

Status: Prototype Turbo Commander (680T) first flown on 31 December 1964; FAA Type Certification 15 September 1965; first customer deliveries May 1966. Model 680V certificated June 1967; Model 681 certificated 20 March 1969. Prototype 690 first flown 3 March 1969 and certificated on 19 July 1971.

Notes: The Model 680T was the original Aero Commander Turbo Commander; Model 680V had the gross weight increased and 680W had improved engines. The Model 681 introduced further improvements and the name Hawk Commander was used for a time, but was dropped again in 1971 when the improved Turbo Commander 681B was introduced. The Turbo Commander 690 succeeded the 681B in 1971 and was followed in 1973 by the Turbo Commander 690A with further improvements and a long dorsal fin.

ROCKWELL (NORTH AMERICAN) SABRE AND SABRELINER

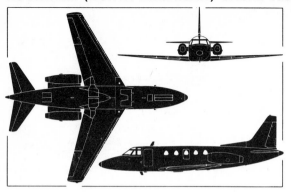

Derived from the military T-39 Sabreliner are several commercial versions for business use, including the Sabre 75A (photograph) and Sabreliner 60 (silhouette)

Country of Origin: USA.

Type: Business and executive transport.

Power Plant: Two (Srs 40) 3,000 lb st (1 360 kgp) Pratt & Whitney JT12A-6A or (Srs 40, 60, 75) 3,200 lb st (1 497 kgp) JT12A-8 turbojets or (Srs 75A) 4,315 lb st (1 961 kgp) General Electric CF 700-2D-2 turbofans.

Performance: Max cruising speed (40, 60), 563 mph (906 km/h), (75A), 556 mph (895 km/h); best economy cruise (40, 60), 495 mph (797 km/h) at 40,000 ft (12 192 m); (75A), 488 mph (785 km/h) at 4,000 ft (12 192 m); initial rate of climb (40), 4,700 ft/min (23,9 m/sec), (75A), 4,500 ft/min (22,9 m/sec); operating ceiling 45,000 ft (13 716 m); range with max fuel (40 and 60), 1,890 mls (3 040 km), (75A), 1,865 mls (3 000 km).

Weights: Typical empty equipped (40), 10,300 lb (4 672 kg), (60), 11,450 lb (5 195 kg), (75A), 13,200 lb (5 987 kg); max payload, (40), 2,300 lb (1 043 kg), (60), 1,600 lb (726 kg), (75A), 2,200 lb (997 kg); max take-off (40), 19,612 lb (8 895 kg), (60), 20,000 lb (9 070 kg), (75A), 23,000 lb (10 430 kg).

Dimensions: Span, 44 ft 5$\frac{1}{4}$ in (13,54 m); length (40), 43 ft 9 in (13,34 m), (60), 48 ft 4 in (14,73 m), (75A), 47 ft 2 in (14,38 m);

height (50, 60), 16 ft 0 in (4,88 m), (75A), 17 ft 3 in (5,26 m); wing area, 342 sq ft (31,78 m²).

Accommodation: Flight crew of two and up to (40) seven or (60, 75A) ten passengers in executive layouts.

Status: Prototype (NA-246) first flown on 16 September 1958; first production (T-39A) flown on 30 June 1960; first Srs 70 flown on 4 December 1969; two Srs 75A prototypes flown on 18 October 1972 and 1 December 1972. Initial Type Approval 23 March 1962; Srs 40 approved on 17 April 1963, Srs 60 on 28 April 1967, Srs 70 on 17 June 1970, Srs 75A in December 1973. Production totals, over 125 Srs 40, over 40 Srs 60, over 20 Srs 70/75 (to end-1973).

Notes: The prototype NA-246 was a private venture prototype to meet a USAF requirement (see *Military* volume, page 192), and the type was offered on the commercial market as the Sabreliner Srs 40. It was joined in 1967 by the Sabreliner 60 with lengthened fuselage. The Sabreliner 70 was introduced in 1970 with a deepened fuselage and the same JT12A-8 engines; its name was changed to Sabre 75 in 1971 and it was superseded by the Sabre 75A in 1973 with turbofan engines. The name Sabre instead of Sabreliner was favoured for all variants after 1971.

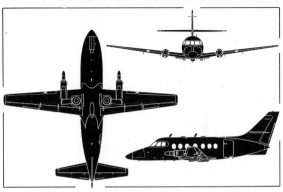

Examples of the original Handley Page JetStream 100, as shown in the photograph and silhouette, will be joined in service by Scottish Aviation-built aircraft

Country of Origin: United Kingdom.

Type: Business and executive transport and commuter.

Power Plant: Two 940 eshp Turboméca Astazou XVI turboprops.

Performance: Max cruising speed, 278 mph (448 km/h) at 12,000 ft (3 660 m) and 254 mph (409 km/h) at 22,000 ft (6 705 m); initial rate of climb, 2,500 ft/min (12,7 m/sec); service ceiling, 26,000 ft (7 928 m); range with typical payload, 630 mls (1 016 km); range with max fuel, 1,382 mls (2 224 km).

Weights: Basic operating (executive) 8,800 lb (3 992 kg), (airliner) 8,680 lb (3 937 kg); max payload (executive) 3,400 lb (1 542 kg), (airliner) 3,570 lb (1 619 kg); max take-off, 12,500 lb (5 670 kg).

Dimensions: Span, 52 ft 0 in (15,85 m); length, 47 ft $1\frac{1}{2}$ in (14,37 m); height, 17 ft $5\frac{1}{2}$ in (5,32 m); wing area, 270 sq ft (25,08 m²).

Accommodation: Flight crew of two and typical layout for (executive) up to 12 or (commuter airline) up to 18 passengers.

Status: Prototypes (HP Jetstream 1) first flown 18 August 1967; 28 December 1967; 8 March 1968 and 8 April 1968; prototype Series 3M (military) first flown 21 November 1968. First Scottish Aviation Jetstream T Mk 1 flown on 13 April 1973. Production, about 35 by HP; 26 by Scottish Aviation for RAF (to 1974).

Notes: The Jetstream project originated in the Handley Page Aircraft company at Radlett, it being intended primarily for the executive market with a secondary application for third-level airline use. Over 180 Jetstreams were on order by mid-1969 when Handley Page suffered financial collapse, and only about 35 were built and 25 delivered. Most of these (all Mk 1s with Astazou XIV engines) were in service in the USA in 1974, and the Riley company had converted one example to have Pratt & Whitney (UACL) PT6A-34 turboprops. This conversion offered a cruising speed of 300 mph (482 km/h) at 15,000 ft (4 572 m) and an optimum range of 1,800 mls (2 900 km), and was being actively pursued as a programme for existing Jetstream 1s. Meanwhile in 1972 the first Jetstream 200 (new designation for the Mk 2) went into service in France with Air Wasteel and Scottish Aviation planned to offer new production Jetstream 200s on the civil market after completing a batch of 26 for the RAF as navigation trainers (see *Military* volume, page 197). The future of this plan depended, however, on options being taken on at least 15 civil Jetstreams.

SMITH AEROSTAR 600, 601 AND SUPERSTAR 700

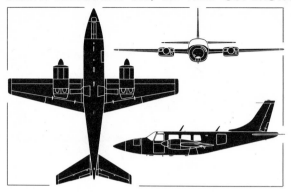

The photograph and silhouette depict the Smith Aerostar 601; other variants of the basic design are externally similar, as described below

Country of Origin: USA.

Type: Business and executive transport.

Power Plant: Two (600) 290 hp Lycoming IO-540-G1B5 or (601 and 601P) 290 hp IO-540-P1A5 or (700, 700P) 300 hp Lycoming IO-540M piston engines.

Performance: Max cruising speed (600), 250 mph (402 km/h) at 10,000 ft (3 050 m), (601), 312 mph (502 km/h) at 25,000 ft (7 620 m), (700), 255 mph (410 km/h) at 10,000 ft (3 050 m); economical cruising speed (600), 225 mph (362 km/h), (601), 275 mph (443 km/h), (700), 178 mph (286 km/h); initial rate of climb (600), 1,850 ft/min (9,35 m/sec), (601), 1,800 ft/min (9,15 m/sec), (700), 2,480 ft/min (12,6 m/sec); service ceiling (600), 22,000 ft (6 705 m), (601), over 30,000 ft (9 145 m), (700), over 24,000 ft (7 315 m); range with max fuel (600), 1,400 mls (2 250 km), (601), 1,410 mls (2 265 km), (700), 1,600 mls (2 575 km).

Weights: Empty equipped (600), 3,425 lb (1 553 kg), (601), 3,700 lb (1 678 kg), (700), 3,900 lb (1 770 kg); max take-off (600), 5,500 lb (2 495 kg), (601), 5,700 lb (2 585 kg), (700), 6,300 lb (2 857 kg).

Dimensions: Span (600, 601), 34 ft 2½ in (10,43 m), (700), 36 ft 8 in (11,18 m); length (600, 601), 34 ft 9¾ in (10,61 m), (700), 35 ft 4 in (10,77 m); height (600, 601), 12 ft 1½ in (3,70 m); wing area (600, 601), 170 sq ft (15,8 m²), (700), 193·5 sq ft (17,96 m²).

Accommodation: Pilot and five passengers in individual seats in cabin.

Status: Prototype Aerostar 320 first flown in November 1966; first Aerostar 600 flown 20 December 1967; first production Aerostar 601 flown on 9 July 1968; prototype Superstar 700 flown 22 November 1972. FAA Type Approvals, (Model 360) 1 May 1967, (Model 400) 4 October 1967, (Model 600) 28 March 1968, (Model 601) 8 November 1968. Production totals, Model 600 and 601 by Smith/Butler/Aerostar, 178; Model 600/601 by Smith, over 50 to 1974.

Notes: First prototype had 160 hp engines when first flown (hence, Model 320) but was re-engined with 180 hp IO-360-E1A units for certification as Model 360 and then with 200 hp IO-360-D1As as Model 400. Production of Model 600 and 601 was initiated by Smith in California, later transferred to Butler Aviation in Texas, then reacquired by Ted Smith in 1972. The latter company then introduced the pressurized 601P and slightly larger 700.

Based on the wings of the Beechcraft Queen Air with a new pressurized fuselage, the Merlin III is shown by both the photograph and silhouette

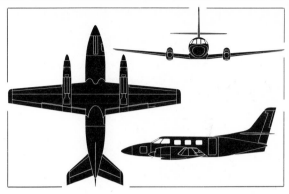

Country of Origin: USA.

Type: Business and executive transport.

Power Plant: Two (IIA) 578 shp Pratt & Whitney (UACL) PT6A-20 or (IIB) 665 hp Garrett AiResearch TPE 331-1-151G or (III) 840 shp TPE 331-3U-303G turboprops.

Performance: Max cruising speed (IIA), 270 mph (435 km/h), (IIB), 295 mph (475 km/h), (III), 316 mph (509 km/h); economic cruising speed (III), 288 mph (463 km/h); initial rate of climb (IIA), 1,950 ft/min (9,9 m/sec), (IIB), 2,570 ft/min (13,1 m/sec), (III), 2,530 ft/min (12,9 m/sec); service ceiling (IIA), 28,000 ft (8 535 m), (IIB), 29,900 ft (9 110 m), (III), 28,900 ft (8 810 m); range with max fuel (IIA), 1,700 ft (2 735 m), (IIB), 1,785 mls (2 872 km), (III), 2,648 mls (4 261 km).

Weights: Empty (IIA), 5,495 lb (2 492 kg), empty equipped (IIB), 6,450 lb (2 926 kg) (III), 7,400 lb (3 356 kg); max take-off, (IIA), 9,800 lb (4 445 kg), (IIB), 10,000 lb (4 536 kg), (III), 12,500 lb (5 670 kg).

Dimensions: Span (IIA, IIB), 45 ft 10½ in (13,98 m), (III), 46 ft 3 in (14,10 m); length (IIA, IIB), 40 ft 1¼ in (12,22 m), (III), 42 ft 2 in (12,85 m); height (IIA, IIB), 14 ft 4 in (4,37 m), (III), 16 ft 8 in

(5,08 m); wing area (IIA, IIB), 279·74 sq ft (25,97 m²).

Accommodation: Crew of two on flight deck and standard arrangement for six or maximum of eight passengers in cabin.

Status: Prototype Merlin IIA first flown on 13 April 1965. Deliveries began (Merlin IIA) 26 August 1966 and (Merlin IIB) June 1968. FAA Type Approvals SA26-T (Merlin IIB) 15 July 1966. SA26-AT (Merlin IIB) 12 June 1968, SA226-T (Merlin III) 27 July 1970. Production totals: Merlin IIA, 33; Merlin IIB, 87; Merlin III, over 20.

Notes: The Merlin II was an outgrowth of earlier Swearingen programmes based on existing business aircraft, and comprised the basic wing structure of the Beech Queen Air and undercarriage of the Twin Bonanza, with a completely new pressurized fuselage. The IIA and IIB differed only in type of power plant, and the IIB was offered initially at a gross weight of 9,300 lb (4 218 kg), later increased as shown in the data here. The Merlin III was a refinement of the IIB, with uprated engines and other small changes. After the Swearingen company became a subsidiary of Fairchild industries in 1971, production was concentrated on the Merlin III and the larger Merlin IV (see page 70), which had common power plants and systems, but different fuselages.

AERO BOERO 95/115/180

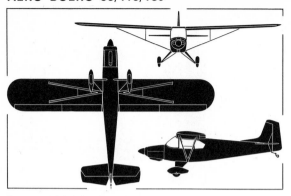

The photograph shows one of the original production Aero Boero 95s, while the silhouette depicts the more refined Model 115 with swept-back fin-and-rudder

Country of Origin: Argentina.

Type: Light sporting aircraft.

Power Plant: One (95 Standard) 95 hp Continental C90 or (95 De Lujo) 100 hp Continental O-200-A or (95B) 150 hp Continental or (95/115) 115 hp Lycoming O-235-C2A or (180) 180 hp Lycoming O-360-A1A piston engine.

Performance: Max cruising speed (95/115), 117 mph (188 km/h), (180), 131 mph (211 km/h), (180 Condor), 125 mph (201 km/h); initial rate of climb (95/115), 1,000 ft/min (5,1 m/sec), (180), 1,180 ft/min (6,0 m/sec); service ceiling (180), 22,000 ft (6 700 m); range with max fuel (95/115 and 180), 495 mls (800 km).

Weights: Empty equipped (95/115), 1,080 lb (490 kg), (180), 1,212 lb (550 kg); max take-off (95/115), 1,697 lb (770 kg), (180), 1,860 lb (844 kg).

Dimensions: Span (95/115), 34 ft 2¼ in (10,42 m), (115BS, 180), 35 ft 2 in (10,72 m); length (95/115), 22 ft 7½ in (6,90 m), (115BS, 180), 23 ft 10¼ in (7,27 m); height (all), 6 ft 10½ in (2,10 m); wing area (95/115), 176·1 sq ft (16,36 m²), (115BS, 180), 177·3 sq ft (16,47 m²).

Accommodation: Normal accommodation in all versions, pilot and two passengers.

Status: Prototype Model 95 first flown on 12 March 1959; first 95/115 flown in March 1969; first 115BS flown in February 1973; first Model 180 delivered in December 1969; first 180RV flown in October 1972. Production totals include about 50 Model 95/115, 20 Model 115BS, 15 Model 180, five 180 RV/RVR and ten 180 Condor by 1974.

Notes: The initial production Model 95 with 95 hp engine was soon followed by the more powerful 95A De Lujo and the 95A Fumigador agricultural versions. The 95/115 introduced a further increase in engine power plus other refinements, and was itself replaced in production early in 1973 by the 115BS with swept-back fin and increased span. The original Aero Boero 180 was a four-seater but the production model seated only three and had the same wing as the 95/115. It was followed in 1972 by the 180RV and the 180RVR (for glider towing) with the same new features as the 115BS. The 180 Condor has provision for a turbo-supercharger and has one passenger seat removed, for better performance at high altitudes in the Andes.

Shown in the photograph (above) and the silhouette (right) is the Airtourer in its basic 100 hp version; more powerful models are externally similar

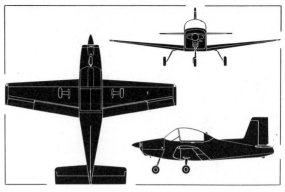

Country of Origin: New Zealand.

Type: Light sporting aircraft.

Power Plant: One 100 hp Continental O-200-A or (T2) 115 hp Lycoming O-235-C2A or (T3) 130 hp R-R Continental O-240-A or (T4) 150 hp Lycoming O-320-E2A or (T5 and T6) O-320-E1A piston engine.

Performance: Max cruising speed (T2), 131 mph (210 km/h), (T4), 140 mph (225 km/h), (T5), 150 mph (241 km/h) ; best economy cruise (T2), 110 mph (177 km/h), (T4), 123 mph (198 km/h), (T5), 134 mph (216 km/h) ; initial rate of climb (T2), 900 ft/min (4,6 m/sec), (T4), 980 ft/min (5,0 m/sec), (T5), 1,100 ft/min (5,6 m/sec) ; service ceiling (T2), 14,000 ft (4 275 m), (T4), 15,500 ft (4 725 m), (T5), 16,000 ft (4 875 m) ; range with max fuel (T2), 710 mls (1 140 km), (T4), 625 mls (1 005 km), (T5), 670 mls (1 075 km).

Weights: Empty equipped (T2), 1,080 lb (490 kg), (T4), 1,165 lb (528 kg), (T5), 1,175 lb (532 kg) ; max take-off (T2, aerobatic), 1,550 lb (703 kg), (T2 normal, T4, T5 aerobatic), 1,650 lb (748 kg), (T4, T5 normal), 1,750 lb (793 kg), (T6 normal), 1,900 lb (862 kg).

Dimensions: Span, 26 ft 0 in (7,92 m) ; length (T2, T4), 21 ft 5$\frac{7}{8}$ in

(6,55 m), (T5, T6), 22 ft 0 in (6,71 m) ; height, 7 ft 0 in (2,13 m) ; wing area, 120 sq ft (11,15 m²).

Accommodation: Two side-by-side in enclosed cabin.

Status: Prototype Victa Airtourer first flown 31 March 1959 ; Airtourer 115 prototype flown on 17 September 1962 ; first production Airtourer 115 flown on 22 February 1963 ; first T3 flown on 27 January 1972 ; prototype T4 flown in September 1968 ; prototype T5 flown in November 1968.

Notes: The Airtourer owes its origin to the Light Aircraft Design Competition organised by the Royal Aero Club of Britain in 1953, which was won by the entry by Henry Millicer. This design was put into production in Australia by Victa Ltd, which built 170 of the 100 hp and 115 hp Airtourers between 1960 and 1966. Production was resumed during 1968 in New Zealand by Aero Engine Services Ltd (AESL) and in 1973 this company merged with Air Parts (NZ) Ltd to form New Zealand Aerospace Industries Ltd. Production of the T2 and T3 versions was continuing in 1974, but few examples of the more powerful T4, T5 and T6 had been delivered for civil use. Among military users of the T6 are the RNZAF, Thailand, Indonesia RAAF and Singapore.

AEROSPATIALE (SOCATA) RALLYE SERIES

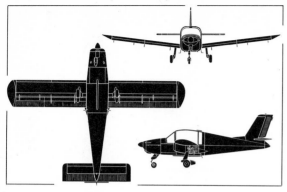

The photograph (above) shows an MS 894A Rallye Minerva while the silhouette (left) depicts the lower-powered MS 880B Rallye 100 Tourisme and Sport model

Country of Origin: France.

Type: Club trainer and private aircraft.

Power Plant: One (880A), 90 hp Continental O-200-A, (880B), 100 hp R-R/Continental O-200-A, (881), 105 hp Potez 4 E-20, (882), 115 hp Potez 4 E-20, (883), 115 hp Lycoming O-235, (884), 125 hp Franklin, (885), 145 hp Continental, (886), 150 hp Continental O-300-C, (887), 125 hp Lycoming O-235-F2A, (890), 145 hp Continental O-300-A, (892), 150 hp Lycoming O-320-E2A, (893), 180 hp O-360-A2A, (894), 220 hp Franklin 6A-350-C1.

Performance: Max speed (880B), 121 mph (195 km/h), (893), 149 mph (240 km/h); cruise speed (880B), 108 mph (173 km/h), (893), 139 mph (224 km/h); initial rate of climb (880B), 541 ft/min (2,75 m/sec), (893), 787 ft/min (4,0 m/sec); service ceiling (880B), 10,500 ft (3 200 m), (893), 11,150 ft (3 400 m); max range (880B), 497 mls (800 km), (893), 590 mls (950 km).

Weights: Empty (880B), 992 lb (450 kg), (893), 1,257 lb (570 kg); max take-off (880B), 1,697 lb (770 kg), (893), 2,315 lb (1 050 kg).

Dimensions: Span (all), 31 ft 6¼ in (9,61 m); length (880B), 22 ft 10½ in (6,97 m), (893), 23 ft 9 in (7,24 m); height (880B), 8 ft 6¼ in (2,60 m), (893), 9 ft 2¼ in (3,67 m); wing area (all), 132 sq ft (12,30 m²).

Accommodation: Two seats side-by-side and (MS880B) two children or one adult or (other variants) two adults on rear seat.

Status: Prototype (MS880) first flown 10 June 1959; MS880B flown on 12 February 1961; MS881, 13 March 1963; MS882, 1 August 1962; MS883, 10 December 1968; MS884, 1967; MS885, 20 April 1961; MS887, 10 February 1972; MS890, 1962; MS892, 13 February 1964; MS893, 7 December 1964; MS894, 12 May 1967. Production totals, prototypes, 2; MS880B, about 900; MS881, 12; MS882, 1; MS883, 77; MS885, 212; MS886, 3; MS887, over 15; MS890, 8; MS892, about 300; MS893, over 500; MS894, over 200. Grand total, over 2,500 by mid-1974.

Notes: All aircraft in the series are basically similar apart from accommodation and power plant. The MS designations were dropped for marketing purposes, the 1974 range comprising the Rallye 100 Sport and Tourisme (MS880B), Rallye 125 (MS887), Rallye 150 GT (MS892), Rallye 180 GT (MS893) and Rallye 220 GT (MS894). The 150 and 180 had also been known as the Commodore, the MS880 as the Club and the 894 as the Minerva.

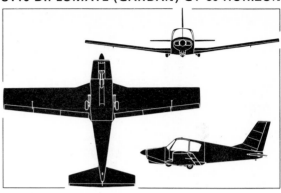

Shown in the photograph (above) is the four-seat ST-10 Diplomate and the silhouette (right) depicts the GY-80 Horizon from which it was derived

Country of Origin: France.

Type: Private and club aircraft.

Power Plant: One (GY-80) 160 hp Lycoming O-320-D or 180 hp Lycoming O-360-A or (ST10) 200 hp Lycoming IO-360-C piston engine.

Performance: Max speed (GY-80-160), 149 mph (240 km/h), (ST10), 174 mph (280 km/h); cruise speed (GY-80-160), 145 mph (234 km/h), (ST10), 165 mph (265 km/h); initial rate of climb (GY-80-160), 690 ft/min (3,5 m/sec), (ST10), 1,003 ft/min (5,1 m/sec); service ceiling (GY-80-160), 13,940 ft (4 250 m), (ST10), 16,400 ft (5 000 m); range with max fuel (GY-80-160), 590 mls (950 km), (ST10), 860 mls (1 385 km).

Weights: Empty (GY-80-160), 1,367 lb (620 kg), (ST10), 1,594 lb (723 kg); max take-off (GY-80-160), 2,425 lb (1 100 kg), (ST10), 2,690 lb (1 220 kg).

Dimensions: Span (both), 31 ft 10 in (9,70 m); length (GY-80), 21 ft 9½ in (6,64 m), (ST10), 22 ft 9¾ in (7,26 m); height (GY-80), 8 ft 6 in (2,60 m), (ST10), 9 ft 5½ in (2,88 m); wing area (both), 139·9 sq ft (13,00 m²).

Accommodation: (GY-80 and ST10) Pilot and three passengers in enclosed cabin.

Status: Prototype GY-80 first flown on 21 July 1960. Prototype ST10 first flown (as Super Horizon 200) on 7 November 1967. Production totals, Horizon, 260 (complete), Diplomate, over 40 to end-1973.

Notes: The GY-80 was designed by Yves Gardan, who had been responsible for several earlier post-war light aircraft, and the prototype was constructed as a private venture. Two years after the prototype first flew (with a 160 hp engine), design rights were sold to Sud-Aviation and production was undertaken by SOCATA (now a Division of Aérospatiale) the 180 hp engine being offered as an optional alternative. Design of an improved and more powerful version of the Horizon was undertaken by SOCATA, originally as the Super Horizon 200 and then as the Provence before the name Diplomate was finally selected. This used many components of the Horizon but had a lengthened fuselage and a more spacious cabin. The Diplomate remained in small scale production in 1974 (only two having been built in 1973) and the users included Varig, the Brazilian airline, which had ordered 12 for use in its pilot training programme.

AUSTER MODEL J SERIES AND HUSKY

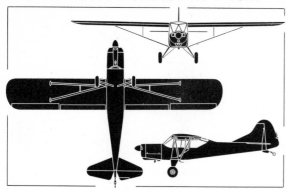

The photograph and the silhouette both depict the D5/180 Husky as finally produced by Beagle, a derivative of the original Auster J/1 Autocrat airframe

Country of Origin: United Kingdom.

Type: Light sporting aircraft, club trainer and agricultural monoplane.

Power Plant: One (Autocrat) 100 hp Blackburn Cirrus Minor 2 or (Aiglet and Autocar) 130 hp de Havilland Gipsy Major 1 or (D/5 Husky) 160 hp Lycoming O-320-A2A piston engine.

Performance: Cruising speed (J/1), 100 mph (161 km/h), (J/5B), 106 mph (170,5 km/h), (D/5), 108 mph (174 km/h); initial rate of climb (J/1), 568 ft/min (2,9 m/sec), (J/5B), 525 ft/min (2,7 m/sec), (D/5), 640 ft/min (3,25 m/sec); service ceiling (J/1), 15,000 ft (4 572 m), (D/5), 12,800 ft (3 900 m); range with max fuel (J/1), 320 mls (515 km), (J/5B), 260 mls (418 km), (D/5), 460 mls (740 km).

Weights: Empty (J/1), 1,052 lb (476 kg), (J/5B), 1,334 lb (603 kg), (D/5), 1,450 lb (658 kg); max take-off (J/1), 1,850 lb (840 kg), (J/5B), 2,400 lb (1 088 kg), (D/5), 2,450 lb (1 111 kg).

Dimensions: Span (except Aiglet), 36 ft 0 in (10,97 m), (Aiglet), 32 ft 0 in (9,75 m); length, (J/1), 23 ft 5 in (7,14 m), (J/5B), 23 ft 4 in (7,11 m), (D/5), 23 ft 4½ in (7,12 m); height (J/1 and J/5), 6 ft 6 in (1,98 m), (D/5), 7 ft 11 in (2,41 m); wing area (all variants except the Aiglet), 185 sq ft (17,19 m²), (Aiglet), 164 sq ft (15,24 m²).

Accommodation: (J/1 and D/5) Three, (J/2, J/4, J/5F, D/4) two, (J/5B, D/6) four in enclosed cabin.

Status: Prototype J/1 first flown in 1945; first J/5B flown in August 1959; first J/1B flown in 1950; first J/5F flown in 1951; first D/4 flown on 12 February 1960; first D/5 flown in April 1960; first D/6 flown 9 May 1960.

Notes: The Auster J series includes the many variants of the classic high-wing Auster produced between 1945 and 1962, examples of which remain in use in various parts of the world in 1974. All were derived, with greater or smaller modifications, from the pre-War Taylorcraft Model C of US origin, by way of war-time Austers built for the British Army. Included in the range were the J/1 Autocrat, J/1A Aiglet, J/1N Alpha, J/2 Arrow, J/3 Atom, J/4 (unnamed), J/5B Autocar, J/5Q Alpine, J/5L Aiglet Trainer and D/4, D/5 and D/6 Husky. Many alternative engine installations were used in addition to the basic production types, and other differences between these various types included the shape and size of the tail unit and the fuselage width.

AUSTER 5, 6, TUGMASTER AND BEAGLE TERRIER

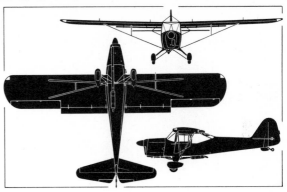

The photographer shows the Auster 6A Tugmaster conversion of the Army AOP variant and the silhouette depicts the Beagle A.61 Terrier

Country of Origin: United Kingdom.

Type: Light sporting aircraft and glider tug.

Power Plant: One (Tugmaster) 145 hp de Havilland Gipsy Major 7 or 10 Mk 1-1 or (Terrier 3) 160 hp Lycoming O-320-B2B.

Performance: Cruising speed (Tugmaster), 108 mph (174 km/h), (Terrier), 107 mph (172 km/h); initial rate of climb (Tugmaster), 810 ft/min (4,1 m/sec), (Terrier), 530 ft/min (2,7 m/sec); service ceiling (Tugmaster), 14,000 ft (4 267 m); range with max fuel (Terrier), 320 mls (515 km).

Weights: Empty (Tugmaster), 1,400 lb (635 kg), (Terrier), 1,600 lb (726 kg); max take-off (Tugmaster), 2,200 lb (997 kg), (Terrier), 2,400 lb (1 088 kg).

Dimensions: Span, 36 ft 0 in (10,97 m); length (Tugmaster), 23 ft 9 in (7,24 m), (Terrier), 23 ft 3 in (7,09 m); height (Tugmaster), 8 ft 4½ in (2,55 m), (Terrier), 8 ft 11 in (2,72 m); wing area, 184 sq ft (17,09 m²).

Accommodation: Standard provision for pilot and one passenger in tandem with optional provision for a second passenger beside the pilot.

Status: First Auster 6A flown in August 1960; prototype Auster

6B flown on 13 April 1961; first Terrier 2 flown on 21 June 1961. Deliveries included 29 Auster 6A Tugmasters, 18 Terrier 1s, 45 Terrier 2s and one Terrier 3.

Notes: Numerous examples of the military Auster 3 (Gipsy Major engine) Auster 4 and 5 (Lycoming O-290) came onto the civil market after being released by the British Army, all these types being war-time derivatives of the pre-war American Taylorcraft Model C lightplane, built in the UK under licence. In addition, Auster built 14 Alpha 5s from scratch for civil use in 1956, these being similar to the military Auster 5s. When ex-Army Auster 6s became available, Auster developed the Auster 6A Tugmaster for use as a glider tug, and about 30 ex-RCAF Auster 6 and 7s found a similar new rôle in Canada. Further evolution produced the Auster 6B, a more fully-equipped three-seater and the marketing of this type was taken over by Beagle as the A.61 Terrier 1. The Terrier 2 had improvements including a luxury interior, Fairey Reed metal airscrew and fibreglass wheel spats. The single Terrier 3 differed only in the type of engine fitted, a Lycoming flat-four replacing the usual in-line unit. Examples of these various Auster derivatives remained in service in 1974, mostly in the United Kingdom.

BEAGLE PUP

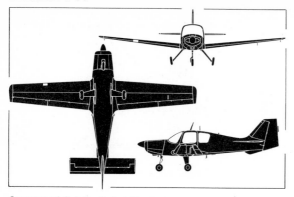

Both the silhouette (left) and the photograph (above) illustrate the Beagle B.121 Pup in its 150 hp Series 2 version, the latter being shown in Swiss service

Country of Origin: United Kingdom.

Type: Light sporting aircraft and club trainer.

Power Plant: One (Srs 1) 100 hp R-R Continental O-200-A or (Srs 2) 150 hp Lycoming O-320-A2B or (Srs 3) 160 hp Lycoming O-320-D2C piston engine.

Performance: Max cruising speed (Srs 1), 118 mph (190 km/h), (Srs 2), 131 mph (211 km/h); best economy cruise (Srs 1), 108 mph (174 km/h), (Srs 2), 115 mph (185 km/h); initial rate of climb (Srs 1), 575 ft/min (2,9 m/sec), (Srs 2), 800 ft/min (4,1 m/sec); service ceiling (Srs 1), 11,200 ft (3 410 m), (Srs 2), 14,700 ft (4 480 m); range with max fuel (Srs 1), 569 mls (915 km), (Srs 2), 633 mls (1 020 km).

Weights: Empty equipped (Srs 1), 985 lb (447 kg), (Srs 2), 1,090 lb (494 kg); max take-off (Srs 1), 1,600 lb (725 kg), (Srs 2), 1,925 lb (873 kg).

Dimensions: Span, 31 ft 0 in (9,45 m); length (Srs 1), 22 ft 11 in (6,99 m), (Srs 2), 23 ft 2 in (7,06 m); height, 7 ft 6 in (2,29 m); wing area, 119·5 sq ft (11,10 m²).

Accommodation: (Srs 1) Two side-by-side or (Srs 2, 3) standard seating for two plus optional provision for one more adult or two children.

Status: Prototype (Srs 1) first flown 8 April 1967; first production Srs 1 flown on 23 February 1968; prototype Srs 2 first flown 4 October 1967 and second prototype Srs 2 on 17 January 1968. Prototype Srs 3 flown on 5 September 1968. Production total (all versions) approximately 169.

Notes: The Pup was an original product of Beagle Aircraft Ltd, set up to specialise in light aircraft design and production but forced into liquidation at the end of 1968 when the British government withdrew its financial backing from the company. At that time, 121 Pups had actually been delivered and another 276 were on order. Aircraft then awaiting delivery or close to completion were subsequently put into service to bring the grand total to more than 160, most of which were still in use in 1974. The Pup Series 1 (or Pup 100) and Series 2 (Pup 150) are externally similar with different engine powers and cabin layouts. The Series 3 (Pup 160) was a four-seater produced primarily for the Iranian Civil Air Training Organisation in Teheran, which acquired six. The Bulldog military trainer (see *Military* volume, page 196) is based on the Pup airframe.

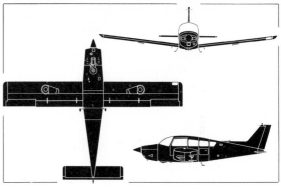

The photograph (above) shows the Beechcraft Sport 19, similar to the original Musketeer, and the silhouette shows the Sierra 24R with retractable gear

Country of Origin: USA.

Type: Private and club aircraft.

Power Plant: One (Sport) 150 hp Lycoming O-320-E2D or (Sundowner) 180 hp Lycoming O-360-A4J or (Sierra 200) 200 hp IO-360-A1B or -A1D piston engine.

Performance: Max cruising speed (Sport), 131 mph (211 km/h), (Sundowner), 143 mph (230 km/h), (Sierra), 161 mph (260 km/h); best economy cruise (Sport), 113 mph (182 km/h), (Sundowner), 123 mph (198 km/h), (Sierra), 128 mph (206 km/h); initial rate of climb (Sport), 700 ft/min (3,55 m/sec), (Sundowner), 888 ft/min (4,5 m/sec), (Sierra), 893 ft/min (4,5 m/sec); service ceiling (Sport), 11,100 ft (3 380 m), (Sundowner), 13,650 ft (4 160 m), (Sierra), 14,350 ft (4 375 m); range with max fuel (Sport), 883 mls (1 420 km), (Sundowner), 860 mls (1 384 km), (Sierra), 682 mls (424 km).

Weights: Empty (Sport), 1,390 lb (630 kg), (Sundowner), 1,425 lb (646 kg), (Sierra), 1,711 lb (776 kg); max take-off (Sport), 2,250 lb (1 020 kg), (Sundowner), 2,450 lb (1 111 kg), (Sierra), 2,750 lb (1 247 kg).

Dimensions: Span, 32 ft 9 in (9,98 m); length, 25 ft 8½ in (7,84 m); height, 8 ft 3 in (2,51 m); wing area, 146 sq ft (13,57 m²).

Accommodation: Pilot and up to (Sport) three or (Sundowner, Sierra) five passengers.

Status: Prototype Model 23 Musketeer first flown 23 October 1961, FAA Type Approval, 20 February 1962 and deliveries began in Autumn 1962. Model 19 Type Approval 9 December 1965; Model 24 Type Approval 7 March 1966. Production total, 2,412 to March 1974.

Notes: Beech introduced a new low-cost all-metal light aircraft as the Musketeer in 1962. Early four-seat Musketeers had the 160 hp Lycoming O-320-D2B engine but the basic Musketeer Custom was enlarged to carry six occupants with a 180 hp O-360-A4G, and the Musketeer Super had the 200 hp IO-360-A2B. For training use the Musketeer Sport had a 150 hp O-320-E2C and normally only two seats, for aerobatic use. A retractable undercarriage was subsequently offered in a variant of the Super. In 1972, Beech dropped the name Musketeer and the three variants became the Sport, Sundowner and Sierra as described above, the fixed-undercarriage Super being discontinued and the Sierra being offered only in the retractable-gear version.

BEECHCRAFT 35 BONANZA

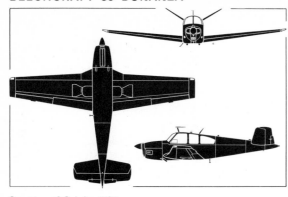

Both the photograph and the silhouette illustrate the Beechcraft Bonanza V35B, latest variant of the distinctive Bonanza with its original "butterfly" tail unit

Country of Origin: USA.

Type: Private, club and business aircraft.

Power Plant: One (Model 35, A35) 185 hp Continental E-185-1 or B35, 35R) 196 hp E-185-8 or (C35, D35, E35, F35) 205 hp E-185-11 or (G35) 225 hp E-225-8 or (H35) 240 hp O-470-G or (J35, K35, M35) 250 hp IO-470-C (N35, P35) 260 hp IO-470-N or (S35, V35) 285 hp IO-520-B or -BA piston engine.

Performance: Max cruising speed (F35), 184 mph (291 km/h), (V35B), 203 mph (327 km/h) at 6,000 ft (1 830 m) ; best economy cruise (F35), 175 mph (282 km/h), (V35B), 164 mph (264 km/h) ; initial rate of climb (F35), 1,100 ft/min (5,6 m/sec), (V35B), 1,136 ft/min (5,8 m/sec) ; service ceiling (F35), 18,000 ft (5 490 m), (V35B), 17,500 ft (5 335 m) ; range with normal fuel (F35), 775 mls (1 240 km), (V35B), 514 mls (827 km) ; range with max fuel (V35B), 1,007 mls (1 620 km).

Weights: Empty (F35), 1,697 lb (770 kg), (V35B), 1,985 lb (900 kg) ; max take-off (F35), 2,750 lb (1 248 kg), (V35B), 3,400 lb (1 542 kg).

Dimensions: Span (F35), 32 ft 10 in (10,0 m), (V35B), 33 ft 5½ in (10,20 m) ; length (F35), 25 ft 2 in (7,67 m), (V35B), 26 ft 4½ in

(8,04 m) ; height (F35), 6 ft 6½ in (2,0 m), (V35B), 7 ft 7 in (2,31 m) ; wing area (F35), 177·6 sq ft (16,49 m²), (V35B), 181 sq ft (16,80 m²).

Accommodation: Pilot and (up to J35) three passengers (K35, N35, P35), up to four (S35, V35) up to five passengers.

Status: Prototype first flown on 22 December 1945. Production deliveries began 1947. FAA Type Approval (Model 35) 25 March 1947 ; (F35) 5 January 1955, (K35) 29 October 1958, (S35) 3 January 1964, (V35B) 24 October 1969. Production total, all models, 9,610 to March 1974.

Notes: The Bonanza, distinguished by its "V" tail, has proved one of the most popular of lightplanes since its introduction in 1947, and has been in continuous production ever since. Apart from progressive increases in engine power and gross weight, significant improvements have been the provision of a fifth seat, starting with the M35, a sixth seat, starting with the S35 and new square wingtips, starting with the M35. A version of the Bonanza with conventional tail unit was introduced in 1959 as the Debonair but since 1967 this model (the Beech 33) has been known as the Bonanza also (see page 135).

The Beechcraft Bonanza A36, shown in both the photograph (above) and the silhouette (right), is an enlarged derivative of the original type, with orthodox tail unit

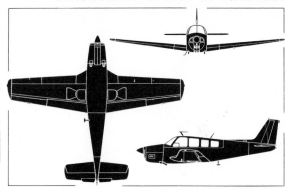

Country of Origin: USA.

Type: Private, club and business aircraft.

Power Plant: One (Model 33, A33) 225 hp Continental IO-470-J or (B33) 225 hp IO-470-K or (C33A, E33A, E33C, F33A, F33C, 36, A36) 285 hp IO-520-B or -BA or (G33) 260 hp IO-470-N piston engine.

Performance: Max cruising speed (F33A), 200 mph (322 km/h), (A36), 195 mph (314 km/h); best economy cruise (F33A), 156 mph (251 km/h), (A36) 167 mph (269 km/h); initial rate of climb (F-33A), 1,136 ft/min (5,8 m/sec), (A36), 1,015 ft/min (5,15 m/sec); service ceiling (F33A), 17,500 ft (5 335 m), (A36), 16,000 ft (4 875 m); range with normal fuel (F33A), 500 mls (804 km), (A36), 460 mls (740 km); range with max fuel (F33A), 980 mls (1 577 km), (A36), 890 mls (1 432 km).

Weights: Empty (F33A), 2,000 lb (907 kg), (A36), 2,040 lb (925 kg); max take-off (F33A), 3,400 lb (1 542 kg), (A36), 3,600 lb (1 633 kg).

Dimensions: Span, 33 ft 5½ in (10,2 m); length (F33A), 25 ft 6 in (7,77 m), (A36), 26 ft 8 in (8,13 m); height (F33A), 8 ft 3 in (2,51 m), (A36), 8 ft 5 in (2,57 m); wing area, 181 sq ft (16,8 m²).

Accommodation: Pilot and (F33A) up to five passengers or (G33) up to four passengers (A36) pilot and five passenger seats, or pilot, passenger and cargo.

Status: Model 33 prototype first flown on 14 September 1959. Production deliveries began 1960 following FAA Type Approval on 13 November 1959. Model 36 introduced in 1968 after Type Approval on 1 May. Production totals to March 1974, Model 33, 492; Model 36, 545.

Notes: The Model 33 appeared in 1959 as a derivative of the original Bonanza (see page 134) from which it differed primarily in having a conventional tail unit. It entered production as the Debonair and successive versions were offered with increased power, higher weights and extra cabin space. In 1967, the name was changed to Bonanza and production continued in 1974 of the F33A version, alongside the V-tailed V35B and the larger Model A36 Bonanza. The latter appeared in 1968, with a larger cabin, large loading doors and provision for rapid conversion to operate in the utility rôle. Several military versions of the A36 Bonanza have also been developed, including QU-22B surveillance drones used by the USAF in SE Asia.

BELLANCA CRUISEMASTER AND VIKING

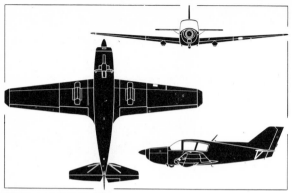

Based on the pre-war Bellanca Cruiser, the Viking 300, shown in both the photograph and the silhouette, was among the best-selling aircraft in its class in 1973

Country of Origin: USA.

Type: Private and club aircraft.

Power Plant: One (260C) 260 hp Continental IO-470-F (Viking 300) 300 hp Continental IO-520-D or Lycoming IO-540-G1E5 or (Turbo Viking) 310 hp Lycoming TIO-540 piston engine.

Performance: Max cruising speed (260C), 186 mph (299 km/h), (Viking 300), 194 mph (312 km/h), (Turbo), 235 mph (378 km/h) ; best economy cruise (360C), 180 mph (290 km/h), (Viking 300), 190 mph (306 km/h) ; initial rate of climb (360C), over 1,500 ft/min (7,6 m/sec), (Viking 300 and Turbo), 1,800 ft/min (9,1 m/sec) ; service ceiling (360C), 22,500 ft (6 860 m), (Viking 300), 21,600 ft (6 584 km), (Turbo), 24,000 ft (7 315 m) ; range with max fuel (360C), 1,000 mls (1 610 km), (Viking 300), 940 mls (1 513 km), (Turbo), 1,220 mls (1 963 km).

Weights: Empty (360C), 1,850 lb (839 kg), (Viking 300), 1,950 lb (884 kg), (Turbo), 2,010 lb (911 kg) ; max take-off (360C), 3,000 lb (1 360 kg), (Viking 300 and Turbo), 3,325 lb (1 508 kg).

Dimensions: Span (all), 34 ft 2 in (10,41 m) ; length (360C), 22 ft 11 in (6,98 m), (Viking 300, Turbo), 23 ft 6 in (7,16 m) ; height (360C), 6 ft 4 in (1,93 m), (Viking 300, Turbo), 7 ft 4 in

(2,24 m) ; wing area (all), 161·5 sq ft (15,00 m²).

Accommodation: Pilot and three passengers.

Status: Original Model 14 first flown in 1937. Model 14-19 Type Approval 26 September 1949 ; Model 14-19-2 on 7 January 1957 and 104 built. Model 14-19-3 prototype flown on 6 November 1958, first production example flown on 20 February 1959. Type Approval on the same day. Viking 300 Type Approval 23 September 1966. Production totals (to 1973), over 700 Vikings, production rate 17 per month.

Notes: The original Bellanca Cruiser of 1937 vintage re-entered production post-war as the Cruisemaster. The Model 14-19-3 introduced a tricycle undercarriage and the 14-19-3C was the first model to dispense with the small outrigged fins on the tailplane, having a broad sweptback single fin and rudder. The Model 17 in 1966 had increased power and was marketed as the Viking, in several versions as noted above, with Lycoming or Continental normally-aspirated or Lycoming turbosupercharged engines. These three models remain in production in 1974, helping Bellanca maintain its position as the fourth largest US producer of light aircraft.

BELLANCA (CHAMPION) CHAMP, CITABRIA AND SCOUT

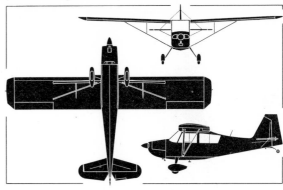

The photograph (above) shows the Bellanca Champion Citabria aerobatic lightplane and the silhouette (right) depicts the Champion Scout with longer wing span

Country of Origin: USA.

Type: Light aircraft.

Power Plant: One (Champ) 60 hp Franklin 2A-120-B or (Citabria) 115 hp Lycoming O-235-C1 or 150 hp Lycoming O-320-A2B or -E2A or (Scout) 150 hp O-320-A2B piston engine.

Performance: Max speed (Champ), 98 mph (158 km/h), (Citabria), 130 mph (209 km/h), (Scout), 128 mph (206 km/h); cruising speed (Champ), 83 mph (133 km/h), (Citabria), 112 mph (180 km/h), (Scout), 125 mph (201 km/h); initial rate of climb (Champ), 400 ft/min (2,03 m/sec), (Citabria), 1,120 ft/min (5,7 m/sec), (Scout), 1,145 ft/min (5,8 m/sec); service ceiling (Citabria), 17,000 ft (5 180 m); range with max fuel (Champ), 300 mls (483 km), (Citabria), 537 mls (865 km), (Scout), 480 mls (772 km).

Weights: Empty (Champ), 750 lb (340 kg), (Citabria), 1,037 lb (470 kg), (Scout), 1,150 lb (522 kg); max take-off (Champ), 1,220 lb (553 kg), (Citabria), 1,650 lb (748 kg), (Scout), 1,650 lb (748 kg), (Scout agricultural), 2,325 lb (1 054 kg).

Dimensions: Span (Champ), 33 ft 1½ in (10,71 m), (Citabria), 33 ft 5 in (10,19 m), (Scout), 34 ft 5½ in (10,50 m); length (Champ), 21 ft 9½ in (6,64 m), (Citabria and Scout), 22 ft 8 in (6,91 m);

height (Champ), 7 ft 0 in (2,13 m), (Citabria and Scout), 6 ft 7¾ in (2,02 m); wing area (Champ), 170 sq ft (15,79 m²), (Citabria), 165 sq ft (15,33 m²), (Scout), 170·2 sq ft (15,81 m²).

Accommodation: Two in tandem.

Status: Original Aeronca Model 7AC Champion introduced in 1946 after Type Approval on 18 October 1945; production totals, over 10,000 up to 1951. Champion Citabria introduced in 1954; production total, over 2,000.

Notes: This design originated pre-war as an Aeronca product and after war-time production for the US Army emerged as the Model 7 Champion, achieving very large-scale production for six years. The design was acquired by Champion Aircraft, which resumed production in 1954 and also developed the fully aerobatic Citabria, with more angular fin and rudder and other changes. A utility version of the Citabria emerged as the Scout and after Bellanca had acquired Champion, a version of the original Aeronca Model 7 went back into production as the Champ. The Bellanca (Champion) Model 8 Decathlon is similar to the Citabria, designed for aerobatic competition flying and a Model 8 Scout was introduced in 1974, with 180 hp engine.

CERVA CE.43 GUÉPARD AND WASSMER WA 4/21

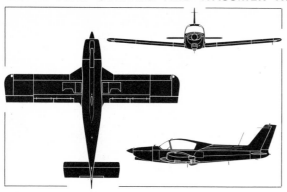

The photograph and silhouette both show the Wassmer WA 4/21, known originally as the Prestige and similar in external appearance to the CE.43 Guépard

Country of Origin: France.

Type: Private and club aircraft.

Power Plant: One (CE.43, WA 4/21), 250 hp Lycoming IO-540-C4B5 or (WA 4/21 option) 235 hp Lycoming O-540-B2B piston engine.

Performance (CE.43): Max cruising speed, 192 mph (310 km/h); economical cruising speed, 161 mph (260 km/h); initial rate of climb, 1,080 ft/min (5,5 m/sec); service ceiling, 17,400 ft (5 300 m); range with max fuel, 1,800 mls (2 900 km).

Weights: Empty (CE.43), 1,863 lb (845 kg), (WA 4/21), 1,774 lb (805 kg); max take-off (CE.43, normal category), 3,527 lb (1 600 kg), (CE.43 utility), 3,220 lb (1 460 kg), (WA 4/21), 3,108 lb (1 410 kg).

Dimensions: Span, 32 ft 9½ in (10,0 m); length (CE.43), 27 ft 6½ in (8,40 m); (WA 4/21), 25 ft 7 in (7,80 m); height (CE.43), 9 ft 2¼ in (2,80 m), (WA 4/21), 9 ft 5 in (2,86 m); wing area, 172 sq ft (16,0 m²).

Accommodation: Pilot and three passengers in enclosed cabin.

Status: Prototype WA 4/21 first flown in March 1967; French type approval, 15 November 1967. Prototype CE.43 flown on 18 May 1971; French type approval, 1 June 1972. Production totals WA 4/21, about 30; CE.43, produced and on order to early 1974, about 30.

Notes: The Wassmer WA 4/21, originally marketed as the Super 4/21 Prestige, was developed from the WA-40A (see page 182), from which it differed in having a more powerful engine, a retractable undercarriage and electrically-operated flaps. It entered production with a 235 hp engine, but the 250 hp engine was subsequently standardised, and a 4/21 with this engine was used to make a 28,000-mile (45 000-km) flight round the world in 45 days in 1968, piloted by Max H Pellissier. During 1971, Wassmer and Siren SA set up a jointly-owned company, CERVA (GIE) to foster development and marketing of an all-metal version of the WA 4/21, designated the CE.43 and named Guépard (Cheetah). Following evaluation of two prototypes and a static specimen, the Guépard was selected to meet a government requirement for a light communications aircraft to be used by the CEV, and 18 were ordered. Subsequently, another five were ordered for use by the SGAC and SFA, and production for the civil market was also under way in 1974.

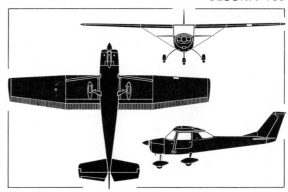

Shown in the photograph is the 1974 model Reims/Cessna FRA150 Aerobat while the silhouette depicts the regular Cessna Model 150 as built in the USA

Country of Origin: USA.

Type: Private and club aircraft.

Power Plant: One (150) 100 hp Continental O-200-A or (FRA-150) 130 hp Lycoming O-235 piston engine.

Performance: Max speed (150), 122 mph (196 km/h), (FRA-150), 130 mph (209 km/h) ; cruising speed (150), 117 mph (188 km/h), (FRA-150), 128 mph (206 km/h) ; initial rate of climb (150), 670 ft/min (3,4 m/sec), (FRA-150), 845 ft/min (4,3 m/sec) ; service ceiling (150), 12,650 ft (3 856 m), (FRA-150), 14,000 ft (4 260 m) ; no-reserves range with standard fuel (150), 565 mls (909 km), (FRA-150), 520 mls (837 km) ; no-reserves range with maximum fuel loads (150), 880 mls (1 416 km) (FRA-150), 810 mls (1 304 km).

Weights: Empty equipped (150), 1,020 lb (463 kg), (FRA-150), 1,080 lb (489 kg) ; max take-off (150), 1,600 lb (726 kg), (FRA-150), 1,650 lb (749 kg).

Dimensions: Span, 33 ft 2 in (10,11 m) ; length, 23 ft 9 in (7,24 m) ; height, 8 ft 7½ in (2,63 m) ; gross wing area, 159,5 sq ft (14,8 m²).

Accommodation: Two side-by-side, with optional provision for two children on "family seat" in place of baggage space behind seats.

Status: Prototype first flown in September 1957 ; FAA Type Approvals, basic Model 150, 10 July 1958, aerobatic A 150, 5 June 1969, Reims F150, 22 December 1966, Reims aerobatic FA150, 8 January 1970. Production totals (to early 1974), US-built Model 150s, 17,978 ; French-built Model 150s, 1,253.

Notes: Among the most successful of all post-war light planes, with production running at more than 2,000 a year in the late 'sixties, the Model 150 was introduced to succeed the early post-war Models 120 and 140, of which 2,164 and 5,560 examples were built, respectively. Models prior to 1966 had unswept vertical tail surfaces and early models had a built-up rear fuselage rather than the wrap-around rear windshield that later became standard. The A150 Aerobat was introduced in 1970, stressed for aerobatics, and examples of both standard and aerobatic types are built by Reims Aviation in France as the F150 and FA150. In 1973, Reims also introduced the FRA-150 with a more powerful engine, data being quoted here for this version. The FRA-150 had no US-built equivalent up to 1974.

CESSNA 170, 172, SKYHAWK, REIMS ROCKET

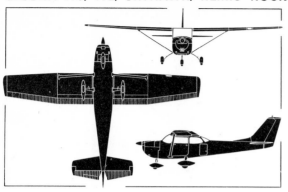

The silhouette (left) shows the Cessna 172K, the best-selling of the range of Cessna lightplanes, and the photograph (above) illustrates the related Reims Rocket

Country of Origin: USA (and France).

Type: Private and club aircraft.

Power Plant: One (172 thru 172H) 145 hp Continental O-300-A, -B, -C, -D or (172I and later) 150 hp Lycoming O-320-E2D or (F172) 145 hp R-R/Continental O-300-D or (FR172) 210 hp R-R/Continental IO-360-D piston engine.

Performance: Max cruising speed (172), 131 mph (211 km/h), (Rocket), 144 mph (232 km/h); best economy cruise (172), 117 mph (188 km/h), (Rocket), 105 mph (169 km/h); initial rate of climb (172), 645 ft/min (3,25 m/sec), (Rocket), 880 ft/min (4,4 m/sec); service ceiling (172), 13,100 ft (3 993 m), (Rocket), 17,000 ft (5 182 m); range with standard fuel (172), 615 mls (989 km), (Rocket), 580 mls (933 km); range with max fuel (172), 820 mls (1 320 km), (Rocket), 1,010 mls (1 625 km).

Weights: Empty (172), 1,300 lb (590 kg), (Rocket), 1,430 lb (649 kg); max take-off (172), 2,300 lb (1 043 kg), (Rocket), 2,550 lb (1 157 kg).

Dimensions: Span, 35 ft 10 in (10,92 m); length (172), 26 ft 11 in (8,21 m), (Rocket), 26 ft 9½ in (8,17 m); height, 8 ft 9½ in (2,68 m); wing area, 175·5 sq ft (16,3 m²).

Accommodation: Pilot and three passengers in enclosed cabin, with optional provision for two children on a "family seat" in baggage space at rear.

Status: Production deliveries began in 1955, with FAA Type Approval on 4 November 1955. Reims F172 prototype first flown 4 January 1963, Type Approval on 9 November 1964. First FA172 Rocket flown 12 January 1967, first production flown 2 February 1968, Type Approval 20 December 1967. Production (to early 1974), 172/Skyhawk, 20,014; F172, 947; Rocket, 447.

Notes: Cessna built 5,136 Model 170s between 1948 and 1957, and introduced the Model 172 in 1955 as a successor, the principal difference being the switch from tailwheel to nosewheel layout. Since then, the Model 172 has undergone progressive improvement year by year, and has become the best-selling of all Cessna light planes. A *de luxe* version is known as the Skyhawk. The Model 172 is also built by Reims Aviation as the F172, and a more powerful version as the FR-172 Reims Rocket. Until 1972, F172s were powered by Rolls-Royce built Continental engines, a switch then being made to the Lycoming O-320. The Cessna 175 (2,119 built, 1958–1963) was a 175 hp variant similar to early 172s.

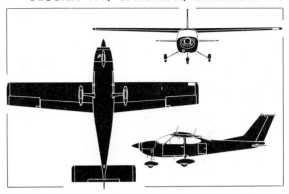

Depicted in the silhouette (right) is the Cessna 177A Cardinal, and the photograph (above) shows the Cardinal RG with retractable undercarriage

Country of Origin: USA.

Type: Private and light business aircraft.

Power Plant: One (177, Cardinal) 180 hp Lycoming O-360-AlF6 or (RG) 200 hp Lycoming IO-360-AlB6 piston engine.

Performance: Max cruising speed (177), 143 mph (230 km/h), (RG), 171 mph (275 km/h) ; best economy cruise (177), 125 mph (201 km/h), (RG) 139 mph (223 km/h) ; initial rate of climb (177), 840 ft/min (4,25 m/sec), (RG), 925 ft/min (4,7 m/sec) ; service ceiling (177), 14,600 ft (4 450 m), (RG), 17,100 ft (5 210 m) ; range with standard fuel (177), 790 mls (1 271 km), (RG), 1,210 miles (1 945 m) ; range with maximum fuel (177), 965 miles (1 553 km).

Weights: Empty (177), 1,450 lb (657 kg), (RG), 1,660 lb (753 kg) ; max take-off (177), 2,500 lb (1 133 kg), (RG), 2,800 lb (1 270 kg).

Dimensions: Span, 35 ft 6 in (10,82 m) ; length, 27 ft 3 in (8,31 m) ; height, 8 ft 7 in (2,62 m) ; gross wing area, 174·0 sq ft (16,20 m²).

Accommodation: Pilot and three passengers in two pairs of seats in enclosed cabin.

Status: Deliveries began 1967 following FAA Type Approval on

16 February. Model 177RG Type Approval on 11 August 1970. Production quantities (to early 1974), 177/Cardinal, 2,050 ; Cardinal RG, 398 ; Reims Cardinal RG (to end-1973), 93.

Notes: The Cessna Model 177 was introduced as a"step-up" aeroplane for owners of the Model 172 series (see page 140), featuring more power and better performance. Unlike the earlier four-seat low-powered models, it had a cantilever wing. The original Model 177 was powered by a 150 hp Lycoming O-320-E2D engine, changed in the Model 177A in 1968, and subsequent models, to the 180 hp -AlF6 variant, for which version data are quoted here. With various *de luxe* features incorporated, the Model 177 is known as the Cardinal, and in 1970 a further version was added to the range, with a retractable undercarriage, this being the Cardinal RG. The last-mentioned variant is also produced in France by Reims Aviation. Under a US Navy contract, one Cardinal was fitted with a Curtiss-Wright Wankel-type rotary engine for flight testing, and another programme, sponsored by NASA, had a Cardinal fitted with an advanced technology wing with 37 per cent less area, and having spoilers and a powerful flap system to provide the required lift and control.

CESSNA 182, SKYLANE

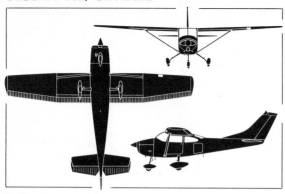

The photograph (above) shows the 1974 model Cessna Skylane, this being the de luxe version of the Cessna 182M depicted in the silhouette (left)

Country of Origin: USA.

Type: Private and light business aircraft.

Power Plant: One 230 hp Continental O-470-L or -R piston engine.

Performance: Max cruising speed (182), 157 mph (253 km/h), (Skylane), 160 mph (257 km/h); best economy cruise (182), 112 mph (180 km/h), (Skylane), 115 mph (185 km/h); initial rate of climb (182 and Skylane), 890 ft/min (4,5 m/sec); service ceiling (182, Skylane), 17,700 ft (5 395 m); range with standard fuel (182), 860 mls (1 384 km), (Skylane), 885 mls (1 424 km); range with max fuel (182), 1,135 mls (1 826 km), (Skylane), 1,160 mls (1 865 km).

Weights: Empty (182), 1,595 lb (723 kg), (Skylane), 1,645 lb (746 kg); useful load (182), 1,355 lb (615 kg), (Skylane), 1,305 lb (592 kg); maximum take-off weight (182 and Skylane), 2,950 lb (1 338 kg).

Dimensions: Span, 35 ft 10 in (10,92 m); length, 28 ft 2 in (8,59 m); height, 9 ft 1½ in (2,78 m); wing area, 174 sq ft (16,2 m²).

Accommodation: Pilot and three passengers in two pairs of seats side-by-side.

Status: Production deliveries began 1956, following initial FAA Type Approval on 2 March. Production quantities (to early 1974), 13,778 (including assembly of US-built components by FMA in Argentina).

Notes: The Cessna 182 was another in the range of "step-up" models, offering more speed, range and extra useful loads than were available in the lower-priced single-engined models. The original version was certificated at a gross weight of 2,550 lb (1 156 kg), with subsequent increases to 2,650 lb (1 202 kg) and then to 2,800 lb (1 270 kg) before the current figure quoted here. The *de luxe* version of the Model 182 is known as the Skylane and the performance quoted here for this version are for the aircraft with "speed fairings" fitted to the landing gear, these fairings being optional on the basic 182 also. The name Skylane should not be confused with the Super Skylane name used for the passenger versions of the Model 206 (see page 79), which is generally similar in appearance to the Model 182 but has more power, a larger cabin and is intended primarily for use in the utility rôle. The Model 182 is among the Cessna types assembled in Argentina by FMA at Cordoba, where the first A182J was completed in August 1966.

Shown in the photograph is the 1974 Cessna Centurion II, with full avionics fit; the silhouette depicts the externally similar Model 210J Centurion

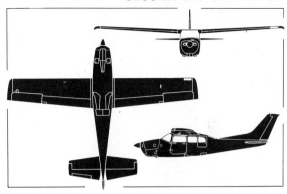

Country of Origin: USA.

Type: Private and light business aircraft.

Power Plant: One (210 three 210C) 260 hp Continental IO-470-S or (210D to 210J) 285 hp Continental IO-520-J or (T-210F, G, H, J) 285 hp Continental TSIO-520-H or (210K, T-210K and subsequent) 300 hp Continental IO-520-L piston engine.

Performance: Max cruising speed (210), 188 mph (303 km/h), (Turbo), 219 mph (352 km/h) at 24,000 ft (7 315 m) and 195 mph (314 km/h) at 10,000 ft (3 050 m); best economy cruise (210), 154 mph (248 km/h), (Turbo), 175 mph (282 km/h) at 24,000 ft (7 315 m) and 140 mph (225 km/h) at 10,000 ft (3 050 m); initial rate of climb (210), 860 ft/min (4,35 m/sec), (Turbo), 930 ft/min (4,7 m/sec); service ceiling (210), 15,500 ft (4 755 m), (Turbo), 28,500 ft (8 687 m); range with normal fuel (210), 900 mls (1 448 km), (Turbo), 955 mls (1 537 km); range with max fuel (210), 1,250 mls (2 012 km), (Turbo), 1,330 mls (2 140 km).

Weights: Empty (210), 2,120 lb (962 kg), (Turbo), 2,235 lb (1 014 kg); maximum take-off (210 and Turbo), 3,800 lb (1 724 kg).

Dimensions: Span, 36 ft 9 in (11,2 m); length, 28 ft 3 in (8,61 m);

height, 9 ft 8 in (2,95 m); wing area, 175 sq ft (16,4 m²).

Accommodation: Pilot and (models to 210J/T-210J) three passengers or (210K/T-210K and subsequent) five passengers in pairs of seats.

Status: Prototype first flown in January 1957; FAA Type Approval 20 April 1959 with deliveries starting in 1959. First T210G flown 18 June 1965. Type Approval 23 August 1966. Production totals (to early 1974), 3,585.

Notes: The Cessna 210 was introduced at the top of the single-engined line in 1959, being the first of the "200 series" aircraft, and the first of the Cessna high-wing types to have a retractable undercarriage. Original versions were conventionally strut-braced, including the first of the turbosupercharged models, the T210F of 1966. The 1967 models, both "plain" and turbo, introduced a cantilever wing and enlarged tail surfaces. The range was further extended in 1971 when a higher standard of avionics equipment and some improvements in the cabin furnishing were introduced in the Centurion II and Turbo-Centurion II; the more simply-equipped Centurion I and Turbo-Centurion I remained available and were externally indistinguishable.

DE HAVILLAND DHC-1 CHIPMUNK

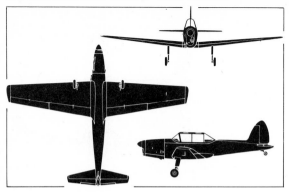

The de Havilland Chipmunk, as depicted in the photograph and silhouette, was built both in Canada and the UK for military and civil use

Country of Origin: Canada.
Type: Private and club aircraft.
Power Plant: One 145 hp Gipsy Major 10 Mk 2 piston engine.
Performance: Max speed, 138 mph (222 km/h) at sea level; cruising speed, 119 mph (191 km/h) at sea level; initial rate of climb, 840 ft/min (4,3 m/sec); service ceiling, 15,800 ft (4 820 m); range with max fuel, 280 mls (445 km) at 116 mph (187 km/h) at 5,000 ft (1 525 m).
Weights: Empty, 1,425 lb (647 kg); max take-off, 2,100 lb (953 kg).
Dimensions: Span, 34 ft 4 in (10,46 m); length, 25 ft 5 in (7,75 m); height, 7 ft 0 in (2,13 m); wing area, 172 sq ft (15,98 m²).
Accommodation: Two in tandem, with dual controls.
Status: Prototype first flown 22 May 1946. Production deliveries began 1947. First British production completed September 1949. Production totals, DHC-1B-1, 157; DHC-1B-2, 60; T Mk 10, 740; T Mk 20, 231; Mk 21, 29; by OFEMA in Portugal, 60.
Notes: The Chipmunk was the first post-war product of the Canadian de Havilland company and its first original design, being intended for both civil and military use. After the Chipmunk had entered production in the UK to meet RAF needs (see *Military* volume, page 170) a few examples were built for civil use as Mk 21s, but most of the privately-owned examples are Mk 22s, these having been offered for sale from 1966 onwards after service with the RAF. Larger-capacity fuel tanks in the wings were the distinguishing feature of the Chipmunk 22A, and five Mk 23s were single-seat agricultural versions. Several similar conversions in Australia were known as Sasin SA-29 Spraymasters, and another Australian variant, the Aerostructures Sundowner, had a 180 hp Lycoming O-360 engine. Another one-off engine installation for special purposes was a 210 hp Continental IO-360-C fitted in a converted Canadian-built example of the Chipmunk by J P Huneault in 1969 and increasing the max cruising speed to 160 mph (257 km/h). A major modification of a Chipmunk by Art Scholl, for aerobatic purposes, included fitting a 260 hp Lycoming GO-435, new wings and a retractable undercarriage. With delivery of Bulldogs to the RAF, started in 1973, further quantities of Chipmunks began to reach the civil market, the only examples remaining in service with the RAF being those used in the ATC air experience flights and for which a further ten-year life was planned.

DRUINE D.5 TURBI AND D.31 TURBULENT

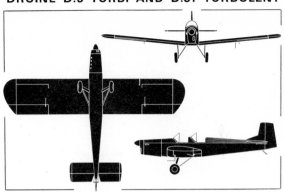

The silhouette (right) shows the two-seat D.5 Turbi and the photograph (above) depicts the smaller D.31 Turbulent, as used by the Tiger Club for many years

Country of Origin: France.

Type: Light sporting aircraft.

Power Plant: One (D.5) 62 hp Walter Mikron II or 85 hp Continental C85-12 or similar (D.31) 45 hp Rollason Ardem 4CO2 Mk IV or 55 hp Ardem Mk V or similar.

Performance: Max speed (D.5/85), 120 mph (193 km/h), (D.31), 109 mph (176 km/h), cruising speed (D.5/85), 90 mph (145 km/h), (D.31), 87 mph (141 km/h); initial rate of climb (D.5/85), 500 ft/min (2,5 m/sec), (D.31), 450 ft/min (2,3 m/sec); ceiling (D.5/85), 10,000 ft (3 050 m), (D.31), 9,000 ft (2 740 m); range with max fuel (D.31), 250 mls (400 km).

Weights: Empty (D.5/85), 830 lb (376 kg), (D.31), 395 lb (179 kg); max take-off (D.5/85), 1,240 lb (562 kg), (D.31), 620 lb (281 kg).

Dimensions: Span (D.5), 28 ft 9 in (8,76 m), (D.31), 21 ft 7 in (6,58 m); length (D.5), 22 ft 0 in (6,71 m), (D.31), 17 ft 6 in (5,33 m); height (D.5), 5 ft 0 in (1,52 m), (D.31), 5 ft 0 in (1,52 m); wing area (D.5), 139 sq ft (12,9 m²), (D.31), 77·5 sq ft (7,20 m²).

Accommodation: (D.5) Two in tandem in open cockpits (D.31) pilot only in open cockpit. Both types sometimes fitted with enclosed cockpits.

Status: Prototype D.3 Turbulent first flown in 1951. First Rollason-built D.31 Turbulent flown on 1 January 1958.

Notes: The original D.3 was designed by Roger Druine primarily for amateur production and many examples have been built all over the world. The prototype D.3 had an Ava engine and early examples had a 25 hp converted Volkswagen engine; many other power plants have been used, including the 30 hp Porsche or Ardem units. The D.31 is a refined version, produced in some quantity by Rollason Aircraft and Engines in the UK and data are quoted for this version. Rollason also built a few D.31As, with improved wing spar and other modifications necessary to obtain a full C of A, whereas the D.31 qualifies only for a Special Category C of A. A version known as Turbulent D was built by Stark Flugzeugbau in Germany with an adapted Volkswagen engine. The D.5 was designed as a two-seat variant of the Turbi, and exists primarily in home-built examples. The most common engine is the 45 hp Beaussier 4 B02 but other installations have included the 62 hp Walter Mikron II, 65 hp Continental, 52 hp Zündapp, 75 hp Minié or 75 hp Regniér, plus the 85 hp version for which data are given here.

DRUINE (AND ROLLASON) D.62 CONDOR

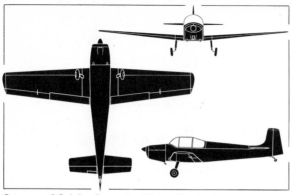

Two Rollason-built Condors are shown in the photograph, both examples being the D.62B production version. The silhouette also depicts the standard aircraft

Country of Origin: France (and United Kingdom).

Type: Light sporting aircraft and club trainer.

Power Plant: One 90 hp Continental C90 or (D.62A and D.62B) 100 hp R-R Continental O-200-A or (D.62C) 130 hp R-R Continental O-240 engine.

Performance (D.62B): Max speed, 127 mph (204 km/h); max cruising speed, 115 mph (185 km/h); best economy cruise, 107 mph (172 km/h); initial rate of climb, 610 ft/min (3,1 m/sec); service ceiling, 12,000 ft (3 650 m); range with max fuel, 328 mls (528 km).

Weights: Empty, 920 lb (417 kg); maximum take-off weight, 1,475 lb (670 kg).

Dimensions: Span, 27 ft 6 in (8,38 m); length, 22 ft 6 in (6,86 m); height, 7 ft 9 in (2,36 m); wing area, 119·8 sq ft (11,13 m²).

Accommodation: Two side by side in enclosed cockpit, with individual doors on each side, upward-opening.

Status: First French-built example flown in 1955. First Rollason-built D.62 flown in May 1961. First Rollason D.62A flown August 1963; first Rollason D.62B flown December 1964; first Rollason D.62C flown March 1970.

Notes: Roger Druine designed the prototype D.60 Condor on the basis of his experience with the Turbi (see page 145), with the intention that it should include various refinements and modifications and should be factory produced. The D.60 had a 60 hp CNA D4 engine and Druine's initial production version, the D.61, had a 65 hp Continental A65. The D.62 was designed to be powered by the 90 hp Continental, and this version was adopted for production in the UK by Rollason in 1961, when a single example was built. Two D.62As were pre-production models and the D.62B was the principal production version, more than 40 having been built by 1974. After the first four D.62Bs, wing flaps were introduced and other changes had been made to the original design to allow the Condor to qualify for a normal category British C of A. Six D.62Cs featured more powerful engines and had provision for glider towing; they were distinguishable by the end-plates at the wing tips. A simplified version of the Condor was also offered by Druine for amateur construction, designated D.610, and the D.620 designation applied to a version of the D.62 fitted with VHF radio and wing flaps. Construction of the Condor is of wood throughout, with fabric wing covering and plywood fuselage skin.

FFA AS.202 BRAVO

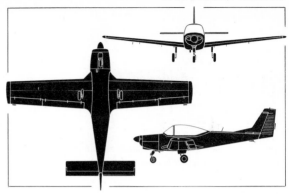

Jointly developed in Italy and Switzerland, the FFA AS.202 Bravo is produced in Switzerland, initially in the AS.202/15 version illustrated in the photograph and silhouette

Country of Origin: Switzerland.

Type: Light private aircraft.

Power Plant: One 150 hp Lycoming O-320-E2A piston engine.

Performance: Max speed, 131 mph (211 km/h) at sea level; max cruising speed, 131 mph (211 km/h) at 8,000 ft (2 440 m); best economy cruise, 126 mph (203 km/h) at 10,000 ft (3 050 m); initial rate of climb, 633 ft/min (3,2 m/sec); service ceiling, 14,000 ft (4 265 m); no reserves range with max fuel, 574 mls (925 km).

Weights: Empty, 1,388 lb (630 kg); max payload (aerobatic), 386 lb (175 kg), (utility), 595 lb (270 kg); max take-off (aerobatic), 1,951 lb (885 kg); max take-off (utility), 2,202 lb (999 kg).

Dimensions: Span, 31 ft 11¾ in (9,75 m); length, 24 ft 7¼ in (7,50 m); height, 9 ft 2¼ in (2,81 m); wing area, 149 sq ft (13,86 m²).

Accommodation: Two side-by-side with provision (in utility version) for third occupant to rear, in space normally available for baggage storage.

Status: Prototype (Swiss-built) first flown on 7 March 1969; second prototype (Italian-built) first flown on 7 May 1969; pre-production model first flown on 16 June 1969 and first production

aircraft flown on 22 December 1971. Swiss Type Approval, 15 August 1972. Production, about 20 by end 1973, from initial batch of 50 in hand.

Notes: The Bravo has been developed jointly in Switzerland (by Flug & Fahrzeugwerke) and Italy (by SIAI-Marchetti), on the basis of an original SIAI-Marchetti design. Prototypes were built and tested in each country and a production line was then set up in Switzerland at Altenrhein, from which the first production aircraft were delivered towards the end of 1972. The AS.202 is a conventional low-wing monoplane of all-metal construction, and has dual controls as standard. The first production batch are all of the AS.202/15 version as described here, with provision for a third occupant when operating in the utility category, although only two are carried in the aerobatic configuration. The rearward-sliding canopy over the cockpit is jettisonable in an emergency, and a hydraulic system is fitted for operation of the independent disc brakes on the main wheels. Also under development is the AS.202/10, which will be only a two-seater, powered by a 115 hp Lycoming O-235-C2A engine and expected to be marketed in due course at lower cost.

FUJI FA-200 AERO SUBARU

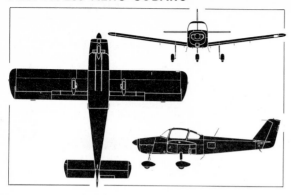

The photograph and silhouette show the Fuji FA-200 Aero Subraru, the first Japanese light aircraft to achieve large-scale production since the end of World War II

Country of Origin: Japan.
Type: Private and club aircraft.
Power Plant: One 160 hp Lycoming O-320-D2A or 180 hp Lycoming IO-360-B1B piston engine.
Performance: Max cruising speed (-160), 122 mph (196 km/h), (-180), 127 mph (204 km/h); best economy cruise (-160), 102 mph (164 km/h), (-180), 104 mph (167 km/h); initial rate of climb, (-160), 680 ft/min (3,4 m/sec), (-180), 760 ft/min (3,9 m/sec); service ceiling (-160), 11,400 ft (3 480 m), (-180), 13,700 ft (4 175 m); range with max fuel (-160), 700 mls (1 125 km), (-180), 615 mls (970 km).
Weights: Empty (-160), 1,336 lb (620 kg), (-180), 1,433 lb (650 kg); max take-off (-160, normal), 2,335 lb (1 060 kg), (-160 aerobatic), 1,940 lb (880 kg), (-180 normal), 2,535 lb (1 150 kg), (-180 aerobatic) 2,072 lb (940 kg).
Dimensions: Span, 30 ft 11 in (9,42 m); length (-160), 26 ft 1 in (7,96 m), (-180), 26 ft 2¼ in (7,98 m); height, 8 ft 6 in (2,59 m); wing area, 150·7 sq ft (14,0 m²).
Accommodation: Pilot and three passengers in two pairs of seats in enclosed cabin.

Status: Prototype first flown on 12 August 1965. Japanese Type Approval, -160 normal category, 1 March 1966, -160 aerobatic (two-seats), 29 July 1967; -180 normal and aerobatic categories, 28 February 1968. Production deliveries began 1968; total built to end-1973, 300.
Notes: The FA-200 is the first light aircraft of wholly original design produced by the Fuji company, which had previously been responsible for the production of some US designs under licence and for the T1 jet trainer (see *Military* volume, page 173). It is also the first Japanese light aircraft to achieve substantial sales in the export market, some half of total production to date having been sold outside Japan. The -160 and -180 versions differ only in power plant and resultant performance variation. One Aero Subaru was modified by Fuji for STOL research as the FA-203S, being fitted with full-span leading-edge flaps and full-span trailing-edge "flaperons" combining the functions of flaps and ailerons. The aircraft is named for the Pleiades group of six stars, recalling that the present Fuji company was formed by a merger of six concerns including the original Nakajima aircraft company, responsible for many of Japan's best aircraft up to 1945.

GAZUIT-VALLADEAU GV10 GAZELLE

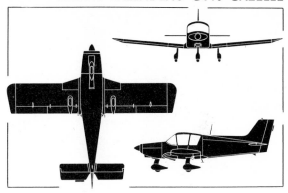

Shown in the photograph is the prototype Gazuit-Valladeau GV-103 lightplane, and the silhouette depicts the production model GV10 Gazelle

Country of Origin: France.

Type: Private and club aircraft.

Power Plant: One (-20) 115 hp Lycoming O-235 or (-31) 150 hp Lycoming O-320 piston engine.

Performance: Max speed (-20), 134 mph (215 km/h), (-31), 152 mph (245 km/h); cruising speed (-20), 118 mph (190 km/h), (-31) 140 mph (225 km/h); initial rate of climb (-20), 590 ft/min (3,0 m/sec), (-31), 787 ft/min (4,0 m/sec); service ceiling (-20), 11,480 ft (3 500 m), (-31), 14,760 ft (4 500 m); range with max fuel (-20), 466 mls (750 km), (-31), 683 mls (1 100 km).

Weights: Empty (-10), 1,157 lb (525 kg), (-31), 1,212 lb (550 kg); max take-off (-20), 1,653 lb (750 kg), (-31), 2,182 lb (990 kg).

Dimensions: Span, 28 ft 8½ in (8,75 m); length, 21 ft 7¾ in (6,60 m); height, 8 ft 3½ in (2,50 m); wing area, 130·25 sq ft (12,10 m²).

Accommodation: (-20) Two side by side or (-31) pilot and three passengers in enclosed cabin; dual controls standard in training version, optional otherwise.

Status: Prototype (GV-103) first flown on 1 May 1969. Pre-

production examples flown in 1970/71; production deliveries began 1973 following French and FAA certification completed during April 1972.

Notes: This light aircraft was designed by two engineers, MM Gazuit and Valladeau, who had previous experience with, respectively, Morane-Saulnier and Wassmer and who had jointly formed a company to provide maintenance facilities for light aircraft, particularly Jodel types. Out of this experience, the GV-103 prototype was designed to meet the particular requirements of French flying clubs, with emphasis upon low cost, good handling and suitability for aerobatics. In production form the type is known as the GV10 Gazelle, and two versions were offered in the first instance—the -20 aerobatic model as a two-seater and the -31 four-seat tourer. While production of an initial batch of these variants was under way in 1973, a version with a 180 hp engine and optional fifth seat was reported to be under development. The Gazelle incorporates certain components fabricated in glass-fibre in its construction, and dual controls are provided as standard on the training version and optional on other variants. Wheel fairings, moulded from laminated plastics, are also optional.

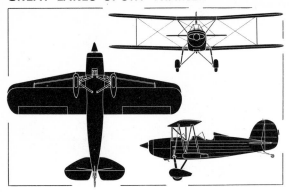

The photograph shows a home-built version of the Great Lakes Biplane, put back into production in 1973 in the version shown in the silhouette

Country of Origin: USA.
Type: Sporting biplane.
Power Plant: One 140 hp Lycoming O-290 or 160 hp Lycoming O-320-B3B flat-four piston engine.
Performance: Max speed (160 hp), 125 mph (201 km/h), (140 hp), 120 mph (193 km/h); max cruising speed (160 hp), 115 mph (185 km/h), (140 hp), 110 mph (177 km/h); initial rate of climb (160 hp), 1,500 ft/min (7,6 m/sec), (140 hp), 720 ft/min (3,65 m/sec); service ceiling (160 hp), 14,000 ft (4 260 m), (140 hp), 12,400 ft (4 267 m); range with max fuel (160 hp), 360 mls (580 km).
Weights: (160 hp) Empty, 1,025 lb (465 kg); max take-off, 1,618 lb (734 kg).
Dimensions: Span, 26 ft 8 in (8,13 m); length, 20 ft 4 in (6,20 m); height, 7 ft 4 in (2,24 m); wing area, 187·6 sq ft (17,43 m²).
Accommodation: Two in tandem open cockpits.
Status: Original Sport Trainer developed in 1930. Production resumed in 1973, production rate about two a month.
Notes: The Great Lakes 2T-1A biplane, powered by a 100 hp American Cirrus in-line engine or Menasco radial, was a popular

sporting aircraft pre-war, being a product of the Great Lakes Company in Cleveland, Ohio. A few surviving examples became prized as antiques by the 'seventies, and growing interest in and enthusiasm for "old-style" flying in an open-cockpit biplane led Mr Douglas Champlin to decide to put the Great Lakes back into production. The assets and manufacturing rights of the original company were acquired in February 1972 and Great Lakes Aircraft Company was formed in Wichita, Kansas. Without changing the overall configuration of the aircraft, the new company introduced certain modifications, the most obvious being an uprated engine— 140 hp or 160 hp Lycoming flat-fours being offered. A sprung, steerable tail wheel and disc brakes on the mainwheels are other new features, and the standard of cockpit instrumentation (with provision for full dual control if required) is modernised. The Great Lakes biplane has acquired an excellent reputation for its aerobatic qualities and its availability as a production aircraft 40 years after it first appeared is a tribute to its flying qualities. It was one of the very few biplanes available for purchase as production items in 1974, although the configuration was still favoured by a number of designers for home-built aircraft.

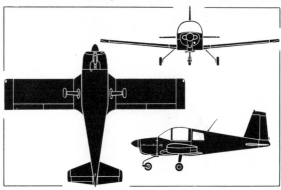

The photograph depicts the four-seat Grumman American AA-5 Traveler and the silhouette shows the similar but lower-powered two-seat AA-1 Yankee

Country of Origin: USA.

Type: Light sporting aircraft and club trainer.

Power Plant: One (AA-1 and AA-1A) 108 hp Lycoming O-235-C2C or (AA-5) 150 hp Lycoming O-320-E2G piston engine.

Performance: Max cruising speed (AA-1, 1A), 134 mph (216 km/h), (AA-5), 140 mph (225 km/h); best economy cruise (AA-1, -1A), 114 mph (183 km/h), (AA-5), 129 mph (207 km/h); initial rate of climb (AA-1, 1A), 720 ft/min (3,6 m/sec), (AA-5), 660 ft/min (3,35 m/sec); service ceiling (AA-1), 11,000 ft (3 350 m), (AA-1A), 12,425 ft (3 787 m), (AA-5), 12,650 ft (3 855 m); range with max fuel (AA-1, -1A), 515 mls (830 km), (AA-5), 500 mls (805 km).

Weights: Empty (AA-1), 963 lb (437 kg), (AA-1A), 968 lb (439 kg), (AA-5), 1,025 lb (465 kg); max take-off (AA-1, -1A), 1,500 lb (680 kg), (AA-5), 2,200 lb (998 kg).

Dimensions: Span (AA-1, 1A), 24 ft 6 in (7,47 m), (AA-5), 31 ft 6 in (9,60 m); length (AA-1, -1A), 19 ft 3 in (5,86 m), (AA-5), 22 ft 0 in (6,71 m); height, 6 ft 9½ in (2,07 m), (AA-5), 8 ft 8½ in (2,65 m); wing area (AA-1, -1A), 100·92 sq ft (9,38 m²), (AA-5), 140·12 sq ft (13,02 m²).

Accommodation: (AA-1, -1A, Tr-2) Two side-by-side or (AA-5) pilot and three passengers in individual seats, in enclosed cabin.

Status: Prototype (BD-1) first flown on 11 July 1963; FAA Type Approval of AA-1, 29 August 1967; first production AA-1 flown 30 May 1968; first AA-1A flown on 25 March 1970; first production AA-1A flown on 6 November 1970; FAA Type Approval of AA-1A, 14 January 1971; Tr-2 deliveries began October 1971; prototype AA-5 flown on 21 August 1970; FAA Type Approval of AA-5, 12 November 1971.

Notes: The original AA-1 Yankee was designed (as the BD-1) by Jim Bede and was put into production by American Aviation Corporation, 456 examples being delivered. It was succeeded by the AA-1A Trainer which has dual controls as standard to facilitate its use as a trainer, and the Tr-2, which is similar but with a higher standard of equipment. More than 575 AA-1A/Tr-2s had been delivered by 1973, when production of both was continuing under the Grumman American name after Grumman Aerospace had acquired American Aviation. The four-seat AA-2 Patrol with 180 hp Lycoming engine did not go into production, the AA-5 Traveler being chosen instead, and over 300 had been built by 1973.

HAL HUL-26 PUSHPAK

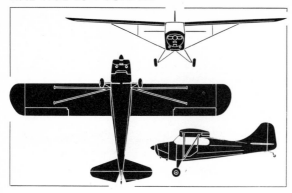

The majority of Hindustan HUL-26 Pushpaks are operated by Indian flying clubs, but the example illustrated by the photograph operates with the Singapore Flying Club

Country of Origin: India.

Type: Light aircraft.

Power Plant: One 90 hp Continental C90-8F piston engine.

Performance: Max speed, 90 mph (144 km/h); cruising speed, 70–85 mph (112–136 km/h); initial rate of climb, 500 ft/min (2,5 m/sec); service ceiling, 14,000 ft (4 270 m); absolute ceiling, 15,400 ft (4 697 m); range with max fuel, 250 mls (400 km); endurance, approx 3 hours.

Weights: Empty, 870 lb (395 kg); maximum take-off weight, 1,350 lb (613 kg).

Dimensions: Span, 37 ft 6 in (11,43 m); length, 27 ft 7 in (8,41 m); height, 7 ft 9 in (2,36 m); wing area, 200 sq ft (18,58 m²).

Accommodation: Two side-by-side in enclosed cabin. Individual doors on each side.

Status: Prototype first flown 28 September 1958. Production total, 147, completed 1969.

Notes: The Pushpak was the second aircraft of original design developed and built at the Bangalore Division of Hindustan Aircraft Ltd (now Hindustan Aeronautics), following the successful launching of the HT-2 basic trainer for the Indian Air Force (see *Military*

volume, page 175) and the licence-production of Prentice trainers and Vampire fighters. The decision to build a light aircraft, taken in 1958, was based on the needs of the Indian flying club movement for a simple, inexpensive training aircraft coupled with Hindustan's wish to broaden its own experience of indigenous design and development activity. Designs were quickly prepared and construction of a prototype, started on 7 August 1958, was completed in only seven weeks. Of entirely conventional layout and all-metal construction, the Pushpak met the requirements for which it was intended virtually the entire production run passing into the hands of Indian flying clubs, where Pushpaks continue to serve in some quantity. A single example was flown with the 90 hp PE-90 engine, designed and built by HAL's Engine Division, also at Bangalore, but no production of this engine took place. During 1958, Hindustan began work on a four-seat development of the Pushpak design and a prototype flew in November 1959, followed by a second in November 1960. This version was known as the Krishak, and although it was not produced in civil guise, an AOP and liaison variant of the same design went into production for the Indian Air Force (see *Military* volume, page 147).

Sport and touring aircraft

JODEL D.9 BEBE, D.11 CLUB

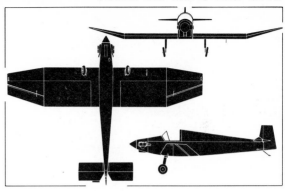

The silhouette (right) depicts the original Jodel D.9 Bébé and the photograph shows a D.120 variant built by Wassmer Aviation as a de luxe derivative

Country of Origin: France.

Type: Light aircraft.

Power Plant: One (D.9) 25 hp Poinsard or similar (D.92) 25 hp Volkswagen or similar (D.11) 45 hp Salmson or similar (D.112) 65 hp Continental, (D 117 and D 119) 90 Continental or similar piston engine.

Performance: Max speed (D.9), 100 mph (160 km/h), (D.112), 118 mph (190 km/h); max cruise (D.9), 85 mph (137 km/h), (D.112), 105 mph (170 km/h); best economy cruise (D.112), 93 mph (150 km/h); initial rate of climb (D.5), 590 ft/min (3,0 m/sec), (D.112), 632 ft/min (3,2 m/sec); range with max fuel (D.9), 250 mls (400 km), (D.112), 373 mls (600 km).

Weights: Empty (D.9), 420 lb (190 kg), (D.112), 600 lb (270 kg); maximum take-off weight, (D.9), 705 lb (320 kg), (D.112), 1,145 lb (520 kg).

Dimensions: Span (D.9), 22 ft 11 in (7,00 m), (D.112), 26 ft 10 in (8,2 m); length (D.9), 17 ft 10½ in (5,45 m), (D.112), 20 ft 10 in (6,36 m); height (D.9), 5 ft 0 in (1,52 m); wing area (D.9), 96·8 sq ft (9,0 m²), (D.112), 137 sq ft (12,72 m²).

Accommodation: (D.9) Pilot only in open or optionally enclosed cockpit or (D.11 series) two seats side-by-side in enclosed cockpit with rearward- or side-opening canopy.

Status: Prototype D.9 first flown in January 1948; first D.11 flown on 5 May 1950. Many hundreds built.

Notes: The Bébé, jointly designed by MM Joly and Delmontez (hence JoDel) was one of the first post-war designs for amateur construction and has proved to be one of the most successful. Nearly 600 D.9 variants were built by individuals and companies in various parts of the world. From the single-seat D.9, the Jodel team developed the D.11 two-seater of similar design and construction, and this basic design then evolved through a variety of sub-variants distinguished primarily by different engines. These differences were indicated by designations from D.111 to D.119, some being factory production versions, built by Société Aéronautique Normande (SAN), Alpavia and Wassmer in France and by Aero Difusión in Spain. Wassmer developed the D.120 Paris-Nice as a de luxe variant of the D.117 and further development of the basic design by Centre Est Aeronautique (CEA) led eventually to the DR100 series, produced in large numbers by CEA and, later, Avions Pierre Robin (see page 171).

JODEL (SAN, ROBIN) D.140 MOUSQUETAIRE AND ABEILLE

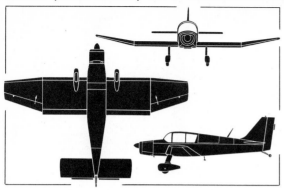

The photograph (above) shows the original production Jodel D.140 Mousquetaire and the silhouette (left) depicts the D.140E Mousquetaire IV

Country of Origin: France.

Type: Private and club aircraft.

Power Plant: One 180 hp Lycoming O-360-A2A piston engine.

Performance: Max speed (D.140), 155 mph (250 km/h), (D.140E), 158 mph (255 km/h); max cruising speed (D.140), 143 mph (230 km/h), (D.140E), 149 mph (240 km/h); best economy cruise (D.140), 137 mph (220 km/h), (D.140E), 125 mph (200 km/h); initial rate of climb (D.140), 985 ft/min (5,0 m/sec), (D.140E), 750 ft/min (3,8 m/sec); service ceiling (D.140), 14,760 ft (4 500 m), (D.140E), 16,400 ft (5 000 m); range with max fuel (D.140), 745 mls (1 200 km), (D.140E), 870 mls (1 400 km).

Weights: Empty (D.140), 1,323 lb (600 kg), (D.140E), 1,367 lb (620 kg), max take off (D.140 and D.140E), 2,645 lb (1 200 kg).

Dimensions: Span, 33 ft 8¼ in (10,27 m); length, 25 ft 8 in (7,82 m); height, 6 ft 9 in (2,05 m); wing area, 199·13 sq ft (18,50 m²).

Accommodation: Pilot and three or four passengers in enclosed cabin.

Status: Prototype first flown 4 July 1958. First production model flown on 1 November 1958. Production quantities (approximate):

D.140 and D.140A, 52; D.140B, 61; D.140C, 53; D.140E, over 50; D.140R, over 20.

Notes: Société Aéronautique Normande, one of the companies that acquired production rights for the Jodel D.11 (see page 153), of which it built 225 in the D.117 version, went on to develop the basic design into a new four-seat version, the D.140 Mousquetaire. It retained the Jodel wing, but had an enlarged fuselage and a redesigned tail unit. The first production examples were the D.140 and the similar D.140A. The D.140B had revised interior arrangements and the D.140C Mousquetaire III introduced a new swept-back fin-and-rudder. Another change was made in the tail of the D.140E Mousquetaire IV, with the tailplane being of the all-moving type, and the wing area was increased. A special version was also developed for glider and banner towing, as the D.140R Abeille, the changes including more extensive cockpit glazing to improve the view rearward. After the SAN company closed down in 1969, production of the Mousquetaire and Abeille was continued for a time by the Robin company, which, under its earlier name of Centre Est Aviation, had also developed its own versions of the original Jodel (see page 153).

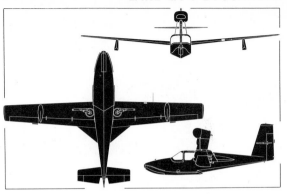

The Lake LA-4 Buccaneer, shown in the photograph and silhouette, is one of the few light amphibians in production in 1974

Country of Origin: USA.

Type: Private sporting amphibian.

Power Plant: One (LA-4), 180 hp Lycoming O-360-A1A or (LA-4T), O-360-A1D with Rajay turbosupercharger or (LA-4-200), 200 hp IO-360-A1B piston engine.

Performance: Max cruising speed (LA-4), 131 mph (211 km/h), (LA-4-200), 150 mph (241 km/h); best economy cruise (LA-4) 125 mph (201 km/h); initial rate of climb (LA-4), 800 ft/min (4,1 m/sec); (LA-4-200), 1,200 ft/min (6,1 m/sec); service ceiling (LA-4), 14,000 ft (4 270 m), (LA-4-200), 14,700 ft (4 480 m); range with max fuel (LA-4), 627 mls (1 010 km), (LA-4-200), 847 mls (1 363 km).

Weights: Empty (LA-4), 1,575 lb (714 kg), (LA-4-200), 1,600 lb (726 kg); max take-off (LA-4), 2,400 lb (1 089 kg), (LA-4-200), 2,690 lb (1 220 kg).

Dimensions: Span, 38 ft 0 in (11,58 m); length, 24 ft 11 in (7,60 m); height, 9 ft 4 in (2,84 m); wing area, 170 sq ft (15,8 m²).

Accommodation: Pilot and three passengers in two pairs of seats in enclosed cabin.

Status: Prototype LA-4P first flown in November 1959; initial

FAA Type Approval 21 June 1960; production LA-4 Type Approval 26 July 1960. Production totals, prototype, 1; pre-production LA-4A, two; LA-4, LA-4S, LA-4T and LA-4-200, over 600 by end of 1973, with production then continuing at an average rate of 5–6 per month.

Notes: The Buccaneer is the most successful light amphibian of recent years, having been designed basically shortly after the end of World War II by David Thurston. A prototype called the Colonial C-1 Skimmer flew in May 1948, and was developed into the C-2 for production by Colonial Aircraft Corporation. Lake Aircraft acquired the rights in 1959 and further developed the design into the LA-4, the prototype LA-4P being dimensionally similar to the C-2. Two pre-production LA-4As had the now-standard increased span, and the production LA-4 also had a longer bow, more powerful engine and other changes. Variants of the basic production model were the LA-4S, a pure seaplane version with the landing gear and hydraulic actuation equipment removed; and the LA-4T with turbosupercharged engine. These versions were superseded by the LA-4-200 in 1970, with more powerful engine and other refinements.

MALMO MFI-9 JUNIOR AND BOLKOW BO 208

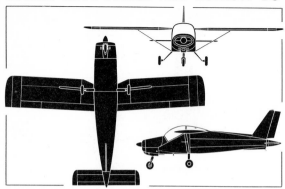

The Bölkow-built version of the original Malmo MFI-9 light aircraft is shown in the photograph (above) and the silhouette shows the BO 208C variant

Country of Origin: Sweden/Federal Germany.
Type: Light Aircraft.
Power Plant: One 100 hp Rolls-Royce/Continental O-200-A piston engine.
Performance: Max cruising speed (MFI-9B), 145 mph (236 km/h), (BO 208C), 130 mph (209 km/h); best economy cruise, (MFI-9B), 130 mph (209 km/h); initial rate of climb (MFI-9B), 900 ft/min (4,5 m/sec), (BO 208C), 785 ft/min (4,0 m/sec); service ceiling (MFI-9B), 15,000 ft (4 500 m), (BO 208C), 14,100 ft (4 300 m); range with max payload (MFI-9B), 500 mls (800 km); range with max fuel (BO 208C), 620 mls (1 000 km).
Weights: Empty (MFI-9B), 750 lb (340 kg), (BO 208C), 835 lb (380 kg); max take-off (MFI-9B), 1,270 lb (575 kg), (BO 208C), 1,390 lb (630 kg).
Dimensions: Span (MFI-9), 24 ft 4 in (7,43 m), (BO 208C), 26 ft 4 in (8,02 m); length (landplane), 19 ft 2 in (5,85 m), (seaplane), 20 ft 0 in (6,10 m); height (landplane), 6 ft 7 in (200 m), (seaplane), 7 ft 6½ in (2,30 m); wing area (MFI-9), 93 sq ft (8,70 m²), (BO 208C), 100 sq ft (9,37 m²).
Accommodation: Two side-by-side in enclosed cabin.

Status: Prototype (BA-7) first flown on 10 October 1958. First prototype MFI-9 flown on 17 May 1961 and first production model flown on 9 August 1962. First BO 208 flown on April 1962. Production totals include 25 MFI-9 and about 200 BO 208s.
Notes: This sporting light aircraft and club trainer was designed in the USA by Bjorn Andreasson and constructed by the designer as a homebuilt project. It subsequently entered production in Sweden after the designer joined A B Malmo Flygindustri, and 25 of the initial version were built. A similar version was put into production in Germany by Bolkow GmbH and both companies subsequently introduced a larger wing on their MFI-9B and BO 208B versions. The final German model, production of which had ended by 1970, was the BO 208C with the big wing and other improvements. A military version, the MFI-9B Militrainer, was also built in small quantities in Sweden and was used in support of Biafran forces in the war with Nigeria. The same configuration was adopted for the MFI-15 and MFI-17, which appeared in 1969 and are available in civil and military guise (see *Military* volume, page 195). Examples of the MFI-17 were used to drop supplies to areas of Ethiopia affected by drought during 1974.

Sport and touring aircraft

MAULE M-4

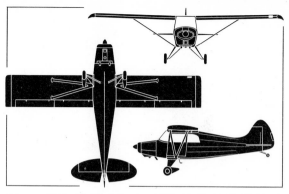

Both the photograph (above) and the silhouette (right) depict the Continental-engine version of the Maule M-4, known as the Rocket

Country of Origin: USA.

Type: Private and club aircraft.

Power Plant: One (M-4, M-4C, M-45, M-4T) 145 hp Continental O-300-A or -B, or (M-4-210) 210 hp Continental IO-360-A or (M-4-220) 220 hp Franklin 6A-350-C1 or (M-4-180) 180 hp Franklin 6A-335-B1A piston engine.

Performance: Max cruising speed (M-4), 150 mph (241 km/h), (-210), 165 mph (265 km/h); initial rate of climb (M-4), 700 ft/min (3,55 m/sec), (-210), 1,250 ft/min (6,3 m/sec); service ceiling (M-4), 12,000 ft (3 650 m), (-210) 18,000 ft (5 500 m); range with max fuel (M-4), 700 mls (1 125 km), (-210), 680 mls (1 090 km).

Weights: Empty (M-4), 1,100 lb (499 kg), (-210), 1,220 lb (553 kg); max take-off (M-4), 2,100 lb (953 kg), (-210), 2,300 lb (1 043 kg).

Dimensions: Span, 30 ft 10 in (9,40 m); length, 22 ft 0 in (6,71 m); height, 6 ft 2½ in (1,89 m); wing area, 152·5 sq ft (14,17 m²).

Accommodation: Pilot and three passengers in enclosed cabin.

Status: Prototype Bee Dee M-4 first flown 8 September 1960. FAA Type Approvals, Bee Dee M-4, 10 August 1961; M-4, 21 February 1963; M-4C, 7 October 1965; M-4S, M-4T, 15 March 1966; M-4-210, 24 September 1964; M-4-220, 18 October 1966; M-4-180, 12 October 1970; M-5, 28 December 1973. Production rate, 1973, 8–10 per month.

Notes: This aircraft originated as a home-built, the Bee Dee M-4, named for its designer B D Maule. A company was subsequently formed to produce the type in quantity and it has sold steadily in the US market since 1963. The four different engines noted above distinguish the four named versions of the M-4, which are the Jetasen with the 145 hp Continental, Astro-Rocket with the Franklin, Rocket with the 210 hp Continental and Strata-Rocket with the 220 hp Franklin. The C suffix on any of the above models indicates installation of larger rear doors to facilitate cargo loading and the T suffix indicates a version with no rear door and no rear seats. About 250 M-4 variants, including Jetasens, Rockets and Strata-Rockets were built at Jackson, Michigan before the company moved to its present base at Moultrie in Georgia, where 472 M-4s had been produced by early 1974. During 1971, Maule flew the M-5-220C Lunar Rocket, a version of the M-4 with larger flaps and other features to provide STOL characteristics.

157

MBB (SIAT, CASA) FLAMINGO

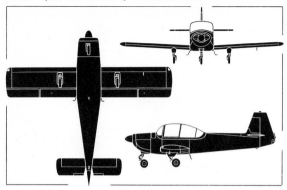

The photograph shows one of the original SIAT-built 223 Flamingo trainers used by Swissair and the silhouette depicts the standard model now built by CASA in Spain

Country of Origin: Federal Germany.

Type: Private and club aircraft and trainer.

Power Plant: One 200 hp Lycoming (A1) IO-360-C1B or (K1) AIO-360 piston engine.

Performance: Max speed (A1), 151 mph (243 km/h), (K1), 155 mph (249 km/h); typical cruise (A1), 134 mph (216 km/h), (K1), 138 mph (222 km/h); initial rate of climb (A1), 846 ft/min (4,3 m/sec), (K1), 1,220 ft/min (6,2 m/sec); service ceiling (A1), 12,300 ft (3 750 m), (K1), 17,390 ft (5 300 m); range with max fuel (A1), 715 mls (1 150 km).

Weights: Empty, 1,510 lb (685 kg); max take-off (A1 normal), 2,315 lb (1 050 kg), (A1, utility), 2,160 lb (980 kg), (K1), 1,810 lb (821 kg).

Dimensions: Span, 27 ft 2 in (8,28 m); length, 24 ft 4½ in (7,43 m); height, 8 ft 10¼ in (2,70 m); gross wing area, 123·8 sq ft (11,50 m²).

Accommodation: (A1) Two seats side-by-side or (K1) pilot only in enclosed cabin.

Status: Prototype first flown on 1 March 1967. Production total (by MBB) 50, completed early 1972. First Hispano-built example flown on 14 February 1972.

Notes: The Flamingo was the winner of a design competition organized during 1962 by the Wissenschaftliche Gesellschaft für Luft- und Raumfahrt, with the backing of the Ministry of Economics. to find a suitable training aircraft on which German flying clubs could standardize. Lack of funds, however, prevented large-scale production of the design being initiated and construction of a proto-type was protracted. The design was a product of the SIAT company, which was absorbed into the MBB group before production began. A batch of 50 was then completed in Germany, including 10 for use by Swissair at its pilot training school and 15 for the Turkish Air Force. Production was then transferred to Spain, where Hispano SA began work on a batch of 50 before itself being taken over by CASA. Initial deliveries from the Spanish production line were for use by the Spanish Air Force in the liaison rôle. The basic version of the Flamingo, the MBB 223A1, is equipped as a two-seater but has space provision to the rear of the cabin for a folding seat for one adult or two children, in place of baggage. The MBB 223K1 is normally flown solo in the aerobatic rôle, being stressed to +6g and −4g at the reduced aerobatic weight.

MBB (BOLKOW) BO 209 MONSUN

An unusual feature of the MBB (originally Bölkow) BO 209 Monsun is its optionally retractable nose wheel, as shown in the illustration above and left

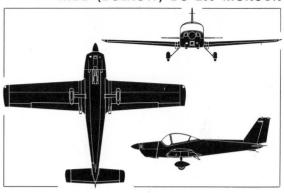

Country of Origin: Federal Germany.
Type: Private and club aircraft.
Power Plant: One 150 hp Lycoming O-320-E1C, E1F or E2C or 160 hp Lycoming IO-320-D1A or (BO 209S) 130 hp R-R Continental O-240 piston engine.
Performance: Max cruising speed (-150), 155 mph (250 km/h), (-160), 170 mph (274 km/h), (S), 146 mph (235 km/h); best economy cruise (-150), 149 mph (239 km/h), (160), 151 mph (243 km/h), (S), 132 mph (213 km/h); initial rate of climb (150), 1,045 ft/min (5,3 m/sec), (160), 1,180 ft/min (6,0 m/sec), (S), 748 ft/min (3,8 m/sec); service ceiling (150), 16,400 ft (5 000 m), (160), 18,100 ft (5 520 m); range with max fuel (150), 620 mls (1 000 km), (160), 745 mls (1 200 kH), (S), 685 mls (1 100 km).
Weights: Empty (150), 1,045 lb (474 kg), (160), 1,067 lb (484 kg), (S), 925 lb (420 kg); max payload, 504 lb (229 kg); maximum take-off weight (150, 160), 1,807 lb (820 kg), (S), 1,675 lb (760 kg).
Dimensions: Span (150, 160), 27 ft 6¾ in (8,40 m), (S), 29 ft 7¼ in (9,025 m); length, 21 ft 7¾ in (6,60 m); height, 7 ft 2½ in (2,20 m); wing area (150, 160), 110 sq ft (10,22 m²), (S), 116·3 sq ft (10,82 m²).

Accommodation: Two seats side-by-side in enclosed cabin.
Status: Prototype (MHK-101) first flown on 22 December 1967; prototype BO 209 first flown on 28 May 1969. Production deliveries began early 1970, completed early 1972. Total production, 100.
Notes: This design owes its origin to the work of Dipl-Ing Hermann Mylius, who was responsible, while the technical director of the former Bolkow company (later absorbed into MBB), for a prototype light aircraft designated the MHK-101. This was adapted for production by Bolkow as the BO 209, and eventually appeared in three different variants. Two of these differed only in the type of engine fitted, and either could have, as an option, a retractable nosewheel, although the main wheels remained fixed in each case. The third variant, the BO 209S, was intended specifically for use as a club trainer, with a lower powered engine, fixed nose wheel and no provision for wing folding. The wing-folding feature was originally provided in the basic BO 209 design to facilitate hangar stowage and to permit it to be towed behind a car. Early in 1974, Monsun Flugzeugbau was set up to resume production of the BO 209 at Weiden.

MOONEY M-10, ALON A-2, FORNAIRE F-1 AIRCOUPE, ERCOUPE

Sport and touring aircraft

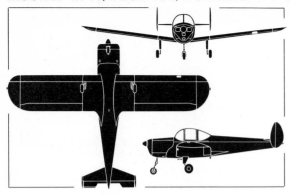

Both the photograph and the silhouette depict the Alon A-1 Aircoupe, one of the final production versions of the original pre-war Ercoupe lightplane

Country of Origin: USA.

Type: Light Aircraft.

Power Plant: One (415-C, -D) 75 hp Continental C75-12 or (415-E, -G) 85 hp C85-12 or (F-1, F-1A, A-2, M-10) 90 hp C90-12F or C90-16F piston engine.

Performance: Max speed (415-C), 120 mph (192 km/h), (A-2), 129 mph (208 km/h); cruising speed (415-C), 110 mph (177 km/h), (A-2), 112 mph (180 km/h); initial rate of climb (415-C), 560 ft/min (2,85 m/sec), (A-2), 640 ft/min (3,25 m/sec); service ceiling (415-C), 11,000 ft (3 360 m), (A-2), 17,300 ft (5 273 m); range with max fuel (415-C), 350 mls (560 km), (A-2), 455 mls (732 km).

Weights: Empty (415-C), 815 lb (370 kg), (A-2), 930 lb (422 kg); maximum take-off weight, (415-C), 1,400 lb (634 kg), (A-2), 1,450 lb (657 kg).

Dimensions: Span, 30 ft 0 in (9,14 m); length, 20 ft 9 in (6,32 m); height, 6 ft 3 in (1,90 m); wing area, 142·6 sq ft (13,2 m²).

Accommodation: Two side-by-side in enclosed cockpit.

Status: Prototype (310) first flown in October 1937. Entered production 1940. First A-2 flown on 24 October 1964. FAA Type

Approvals: 415-C, 25 March 1940; 415-CD, 19 August 1947; 415-D, 13 June 1947; 415-E, 8 July 1948; 415-F, 28 January 1949; F-1, 18 September 1956; F-1A, 22 December 1959; A-2, 12 November 1964; A-2A, 21 June 1967; M10, 27 September 1968. Production totals, Erco Model 415s, over 5,000; Fornaire F-1/F-1A, over 1,000; Alon A-2/A-2A, about 300; Mooney M10, about 20.

Notes: The original Ercoupe was designed by Fred Weick with an unusual two-control system that eliminated rudder pedals and was claimed to make the aircraft spin-proof; elevator control was effected by pushing or pulling back on the horizontal column to which the control wheel was attached, the latter moving both ailerons and rudders in response to a single movement. The first 112 had 65 hp A-65 engines but the major production model was the 75 hp Ercoupe 415-C described above; many examples survive. The basic design has been produced successively by other companies as the Fornaire F-1, the Alon A-2 Aircoupe, the Mooney A-2A and finally the Mooney M-10 Cadet. The Alon version introduced conventional three-axis controls and the Cadet had a single fin and rudder.

MOONEY M-20 RANGER, CHAPARRAL, STATESMAN, EXECUTIVE

A 1971 model Mooney Ranger is shown in the photograph (above) and the silhouette (right) depicts the same variant, production of which was resumed in 1974

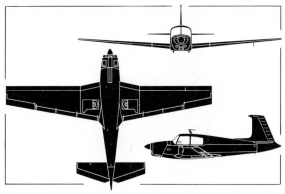

Country of Origin: USA.

Type: Private, club and business aircraft.

Power Plant: One (M-20) 150 hp Lycoming O-320 or (M-20A, M-20B) 180 hp O-360-AlA or (M-20C, M-20D) O-360-AlD or -A2D or (M-20E, M-20F) 200 hp IO-360-AlA or (M-20G) 180 hp O-360-AlD piston engine.

Performance: Max cruising speed (M-20C), 168 mph (270 km/h), (M-20F), 176 mph (283 km/h); best economy cruise, 128 mph (206 km/h), (M-20F), 118 mph (190 km/h); initial rate of climb (M-20C), 800 ft/min (4,1 m/sec), (M-20F), 1,080 ft/min (5,5 m/sec); service ceiling (M-20C), 17,200 ft (5 243 m), (M-20F), 16,000 ft (4 877 m); range with max fuel (M-20C), 800 mls (1 287 km), (M-20F), 954 mls (1 535 km).

Weights: Empty (M-20C), 1,525 lb (691 kg), (M-20F), 1,640 lb (743 kg); max take-off (M-20C), 2,575 lb (1 168 kg), (M-20F), 2,740 lb (1 243 kg).

Dimensions: Span (all), 35 ft 0 in (10,67 m); length (M-20C), 23 ft 2 in (7,06 m), (M-20F, M-20G), 24 ft 0 in (7,32 m); height (all), 8 ft 4 in (2,54 m); wing area (all), 167 sq ft (15,51 m²).

Accommodation: Pilot and three passengers in two pairs of seats in enclosed cabin.

Status: Prototype M-20 first flown on 10 August 1963. Prototype M-20C (M-21) first flown on 23 September 1961 and first production on 7 November 1961. FAA Type Approvals, M-20, 24 August 1955, M-20A, 13 February 1958; M-20B, 14 December 1960; M-20C, 20 October 1961; M-20D, 15 October 1962, M-20E, 4 September 1963; M-20F, 25 July 1965, M-20G, 13 November 1967. Production totals, over 5,000 of all versions.

Notes: The Mooney M-20 series was in production for 15 years and all models are recognisable by the forward sweep of the fin. The M-20C and M-20F were at one time known as the Mark 21 and Super-21 but the final production versions were known as the Ranger (M-20C), the Chaparral (M-20E), Executive (M-20F) and Statesman (M-20G). After the Mooney company had been acquired by Butler, the Ranger, Chaparral and Statesman were briefly known as the Aerostar 200, 201 and 220, distinguished by the "button-hook" fairing at the fin tip. Production was resumed in 1974 after the rights were acquired by Republic Steel Corp. The Mooney M-22 was a larger, pressurized variant of the M-20 design and few were built.

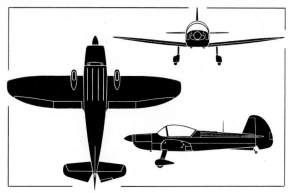

The silhouette (left) depicts the CAP 10 two-seat light aircraft and the photograph (above) shows the generally-similar aerobatic CAP 20 single-seater

Country of Origin: France.

Type: Aerobatic light plane.

Power Plant: One (CAP 10) 180 hp Lycoming IO-360-RCF, (CAP 20) 200 hp Lycoming AIO-360-BIB or (CAP 20C and 20E) 260 hp Lycoming IO-540 piston engine.

Performance: Max speed (CAP 10), 168 mph (280 km/h); max cruising speed (CAP 10), 149 mph (240 km/h), (CAP 20), 211 mph (340 km/h); initial rate of climb (CAP 10), 1,180 ft/min (6,0 m/sec); service ceiling (CAP 10), 18,050 ft (5 500 m); range with max fuel (CAP 10), 745 mls (1 200 km).

Weights: Empty (CAP 10), 1,168 lb (530 kg), (CAP 20), 1,410 lb (640 kg); max take-off (CAP 10 aerobatic), 1,666 lb (756 kg), (CAP 10 utility), 1,829 lb (830 kg), (CAP 20 aerobatic), 1,675 lb (760 kg).

Dimensions: Span (CAP 10), 26 ft 5¼ in (8,06 m), (CAP 20), 26 ft 4¾ in (8,04 m); length (CAP 10), 23 ft 11½ in (7,30 m), (CAP 20), 23 ft 7¾ in (7,21 m); height (CAP 10), 8 ft 4½ in (2,55 m); wing area (both), 116·8 sq ft (10,85 m²).

Accommodation: (CAP 10) Two side-by-side, (CAP 20) pilot only in enclosed cockpit.

Status: Prototype CAP 10 first flown in August 1968; French type approval 4 September 1970. First CAP 20 flown on 29 July 1969. Production, CAP 10, 50 built to mid-1973; CAP 20, one prototype and eight production.

Notes: The CAP 10 was developed from the Piel Emeraude (see page 165) by the CAARP company, which assumed responsibility for Emeraude production from Scintex in 1965. More powerful than the Emeraude, the CAP 10 was stressed to be fully aerobatic and a batch of 30 was built for use as aerobatic trainers by *l'Armée de l'Air* at its basic flying training school and the *Equipe Voltige Aerienne* (EVA). Deliveries for civil use began at the end of 1972, from the production line established by Avions Mudry. The CAP 20 was developed jointly by CAARP and Mudry as a single-seat aerobatic aircraft for use in World Aerobatic Championships. Six have been acquired by the EVA. Variants designated CAP 20A to CAP 20E, tested in 1973 and 1974, incorporate various modifications designed to improve the performance and precision with which aerobatic manoeuvres can be flown, and it was expected that the EVA team's aircraft would eventually be modified in the light of these tests.

Both the photograph and the silhouette depict the Lake Commander, distinguished from the earlier Darter Commander by its back-swept fin-and-rudder

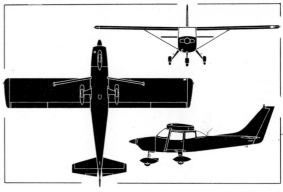

Country of Origin: USA.

Type: Private and club aircraft.

Power Plant: One (Darter) 150 hp Lycoming O-320-A or (Lark) 180 hp Lycoming O-360-A2F piston engine.

Performance: Max (Darter), 133 mph (214 km/h), (Lark), 138 mph (222 km/h); max cruise (Darter), 128 mph (206 km/h), (Lark), 132 mph (212 km/h) at 7,500 ft (2 285 m); initial rate of climb (Darter), 785 ft/min (4,0 m/sec), (Lark), 750 ft/min (3,8 m/sec); service ceiling (Darter), 13,000 ft (3 960 m), (Lark), 13,000 ft (3 960 m); range with max fuel (Darter), 510 mls (821 km), (Lark), 525 mls (845 km).

Weights: Empty (Darter), 1,280 lb (580 kg), (Lark), 1,450 lb (657 kg); max take-off (Darter), 2,250 lb (1 020 kg), (Lark), 2,450 lb (1 110 kg).

Dimensions: Span, 35 ft 0 in (10,67 m); length (Darter), 22 ft 6 in (6,86 m), (Lark), 24 ft 11 in (7,59 m); height (Darter), 9 ft 4 in (2,84 m), (Lark), 10 ft 1 in (3,07 m); wing area, 181 sq ft (16,81 m²).

Accommodation: Pilot and three passengers in enclosed cabin.

Status: Prototype Volaire 10 first flown 1960; FAA Type Approvals,

Volaire 10, 30 November 1961; Volaire 10A, 1 June 1965; Lark Commander, 26 September 1967. Production totals, Volaire 10, 3; Aero Commander 100A, 13; Volaire 10A, 6; Aero Commander 100/Darter Commander, about 200; Lark Commander, over 200.

Notes: The Volaire 10 was a simple all-metal light aircraft developed and certificated by Volaircraft Inc of Aliquippa, Penn, with a 135 hp Lycoming O-290-D2C engine. Limited production was initiated, supplemented by the more powerful Model 10A, but the production total had scarcely reached double figures when design and production rights in the two models were acquired by Aero Commander. On 30 September 1965, the names of the Model 10 and Model 10A were changed to Aero Commander 100A and· 100 respectively; the former was quickly dropped but production of the latter continued and the name Darter Commander was adopted in due course. In 1967, Aero Commander, by then a division of North American Rockwell, introduced an uprated version, the Model 100-180 Lark Commander, featuring a swept-back fin and other refinements. Design rights in both types were sold at the end of 1971 to Phoenix Aircraft, which planned to continue production as the Model 150 and Model 180.

PARTENAVIA P.64 AND P.66 OSCAR

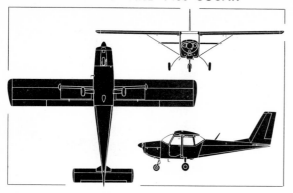

The photograph (above) shows the P.66B Oscar 150 version of the Partenavia lightplane, the silhouette (left) also depicting the P66 variant

Country of Origin: Italy.

Type: Private and club aircraft.

Power Plant: One (P.64 and Oscar -180) 180 hp Lycoming O-360-AIA or (Oscar -200) 200 hp IO-360-AIB or (Oscar -100) 115 hp Lycoming O-235-C1B or (Oscar -150) 150 hp Lycoming O-320-E2A piston engine.

Performance: Max speed (-180), 162 mph (260 km/h), (-100), 134 mph (215 km/h); max cruise (-180), 149 mph (240 km/h), (-100), 118 mph (190 km/h); initial rate of climb (-180), 984 ft/min (5,0 m/sec), (-100), 728 ft/min (3,7 m/sec); service ceiling (-180), 16,400 ft (5 000 m), (-100), 13,125 ft (4 000 m); range with max fuel (-180), 650 mls (1 046 km), (-100), 375 mls (600 km).

Weights: Empty (-180), 1,477 lb (670 kg), (-200), 1,521 lb (690 kg), (-100), 1,235 lb (560 kg), (-150), 1,344 lb (610 kg); max take-off (-180), 2,425 lb (1 100 kg), (-200), 2,546 lb (1 155 kg), (-100), 1,808 lb (820 kg), (-150), 2,050 lb (930 kg).

Dimensions: Span (all), 32 ft 9¼ in (9,99 m); length (-180, -200), 23 ft 8¾ in (7,23 m), (-100, -150), 23 ft 3¼ in (7,09 m); height (all), 9 ft 1 in (2,77 m); wing area (all), 144·2 sq ft (13,40 m²).

Accommodation: Pilot and (-180, -200) three or (-100) one or (-150) two passengers in enclosed cabin.

Status: Prototype P.64 first flown on 2 April 1965; production deliveries began spring 1966; prototype P.64B Oscar-180 flown in early summer 1967; first Oscar -200 flown May 1970. Production quantities include over 70 Oscar-180, about 12 Oscar-200, over 100 Oscar-100 and about 70 Oscar-150 by end-1973, plus over 20 in South Africa by AFIC (Pty) Ltd.

Notes: The Oscar was designed by Ing Luigi Pascale as a successor to the P.57 Fachiro, and became one of the most successful of Italian light aircraft. The initial version was the four-seat P.64, followed by the refined P.64B, sometimes known as Oscar B before being designated Oscar-180 and Oscar-200 according to the type of engine fitted. The P.66 series was derived from the basic Oscar in order to offer two- and three-seat versions. Apart from the cabin arrangements and engine power, there are few differences between the P.64 and P.66. In 1967, AFIC (Pty) Ltd was founded in South Africa to build the P.64B under licence as the RSA-200 Falcon, with either 180 hp or 200 hp engine but these plans were subsequently suspended pending completion of manufacturing facilities.

PIEL (AND SCINTEX) C.P.30 EMERAUDE

Powered by a Rolls-Royce/Continental engine, the C.P. 1310 variant of the Piel (Scintex) Super Emerande is shown in both the photograph and the silhouette

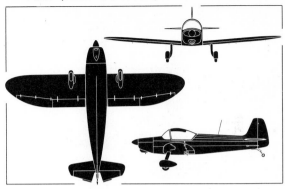

Country of Origin: France.

Type: Private aircraft.

Power Plant: One (C.P.30) 65 hp Continental A65 or (C.P. 301) 90 hp Continental C90 or other similar engines up to 150 hp.

Performance: Max cruising speed (C.P.301), 124 mph (200 km/h), (C.P.320), 137 mph (230 km/h); best economy cruise (C.P.301), 116 mph (187 km/h), (C.P.320), 127 mph (205 km/h); initial rate of climb (C.P.301), 551 ft/min (2,8 m/sec), (C.P.320), 787 ft/min (4,0 m/sec); service ceiling (C.P.301), 13,125 ft (4 000 m), (C.P.320), 14,100 ft (4 300 m); range (C.P.301), 620 mls (1 000 km), (C.P.320), 620 mls (1 000 km).

Weights: Empty (C.P.301), 838 lb (380 kg), (C.P. 320), 903 lb (410 kg); max take-off (C.P. 301), 1,433 lb (650 kg), (C.P.320), 1,543 lb (7 000 kg).

Dimensions: Span (all), 26 ft 4½ in (8,04 m); length (C.P.301), 20 ft 8 in (6,30 m), (C.P.320), 21 ft 2 in (6,45 m); height (C.P. 301), 6 ft 0¾ in (1,85 m), (C.P.320), 6 ft 2¾ in (1,90 m); wing area, 116·7 sq ft (10,85 m²).

Accommodation: Two side-by-side in enclosed cockpit.

Status: First C.P.30 flown in 1962; first production example flown in 1953. First Garland-Bianchi (Fairtravel) Linnet flown on 1 September 1958. Production quantities include 114 C.P.301A, 21 C.P.301B, 84 C.P.301C, 31 Super Emeraude, 3 Linnets and many amateur-built examples.

Notes: The Emeraude was designed by Claude Piel to be suitable for amateur construction, although over 200 examples were factory-built. About half these were C.P.301As, built by four companies in France; other variants were the C.P.301B with strengthened airframe and other changes; C.P.301C with 95 hp engine, sliding canopy etc; C.P.301S built in Germany; C.P.315 with 105 hp Potez engine and C.P. 1310, 1315 and 1330 Super Emeraude with 100 hp R-R/Continental O-200-A engine. Amateur-built versions took designations from C.P.302 to C.P. 323A and have a variety of refinements and special features, the C.P. 320 described above being a typical example, similar to the Super Emeraude. The C.P.301 was built in Britain as the Linnet, originally by Garland Aircraft, then by Fairtravel, but plans for quantity production by these companies did not proceed. Among the companies that built the Emeraude in France was CAARP, which used it as the basis for development of its own CAP 10 design (see page 162).

PIPER PA-18 SUPER CUB

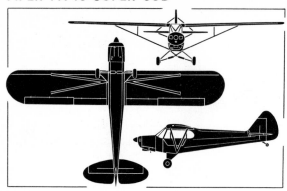

Directly derived from the famous pre-war Cub, the Piper PA-18 Super Cub, shown in the photograph and the silhouette, was the only high-wing Piper in production in 1974

Country of Origin: USA.

Type: Private and club aircraft.

Power Plant: One (PA-18) 90 hp Continental C90-12F or -8F or (PA-18-125) 125 hp Lycoming O-290-D or (PA-18-135) 135 hp O-290-D2 or (PA-18-150) 150 hp Lycoming O-320 or (PA-18S) 108 hp Lycoming O-235-C1 engine.

Performance (PA-18-150): Max cruising speed, 115 mph (185 km/h); best economy cruise, 105 mph (169 km/h); initial rate of climb, 960 ft/min (4,9 m/sec); service ceiling, 19,000 ft (5 795 m); range with max fuel, 460 mls (735 km).

Weights: (PA-18-150), Empty, 930 lb (422 kg); max take-off, 1,750 lb (794 kg).

Dimensions: Span, 35 ft 2½ in (10,73 m); length (landplane), 22 ft 7 in (6,88 m), (seaplane), 23 ft 11 in (7,28 m); height, 6 ft 8½ in (2,02 m); wing area, 178·5 sq ft (16,58 m²).

Accommodation: Two in tandem in enclosed cabin.

Status: Prototypes flown in 1949. FAA Type Approval, 18 November 1949 for initial model, and successive variants approved up to the PA-18-150 on 1 October 1954. Production total, over 6,600; production rate about one a week in 1973.

Notes: The Super Cub was one of the series of high-wing light-planes evolved by Piper in the first few post-war years. Retaining many well-tried Piper features, it introduced all-metal wings and entered production with a 90 hp engine. Subsequently, versions were offered with 108 hp, 125 hp, 135 hp and finally 150 hp engines and the last-mentioned version remained in production as the only high-wing Piper design in 1974. Many Super Cubs were built for agricultural duties, designated PA-18A, with a hopper in the fuselage in place of the rear seat. Other high-wing Pipers are still flying, all these types, like the PA-18, having tail wheel landing gear. They include versions of the original J-3 with 40 hp, 50 hp or 65 hp Continental engine, or 50 hp, 60 hp or 65 hp Franklin engine, or 50 hp or 65 hp Lycoming engine; the PA-11 with 65 hp Continental; the J-4 series with 50 hp or 75 hp Continental; the J-5 series with 75 hp or 80 hp Continental or 75 hp Lycoming; ex-military (L-4) examples of the J-3, J-4 and J-5; the PA-12 Super Cruiser with 100 hp Lycoming; the PA-14 Family Cruiser with 115 hp Lycoming; the PA-15 Vagabond with 65 hp Lycoming and the PA-20 Pacer with 115 hp, 125 hp or 135 hp Lycoming engine. Military versions of the PA-18 were designated PA-19 by Piper.

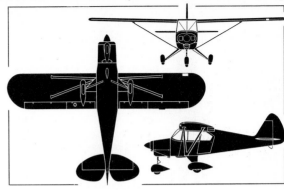

The photograph (above) depicts the PA-22 Colt, lowest-powered of the Tri-Pacer derivatives, and the silhouette (right) shows the PA-22-160 version

Country of Origin: USA.

Type: Private and club aircraft.

Power Plant: One (PA-22) 125 hp Lycoming O-290-D or (PA-22-108) 108 hp Lycoming O-235-C1B or (PA-22-135) 135 hp Lycoming O-290-D2 or (PA-22-150) 150 hp Lycoming O-320-A2A or (PA-22-160) 160 hp Lycoming O-320-B2A or B2B engine.

Performance: Max speed (-108), 120 mph (193 km/h), (-160), 141 mph (226 km/h); cruising speed (-108), 108 mph (174 km/h), (-160), 134 mph (214 km/h); initial rate of climb (-108), 610 ft/min (3,1 m/sec), (-160), 800 ft/min (4,1 m/sec); service ceiling, (-108), 12,000 ft (3 660 m), (-160), 16,500 ft (5 030 m); range with standard fuel (-108), 324 mls (520 km), (-160), 536 mls (863 km); range with max fuel (-108), 690 mls (1 110 km), (-160), 655 mls (1 055 km).

Weights: Empty (-108), 940 lb (426 kg), (-160), 1,110 lb (504 kg); max take-off (-108), 1,650 lb (748 kg), (-160), 2,000 lb (908 kg).

Dimensions: Span (-108), 30 ft 0 in (9,14 m), (-160), 29 ft $3\frac{1}{8}$ in (8,9 m); length, 20 ft 0 in (6,10 m), (-160), 20 ft $7\frac{1}{4}$ in (6,28 m); height (-108), 6 ft 3 in (1,90 m), (-160), 8 ft 4 in (2,54 m); wing area (-108), 147 sq ft (13,66 m²), (-160), 147·5 sq ft (13,7 m²).

Accommodation: (PA-22-108) Two seats side-by-side (other PA-22 models) Pilot and three passengers in enclosed cabin.

Status: Prototype first flown 1950. FAA Type Approvals, PA-22, 20 December 1950; PA-22-135, 5 May 1952; PA-22-150, 3 September 1954; PA-22-160, 27 August 1957; PA-22-108, 21 October 1960.

Notes: The Tri-Pacer, as the name suggested, was a tricycle under-carriage version of the PA-20 Pacer, and of the several thousand built many are still flying; they are the only high-wing Pipers with nosewheel gear. The 135, 150 and 160 hp versions of the Tri-Pacer were also certificated as seaplanes (PA-22S) with twin Edo floats, in which case only three persons could be accommodated. Skis could also be fitted to the nose and main wheel legs for snow and ice operations. In 1958, a version of the PA-22-150 was marketed as the Caribbean, at a lower price than the more fully equipped Tri-Pacer, and in 1961 a two-seat, 108 hp version of the basic PA-22 design was introduced as the Colt. This was the final member of the PA-22 family, some 1,600 being built by the time production ended in 1963.

PIPER PA-24 COMANCHE

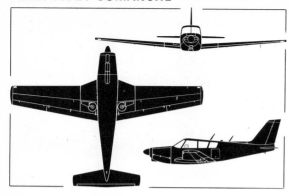

Shown in the photograph (above) is a 1960-model Comanche, representative of all versions; the silhouette (left) illustrates the final production version, PA-24-260

Country of Origin: USA.

Type: Private and light business aircraft.

Power Plant: One (PA-24) 180 hp Lycoming O-360-AIA or (-250) 250 hp Lycoming O-540-AIA or (-260) 260 hp Lycoming O-540-E4A5 or (Turbo C) 260 hp Lycoming IO-540-R1A5 or (-400) 400 hp Lycoming IO-720-AIA piston engine.

Performance: Max speed (-260), 195 mph (314 km/h), (Turbo C), 242 mph (389 km/h), (-400), 223 mph (359 km/h); max cruise (-260), 185 mph (298 km/h), (Turbo C), 228 mph (318 km/h), (-400), 213 mph (343 km/h); initial rate of climb (-260 and Turbo C), 1,320 ft/min (6,7 m/sec), (-400), 1,600 ft/min (8,1 m/sec); service ceiling (-260), 19,500 ft (5 945 m), (Turbo C), 25,000 ft (7 620 m), (-400), 19,500 ft (5 945 m); range with standard fuel (-260), 800 mls (1 285 km), (Turbo C), 975 mls (1 569 km), (-400), 1,250 mls (2 010 km); range with max fuel (-260), 1,225 mls (1 970 km), (Turbo C), 1,490 mls (2 398 km), (-400), 1,700 mls (2 735 km).

Weights: Empty (-260), 1,773 lb (804 kg), (Turbo C), 1,894 lb (859 kg), (-400), 2,110 lb (857 kg); max take-off (-260 and Turbo C), 3,200 lb (1 451 kg), (-400), 3,600 lb (1 633 kg).

Dimensions: Span, 36 ft 0 in (10,97 m); length (-260), 25 ft 0 in (7,62 m), (-400), 7 ft 10 in (2,39 m); wing area, 178 sq ft (16,53 m²).

Accommodation: Pilot and three passengers in enclosed cabin, with optional provision (in Comanche B and C models) for a third pair of seats.

Status: Prototype PA-24 first flown on 24 May 1956; first production aircraft flown on 21 October 1957. FAA Type Approvals, PA-24, 20 June 1957; PA-24-250, 18 April 1958; PA-24-260, 19 June 1964; PA-24-400, 27 December 1963.

Notes: The Comanche was the first of the Piper low-wing single-engined light aircraft to reach production status and well over 4,000 have been produced. The initial production model had a 180 hp engine but by 1964 the range had been extended to cover four models of different power, as outlined above and including a 400 hp model that was, at the time produced, the fastest single-engined four-seater in production. The Comanche B and C series included provision for a fifth and sixth seat, and in 1970 a turbosupercharged version of the Comanche C was added to the range. By 1973, all but the 260 hp Comanche C had ceased production.

The photograph shows the 1973 model Piper Cherokee "2+2" Cruiser and the silhouette (right) depicts the larger PA-28-235 Pathfinder

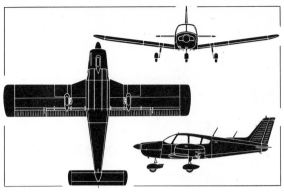

Country of Origin: USA.

Type: Private and club aircraft.

Power Plant: One (Cruiser and Warrior) 150 hp Lycoming O-320-E3D or (Archer) 180 hp Lycoming O-360-A3A or (Arrow II) 200 hp Lycoming IO-360-C1C or (Pathfinder) 235 hp Lycoming O-540-E4B5 piston engine.

Performance: Max cruising speed (Cruiser), 135 mph (217 km/h), (Arrow), 165 mph (266 km/h), (Pathfinder), 152 mph (245 km/h); best economy cruise (Cruiser), 115 mph (185 km/h); initial rate of climb (Cruiser), 631 ft/min (3,2 m/sec), (Arrow), 900 ft/min (4,6 m/sec), (Pathfinder), 800 ft/min (4,1 m/sec); service ceiling (Cruiser), 10,950 ft (3 340 m), (Arrow), 15,000 ft (4 575 m), (Pathfinder), 12,000 ft (3 665 m); range with max fuel (Cruiser), 780 mls (1 255 km), (Arrow), 900 mls (1 445 km), (Pathfinder), 1,066 mls (1 716 km).

Weights: Empty (Cruiser), 1,283 lb (582 kg), (Arrow), 1,499 lb (680 kg), (Pathfinder), 1,550 lb (703 kg); max take-off (Cruiser), 2,150 lb (975 kg), (Arrow), 2,650 lb (1 202 kg), (Pathfinder), 3,000 lb (1 360 kg).

Dimensions: Span (all), 32 ft 0 in (9,75 m); length (Cruiser), 23 ft 3½ in (7,10 m), (Arrow), 24 ft 7¼ in (7,50 m), (Pathfinder), 24 ft 1¼ in (7,35 m); height (Cruiser & Pathfinder), 7 ft 9¾ in (2,38 m); (Arrow), 8 ft 0 in (2,44 m); wing area (all), 170 sq ft (15,79 m²).

Accommodation: (Cruiser) Two side-by-side and rear seat for two children or one adult. (Flite Liner) two side-by-side, (Archer) pilot and three passengers, (Arrow II) pilot and three passengers, (Pathfinder) pilot and three passengers.

Status: Prototype PA-38 Cherokee first flown 1959; FAA Type Approval on 31 October 1960; first production Cherokee flown 10 February 1961. Total production, over 20,000 by 1974.

Notes: Versions include the original PA-28-160 Cherokee with 160 hp engine; the PA-28-140 Cherokee Cruiser with "2+2" seating and Flite Liner with only two seats, for club training use; the PA-28-180 full four seater with 180 hp engine, which was marketed as the Challenger in 1973 and the Archer in 1974; the PA-28-235 with 235 hp engine, known successively as the Charger and the Pathfinder; the PA-28-200R Arrow, similar to the Archer but with retractable undercarriage; and the PA-28-151 Warrior, similar in most respects to the Archer, but introducing a new wing, with tapered outer panels.

PIPER PA-32 CHEROKEE SIX

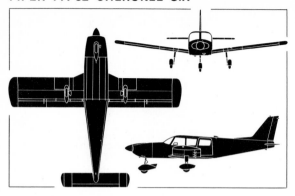

Largest of the Piper single-engined range in 1974, the Cherokee Six is used primarily as a light utility transport or family tourer

Country of Origin: USA.

Type: Tourer and light business aircraft.

Power Plant: One (PA-32-260) 260 hp Lycoming O-540-E or (PA-32-300 and PA-32S-300), 300 hp Lycoming IO-540-K piston engine.

Performance: Max speed (-260), 166 mph (267 km/h), (-300), 174 mph (279 km/h); cruise speed on 75 per cent engine power (-260), 158 mph (254 km/h), (-300), 168 mph (320 km/h); initial rate of climb (-260), 850 ft/min (4,3 m/sec), (-300), 1,050 ft/min (5,3 m/sec); service ceiling (-260), 14,500 ft (4 420 m), (-300), 16,250 ft (4 950 m); range with standard fuel (-260), 660 mls (1 062 km), (-300), 630 mls (1 015 km); range with max fuel (-260), 1,110 mls (1 786 km), (-300), 1,060 mls (1 705 km).

Weights: Empty (-260), 1,706 lb (774 kg), (-300), 1,799 lb (816 kg); max take-off (-260, -300), 3,400 lb (1 542 kg).

Dimensions: Span, 32 ft 9½ in (9,99 m); length, 27 ft 8¾ in (8,45 m); height, 7 ft 11 in (2,41 m); wing area, 174·5 sq ft (16,21 m²).

Accommodation: Pilot and five passengers with optional provision for sixth passenger seat in cabin.

Status: Prototype PA-32 first flown on 6 December 1963; first production model flown on 17 September 1964. FAA Type Approval, PA-32-260, 4 March 1965; PA-32-300, 27 May 1966; PA-32S-300, 14 February 1967. Production rate between 20 and 30 per month in 1973.

Notes: The Cherokee Six was evolved from the PA-28 Cherokee (see page 169) as a six-seat addition to the Piper range, becoming the largest of its single-engined types. It has the same general structure as the PA-28 but is larger overall and has a more extensive range of equipment available for optional installation. After an initial batch of PA-32s had been built as six-seaters with 260 hp engines, the cabin layout was revised to permit accommodation of a seventh occupant, and a second version was introduced, with 300 hp engines. The latter variant has also been certificated as a float-plane (PA-32S), using two Edo floats and a propeller of increased diameter. An optional feature is a large loading door, upwards hinged, to give access to the cabin from the rear; with the passenger seats removed, the Cherokee Six can carry a stretcher with one or two attendants, and has 110 cu ft (3,11 m³) space available in the cabin for cargo. The PA-34 (see page 119) was developed as a twin-engined derivative of the PA-32.

*Evolved from the original Jodel lightplane designs, the DR 1050
(photograph) and DR 221 Dauphine were built successively by
Centre Est and Avions Pierre Robin*

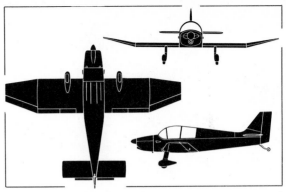

Country of Origin: France.

Type: Private and club aircraft.

Power Plant: One (DR 220) 100 hp R-R Continental O-200-A
or (DR 221) 115 hp Lycoming O-235-C2A or (DR 250) 150 hp
Lycoming O-320-A2B or 160 hp O-320-D2A piston engine.

Performance: Max cruising speed (DR 220), 125 mph (200 km/h),
(DR 221), 142 mph (229 km/h), (DR 250), 152 mph (245 km/h);
best economy cruise (DR 221), 130 mph (210 km/h), (DR 250),
155 mph (250 km/h); initial rate of climb (DR 220), 690 ft/min
(3,5 m/sec), (DR 221), 690 ft/min (3,5 m/sec), (DR 250), 780
ft/min (4,0 m/sec); service ceiling (DR 220), 13,125 ft (4 000 m),
(DR 221), 13,125 ft (4 000 m), (DR 250), 16,400 ft (5 000 m);
range with max fuel (DR 220), 600 mls (966 km), (DR 221), 565
mls (910 km), (DR 250), 1,000 mls (1 600 km).

Weights: Empty (DR 220), 970 lb (440 kg), (DR 250), 1,100 lb
(500 kg); max take-off (DR 220), 1,720 lb (780 kg), (DR 221),
1,830 lb (830 kg), (DR 250), 2,120 lb (960 kg).

Dimensions: Span, 28 ft $7\frac{1}{4}$ in (8,72 m); length (DR 220), 22 ft
8 in (6,90 m), (DR 221), 22 ft $9\frac{1}{2}$ in (6,95 m), (DR 250), 22 ft
$10\frac{3}{4}$ in (6,98 m); height, 6 ft 2 in (1,88 m); wing area, 146·4 sq ft

(13,60 m²).

Accommodation: Two side-by-side plus (DR 220) provision for
two children on rear bench seat or (DR 221) provision for one adult
or two children on rear seat or (DR 250) two passengers.

Status: Prototype DR 250 first flown on 2 April 1965. Prototype
DR 220 first flown on 5 February 1966. Prototype DR 221 first
flown on 18 February 1967. Production totals, DR 250, 102; DR
220/220A, 84; DR 221, 62.

Notes: The Avions Pierre Robin company was formed in 1957 (as
Centre Est Aéronautique) to develop and produce light aircraft
designed by Jean Delemontez (see page 153), based on the Jodel
wing. The first product was the DR 100, and the DR 1050/DR 1051
Ambassadeur, Sicile and Sicile Record production versions, about
330 of which were built. These three-seaters were followed by the
similar DR 250 Capitaine described above, which became the basic
four-seater of the company's range, being followed by the DR
220/DR 220A "2+2" and the DR 221 Dauphin. The DR 220A
differed from the DR 220 in having a strengthened airframe and
different landing gear. Derivatives of this same basic design with a
nosewheel undercarriage are described on the next page.

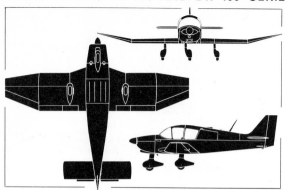

Introduction of a nosewheel landing gear by Avions Pierre Robin distinguished such Jodel derivatives as the DR 380 Prince (photograph) and DR 253 Regent (silhouette)

Country of Origin: France.

Type: Private and club aircraft.

Power Plant: One (DR 300/108, DR 400/2+2) 108 hp Lycoming O-235-C2A, (DR 315) 115 hp O-235-C2A, (DR 300/125, 400/125) 125 hp O-235-F2B, (DR 300/140, DR 340, DR 400/125) 140 hp Lycoming O-320-E, (DR 300/180, DR 380, DR 400/180) 180 hp Lycoming O-360-A, (DR 360, DR 400/160) 160 hp O-360-E piston engine.

Performance: Max cruising speed (300/108), 162 mph (295 km/h), (400/180), 164 mph (265 km/h); best economy cruise (300/108), 134 mph (215 km/h), (400/180), 155 mph (249 km/h); initial rate of climb (300/108), 689 ft/min (3,5 m/sec), (400/180), 825 ft/min (4,2 m/sec); service ceiling (300/108), 13,125 ft (4 000 m), (400/180), 20,000 ft (6 100 m); range with max fuel (300/108), 574 mls (925 km), (400/180), 913 mls (1 470 km).

Weights: Empty (300/108), 1,102 lb (500 kg), (400/180), 1,301 lb (590 kg); max take-off (300/108), 1,851 lb (840 kg), (400/180), 2,425 lb (1 100 kg).

Dimensions: Span (all), 28 ft 7¼ in (8,72 m); length (300/108), 22 ft 10 in (6,96 m), (400/180), 23 ft 6¾ in (7,18 m); height (all),

7 ft 3¾ in (2,23 m); wing area (all), 146·4 sq ft (13,60 m²).

Accommodation: (300/108, 400/2+2) Two side-by-side and provision for two children in rear seat or (300/125, 400/125) two side-by-side and provision for one adult or two children on rear seat or (DR 400/180) pilot and up to four passengers or (others) pilot and three passengers.

Status: Prototype DR 253 flown on 30 March 1967; first production on 16 June 1967; prototype 300/108 flown 29 May 1970; 300/125 flown June 1970; 300/140 flown 25 March 1970; 300/180R flown 28 May 1970; DR 315 flown 31 March 1968; DR 340 flown on 27 February 1968; DR 360 flown on 27 March 1968; DR 380 flown on 15 October 1968; DR 400/125 and /180 flown June 1972, 400/180R, November 1972. Production totals, DR 253, 93; DR 300 variants, 130; DR 340, 60; DR 360, 24; DR 380, 22; DR 400 series, over 160 to end of 1973.

Notes: Names of these types are: DR 300 and 400/125, Petit Prince, DR 300/140, l'Acrobat; DR 300/180R and 400/180R, Remorqueur (glider tug); DR 315 Cadet; DR 340 and 400/140, Major; DR 360, Major 160, DR 380, Prince, DR 400/160, Chevalier and DR 400/180, Régent.

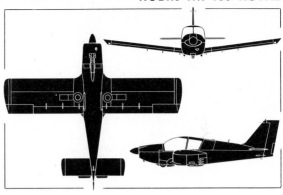

The photograph (above) illustrates an early-production Robin HR.100/210 and the more powerful HR.100/320 with retractable undercarriage is shown in the silhouette (right)

Country of Origin: France.

Type: Private and club aircraft.

Power Plant: One (200) 200 hp Lycoming IO-360-A1D6 or (210F and 210R) 210 hp Continental IO-360-D or (235) 235 hp Lycoming O-540 or (320) 320 hp Teledyne Continental Tiara 6-320 piston engine.

Performance: Max cruising speed (200), 155 mph (250 km/h), (210F), 158 mph (254 km/h), (320), 199 mph (320 km/h) ; initial rate of climb (200), 1,004 ft/min (5,1 m/sec), (210F), 1,000 ft/min (5,1 m/sec), (310), 1,770 ft/min (9 m/sec) ; service ceiling (200), 16,725 ft (5 100 m), (210F), 16,400 ft (5 000 m), (320), over 19,700 ft (6 000 m) ; range with standard fuel (200), 750 mls (1 210 km), (210F), 850 mls (1 370 km) ; range with max fuel (200), 1,590 mls (2 560 km), (210F), 1,675 mls (2 700 km), (320), 1,430 mls (2 300 km).

Weights: Empty (200), 1,543 lb (700 kg), (210F), 1,565 lb (710 kg), (320), 1,764 lb (800 kg) ; max take-off (200), 2,645 lb (1 200 kg), (210F), 2,755 lb (1 250 kg), (320), 3,086 lb (1 400 kg).

Dimensions: Span, 29 ft 9½ in (9,08 m) ; length (200), 24 ft 1 in (7,34 m), (210F), 24 ft 3 in (7,39 m), (320), 24 ft 10¾ in (7,59 m) ;

height, 7 ft 5 in (2,26 m) ; wing area, 163·6 sq ft (15,2 m²).

Accommodation: Pilot and three passengers in enclosed cabin.

Status: Prototype first flown on 3 April 1969 ; prototype 210F first flown 8 April 1971 ; prototype 320 first flown November 1972 ; prototype 235R first flown 6 March 1974.

Notes: The HR100 series of aircraft was designed by Christophe Heintz, marking a break in the Robin association with Delmontez, designer of the original Jodel light aircraft. A prototype was built as the HR1 and this aircraft, together with three pre-production examples had the 180 hp Lycoming engine. The initial production batch of HR.100/200s had a 200 hp engine, about 30 being built before the HR 100/210 became the standard version in 1973. This was produced primarily in the 210F version with fixed nosewheel undercarriage but a 235R retractable version was also being offered in 1974. The retractable gear was first flown on the HR.100/320, sometimes known as the Tiara, and this version was being prepared for production in 1974. A 180 hp version of the fixed-gear Royal has also been planned by Robin for introduction in 1975, and a six-seat HR 100/4+2 was expected to fly in 1974, with 320 hp Tiara engine.

ROBIN HR 200 CLUB AND ACROBIN

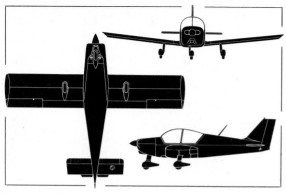

Smaller and cheaper than the HR.100 (previous page), the HR.200 is available in fully-aerobatic and club variants, as illustrated by the photograph and silhouette

Country of Origin: France.
Type: Private and club aircraft.
Power Plant: One (Club) 108 hp Lycoming O-235-C2A or (Acrobin) 125 hp Lycoming O-235 or 160 hp Lycoming IO-320 piston engine.
Performance: Max speed (Club), 143 mph (230 km/h), (Acrobin 160), 169 mph (272 km/h); max cruise (Club), 133 mph (215 km/h), (Acrobin 160), 154 mph (248 km/h); initial rate of climb (Club) 670 ft/min (3,4 m/sec), (Acrobin 160), 1,278 ft/min (6,5 m/sec); service ceiling, 13,000 ft (3 962 m), (Acrobin 160), 19,700 ft (6 000 m); range with max fuel (Club), 670 mls (1 078 km), (Acrobin 160), 540 mls (870 km).
Weights: Empty (Club), 1,102 lb (500 kg), (Acrobin 160), 1,150 lb (520 kg); max take-off (Club), 1,670 lb (760 kg), (Acrobin 160), 1,750 lb (800 kg).
Dimensions: Span, 27 ft 6½ in (8,40 m); length, 21 ft 11 in (6,68 m); height, 7 ft 1¾ in (2,18 m); wing area, 135·6 sq ft (12,6 m²).
Accommodation: Pilot and passenger side-by-side in enclosed cabin.
Status: Prototype (Club) first flown on 29 July 1971; first pro-

duction (Club) flown on 16 April 1973. First Acrobin-125 and Acrobin-160 flown in May 1973.
Notes: Second of the all-metal light aircraft designed by Christophe Heintz for production by Robin, the HR 200 was evolved specifically for flying club and school use, with full aerobatic capability. The basic version, sometimes referred to as the HR200/100, has a 108 hp engine in its production form and has been named Club, as it is not suitable for the full range of aerobatics on this power. The HR200/125 and the fully-aerobatic HR200/160 are named the Acrobin, and production in 1974 was concerned only with the latter version, together with the Club. An unusual feature of the HR200 is that the one-piece canopy over the seats slides forwards to allow access to the cabin. The standard version has a bench seat for the two occupants but individual seats are available as an option, and there is provision for 55 lb (25 kg) of baggage behind the seats. Despite the fixed landing gear, the Club and Acrobin have a very high performance for aircraft of their weight class, and have helped the Robin company to maintain a leading position among light aircraft manufacturers, following their success with design based on the Jodel wing.

Sport and touring aircraft

The photograph (above) shows a 1974 model Rockwell Commander 112A and the silhouette (right) also depicts the basic Model 112 with retractable landing gear

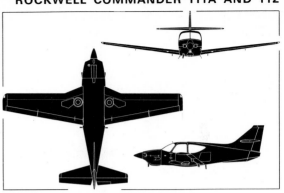

Country of Origin: USA.

Type: Private and club aircraft.

Power Plant: One (111A) 180 hp Lycoming IO-360-A1CG or (112) 200 hp Lycoming IO-360-C1DG.

Performance (112A): Max speed, 170 mph (274 km/h); max cruise, 162 mph (261 km/h) at 7,500 ft (2 285 m) at 75 per cent max power; initial rate of climb, 890 ft/min (4,5 m/sec); service ceiling, 16,000 ft (4 875 m); range with max fuel, 1,180 mls (1 900 km).

Weights (112A): Empty, 1,413 lb (641 kg); max take-off, 2,650 lb (1 202 kg).

Dimensions: Span, 32 ft 10¾ in (10,03 m); length, 25 ft 0 in (7,62 m); height, 8 ft 5 in (2,57 m); wing area, 152 sq ft (14,12 m²).

Accommodation: Pilot and three passengers in two pairs of seats in enclosed cabin.

Status: Prototype Model 112 first flown on 4 December 1970, followed by four more prototypes for test and certification. Prototype Model 111 first flown on 11 September 1971. FAA Type Approval, mid-1972. Production deliveries (112) began mid-1972. Production total, Model 112, 115 by January 1974; Model 112A, pro-

duction continuing at about 10 per month.

Notes: The Model 112 was the first totally new light aircraft evolved by the Rockwell company, following its acquisition of the Aero Commander company and merger with North American. As a high-performance four-seater it was designed to compete with such types as the Cessna Cardinal RG, Piper Cherokee Arrow and Beechcraft Sierra 200. Maximum attention was placed upon comfort, leading to a wider-than-average cabin at some cost to maximum and cruising speeds. Flight testing and evaluation took rather longer than usual for a light plane, since the design was completely unrelated to any previous type, and was delayed by the loss of one of the prototypes in October 1971 due to tailplane flutter in a high speed dive. Certification was held up until a modified rear fuselage structure and elevator tab control system had been tested and incorporated in 45 aircraft already completed. The prototype Model 112s were powered by 180 hp engines but the 200 hp unit was adopted for production 112s and (1974 model) 112As, the lower powered engine remaining standard for the Model 111A, which differed in having a fixed nose-wheel undercarriage. Production of the Model 111A had not begun by mid-1974.

SCHEIBE SF-25 FALKE, SF-28, SF-29

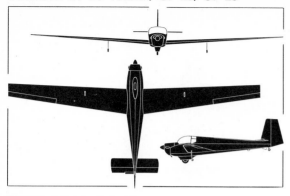

The silhouette (left) shows a Scheibe SF-25 Falke motor-glider and the photograph (above) depicts a Slingsby T.61A Falcon, the license-built version

Country of Origin: Federal Germany.

Type: Powered sailplane.

Power Plant: One (SF-25B and SF-28) 45 hp Stamo MS 1500 or (SF-25C, SF-28A), 60 hp Sportavia-Limbach SL 1700 EA or (SF-29) 30 hp Hirth O-17 piston engine.

Performance: Max speed (SF-25B, SF-29), 100 mph (160 km/h), (SF-25C, SF-28A), 112 mph (180 km/h); cruising speed (SF-25C, SF-28A), 100 mph (160 km/h), (SF-29), 87 mph (140 km/h); initial rate of climb (SF-25B, SF-29), 400 ft/min (2,0 m/sec), (SF-25C), 433 ft/min (2,2 m/sec); service ceiling (SF-25C, SF-28A), 16,400 ft (5 000 m); range (SF-25B), 220 mls (350 km), (SF-25C), 372 mls (600 km), (SF-28A), 311 mls (500 km), (SF-29), 186 mls (300 km).

Weights: Empty (SF-25B), 739 lb (335 kg), (SF-25C), 826 lb (375 kg), (SF-28A), 882 lb (400 kg), (SF-29), 573 lb (260 kg); max take-off (SF-25B), 1,168 lb (530 kg), (SF-25C), 1,278 lb (580 kg), (SF-28A), 1,300 lb (590 kg), (SF-29), 816 lb (370 kg).

Dimensions: Span (SF-25B), 50 ft $0\frac{1}{4}$ in (15,25 m), (SF-28A), 53 ft $5\frac{3}{4}$ in (16,30 m), (SF-29), 49 ft $2\frac{1}{2}$ in (15,00 m); length (SF-25B), 24 ft $10\frac{1}{2}$ in (7,58 m), (SF-28A), 26 ft 9 in (8,15 m),

(SF-29), 22 ft $1\frac{1}{2}$ in (6,75 m); height (SF-25B, 26C, 28A), 5 ft $0\frac{1}{4}$ in (1,53 m), (SF-29), 4 ft 3 in (1,30 m); wing area (SF-25B), 188·5 sq ft (17,50 m²), (SF-28A), 197·5 sq ft (18,35 m²), (SF-29), 134·5 sq ft (12,50 m²).

Accommodation: (SF-25B, C) Two side-by-side or (SF-28, 28A) two in tandem or (SF-29) pilot only in enclosed cockpit.

Status: Production totals include more than 250 SF-25B by Scheibe and 80 by Sportavia in Germany and 35 by Slingsby in UK; over 50 SF-25C by Scheibe and 20 by Sportavia; about 20 SF-28 by 1973.

Notes: Scheibe was one of the first companies to popularise the motor glider with its SF-24 Motorspatz. This was followed by the even more successful SF-25 Falke (Falcon), which has been built by two companies in Germany and one in the UK (Slingsby, as the T.61). The SF-25C differs from the SF-25B in having a more powerful engine, and the SF-28 and SF-28A are respectively equivalent to the SF-25B and SF-25C but with tandem seating. The SF-29, first flown in 1973, is a further variant of the same design, being a single-seater of lower weight and power.

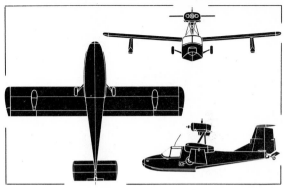

Both photograph and silhouette depict the Schweizer (originally Thurston) Teal II, the former showing how the main wheels remain exposed when retracted for water operation

Country of Origin: USA.

Type: Private sporting amphibian.

Power Plant: One 150 hp Lycoming O-320-A3B piston engine.

Performance: Max speed, 120 mph (193 km/h); max cruise, 116 mph (187 km/h); best economy cruise, 110 mph (177 km/h); initial rate of climb, 650 ft/min (3,3 m/sec); service ceiling, 12,000 ft (3 660 m); range with standard fuel, 472 mls (759 km); range with max fuel, 748 mls (1 203 km).

Weights: Empty, 1,435 lb (651 kg); max take-off, 2,200 lb (998 kg).

Dimensions: Span, 31 ft 11 in (9,73 kg); length, 23 ft 7 in (7,19 m); height, 9 ft 5 in (2,87 m); wing area, 157 sq ft (14,59 m²).

Accommodation: Two side-by-side in enclosed cockpit.

Status: Prototype first flown in June 1968. FAA Type Approval, 28 August 1969. Production, 15 TSC-1A Teal I, about 8 TSC-1A1, about 20 TSC-1A2 built or on order up to 1974.

Notes: The Teal is one of the few light amphibians in production and examples are in use in several parts of the world, including Hawaii, Finland, Canada, Ivory Coast, Australia, the USA and the UK. The design was developed by David Thurston, who had previously been responsible for the Lake LA-4 and Colonial Skimmer (see page 155) and was originally produced by Thurston Aircraft Corp. A batch of 15 Model TSC-1A amphibians was built by Thurston, and then a series of modifications was introduced in the TSC-1A1, including new fuel tanks in the wing leading edges, an optional tank in the hull, and independent tailwheel retraction. Production of this model continued for a time after the Thurston company had been acquired by Schweizer Aircraft early in 1972, but ended during 1973 in favour of the improved TSC-1A2 Teal II version. The latter, first flown in October 1972, had increased gross weight and slotted trailing-edge flaps. The Teal II is designed with the needs of the sportsman pilot particularly in mind—for example, the back of the seat folds down to provide access to the baggage compartment and to allow the occupant to stand comfortably in the cabin when fishing. The main wheels and legs do not retract but merely swing up to clear the hull during water operations; oddly, the drag increases when the wheels are up and the Teal is 3 mph (4,8 km/h) faster with the wheels down that with the gear retracted. A pure 'boat version of the Teal has been projected as the TSC-1 T-Boat.

SIAI-MARCHETTI S.205 AND S.208

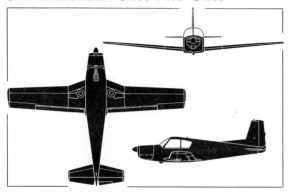

Shown in the photograph (above) is the SIAI-Marchetti S.205/F with fixed landing gear while the silhouette (left) depicts the S.205/20R with retractable undercarriage

Country of Origin: Italy.

Type: Private and club aircraft.

Power Plant: One (S.205-18) 180 hp Lycoming O-360-AIA or (S.205-20) 200 hp Lycoming IO-360-AIA or (S.205-22) 220 hp Franklin 6A-350-C1 or (S.208) 206 hp Lycoming O-540-E9A5 piston engine.

Performance: Max speed (-18F), 146 mph (235 km/h), (-22R), 183 mph (295 km/h), (S.208), 199 mph (320 km/h); max cruise (-18F), 134 mph (215 km/h), (-22R), 175 mph (281 km/h), (S.208), 187 mph (300 km/h); initial rate of climb (-18F), 690 ft/min (3,5 m/sec), (-22R), 1,160 ft/min (5,9 m/sec); service ceiling (18F), 14,750 ft (4 500 m), (22R), 20,330 ft (6 200 m); range with max payload (18F), 765 mls (1 230 km), (22R), 823 mls (1 325 km); range with max internal fuel (S.208), 746 mls (1 200 km); range with max fuel, including tip tanks (S.208), 1,250 mls (2 000 km).

Weights: Empty (18F), 1,565 lb (710 kg), (22R), 1,635 lb (750 kg), (S.208), 1,720 lb (780 kg); max take-off (18F), 2,645 lb (1 200 kg), (22R), 2,976 lb (1 750 kg), (S.208), 3,307 lb (1 500 kg).

Dimensions: Span (all), 35 ft $7\frac{1}{2}$ in (10,86 m); length (all), 26 ft 3 in (8,00 m); height (all), 9 ft $5\frac{3}{4}$ in (2,89 m); wing area (all), 173 sq ft (16,09 m²).

Accommodation: Pilot and (S.205) three or (S.208) four passengers in enclosed cabin.

Status: Three prototypes completed 1964/65. First production model flown February 1966. First S.208 flown on 22 May 1967. Production totals, nearly 500 S.205s of all variants; nearly 100 S.208s by 1974.

Notes: The S.205 was an original design by the SIAI-Marchetti company, intended to provide a basis for the company to re-enter the light aircraft market. The prototypes were powered by 180 hp Lycoming engines but production models were offered with three choices of power plant as indicated above. They also provided an option between fixed or retractable landing gear, indicated by F or R as a designation suffix. Production of the S.205 series ended in 1972, and included 62 airframes assembled in the US as Waco S.220 Velas. The S.208 was a derivative of the S.205, with the same wing but a modified cabin, more powerful engine and stronger structure.

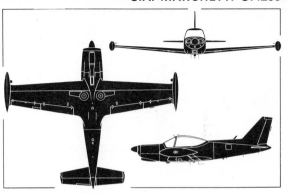

The photograph (above) illustrates a SIAI-Marchetti SF.260 operated by the Sabena pilot training school in Belgium and the silhouette (right) shows the standard version

Country of Origin: Italy.

Type: Private and club aircraft.

Power Plant: One 260 hp Lycoming O-540-E4A5 piston engine.

Performance: Max speed, 235 mph (375 km/h); max cruising speed, 214 mph (345 km/h) at 10,000 ft (3 050 m); initial rate of climb, 1,770 ft/min (9,0 m/sec); service ceiling, 21,370 ft (6 500 m); range with max fuel, 1,275 mls (2 050 km).

Weights: Empty, 1,543 lb (700 kg); max take-off (utility), 2,430 lb (1 102 kg), (aerobatic), 2,205 lb (1 000 kg).

Dimensions: Span, 26 ft 11¾ in (8,25 m); length, 23 ft 0 in (7,02 m); height, 8 ft 6 in (2,60 m); wing area, 108·5 sq ft (10,10 m²).

Accommodation: Two seats side-by-side and third seat in rear for one adult or two children.

Status: Prototype (F.250) first flown on 15 July 1964 FAA Type Approval (SF.260), 1 April 1966. Production total, over 100 (to 1974).

Notes: This attractive light aircraft is one of a series of designs by Dott Ing Stelio Frati, who has been responsible for several outstanding aircraft in this category since World War II. It is distinguished by the one-piece rearward sliding canopy, giving excellent all-round view, and wing-tip fuel tanks. The prototype was built by Aviamilano and had a 250 hp Lycoming engine; production was handled by SIAI-Marchetti, the designation changing to SF-260 and the engine being uprated to 260 hp, as indicated by the designation change. In addition to its use as a high performance club and touring aircraft, the SF-260 has been adopted by Air France and Sabena for use at their pilot training schools, and also provided the basis for the SF.260M military trainer and light attack aircraft (see *Military* volume, page 198). The high performance of the SF-260 is indicated by its record-breaking ability, two closed-circuit records in the FAI Class C-1-b having been set up with flights made in California in 1969 with speeds of 200·4 mph (322,52 km/h) over 1,000 km and 229·6 mph (369,43 km/h) over 100 km. Following production of two batches of SF.260s to the initial production standard and with the characteristics described here, SIAI-Marchetti put in hand a further batch of 50 during 1973, incorporating structural and aerodynamic improvements that had been evolved for the SF.260M. These include a revised wing leading edge profile to improve the handling at the stall and various improvements to the flight controls.

SPORTAVIA AVION-PLANEUR RF4 AND RF5

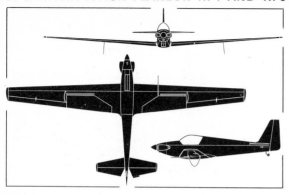

Both the single-seat Sportavia RF4 and two-seat RF5 are shown in the photograph (above) and the silhouette (left) depicts the single-seat RF4D

Country of Origin: Federal Germany.

Type: Sporting powered sailplane.

Power Plant: One (RF4D) 40 hp Rectimo-converted VW or (RF5 and RF5B) 68 hp Sportavia-Limbach SL 1700E Comet piston engine.

Performance: Max cruising speed (RF4D), 112 mph (180 km/h), (RF5), 118 mph (190 km/h), (RF5B), 109 mph (175 km/h); best economy cruise (RF4D), 100 mph (160 km/h), (RF5 and 5B), 75 mph (120 km/h); initial rate of climb (RF4D), 690 ft/min (3,5 m/sec), (RF5), 590 ft/min (3,0 m/sec), (RF5B), 630 ft/min (3,2 m/sec); service ceiling (RF4D), 19,700 ft (6 000 m), (RF5), 19,675 ft/min (6 000 m), (RF5B), 18,050 ft (5 500 m); range with max fuel (RF-4D), 422 mls (680 km), (RF5), 472 mls (760 km), (RF5B), 260 mls (420 km).

Weights: Empty (RF4D), 584 lb (265 kg), (RF5), 921 lb (418 kg), (RF5B), 1,014 lb (460 kg); max take-off (RF4D), 859 lb (390 kg), (RF5), 1,455 lb (660 kg); (RF5B), 1,499 lb (680 kg).

Dimensions: Span (RF4D), 36 ft 11¼ in (11,26 m), (RF5), 45 ft 1 in (13,74), (RF5B), 55 ft 10 in (17,02 m); length (RF4D), 19 ft 10¼ in (6,05 m), (RF5), 25 ft 7¼ in (7,80 m), (RF5B), 25 ft 3½ in (7,71 m); height (RF4D), 5 ft 1¾ in (1,57 m), (RF5 and 5B), 6 ft 5 in (1,96 m); wing area (RF4D), 121·7 sq ft (11,30 m²), (RF5), 163·2 sq ft (15,16 m²), (RF5B), 204·5 sq ft (19,00 m²).

Accommodation: (RF4) Pilot only or (RF5 and RF5B) two in tandem.

Status: Prototype Avion-Planeur RF101 first flown 6 July 1960. Prototype RF5 first flown in January 1968; first RF5B flown in May 1971. Production includes 95 RF3, 160 RF4D, 120 RF5 and 30 RF5B.

Notes: The RF4 and RF5 are among the most successful of aircraft in the motor-glider category, being in essence sailplanes with a small engine which makes them independent of tows for take-off and to give extended duration of flight. The design originated in 1960 in France as the RF01, developed by Rene Fournier and called the Avion-Planeur. The RF2 and RF3 were produced in France by Alpavia and responsibility for the Avion-Planeur series was then transferred to Sportavia in Germany. The RF5 is basically a two-seat version of the RF4, and the RF5B has improved performance; a further derivative of the RF5B is the RF55 with a 60 hp Franklin 2A-120-A.

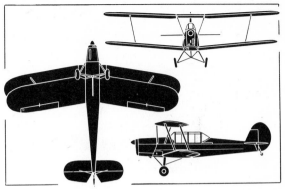

The silhouette (right) shows a standard Stampe S.V.4C and the photograph (above) depicts an example modified as a single-seater for use by the Tiger Club

Country of Origin: Belgium.

Type: Sporting biplane.

Power Plant: One (S.V.4B) 130 hp de Havilland Gipsy Major 10 or (S.V.4C) 140 hp Renault 4 Pei or (S.V.4D) 145 hp R-R/Continental IO-340-A or (S.V.4L) 152 hp Lycoming O-320-E2A piston, engine.

Performance: Max speed (S.V.4B), 122 mph (200 km/h), (S.V.4C), 127 mph (204 km/h); cruise speed (S.V.4B), 105 mph (169 km/h), (S.V.4C), 109 mph (175 km/h); service ceiling (S.V.4B), 18,000 ft (5 500 m), (S.V.4C), 16,400 ft (5 000 m).

Weights: Empty equipped (S.V.4B), 1,056 lb (480 kg), (S.V.4C), 1,104 lb (500 kg); max take-off (S.V.4B and S.V.4C), 1,716 lb (780 kg).

Dimensions: Span, 27 ft 6 in (8,38 m); length, 22 ft 10 in (6,96 m); height, 9 ft 1 in (2,77 m); wing area, 194·3 sq ft (18,03 m²).

Accommodation: Two in tandem in open cockpits.

Status: Prototype S.V.4 first flown in 1933. Pre-war production followed by production of 65 S.V.4Bs post-war in Belgium; total of 700 S.V.4Cs built in France by Nord post-war.

Notes: The Stampe biplane, which became a well-known mount for aerobatic displays in many parts of the world in the 'sixties, originated in Belgium in 1933, having been designed by Jean Stampe, who was the Belgian agent for de Havilland. The original S.V.4 showed signs of the influence of de Havilland design practice, and was comparable in performance to the D.H.82 Tiger Moth. It was adopted by the Belgian and French air forces and large-scale production began to meet these and other orders, but was halted when Belgium was occupied. Between 1944 and 1946, Nord built 700 S.V.4Cs in France, primarily for use by the Armée de l'Air and French flying clubs, and Jean Stampe then formed the Stampe et Renard company in Belgium to complete an order for 65 for the Belgian Air Force, the latter aircraft differing from all previous versions in having enclosed cockpits. Many ex-French and ex-Belgian aircraft eventually passed into use with flying clubs and private owners, and several were modified for special aerobatic displays, usually as single seaters. In particular, Stampes equipped the widely-admired Rothmans Aerobatic Team when it was first formed in the UK. The S.V.4D was a single prototype developed by Stampe et Renard and the S.V.4L was a single converted airframe in France, both these aircraft having new power plants.

WASSMER WA 40 SUPER IV, WA 41 BALADOU

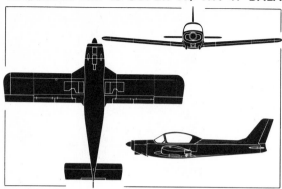

Shown in the silhouette (left) is the Wassmer WA 40A Sancy with retractable undercarriage and the photograph (above) illustrates the fixed-gear WA 41 Baladou

Country of Origin: France.

Type: Private and club aircraft.

Power Plant: One 180 hp Lycoming (WA 40) O-360-A1A or (WA 41) O-360-A2A piston engine.

Performance: Max cruising speed (WA 40), 165 mph (265 km/h), (WA 41), 149 mph (240 km/h); best economy cruise (WA 40), 155 mph (250 km/h), initial rate of climb (WA 40), 985 ft/min (5,0 m/sec), (WA 41), 787 ft/min (4,0 m/sec); service ceiling (WA 40), 18,040 ft (5 500 m), range with max fuel (WA 40), 775 mls (1 250 km), (WA 41), 826 mls (1 330 km).

Weights: Empty (WA 40), 1,433 lb (650 kg), (WA 41), 1,565 lb (710 kg); max take-off (WA 40 and WA 41), 2,645 lb (1 200 kg).

Dimensions: Span (all), 32 ft 9½ in (10,0 m); length (all), 24 ft 11¼ in (7,60 m); height (WA 40), 8 ft 6 in (2,60 m), (WA 41), 9 ft 5 in (2,86 m); wing area (all), 172 sq ft (16,0 m²).

Accommodation: Pilot and three or four passengers in enclosed cabin.

Status: Prototype (WA 40) first flown on 8 June 1959; French type approval 9 June 1960. First WA 40A flown in January 1963; French type approval 4 March 1963. Prototype WA 41 flown in March 1965.

Production totals: WA 40, 2 prototypes plus 50, WA 40A, 128; WA 41, over 60.

Notes: The Wassmer company, founded in 1905 and concerned for many years with the production of propellers and aircraft repairs and maintenance, set up a design department in 1955. Its first product was a variant of the Jodel design (see page 153), the D.120 Paris Nice, and more than 300 Jodel types were built by the company. The first original design was the WA 40 Super IV, a conventional low-wing monoplane with retractable nosewheel landing gear, manually operated. After the first production batch of 50 had been completed, the WA 40A emerged, with a swept-back fin and rudder, optional electrical operation of the landing gear and other refinements. To distinguish between equipment standards, names were adopted as suffixes to Super IV, being Pariou for the basic model, Baladou for the de luxe standard and Sancy for the IFR-equipped version. The WA 41 Baladou was introduced in 1965 and differed from the WA 40A primarily in having a fixed landing gear. The type was further developed into the WA 4/21 (see page 138), and also provided Wassmer with the basis for developing the all-plastics WA 50 series (page 183).

Of all-plastics construction, the Wassmer WA 51 Pacific (photograph and silhouette) and its related WA 52 and WA 54 have been in production since 1971

Country of Origin: France.
Type: Private and club aircraft.
Power Plant: One (WA 51) 150 hp Lycoming O-320-E2A or (WA 52) 160 hp IO-320 or (WA 54) 180 hp Lycoming O-360 piston engine.
Performance: Max speed (WA 51), 146 mph (235 km/h), (WA 54), 174 mph (280 km/h); cruising speed (WA 51), 138 mph (222 km/h), (WA 52), 155 mph (250 km/h), (WA 54), 161 mph (260 km/h); initial rate of climb (WA 51), 787 ft/min (4,0 m/sec), (WA 54), 1,375 ft/min (7,0 m/sec); service ceiling (WA 51), 14,450 ft (4 400 m); range with max fuel (WA 51), 565 mls (910 km), (WA 52, WA 54), 870 mls (1 400 km).
Weights: Empty (WA 51), 1,320 lb (600 kg), (WA 52), 1,344 lb 610 kg), (WA 54), 1,356 lb (615 kg); max take-off (WA 51), 2,292 lb (1 040 kg), (WA 52), 2,380 lb (1 080 kg), (WA 54), 2,447 lb (1 110 kg).
Dimensions: Span (all), 30 ft 10 in (9,40 m); length (WA 51, WA 52), 23 ft 11½ in (7,30 m), (WA 54), 24 ft 3½ in (7,40 m); height (all), 7 ft 5 in (2,26 m); wing area (all versions), 40·68 sq ft (12,40 m²).

WASSMER WA 51, WA 52, WA 54

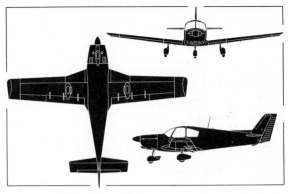

Accommodation: Pilot and three passengers in two pairs of seats in enclosed cabin.
Status: Prototype (WA 50) first flown on 22 March 1966; first WA 51 flown on 17 May 1969; WA 52 deliveries began 1971; first WA 54 flown 20 February 1973. Production, 100 of all three variants delivered by 18 January 1974, with production continuing at 4–5 per month.
Notes: The WA 50 prototype was a departure from previous Wassmer tradition in that the airframe structure was wholly constructed in plastics material. Its development was officially sponsored, and after thorough flight and static testing the design was put into production as the WA 51 Pacific. Whereas the WA 50 had a retractable landing gear, the production article had a fixed and spatted undercarriage and other small modifications, whilst retaining the 150 hp Lycoming engine as used in the prototype in 1971, the WA 51A replaced the WA 51 in production, with various improvements. The WA 52 Europa or Trans-Pacific and WA 54 Atlantic differ from the WA 51 primarily in having progressive increases of engine power and featuring variable pitch propellers. The WA 54 also features revised main gear and improved nosewheel steering.

WINDECKER AC-7 EAGLE

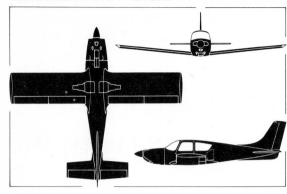

Both the photograph and the silhouette show the Windecker Eagle 1, the former showing the third prototype in production configuration

Country of Origin: USA.

Type: Private and light business aircraft.

Power Plant: One 285 hp Continental IO-520-C flat-six piston engine.

Performance: Max speed, 211 mph (340 km/h); max cruising speed, 207 mph (333 km/h); initial rate of climb, 1,220 ft/min (6,2 m/sec); service ceiling, 18,000 ft (5 475 m); range with max fuel, 1,232 mls (1 982 km).

Weights: Empty, 2,150 lb (975 kg); max take-off and landing, 3,400 lb (1 542 kg).

Dimensions: Span, 32 ft 0½ in (9,76 m); length, 28 ft 6¾ in (8,70 m); height, 9 ft 7 in (2,92 m), wing area, 167 sq ft (15,51 m²).

Accommodation: Pilot and three passengers in two pairs of seats in enclosed cabin.

Status: Prototype Windecker all-plastics aircraft first flown on 7 October 1967; prototype Eagle flown on 26 January 1969; second prototype flown on 29 September 1969; FAA Type Approval 18 December 1969; first delivery 7 October 1970. Production total to end 1973, seven.

Notes: The Windecker Eagle is the outgrowth of a research programme in the use of reinforced plastics for structural components. Under licence from the Dow Chemical Company, which developed the basic material used, the Windecker company produced an all-plastics aircraft wing in 1960, and conducted flight tests on a conventional aircraft. On the basis of this successful research, a prototype was then built to Windecker design, using reinforced glass fibre materials for all structural components. For test purposes, this prototype had a fixed undercarriage and various other features that were not acceptable for a production type; the Eagle was evolved subsequently, with retractable nosewheel landing gear and other refinements, as a high-performance four-seat light aircraft. An unrestricted FAA Type Approval was obtained for the Eagle at the end of 1969 and small-scale production began in 1970. The production rate has been limited by the company's lack of working capital, but a process of continuous design refinement has been maintained pending the availability of finance to re-launch production. During 1973, one Eagle was acquired by the USAF, with the designation YE-5, to be used in trials on the radar-detectability of aircraft of plastics construction.

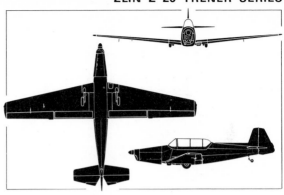

Shown in the photograph (above) is the single-seat Zlin 2526A aerobatic version and the silhouette (right) depicts the standard two-seat Z526

Country of Origin: Czechoslovakia.

Type: Private and club trainer and aerobatic aircraft.

Power Plant: One (Z 226, Z326, Z526) 160 hp Walter Minor 6-III or (Z 526F, AF) 180 hp M 137 or (Z 526L) 200 hp Lycoming AIO-360B or (Z 526AFS, Z 726) 185 hp M 137A.

Performance: Max speed (Z 226), 137 mph (220 km/h), (Z 526F), 152 mph (244 km/h) ; cruise speed (Z 226), 121 mph (195 km/h), (Z 526F), 130 mph (210 km/h) ; initial rate of climb (Z226), 950 ft/min (4,8 m/sec), (Z 526F), 1,181 ft/min (6,0 m/sec) ; service ceiling (Z 226), 17,390 ft (5 300 m), (Z 526F), 17,060 ft (5 200 m) ; range with standard fuel (Z 226), 300 mls (480 km), (Z 526F), 295 mls (480 km) ; range with wing-tip tanks (Z 526F), 520 mls (840 km).

Weights: Empty equipped (Z 226), 1,257 lb (570 kg), (Z 526F), 1,465 lb (665 kg) ; max take-off (Z 226), 1,808 lb (820 kg), (Z 526F), 2,150 lb (975 kg).

Dimensions: Span (Z 226), 33 ft 9 in (10,28 m), (Z 526F), over tip tanks, 35 ft 11½ in (10,96 m) (Z 526AFS), 29 ft 0 in (8,84 m) ; length (Z 226, Z 526AFS), 25 ft 7 in (7,8 m), (Z 526F), 26 ft 3 in (8,00 m) ; height, 6 ft 9 in (2,06 m) ; wing area (Z 226), 160·4 sq ft (14,9 m²), (Z526F), 166·3 sq ft (15,45 m²), (Z 526AFS), 149 sq ft (13,81 m²).

Accommodation: Two in tandem or (aerobatic versions, A suffix), pilot only in enclosed cockpit.

Status: Prototype Z 26 first flown in 1947. Z 126 appeared in 1953. Z 226 appeared in 1955. First Z 326 flown in 1957. Prototype Z 526F flown in 1968. Prototype Z 526L flown in August 1969. Prototype Z 526AFS flown in October 1970. Z 726 appeared in 1973. Production, over 1,700 of all versions.

Notes: The Zlin Z 26 Trenér was designed to an official requirement for a basic trainer for military and club use. Variants fall into four categories—with fixed or retractable undercarriages and with one or two seats. The Z 26, Z.126 and Z 226 were fixed-gear two-seaters, the first single-seat aerobatic version being the Z 226A in 1956, named the Akrobat. The Z 326 Trenér-Master was the first to have retractable gear, also a feature of the Z 526 and Z 726 variants. Single-seaters are the Z 326A, Z 526A, Z526AF and Z 526AFS, with reduced-span wings. The Z 526L was developed primarily for export, with an American power plant, but few were built. The Z 726 was developed in 1973, primarily for aerobatic competitions.

ZLIN Z 42 AND Z 43

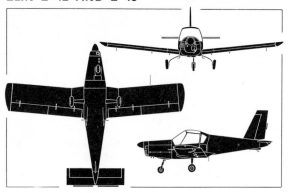

The photograph (above) shows the four-seat Zlin Z 43 while the silhouette (left) depicts the similar but lower-powered Z 42 two-seater

Country of Origin: Czechoslovakia.
Type: Private and club aircraft.
Power Plant: One (Z 42) 180 hp Avia M 137A or (Z 43) 210 hp Avia M337 piston engine.
Performance: Max speed (Z 42), 143 mph (230 km/h), (Z 43), 146 mph (235 km/h); cruise (Z 42), 124 mph (200 km/h), (Z 43), 130 mph (210 km/h); initial rate of climb (Z 42), 846 ft/min (4,3 m/sec), (Z 43), 689 ft/min (3,5 m/sec); service ceiling (Z 42), 13,450 ft (4 100 m), (Z 43), 12,465 ft (3 800 m); range with normal fuel (Z 42), 372 mls (600 km), (Z 43), 375 mls (610 km); range with max fuel (Z 42), 683 mls (1 100 km), (Z 43), 680 mls (1 100 km).
Weights: Empty (Z 42), 1,332 lb (600 kg), (Z 43), 1,609 lb (730 kg); max take-off (Z 42, normal), 2,138 lb (970 kg), (Z 42, aerobatic), 1,851 lb (840 kg), (Z 43, normal), 2,976 lb (1 350 kg), (Z 43 utility), 2,204 lb (1 000 kg).
Dimensions: Span (Z 42), 29 ft 10¾ in (9,11 m), (Z 43), 32 ft 0¼ in (9,76 m); length (Z 42), 23 ft 2¼ in (7,07 m), (Z 43), 25 ft 5 in (7,75 m); height (Z 42), 8 ft 10 in (2,69 m), (Z 43), 9 ft 6½ in (2,91 m); wing area (Z 42), 141·5 sq ft (13,15 m²), (Z 43), 156·1

sq ft (14,50 m²).
Accommodation: (Z 42) Two seats side-by-side or (Z 43) pilot and three passengers in enclosed cabin.
Status: Prototype Z 42 first flown on 17 October 1967; prototype Z 43 first flown on 10 December 1968. Production totals to 1973, Z 42, over 70, Z 43, over 20.
Notes: These two light aircraft are the latest types to carry the famous Zlin name, which became well-known pre-war and has been retained for the products of the Moravan works of the now State-owned Czech aircraft industry. The Z 42 was conceived basically as an updated replacement for the Zlin 26-726 series (see page 185), featuring side-by-side rather than tandem seating and other refinements in line with contemporary practice. The Zlin 43 emerged a year after the 42 as a four-seat derivative, featuring a more powerful engine and a widened centre fuselage; some 80 per cent of structural components are common to the two types. Up to 1974, virtually all Zlin 42 and 43 production had been to meet the demand of the Czech flying clubs. Variants of both the Z 42 and Z 43 have been developed with Lycoming engines and are available for export to Western nations.

Originally built by North American Rockwell, the Quail Commander, shown in the photograph and silhouette, is now produced in Mexico

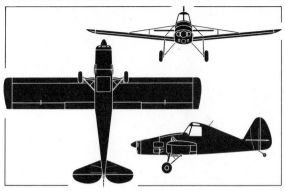

Country of Origin: Mexico (and USA).

Type: Agricultural monoplane.

Power Plant: One (Sparrow) 235 Lycoming O-540-B2B5 or (Quail) 290 hp Lycoming IO-540-G1C5 piston engine.

Performance: Max cruising speed (Sparrow), 105 mph (169 km/h), (Quail), 115 mph (185 km/h); normal operating speed (Sparrow and Quail), 90–100 mph (145–161 km/h); initial rate of climb (Sparrow), 650 ft/min (3,3 m/sec), (Quail), 850 ft/min (4,3 m/sec); service ceiling (Sparrow), 14,000 ft (4 265 m), (Quail), 16,000 ft (4 875 m); range with max fuel (Sparrow and Quail), 300 mls (483 km).

Weights: Empty (Sparrow), 1,600 lb (726 kg); max payload (Sparrow), 1,400 lb (635 kg), (Quail), 1,600 lb (726 kg); max take-off (Sparrow), 3,400 lb (1 542 kg), (Quail), 3,600 lb (1 633 kg).

Dimensions: Span, 34 ft 9 in (10,59 m); length, 23 ft 6 in (7,16 m); height, 7 ft 7 in (2,31 m); wing area, 182 sq ft (16,90 m²).

Accommodation: Pilot only, in enclosed cockpit with open side panels.

Status: First production A-9 completed January 1963 and de-

liveries began March 1963. Prototype B-1 flown 15 January 1966; production deliveries began 1 April 1966. FAA Type Approvals, A-9A, 25 March 1964; B-1, 11 March 1966; B-1A, 13 February 1967.

Notes: Origin of this design was the CallAir series of agricultural monoplanes, going back to the A-5 of 1956 with a 150 hp Lycoming O-320-A2A and the A-6 with a 180 hp Lycoming O-360-A1A. The more powerful A-9 was purchased by Aero Commander and marketed as the Ag Commander until this company was absorbed by Rockwell and merged with North American. The original A-9A was then re-named the Sparrow Commander and a further version with a more powerful motor was introduced as the Quail Commander. The CallAir B-1, which in prototype form had been powered by a 400 hp IO-720-A1A, was also added to the North American Rockwell range as the Snipe Commander with a 450 hp Pratt & Whitney R-985 radial engine. However, NR built only nine Snipe Commanders before it was discontinued, and rights in the Sparrow and Quail were sold to Aeronautica Agricola Mexicana SA in 1971. The first Mexican example of the Sparrow Commander flew early in 1972.

AIR PARTS FLETCHER FU-24

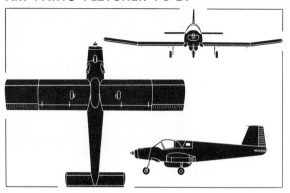

Both the photograph and the silhouette show the standard 300-hp version of the Air Parts Fletcher FU-24 of which turboprop versions are also in use

Country of Origin: New Zealand (and USA).

Type: Agricultural monoplane.

Power Plant: One (FU-24) 300 hp R-R Continental IO-520-F or (FU-24-950) 400 hp Lycoming IO-720 piston engine or (1284) 665 shp Garrett AiResearch TPE 331-1-101 turboprop.

Performance: Max cruising speed (F-24), 112 mph (180 km/h), (FU-24-950), 122 mph (196 km/h), (1284), 145 mph (233 km/h); initial rate of climb (FU-24), 625 ft/min (3,15 m/sec), (FU-24-950), 630 ft/min (3,2 m/sec), (1284), 1,250 ft/min (6,35 m/sec); service ceiling (FU-24, FU-24-950), 16,000 ft (4 875 m), (1284), 30,000 ft (9 145 m); range with max fuel (FU-24), 371 mls (597 km), (FU-24-950), 440 mls (708 km), (1284), 530 mls (853 km).

Weights: Basic operating (FU-24), 2,210 lb (1 002 kg), (FU-24-950), 2,616 lb (1 186 kg), (1284), 3,147 lb (1 427 kg); max agricultural payload (FU-24), 1,870 lb (848 kg), (FU-24-950), 2,320 lb (1 052 kg), (1284), 3,000 lb (1 360 kg); max take-off (FU-24), 4,470 lb (2 027 kg), (FU-24-950), 5,430 lb (2 463 kg), (1284), 6,500 lb (2 948 kg).

Dimensions: Span (FU-24, FU-24-950), 42 ft 0 in (12,81 m), (1284), 44 ft 0 in (13,41 m); length (FU-24), 31 ft 10 in (9,69 m),

(FU-24-950), 32 ft 9 in (9,98 m), (1284), 35 ft 3 in (10,74 m); height (all), 9 ft 4 in (2,84 m); wing area (FU-24, FU-24-950), 294 sq ft (27,31 m²), (1284), 308 sq ft (28,6 m²).

Accommodation: Pilot and provision for one passenger in agricultural version and up to (FU-24) five or (FU-24-950) seven or (1284) nine passengers.

Status: Prototype Fletcher FU-24 first flown in July 1954. First production example flown in December 1954. First 1284 flown early 1970. Production totals, 100 in USA by Fletcher, over 70 in New Zealand by Air Parts (by end-1973).

Notes: The FU-24 was an original product of the Fletcher Aviation Corporation of California, and was developed primarily to meet the requirements of the New Zealand agricultural industry. An initial batch of 100 airframes was built in the USA for assembly in New Zealand, and these had 260 hp Continental engines. Subsequently, manufacturing rights were obtained by Air Parts (NZ) Ltd and the 300 hp and 400 hp versions described here entered production. In addition, some turboprop models were developed, these being the Fletcher 1060 with 500 shp Pratt & Whitney PT6A-20, Fletcher 1160 with 530 hp TPE 331 and Fletcher 1284 described here.

One of the few aircraft of original design to be developed and produced in Mexico in recent years, the Anahuac Tauro is shown in both silhouette and photograph

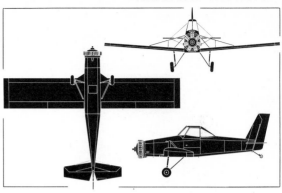

Country of Origin: Mexico.

Type: Agricultural monoplane.

Power Plant: One 300 hp Jacobs R-755-A2M1 or 350 hp R-755-SM piston radial engine.

Performance: Max speed, 120 mph (193 km/h) at sea level; max cruising speed, 90 mph (145 km/h) at sea level; best economy cruise, 85 mph (137 km/h) at 5,000 ft (1 525 m); initial rate of climb, 500 ft/min (2,53 m/sec); service ceiling, 14,000 ft (4 250 m); range with max fuel, 233 mls (375 km).

Weights: Empty, 1,973 lb (895 kg); max take-off, 3,542 lb (1 606 kg).

Dimensions: Span, 37 ft 6½ in (11,43 m); length, 26 ft 11¼ in (8,21 m); height, 7 ft 8 in (2,34 m); wing area, 217·89 sq ft (20,24 m²).

Accommodation: Pilot only, in enclosed, ventilated cockpit.

Status: Prototype first flown on 3 December 1968; first production example flown on 5 June 1970. Production total seven; production continuing.

Notes: The Anahuac company was founded at Mexico International Airport in 1966 to undertake the development of aircraft specially suited to local needs and conditions. The first project put in hand was this simple agricultural monoplane, for the design of which Ing Arno Gjumlich, the company's chief engineer and designer, was responsible. The Tauro (Bull) follows conventional lines for agricultural aeroplanes, emphasis being placed upon simplicity of construction. The structure is of metal throughout, with fabric covering of the wings and tail unit, and removable aluminium side panels on the fuselage. The hopper in the fuselage forward of the cockpit has a capacity of 190 Imp gal (870 l) of liquid or 1,765 lb (800 kg) of dry insecticide; fuel tanks are in each wing root with an optional extra tank in the fuselage. Versions of the Tauro are available with 300 or 350 hp engines, indicated by an appropriate suffix to the name, and a two-seat variant was under development in 1973 for use as a trainer and to provide for transportation of a ground engineer to operating sites; the data quoted here are for the 300 hp version. After production of an initial small batch of Tauros, a series of modifications was evolved on the basis of early operational experience, and production arrangements for a further batch of modified aircraft were in hand in 1973, with financial support from the Mexican government.

BOEING STEARMAN 75

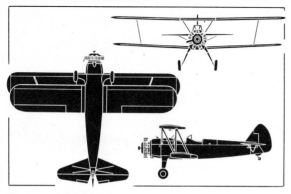

The silhouette depicts the standard Boeing Stearman 75 and the photograph shows a single-seat aerobatic conversion with 650 hp Wasp engine

Country of Origin: USA.

Type: Agricultural (and sporting) biplane.

Power Plant: One 225 hp Lycoming R-680 or 220 hp Continental W-670-6 or 225 hp Jacobs R-755-7 or 450 hp Pratt & Whitney R-985-A6-1 piston radial.

Performance: Max cruising speed, 124 mph (200 km/h); typical cruise, 92–106 mph (148–171 km/h); initial rate of climb, 1,000 ft/min (5,1 m/sec); service ceiling, 11,200 ft (3 413 m); range with max fuel, 375 mls (6p4 km) at 92 mph (148 km/h).

Weights: Basic operating, 2,075 lb (940 kg); max take-off (typical sporting), 2,810 lb (1 275 kg), (agricultural), 4,500 lb (2 040 kg).

Dimensions: Span, 32 ft 2 in (9,80 m); length, 25 ft 0 in (7,62 m); height, 9 ft 2 in (2,79 m); wing area, 297·4 sq ft (27,6 m²).

Accommodation: Pilot only or (sporting model) two in tandem in open cockpits.

Status: Stearman Model 75 prototype flown in 1936; production total (by Stearman and Boeing) in Model 70-76 series, 8,584, plus spares equivalent to 2,242 more complete aircraft.

Notes: As the Kaydet, the Stearman (later Boeing Stearman)

Model 75 was one of the classic training aircraft of the World War II period, on which almost all pilots in the US took their *ab initio* training. Subsequently, as many as half of all Kaydets built were adapted for crop dusting and several hundred were still being used in this rôle in 1974. For this purpose, most examples were re-engined with a Pratt & Whitney R-985, in place of the Lycoming, Continental or Jacobs engines fitted originally, and metal covering of the fuselage was considered necessary as the original fabric covering tended to be destroyed by chemical contamination. Several companies developed special agricultural variants of the Boeing Stearman 75, with various spraying and dusting gear beneath the fuselage and wings, and to improve performance, modifications to the wings were also developed with redesigned tips or in some cases completely new wings. In April 1970, an even more extensive redesign of the Model 75 made its first flight at Honolulu, this being the Murrayair MA-1 Paymaster with a 600 hp Pratt & Whitney R-1340 engine and an enclosed cockpit, and this subsequently entered production, as described on page 192. Several Boeing Stearmans have also been adapted as aerobatic mounts for display purposes, with various modifications.

CESSNA 188 AGWAGON, AGTRUCK, AGPICKUP

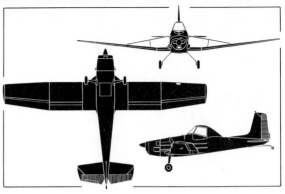

The Cessna AGwagon is shown in both the photograph and silhouette, the AGtruck and AGpickup being externally similar with different engine powers

Country of Origin: USA.

Type: Agricultural monoplane.

Power Plant: One (AGpickup) 230 hp Continental O-470-R or (AGtruck, -wagon) 300 hp Continental IO-520-D piston engine.

Performance: Max cruising speed (AGpickup), 90 mph (145 km/h) at 5,000 ft (1 524 m), (AGwagon, -truck), 114 mph (183 km/h) at 6,500 ft (1 980 m); initial rate of climb (AGpickup), 400 ft/min (2,0 m/sec), (AGtruck, -wagon), 690 ft/min (3,5 m/sec); service ceiling (AGpickup), 6,500 ft (1 981 m), (AGwagon, -truck), 11,100 ft (3 383 m); range (AGpickup), 235 mls (378 km), (AGwagon), 260 mls (418 km), (AGtruck), 390 mls (628 km).

Weights: Empty (AGpickup), 1,950 lb (885 kg), (AGwagon), 2,060 lb (934 kg), (AGtruck), 2,150 lb (975 kg); max take-off (AGpickup), 3,800 lb (1 724 kg), (AGwagon), 4,000 lb (1 814 kg), (AGtruck), 4,200 lb (1 905 kg).

Dimensions: Span (AGpickup, -wagon), 40 ft 8½ in in (12,4 m), (AGtruck), 41 ft 8 in (12,7 m); length (AGpickup), 25 ft 3 in (7,7 m), (AGwagon, -truck), 26 ft 3 in (8,0 m), height (AGpickup), 7 ft 8½ in (2,35 m), (AGwagon, -truck), 7 ft 9½ in (2,38 m); wing area (AGpickup, -wagon), 202 sq ft (18,8 m²), (AGtruck), 205

sq ft (19,0 m).

Accommodation: Pilot only.

Status: Prototype AGwagon first flown on 19 February 1965. FAA Type Approval, 14 February 1966. Production totals (to end-1973), AGwagon, 1,201; AGpickup, 39; AGtruck, 221; production continuing.

Notes: The AGwagon was the first Cessna ag-plane, being a low-wing type of typical design for this duty. Deliveries began in 1966, in two versions, with 230 hp (Model 188) or 300 hp (Model A188) engines; each of these models had a hopper capacity of 200 US gal (1 060 l). In 1972, the Model 188 was marketed under the new name of AGpickup and another new model, the AGtruck, was introduced, with the same 300 hp engine as the AGwagon but having a 280 US gal (1 627 l) hopper and a higher gross weight. The AGtruck also has a slightly longer wing span, and a larger fuel capacity as standard, this latter being only an option on the AGwagon and not available at all on the low-cost AGpickup. The AGpickup is also available with a constant-speed propeller, when the performance is rather better than that quoted here for a fixed-pitch propeller version.

EMAIR (MURRAYAIR) MA-1 PAYMASTER

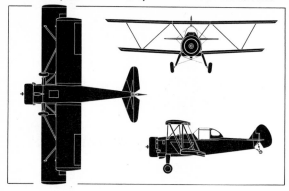

Developed as a variant of the Boeing Stearman 75, the Murrayair MA-1 entered production in 1973 in the form illustrated by photograph and silhouette

Country of Origin: USA.

Type: Agricultural biplane.

Power Plant: One 600 hp Pratt & Whitney R-1340-AN1 Wasp radial piston engine.

Performance: Max cruising and manoeuvre speed, 117 mph (188 km/h).

Weights: Empty, 3,746 lb (1 699 kg); max hopper load, 3,000 lb (1 360 kg); normal take-off and max landing weight, 6,250 lb (2 834 kg); max take-off (agricultural), 7,000 lb (3 175 kg).

Dimensions: Span (upper), 41 ft 8 in (12,70 m); span (lower), 35 ft 0 in (10,67 m); length (tail up), 28 ft 8 in (8,74 m); height, 11 ft 3 in (3,43 m); wing area, 400 sq ft (37,16 m²).

Accommodation: Pilot in fully-enclosed cockpit with space provision (on bench-type seat) for loader mechanic alongside on short-duration flights.

Status: Prototype first flown 27 July 1969. Six pre-production aircraft built 1969–70. FAA Type Approval (Restricted Category) 14 April 1970. Full production initiated 1973, production rate two a month by mid-1974.

Notes: The MA-1 is an evolution of the Boeing-Stearman 75 (see

page 190) and is notable for the size of its hopper, which has a capacity of 62·5 cu ft (1 705 l or 450 US gal) and is larger than that of any other agricultural aircraft currently in use. The MA-1 was evolved during 1969 to meet the requirements of Murrayair, a large-scale agricultural aircraft operator in the Hawaiian Islands that was operating modified Boeing-Stearmans. A prototype was built for Murrayair by Air New Zealand engineers using Boeing Stearman components, although only the tail unit remained unmodified. Apart from the use of an engine of greatly increased power, the MA-1 had increased span of both upper and lower wings, with metal construction introduced in critical areas to permit operations at higher gross weights, and moulded glass fibre panels introduced for the fuselage covering to improve cleaning, maintenance and inspection. Six pre-production MA-1s were built for use by Murrayair in Hawaii, and the success of their operation led to the decision during 1973 to put the design into full-scale production, at an initial rate of one a month, increasing to two-three a month by mid-1974. Production is by the Emair division of Murrayair. Provision is made for rapid conversion between liquid and granular dispersal systems, changeover time being approximately 10 minutes.

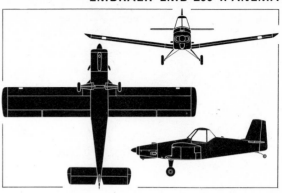

The Embraer Ipanema is shown in both the photograph and the silhouette in its initial production form; more powerful and larger derivatives are under development

Country of Origin: Brazil.

Type: Agricultural monoplane.

Power Plant: One (EMB-200) 260 hp Lycoming O-540-H2B5D or (EMB-201) 300 hp Lycoming IO-540-K1D5 piston engine.

Performance: Max cruising speed, 131 mph (211 km/h); initial rate of climb, 705 ft/min (3,6 m/sec); range with max fuel, 584 mls (941 km).

Weights: Max payload (normal cat), 1,212 lb (550 kg), (restricted cat), 1,763 lb (800 kg); max take-off (normal cat), 3,417 lb (1 550 kg), (restricted cat), 3,968 lb (1 800 kg).

Dimensions: Span, 36 ft 9 in (11,20 m); length, 24 ft 4½ in (7,43 m); height, 7 ft 2½ in (2,20 m); wing area, 193·75 sq ft (18,00 m²).

Accommodation: Pilot only in fully-enclosed cockpit.

Status: Prototype first flown on 30 July 1970. Type Approval, 14 December 1971. Production, about 50 by end of 1973, six a month in 1974.

Notes: The Ipanema was designed to meet specific Brazilian needs for an agricultural aircraft, the specification being drawn up by the Brazilian Ministry of Agriculture and the design being prepared by

the *PAR-Departmento de Aeronaves* of the Aerospace Technical Centre (CTA). Following the creation of the Embraer company as a state-sponsored manufacturing company in 1969, responsibility for the Ipanema was transferred to it, the designation EMB-200 then being assigned. Following successful testing of the prototype, production was launched at the São José dos Campos factory, and the production rate built up steadily to reach six a month by 1974. Initial aircraft were of the EMB-200 standard with a McCauley two-blade fixed-pitch propeller, but a version with a constant-speed propeller, the EMB-200A, was also made available subsequently. During 1973, the Ipanema prototype was converted to EMB-201 standard with a 300 hp engine and this was undergoing testing during 1974. Embraer have also prepared designs for a larger derivative of the Ipanema known as the EMB-210 Formigao, powered by a 400 hp Lycoming IO-720-A1A engine driving a three-bladed constant-speed propeller. This design has the same configuration as the EMB-200 but has larger overall dimensions, a bigger hopper capacity and a gross weight of 4,850 lb (2 200 kg). The span is 39 ft 4½ in (12,00 m) and the overall length is 27 ft 6 in (8,38 m), and a 2,200 lb (1 000 kg) load can be carried.

GRUMMAN G-164 AG-CAT

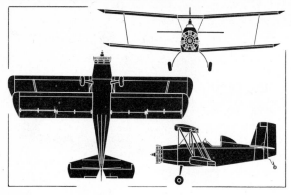

The Grumman G-164A Super Ag-Cat, shown in the photograph above, is externally similar to the original G-164, which had lower weights

Country of Origin: USA.

Type: Agricultural biplane.

Power Plant: One (G-164) 220 hp Continental W-670-6A, 6N or 16, 225 hp or 240 hp W-670-240 or 275 hp Jacobs R-755-A2M1 or (G-164 and G-164A) 450 hp Pratt & Whitney R-985-AN-1, AN-3, AN-25, AN-27, T1B2, T1B3, -39, -39A or AN14B piston radial engine.

Performance: Max permissible speed (G-164), 131 mph (211 km/h), (G-164A), 147 mph (237 km/h); working speed (G-164), 75–95 mph (121–153 km/h), (G-164A), 80–100 mph (129–161 km/h); initial rate of climb (225 hp), 435 ft/min (2,2 m/sec), (240 hp), 600 ft/min (3,05 m/sec), (275 hp), 700 ft/min (3,55 m/sec), (450 hp), 1,080 ft/min (5,5 m/sec).

Weights: Empty, equipped for spraying (225 hp), 2,201 lb (999 kg), (240 hp), 2,233 lb (1 013 kg), (275 hp), 2,239 lb (1 016 kg), (450 hp), 2,690 lb (1 220 kg); max hopper capacity (G-164), 1,200 lb (5 443 kg), (G-164 late and G-164A), 2,000 lb (9 071 kg); certificated max take-off (G-164), 3,750 lb (1 700 kg), (G-164A), 4,500 lb (2 040 kg); max permissible take-off, 6,075 lb (2 755 kg).

Dimensions: Span, 35 ft 11 in (10,95 m); length (W-670), 24 ft 4 in (7,42 m), (R-755), 24 ft 4¼ in (7,43 m), (R-985), 23 ft 4 in (7,11 m); height, 10 ft 9 in (3,27 m); wing area, 328 sq ft (20,47 m²).

Accommodation: Pilot only in (optional enclosed) cockpit.

Status: Prototype first flown 22 May 1957. Production totals, G-164, 400; G-164A, over 650 by end 1973, with production continuing at about 8 per month. FAA Type Approval, G-164, 20 January 1959 in Restricted Agricultural Category, 9 April 1962 in Restricted Patrol and/or Survey Category; G-164A, 4 March 1966.

Notes: The Ag-Cat is a typical agricultural biplane, put into production as part of the Grumman Corporation's effort to diversify into the civil aircraft market. Production was subsequently subcontracted to Schweizer Aircraft of Elmira and marketing became a responsibility of Grumman American Aviation in 1972. A large variety of alternative power plants has been certificated for the Ag-Cat and for the G-164A Super Ag-Cat, which replaced the G-164 after 400 examples had been delivered. The Super Ag-Cat had structural changes for operation at a higher gross weight with an extra 13 US-gal (50-l) fuel tank as standard. Ag-Cats are in service in about 35 countries.

Second design built for agricultural purposes by Hindustan Aeronautics with the HA-31 designation, the Basant (photograph and silhouette) entered production in 1974

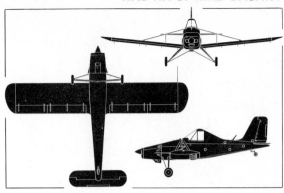

Country of Origin: India.

Type: Agricultural monoplane.

Power Plant: One 400 hp Lycoming TIGO-541-C1A piston engine.

Performance: Max speed (normal category), 140 mph (225 km/h) ; max cruise, 115 mph (185 km/h) at 8,000 ft (2 625 m) ; initial rate of climb (normal cat), 750 ft/min (3,8 m/sec) ; service ceiling, 12,500 ft (3 800 m) ; range with maximum fuel, no payload, 400 mls (645 km) ; range with maximum payload, about 120 mls (193 km).

Weights: Empty, 2,579 lb (1 170 kg) ; hopper capacity, 2,000 lb (910 kg) ; normal operating weight, 4,300 lb (1 950 kg) ; max take-off (restricted cat), 5,004 lb (2 270 kg).

Dimensions: Span, 39 ft 4½ in (12,00 m) ; length, 29 ft 6¼ in (9,0 m) ; height, 8 ft 4½ in (2,55 m) ; gross wing area, 251 sq ft (23,34 m²).

Accommodation: Pilot only, in totally-enclosed heated and ventilated cockpit.

Status: Prototype HA-31 Mk 1 first flown in 1969. Prototype HA-31 Mk 2 first flown 30 March 1972, second prototype in September 1972.

Notes: Hindustan Aeronautics initiated design work on an agricultural monoplane in 1968 and flew a prototype a year later. This HA-31 Mk 1 had a tall nosewheel undercarriage, and a cockpit raised well clear of the basic fuselage top line to obtain a good forward view for the pilot. A 250 hp R-R Continental engine was fitted, and maximum emphasis was placed upon simplicity of manufacture. The HA-31 Mk 1 was not a success, however, and a completely new design was prepared as the HA-31 Mk 2, data for which are given here. The primary rôle for the Mk 2 Basant is the spreading of pesticides and fertilisers, although general utility duties, aerial survey, fire patrol and similar tasks can be undertaken. The Indian Ministry of Agriculture indicated an initial requirement for at least 100 Basants and subject to the satisfactory completion of flight trials, production was expected to begin during 1974. Meanwhile, a small pre-production batch, reported to total six, had been put in hand at the Bangalore works. Hindustan Aeronautics was also developing a 400 hp engine, the HPE.4, as a locally-produced alternative to the Lycoming used in the prototypes, for possible use in later production Basants. The Hindi name Basant is translated as meaning "Spring".

IAR-821, 822, 826, 827

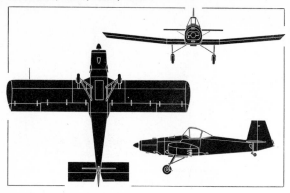

Both the photograph and silhouette show the IAR 822, first variant in this Rumanian series of agricultural aircraft to have a Lycoming engine

Country of Origin: Romania.

Type: Agricultural monoplane.

Power Plant: One (821) 300 hp Ivchenko Al-14RF radial or (822, 826) 290 hp Lycoming IO-540-G1D5 or (827) 400 hp Lycoming IO-720 piston engine.

Performance: Max speed (821), 107 mph (172 km/h), (822), 112 mph (180 km/h); cruising speed (821), 99 mph (160 km/h), (822), 103 mph (165 km/h); initial rate of climb (821), 886 ft/min (4,5 m/sec), (822), 689 ft/min (3,5 m/sec); service ceiling (821), 13,125 ft (4 000 m), (822), 9,850 ft (3 000 m); range with max fuel (821), 161 mls (260 km), (822), 279 mls (450 km).

Weights: Empty (821 and 822), 2,425 lb (1 100 kg); max take-off (821 and 822), 4,188 lb (1 900 kg); (821B), 3,218 lb (1 460 kg), (822B), 3,196 lb (1 450 kg).

Dimensions: Span (all), 42 ft 0 in (12,80 m); length (821), 30 ft 2 in (9,20 m), (821B), 30 ft 8¼ in (9,35 m); (822), 30 ft 10 in (9,40 m), (822B), 31 ft 4 in (9,55 m); height (821), 9 ft 1½ in (2,78 m), (822), 8 ft 6½ in (2,60 m); wing area (all), 279·86 sq ft (26,00 m²).

Accommodation: Pilot only or (IAR-821B, 822B), two in tandem with dual controls.

Status: Prototype IAR-821 first flown in 1967; first IAR-821B flown in August 1968; first IAR-822 flown March 1970; first IAR-822B flown in December 1972. Production, IAR-821, 20; IAR-822/826/827, about 30 by end 1973.

Notes: The IAR-821 originated at the IRMA works in Bucharest and was of conventional agricultural layout. Production began in 1968 and 20 were built, in addition to a small batch of two-seat IAR-821B versions, suitable for use as trainers, glider tugs and for simulated agricultural operations. The design was further developed by the same team of engineers after the ICA aircraft construction factory had been formed at Brasov, and this led to the appearance of the IAR-822, which incorporated numerous refinements and a Lycoming engine. A two-seat version was also built as the IAR-822B, these types being of mixed wood and metal construction. During 1973, an all-metal version appeared as the IAR-826, and a further development of the same design was produced as the IAR-827. With a more powerful engine, this had increased span and length, higher weights, improved flying characteristics and superior operational capability.

The standard single-seat LET Z-37 Cmelak agricultural and utility monoplane is depicted by both the photograph (above) and the silhouette (right)

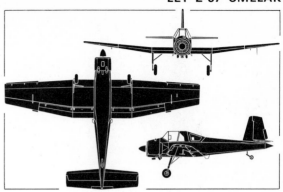

Country of Origin: Czechoslovakia.

Type: Agricultural monoplane.

Power Plant: One 315 hp M 462 RF piston radial engine.

Performance: Cruising speed (agricultural), 106 mph (170 km/h), (freight), (114 mph (183 km/h); agricultural operating speed, 75 mph (120 km/h); initial rate of climb (agricultural), 728 ft/min (3,7 m/sec), (freight), 925 ft/min (4,7 m/sec); service ceiling (freight), 13,125 ft (4 000 m); range with max fuel, 398 mls (640 km).

Weights: Basic operating (without agricultural gear), 2,295 lb (1 043 kg); maximum chemical load, 1,323 lb (600 kg); maximum take-off (agricultural), 4,080 lb (1 850 kg), (freight), 3,855 lb (1 750 kg).

Dimensions: Span, 40 ft 1¼ in (12,22 m); length, 28 ft 0½ in (8,55 m); height, 9 ft 6 in (2,90 m); wing area, 256·2 sq ft (23,8 m²).

Accommodation: Pilot and provision for one other occupant or (Z-237) two pilots with dual controls.

Status: Prototype XZ-37 first flown 29 March 1963. Type certification obtained on 20 June 1966 and deliveries began in same month. Production totals, prototypes, 10; Z-37 and Z-37-A, over 400; Z-237, about 20.

Notes: The Cmelak (Bumble Bee) was developed by the Czech State Aircraft Industry to meet domestic requirements for a crop-sprayer and -duster. Prototypes had the Soviet AI-14RF engine but a licence-built Czech version of the engine was adopted for the production versions. The original Z-37 was followed by the Z-37-A with a number of structural and other modifications designed to extend the operational life. When agricultural gear is not fitted, the Z-37-A can be used as a freight carrier and for general utility purposes, in which case an extra fuel tank is usually fitted in the starboard wing centre section. Provision is made for two external fuel tanks to be carried, these being used to ferry fuel to operating sites. A feature of the Cmelak design is its use of pneumatically-operated double-slotted aluminium flaps. To train agricultural pilots in operating techniques, a two-seat version of the Cmelak was developed, this having two cockpits in tandem beneath a single long canopy, with full dual controls, and being designated the Z-237. Cmelaks have been exported to several countries including Finland, the UK, India, Iraq and Yugoslavia.

PIPER PA-25 PAWNEE AND PA-36 PAWNEE BRAVE

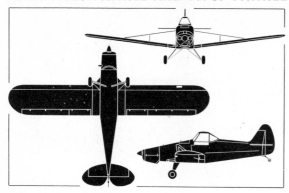

The silhouette (left) shows the Piper PA-25-235 Pawnee "C" and the photograph illustrates the larger PA-36 Pawnee II introduced in 1972

Country of Origin: USA.

Type: Agricultural monoplane.

Power Plant: One (PA-25-150) 150 hp Lycoming O-320-A1A or -A2A or (PA-25-235) 235 hp Lycoming O-540-B2B5 or -B2C5 or (PA-25-260) 260 hp Lycoming O-540-G1A5 or -G2A5 or (Brave) 285 hp Teledyne Continental 6-285A piston engine.

Performance: Max cruising speed (-235), 114 mph (183 km/h); speed for max output (sprayer), 90 mph (145 km/h); speed for minimum application (sprayer), 135 mph (217 km/h); initial rate of climb (-235), 630 ft/min (3,2 m/sec) with spray equipment; range with max fuel (-235), 290 mls (467 km) with no dispersal equipment, 255 mls (410 km) with dusting equipment.

Weights: Empty (-235, no dispersal equipment), 1,420 lb (644 kg), (-235, sprayer), 1,488 lb (675 kg), (Brave, standard), 2,050 lb (930 kg), (Brave, sprayer), 2,170 lb (984 kg); max hopper load (Brave), 1,900 lb (862 kg), (-235), 1,200 lb (544 kg); max take-off (-150), 2,300 lb (1 043 kg), (-235, -260), 2,900 lb (1 315 kg), (Brave), 4,400 lb (1 996 kg).

Dimensions: Span (PA-25), 36 ft 2 in (11,02 m), (PA-36), 39 ft 0 in (11,89 m); length (PA-25), 24 ft 8½ in (7,53 m), (PA-36),

27 ft 4 in (8,33 m); height, (PA-25), 7 ft 2 in (2,18 m); wing area (PA-25), 183 sq ft (17,0 m²), (PA-36), 225 sq ft (20,9 m²).

Accommodation: Pilot only in totally enclosed cockpit, and provision for loader/assistant on temporary seat in hopper.

Status: FAA Type Approvals: PA-25-150, 6 January 1959, PA-25-235, 12 October 1962; PA-25-260, 19 April 1967; PA-36, 1972. Production total, PA-25 all models, over 4,200 by end-1973.

Notes: The original PA-25 Pawnee entered production in 1958 as an addition to the Piper range of light aircraft intended specifically for crop-dusting and spraying. Its configuration followed the recommendations of the Cornell Medical College in respect of pilot safety, the basic design being undertaken on a private basis by Fred Weick before it was acquired for production by Piper. When deliveries began in August 1959, only the PA-25-150 was available, the 235 hp version being introduced in 1962. The latter engine became standard in the Pawnee B version in 1965 and in 1966 further improvements were offered in the Pawnee C, a 260 hp version of which appeared the following year. The larger PA-36 Pawnee Brave (originally known as the Pawnee II) was introduced at the end of 1972.

PZL-101 GAWRON

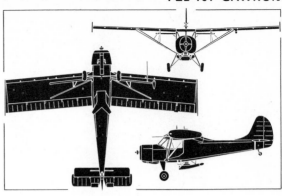

The photograph (above) shows the PZL-101 Gawron in its standard agricultural version and the silhouette (right) depicts the similar PZL-101A

Country of Origin: Poland.
Type: Agricultural monoplane.
Power Plant: One 260 hp AI-14R piston radial engine.
Performance: Max cruising speed, 81 mph (130 km/h); best economy cruise, 75 mph (120 km/h); operating speed, dusting and spraying, 68–80 mph (110–130 km/h); initial rate of climb, 530 ft/min (2,7 m/sec); service ceiling, 11,100 ft (3 380 m); range with normal fuel, 410 mls (660 km); range with max fuel, 708 mls (1 140 km).
Weights: Empty equipped (agricultural), 2,260 lb (1 025 kg), (ambulance), 2,354 lb (1 068 kg); max take-off 3,660 lb (1 660 kg).
Dimensions: Span (endplate tips), 41 ft 7½ in (12,68 m), (laminar tips), 42 ft 9 in (13,03 m); length, 29 ft 6½ in (9,00 m); height, 9 ft 2¾ in (2,81 m); wing area, 256·8 sq ft (23,86 m²).
Accommodation: Pilot and (agricultural) provision for second seat for loader/assistant or (ambulance) two stretchers and one attendant.
Status: Prototype first flown in April 1958. First production example flown in February 1960. Prototype PZL-101AF first flown

on 30 August 1966. Production total, over 350.
Notes: The PZL-101 Gawron (Rook) was evolved in the OKL (Aircraft Construction Centre) in Warsaw as a locally-produced, improved version of the Yakovlev Yak-12, which was itself built under licence in Poland in several different versions. Compared with the Yak-12M, the original PZL-101 differed primarily in having a simplified and lightened structure, and endplates on the wing tips. It was produced in two principal versions, the PZL-101 G-1 agricultural model and the PZL-101 G-2 utility model with fittings for passenger or freight carrying. The PZL-101A followed in 1962, by which time the Gawron had been adopted as the standard agricultural aircraft for the Soviet Bloc countries including the Soviet Union itself. The PZL-101A was produced in three basic versions for agricultural, ambulance and utility duties. The improved PZL-101AF had the 300 hp AI-14RF engine and an increased payload, but did not enter production, and since 1969 production models of the PZL-101A have differed from the original versions by having laminar-flow wing tips in place of the endplates. Among the countries to which Gawrons have been exported are Austria, Finland, India, Spain, Turkey and North Vietnam.

199

ROCKWELL THRUSH COMMANDER (AND SNOW S-2)

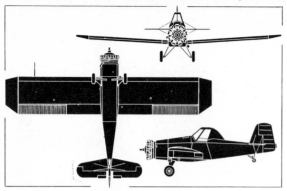

Originally produced as the Snow S-2 series, the Thrush Commander (photograph and silhouette) was Rockwell's only agricultural aeroplane in production in 1974

Country of Origin: USA.

Type: Agricultural monoplane.

Power Plant: One (S-2C) 450 hp Pratt & Whitney R-985-AN-1, -3 or -14B or (S-2C and Thrush) 600 hp R-1340-AN-1 piston radial engine.

Performance: Max cruising speed (S-2C), 115 mph (185 km/h), (Thrush), 110 mph (117 km/h); best economy cruise (S-2C), 105 mph (168 km/h); normal operating speed (Thrush), 95–100 mph (153–177 km/h); initial rate of climb (S-2C), 700 ft/min (3.65 m/sec), (Thrush), 900 ft/min (4,6 m/sec); service ceiling (Thrush), 15,000 ft (4 570 m); range with max payload (S-2C), 550 mls (885 km), (Thrush) 470 mls (756 km).

Weights: Empty (S-2C), 3,210 lb (1 456 kg), (Thrush), 3,700 lb (1 678 kg); hopper capacity (S-2C), 2,000 lb (907 kg), (Thrush), 3,280 lb (1 487 kg); max take-off (S-2C), 5,600 lb (2 540 kg), (Thrush), 6,900 lb (3 130 kg).

Dimensions: Span (S-2C), 44 ft 7 in (13,59 m), (Thrush), 44 ft 5 in (13,54 m); length (S-2C), 28 ft 8 in (8,73 m), (Thrush), 29 ft 4 ½ in (8,95 m); height (S-2C), 8 ft 7 in (2,62 m), (Thrush), 9 ft 2 in (2,79 m); wing area (S-2C), 327·4 sq ft (30,42 m²).

Accommodation: Pilot only.

Status: Snow S-2 prototype first flown in 1956. Production deliveries began 1958. FAA Type Approvals, S-2A, 2 April 1959; S-2B, 29 July 1958; S-2C, 12 May 1961; S-2C-600, 26 April 1962; S-2D, 1 November 1965; S-2R, 2 November 1967. Production totals, S-2A, 36; S-2B, 41; S-2C and S-2C-600, 232; S-2D, 104; Thrush Commander, over 250 to end-1973.

Notes: The Thrush Commander remained in production in 1974 as the only agricultural aeroplane in the Rockwell range. Of typical ag-plane layout, it had originated in 1955 as the Snow S-2, designed by Leland Snow, an experienced agricultural pilot. A series of production Snow models differed primarily in engine type fitted—220 hp Continental W-670 in the S-2A, Pratt & Whitney R-985 in the S-2B and S-2C and R-1340-AN-1 in the S-2C-600. Design rights in the S-2 were acquired by Aero Commander in 1965 and the type was named the Ag Commander in its S-2D version. It was then further improved for production as the Thrush Commander by North American Rockwell and subsequently Rockwell International's General Aviation Divisions. Construction is of steel tube throughout, with light alloy covering.

Agricultural aircraft

TRANSAVIA PL-12 AIRTRUK

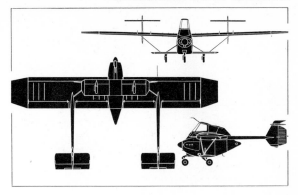

One of the most unusual configurations of any aircraft in production in 1974 is shown in the photograph and silhouette of the Transavia PL-12 Airtruk

Country of Origin: Australia.

Type: Agricultural biplane.

Power Plant: One 300 hp Continental IO-520-D piston engine.

Performance: Max cruising speed (PL-12), 109 mph (175 km/h), (PL-12-U), 117 mph (188 km/h); initial rate of climb (PL-12), 600 ft/min (3,05 m/sec), (PL-12-U), 800 ft (4,1 m/sec); service ceiling, 10,500 ft (3,200 m); range with max payload, 748 mls (1 203 km); range with max fuel, 806 mls (1 297 km).

Weights: Empty (PL-12), 1,800 lb (816 kg), (PL-12-U), 1,830 lb (830 kg); max take-off (PL-12), 4,090 lb (1 855 kg), (PL-12-U), 3,800 lb (1 723 kg).

Dimensions: Span, 39 ft 10½ in (12,15 m); length, 20 ft 10 in (6,35 m); height, 9 ft 2 in (2,79 m); wing area, 252·7 sq ft (23,48 m²).

Accommodation: Pilot and (PL-12) provision for two passengers in rear fuselage and (PL-12-U) up to five passengers in fuselage in place of chemical hopper.

Status: Prototype first flown on 22 April 1965; Australian Type Approval, 10 February 1966, deliveries began December 1966. Prototype PL-12-U first flown December 1970; Type Approval

February 1971 deliveries began during 1971. Production totals (to early 1974) about 60 PL-12 and 4 PL-12-U.

Notes: The unconventional Airtruk was designed by Luigi Pellarini with the special requirements of the agricultural industry in mind. A capacious fuselage was designed around a hopper for insecticide, with the pilot located high above the short nose for best visibility. To avoid contamination of the rear structure by chemicals and to permit direct loading from trucks into the hopper in the fuselage, the tail unit was divided into two separate units, each carried on a single boom. A small stub wing beneath the mainplane proper made the PL-12 a sesquiplane. Production PL-12s, built by Transavia Corporation Pty of Sydney, have gone into service in Australia, Thailand, New Zealand, South Africa, and Kenya, and the first example purchased in Europe was delivered to Denmark in 1973. For general utility duties, cargo carrying and specialised rôles, the PL-12-U was introduced in 1971, this variant having the hopper removed and replaced by up to five passenger seats, of which four are contained on the lower deck and one is rearward facing behind the pilot. The standard PL-12 has a hopper capacity of 180 Imp gal (818 l). Production and assembly is also undertaken in New Zealand.

201

UTVA-65 PRIVREDNIK

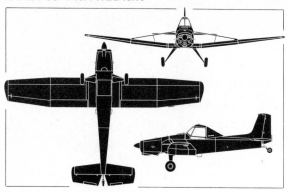

Shown in the photograph and silhouette, the UTVA-65 Privrednik follows conventional layout for modern agricultural monoplanes, and is in production in Yugoslavia

Country of Origin: Yugoslavia.

Type: Agricultural monoplane.

Power Plant: One (Privrednik-GO) 295 hp Lycoming GO-480-G1A6 or (Privrednik-IO) 300 hp IO-540-K1A5 or (Super Privrednik-350) 250 hp IGO-540-A1C piston engine.

Performance: Max speed (GO), 128 mph (206 km/h), (IO), 125 mph (202 km/h), (Super), 140 mph (225 km/h) ; initial rate of climb (GO), 1,053 ft/min (5,35 m/sec), (Super), 590 ft/min (3,0 m/sec) ; range with normal fuel (IO), 373 mls (600 km) ; range with max fuel (IO), 621 mls (1 000 km).

Weights: Basic operating (IO), 2,227 lb (1 010 kg) ; max payload (GO), 1,323 lb (600 kg), (IO), 1,543 lb (700 kg), (Super), 1,455 lb (660 kg) ; max take-off (GO, normal cat), 3,225 lb (1 463 kg), (GO, restricted cat), 4,078 lb (1 850 kg), (IO), 4,123 lb (1 870 kg), (Super, restricted cat), 4,409 lb (2 000 kg).

Dimensions: Span (GO, IO), 40 ft 1 in (12,22 m), (Super), 44 ft 0½ in (13,42 m) ; length (GO, IO), 22 ft 9 in (8,46 m), (Super), 27 ft 9 in (8,46 m) ; height (all), 8 ft 6½ in (2,60 m) ; gross wing area (GO, IO), 209 sq ft (19,4 m²), (Super), 224·85 sq ft (20·89 m²).

Accommodation: Pilot only, in enclosed cockpit.

Status: Prototype first flown in Spring 1965. Production of GO and IO models completed by 1973. Prototype Super Privrednik-350 flown in 1973.

Notes: Although it has the conventional low-wing layout of most contemporary agricultural monoplanes, the Privrednik uses many components of the high-wing UTVA-60 light plane (see *Military* volume, page 154), including the basic wing structure, the tail unit and the landing gear. Two prototypes built in 1964/65 were powered by 270 hp Lycoming GO-480-B1A6 engines, the more powerful -G1A6 version being adopted for the production Privrednik-GO model. The second production series, identified as Privrednik-IO, featured an ungeared engine and other minor changes to conform with Western certification standards. The Super Privrednik-350 was under development in 1973 and was expected to enter production in place of the earlier versions, from which it differed in having larger overall dimensions and a more powerful engine. The plastics hopper forward of the cockpit has a capacity of over 154 Imp gal (700 l) and can accommodate a long-range fuel tank when necessary for ferry and positioning flights.

AEROSPATIALE ALOUETTE II

The photograph above depicts an Aérospatiale Alouette II operated by the Greek airline Olympic Airways. Many Alouette IIs are used on general utility duties

Country of Origin: France.
Type: Five-seat utility helicopter.
Power Plant: One (SA 313B) 360 hp Turboméca Artouste IIC6 turboshaft.
Performance (SA 313B): Max speed, 115 mph (185 km/h) at sea level; max cruise, 102 mph (165 km/h); max inclined climb, 825 ft/min (4.2 m/sec); hovering ceiling (IGE), 5,400 ft (1 650 m), hovering ceiling (OGE), 3,000 ft (920 km); range with max fuel, 186 mls (300 km), with max payload, 62 mls (100 km).
Weights (SA 313B): Empty, 1,973 (895 kg); max take-off, 3,527 lb (1 600 kg).
Dimensions: Rotor diameter, 33 ft 5 in (10,20 m); fuselage length, 31 ft 10 in (9,70 m); height, 9 ft 0 in (2,75 m).
Notes: The SE 313B Alouette II was first flown on 12 March 1955 (as the SE 3130) and was certificated 14 January 1958. This type provided the basis for the most successful European helicopter programme to date, later derivatives being the SA 318C Alouette II Astazou, the SA 315 Lama and SA 316/319 Alouette II. Production of the Alouette II versions, including the Astazou version, totalled 1,291 by early 1973.

AEROSPATIALE ALOUETTE III

The photograph above depicts an Aérospatiale SA316 Alouette III in the markings of Olympic Airways, with emergency flotation bags on the fuselage sides

Country of Origin: France.
Type: Seven-seat light utility helicopter.
Power Plant: One (SA 316B) 570 hp Turboméca Artouste IIIB or (SA 319) 600 shp Astazou XIV turboshaft.
Performance (SA 316B): Max speed 130 mph (210 km/h) at sea level; max cruise, 115 mph (185 km/h); max inclined climb, 885 ft/min (4,5 m/sec); hovering ceiling (IGE), 7,380 ft (2 250 m); range with max fuel, 298 mls (480 km).
Weights (SA 316B): Empty, 2,474 lb (1 122 kg); max take-off, 4,850 lb (2 200 kg).
Dimensions: Rotor diameter, 36 ft 1¾ in (11,02 m); fuselage length, 32 ft 10¾ in (10,03 m); height, 9 ft 10 in (3,0 m).
Notes: The SA 316 Alouette III was a development of the Alouette II, first flown on 28 February 1959. The initial production model was the SA 316A with Artouste IIIB turboshaft, followed by the SA 316B (data above) with higher weights. The SA 316C subsequently replaced it, with Artouste IIID engine. A further improvement came with the SA 319 with an Astazou engine. Over 1,000 Alouette IIIs have been built in France; also in production in India, Romania and Switzerland.

AEROSPATIALE SA 330 PUMA

The photograph above depicts the seventh Aérospatiale Puma in SA330F configuration as a 15–17 passenger civil transport helicopter

Country of Origin: France.
Type: 9–20-seat transport and utility helicopter.
Power Plant: Two (SA 330F) 1,435 shp Turboméca Turmo IVA or (SA 330G) 1,575 shp Turmo IVC turboshafts.
Performance (SA 330F): Max speed, 170 mph (274 km/h); max cruise, 162 mph (261 km/h); max inclined climb, 1,380 ft/min (7,0 m/sec); hovering ceiling (IGE), 6,890 ft (2 100 km), hovering ceiling (OGE), 4,265 ft (1 300 m); range with max fuel, 385 mls (620 km).
Weights: Empty equipped, 7,805 lb (3 540 kg); max take-off, 14,770 lb (6 700 kg).
Dimensions: Rotor diameter, 49 ft 2½ in (15,00 m); fuselage length, 46 ft 1½ in (14,06 m); height, 16 ft 10½ in (5,14 m).
Notes: The SA 330 first flew on 15 April 1965, having been developed by Aérospatiale primarily to meet military requirements. It subsequently became one of the three helicopters in the Anglo-French joint production programme and Westland built 40 SA 330Es for the RAF. The SA 330B and C are French military versions and the SA 330F and G are civil versions, the latter being certificated in 1973 with improved performance.

AEROSPATIALE/WESTLAND GAZELLE

The photograph above depicts an early production Aérospatiale SA341G Gazelle, this being the civil version of the five-seat light utility helicopter

Country of Origin: France.
Type: Five-seat light utility helicopter.
Power Plant: One 592 shp Turboméca Astazou IIIN turboshaft.
Performance: Max cruise, 164 mph (264 km/h) at sea level; economical cruise, 144 mph (233 km/h); max inclined climb, 1,770 ft/min (9,0 m/sec); hovering ceiling (IGE), 9,350 ft (2 850 m); hovering ceiling (OGE), 6,560 ft (2 000 m); range with max fuel, 416 mls (670 km).
Weights: Empty, 2,022 lb (917 kg); max take-off, 3,970 lb (1 800 kg).
Dimensions: Rotor diameter, 34 ft 5½ in (10,50 m); fuselage length, 31 ft 3¼ in (9,53 m); height, 10 ft 4 in (3,15 m).
Notes: The SA 340 prototype first flew on 7 April 1967 and in its SA 341 production form was adopted for joint development and production in France and Britain. The first production examples flew in France and Britain, respectively, on 6 August 1971 and 31 January 1972, initial production being for the armed forces of the two countries, in versions designated SA 341B to SA 341F. The SA 341G received French Type Approval on 7 June 1972 and deliveries for civil use began in 1973.

AGUSTA A 109 HIRUNDO

The photograph above depicts the second prototype of the Agusta A109 Hirundo general purpose helicopter which was expected to enter production in 1974

Country of Origin: Italy.

Type: Six–eight-seat general purpose helicopter.

Power Plant: Two 400 shp Allison 250-C2 turboshafts.

Performance: Max speed, 172 mph (277 km/h) at sea level; economical cruise, 138 mph (223 km/h); max inclined climb, 2,060 ft/min (10,5 m/sec); hovering ceiling (IGE), 11,810 ft (3 600 m); hovering ceiling (OGE), 9,190 ft/min (2 800 m); max range, 457 mls (735 km).

Weights: Empty, 2,645 lb (1 200 kg); max take-off, 5,070 lb (2 300 kg).

Dimensions: Rotor diameter, 36 ft 1 in (11,0 m); fuselage length, 36 ft 7 in (11,15 m); height, 10 ft 6 in (3,20 m).

Notes: Originally designed with a single-engined layout, the A109 was built in its twin-engined form, first flown on 4 August 1971. A second example flew on 27 January 1973, and flight trials and certification then proceeded rapidly, with conclusion by mid-1974. Among the first customers to announce orders was Petroleum Helicopter Industries. A military version is under development carrying missiles, gun pods, etc on stub wings, and the A.123 is a further military derivative.

BELL MODEL 47

The photograph above depicts a Bell 47G-5 three-seat utility helicopter, one of the many variants of the Model 47 which was in production from 1946 to 1974

Country of Origin: USA.

Type: Light utility and training helicopter.

Power Plant: (47G) 200 hp Franklin 6V4-200-C32 or (47G-3B-2A) 280 hp Lycoming TVO-435-F1A piston engine.

Performance: (47G-3B-2A): Max speed, 105 mph (169 km/h); cruising speed, 84 mph (135 km/h); max inclined climb, 990 ft/min (5,0 m/sec); hovering ceiling (IGE), 17,700 ft (5 395 m); hovering ceiling (OGE), 12,700 ft (3 870 m); max range, 247 mls (397 km).

Weights: Empty equipped, 1,893 lb (858 kg); max take-off, 2,950 lb (1 338 kg).

Dimensions: Rotor diameter, 37 ft 1½ in (11,32 m); fuselage length, 31 ft 7 in (9,63 m); height, 9 ft 3¾ in (2,84 m).

Notes: Derived from Bell's original Model 30 helicopter flown in 1943, the Model 47 first flew on 8 December 1945 and was in production until 1974, having become the World's most-produced helicopter. More than 5,000 have been built in the USA, plus many others in Italy by Agusta, by Kawasaki in Japan and by Westland in the UK. The basic Model 47 seats three side-by-side and many are used for agricultural duties. The Kawasaki KH-4 (see page 212) is a four-seat derivative.

BELL MODEL 204

The photograph above depicts an Agusta-built Bell 204B 10-seat general purpose helicopter, fitted with an external winch above the starboard entry door

Country of Origin: USA.

Type: Ten-seat general purpose helicopter.

Power Plant: One 1,100 shp Lycoming T5309A or T5311A turboshaft.

Performance: Max speed, 138 mph (222 km/h); economical cruise, 120 mph (193 km/h); max inclined climb, 1,600 ft/min (8,1 m/sec); hovering ceiling (IGE), 8,200 ft (2 500 m); hovering ceiling (IGE), 2,400 ft (12,2 m/sec); range, 230 mls (370 km).

Weights: Empty, 4,600 lb (2 086 kg); max take-off, 8,500 lb (3 856 kg).

Dimensions: Rotor diameter, 48 ft 0 in (14,63 m); fuselage length, 41 ft 7½ in (12,69 m); height, 14 ft 7 in (4,45 m).

Notes: The Bell Model 204 was designed to meet a US Army requirement for a utility helicopter and entered production in this rôle as the UH-1 Iroquois (see *Military* volume, page 205). The commercial Model 204B was certificated on 4 April 1963 and over 60 were built for the civil market. Others were built under licence in Japan by Fuji (about 20 for civil use) and by Agusta in Italy, whose AB-204B version is also available with General Electric T58 or R-R/Bristol Gnome.

BELL MODEL 205 (AND 214)

The photograph above depicts a Bell 205 15-seat general purpose helicopter, this example being an Agusta-built machine in Italian service

Country of Origin: USA.

Type: General purpose and business helicopter.

Power Plant: One 1,400 shp (derated to 1,250 shp) Lycoming T5313A turboshaft.

Performance: Max speed, 127 mph (204 km/h) at sea level; max cruise, 111 mph (179 km/h) at 8,000 ft (2 440 m); max inclined climb, 1,680 ft/min (8,5 m/sec); hovering ceiling (IGE), 10,400 ft (3 170 m); hovering ceiling (OGE), 6,000 ft (1 830 m); range 344 mls (553 km).

Weights: Empty equipped, 5,197 lb (2 357 kg); max take-off, 9,500 lb (4 309 kg), with external load, 10,500 lb (4 763 kg).

Dimensions: Rotor diameter, 48 ft 0 in (14,63 m); fuselage length, 41 ft 6 in (12,65 m); height, 14 ft 4¾ in.

Notes: Bell's 15-seat Model 205A-1 is the commercial equivalent of the UH-1H (see *Military* volume, page 105), differing from the Model 204B primarily in having a lengthened cabin with increased accommodation. Agusta in Italy and Fuji in Japan hold licences for its production. The Model 214B is under development with 2,930 shp Lycoming T5508D turboshaft and gross weight of 12,400 lb (5 624 kg).

BELL MODEL 206 JETRANGER

The photograph above depicts a Bell 206A JetRanger, built in Italy by Agusta, and fitted with its optional long-leg landing skids

Country of Origin: USA.
Type: Light general purpose five-seat helicopter.
Power Plant: One (206A) 317 shp Allison 250-C18 or (206B) 400 shp 250-C20 or (206L) 420 shp 250-C20B turboshaft.
Performance (206B): Max speed, 140 mph (225 km/h) at sea level; economical cruise, 138 mph (222 km/h) at 5,000 ft (1 525 m); max inclined climb, 1,260 ft/min (6,4 m/sec), hovering ceiling (IGE), 11,300 ft (3 445 m); hovering ceiling (OGE), 5,800 ft (1 770 m); max range, 388 mls (624 km).
Weights: Empty, 1,455 lb (660 kg); max take-off, 3,200 lb (1 451 kg).
Dimensions: Rotor diameter, 33 ft 4 in (10,16 m); fuselage length, 31 ft 2 in (9,50 m); height, 9 ft 6½ in (2,91 m).
Notes: Like the Bell Models 204 and 205, the 206 originated as a military design (see *Military* volume, page 206). The commercial Model 206A was superseded by the more powerful 206B JetRanger II in 1971 and in 1973 Bell announced the 206L Long-Ranger with lengthened cabin and up to seven seats. Several hundred Jet-Rangers are in commercial use, and the type is also built by Agusta in Italy.

BELL MODEL 212

The photograph above depicts a Bell 212, this being essentially a twin-engined version of the Model 205 described and illustrated on the opposite page

Country of Origin: USA.
Type: General purpose and business helicopter.
Power Plant: One 1,250 shp Pratt & Whitney (UACL) PT6T-3 Twin Pac coupled turboshaft.
Performance: Max speed, 126 mph (203 km/h) at sea level; max inclined climb, 1,745 ft/min (8,8 m/sec); hovering ceiling (IGE), 14,700 ft (4 480 m); hovering ceiling (OGE), 10,600 ft (3 230 m); max range, 273 mls (439 km).
Weights: Empty, 5,549 lb (2 517 kg), max take-off (transport wt), 10,000 lb (4 540 kg); max take-off (external load), 11,200 lb (5 080 kg).
Dimensions: Rotor diameter, 48 ft 2¼ in (14,69 m); fuselage length, 42 ft 4¾ in (12,92 m); overall height, 14 ft 4¾ in (4,39 m).
Notes: The Bell Model 212 is a derivative of the Model 205 (see page 206) from which it differs primarily in having two engines coupled to a single gear box. Although the cabin of the Model 212 remains the same size as that of the Model 205, the extra power gives it a greatly enhanced performance and improved load-carrying ability. With suitable avionics, the Bell 212 is approved for IFR operation.

The photograph above depicts a Boeing Vertol 107-II in the markings of New York Airways, which at one time operated from a roof-top heliport in Manhattan

The photograph above depicts a Brantly B-2 light general purpose helicopter operated in the United Kingdom by British Executive Air Services Ltd

Country of Origin: USA (Japan).
Type: Medium lift transport helicopter.
Power Plant: Two 1,250 shp General Electric CT58-110-1 turboshafts.
Performance: Max speed, 168 mph (270 km/h); economical cruise, 144 mph (232 km/h); max inclined climb, 1,440 ft/min (7,3 m/sec); hovering ceiling (IGE), 8,400 ft (2 560 m); hovering ceiling (OGE), 6,600 ft (2 012 m); range, 109 mls (175 km).
Weights: Empty equipped, 10,723 lb (4 868 kg); max take-off and landing, 19,000 lb (8,618 kg).
Dimensions: Rotor diameter, 50 ft 0 in (15,24 m) each; fuselage length, 44 ft 7 in (13,59 m); height, 16 ft 8½ in (5,09 m).
Notes: The Model 107 originated with the Vertol company, the prototype flying on 22 April 1958 with Lycoming T53 engines. A prototype with General Electric T58-GE-6 engines flew on 25 October 1960 as the Boeing-Vertol 107-II-1. New York Airways acquired five before Boeing transferred all commercial Model 107 production to Kawasaki in Japan in 1965. Ten have been built, including three more for NYA, plus one KV-107-IIA with CT58-140-1 engines, first flown 3 April 1968.

Country of Origin: USA.
Type: Two-seat light helicopter.
Power Plant: One 180 hp Lycoming IVO-360-A1A piston engine.
Performance: Max speed, 100 mph (161 km/h) at sea level; max cruise, 90 mph (145 km/h); max inclined climb, 1,900 ft/min (9,7 m/sec); hovering ceiling (IGE), 6,700 ft (2 040 m); max range, 250 mls (400 km).
Weights: Empty, 1,020 lb (463 kg); max take-off, 1,670 lb (757 kg).
Dimensions: Rotor diameter, 23 ft 9 in (7,24 m); length overall, 21 ft 9 in (6,62 m); height, 6 ft 9 in (2,06 m).
Notes: The Brantly B-2 was first flown on 21 February 1953, and an improved B-2 prototype flew on 14 August 1956; after certification in April 1959 this design entered production. Successive models, with various refinements, were the B-2A and B-2B (described above) and the B-2E with 205 hp engine. The Model 305, first flown in January 1964, had a lengthened cabin and four seats. Production ceased in 1970 by which time about 400 B-2s and 50 Model 305s had been built; most of those still flying are operated in the USA.

ENSTROM F-28A AND MODEL 280

FAIRCHILD FH-1100

The photograph above depicts an Enstrom F.28 light general purpose helicopter operated by Twyford Moors Helicopters; an executive model is known as the President

Country of Origin: USA.

Type: Light three-seat personal and business helicopter.

Power Plant: One (F-28A) 205 hp Lycoming HLO-360-C1A or (280) 210 hp Lycoming TLO-360-A1B turbosupercharged piston engine.

Performance: Max speed, 112 mph (180 km/h) at sea level; max cruise, 100 mph (161 km/h); max inclined climb, 950 ft/min (4,8 m/sec); hovering ceiling (IGE), 5,600 ft (1 705 m); hovering ceiling (OGE), 3,400 ft (1 035 m); max range, 237 mls (381 km).

Weights: Empty, 1,450 lb (657 kg); max take-off, 2,150 lb (975 kg).

Dimensions: Rotor diameter, 32 ft 0 in (9,75 m); length overall, 29 ft 6 in (8,99 m); height, 9 ft 2 in (2,79 m).

Notes: The F-28 is derived from an experimental helicopter built by Rudolph J. Enstrom, first flown on 12 November 1960. The first F-28 flew in May 1962, and improved F-28A (data above) was introduced in 1968. More than 130 had been built by the end of 1973. The Model 280 Shark, under development in 1973, is generally similar but has turbosupercharged engine and increased fuel capacity.

The photograph above depicts a Fairchild FH1100, a commercial general purpose helicopter derived from the original Hiller designs for an Army scout

Country of Origin: USA.

Type: Five-seat general purpose helicopter.

Power Plant: One 317 shp Allison 250-C18 turboshaft.

Performance: Max cruising speed, 127 mph (204 km/h) at 5,000 ft (1 525 m); economical cruise, 122 mph (196 km/h); max inclined climb, 1,600 ft/min (8,1 m/sec); hovering ceiling (IGE), 13,400 ft (4 085 m); hovering ceiling (OGE), 8,400 ft (2 560 m); range with full load, 348 mls (560 km).

Weights: Empty, 1,396 lb (633 kg); max take-off, 2,750 lb (1 247 kg).

Dimensions: Rotor diameter, 35 ft 4¾ in (10,79 m); fuselage length, 29 ft 9¾ in (9,08 m); height, 9 ft 3½ in (2,83 m).

Notes: Before its acquisition by Fairchild Industries, the Hiller company developed a light observation helicopter for a US Army fly-off. The design was subsequently re-engineered for the commercial market, with seating capacity increased from four to five, and FAA Type Approval was obtained on 20 July 1964. A production batch of 250 was put in hand, the first being completed in June 1966; some of these have gone into military service in various parts of the world.

The photograph above depicts a Hiller E4, one of the final production variants of the Hiller 360 and United Helicopters UH-12 family of light helicopters

Country of Origin: USA.
Type: Light utility helicopter.
Power Plant: One 305 hp Lycoming VO-540-C2B piston engine.
Performance: Max speed, 96 mph (154 km/h) at sea level; max cruise, 90 mph (145 km/h); max inclined climb, 1,290 ft/min (6,55 m/sec); hovering ceiling (IGE), 9,500 ft (2 900 m); hovering ceiling (OGE), 5,800 ft (1 770 m); range, 437 mls (703 km).
Weights: Empty, 1,759 lb (798 kg); max take-off, 2,800 lb (1 270 kg).
Dimensions: Rotor diameter, 35 ft 5 in (10,80 m); fuselage length, 28 ft 6 in (8,69 m); height, 9 ft 3½ in (2,83 m).
Notes: Originally marketed as the Hiller 360, the UH-12 series of helicopters derived from the work of Stanley Hiller Jr, who flew his first successful helicopter in 1944, at the age of 18. About 2,000 examples were built, more than half for military use, and of those used commercially, many were deployed in the agricultural rôle. Production ended soon after Hiller's company was acquired by Fairchild in 1964, but a considerable number of three-seat UH-12s and similar four-seat E4s remain in use in the USA and other parts of the world.

The photograph above depicts a Hughes 269 operating in support of ground activities by Los Angeles County sheriffs—a growing application for helicopters

Country of Origin: USA.
Type: Light three-seat helicopter.
Power Plant: One (269A) 180 hp Lycoming O-360-C2D or (269B/300) 180 hp HIO-360-A1A or (269C/300C) 190 hp HIO-360-D1A engine.
Performance (300): Max speed, 87 mph (140 km/h) at sea level; economical cruise, 66 mph (106 km/h); max inclined climb, 1,140 ft/min (5,8 m/sec); hovering ceiling (IGE), 7,700 ft (2 350 m); hovering ceiling (OGE), 5,800 ft/min (1 770 m); max range, 300 mls (480 km).
Weights: Empty, 958 lb (434 kg); max take-off (normal), 1,670 lb (757 kg), (restricted) 1,850 lb (839 kg).
Dimensions: Rotor diameter, 25 ft 3½ in (7,71 m); fuselage length, 21 ft 11¾ in (6,80 m); height, 8 ft 2¾ in (2,50 m).
Notes: The Hughes Model 269 was first flown in October 1956 and provided the basis for the company's successful bid for a US Army training helicopter contract. For the commercial market, the two-seat Model 269A was followed by the three-seat Model 269B, which was marketed as the Hughes 300. The Hughes 300C (269C), has increased power and gross weight of 1,900 lb (861 kg).

HUGHES 369/500

KAMOV KA-25K

The photograph above depicts a Hughes 500 (also known as Model 369) operating as a five-seat executive transport, in which rôle many are in service

The photograph above depicts a Kamov Ka-25K—the commercial flying crane version of the Soviet Navy's Ka-25 anti-submarine helicopter

Country of Origin: USA.

Type: Light five-seat helicopter.

Power Plant: One 317 shp (derated to 278 shp) Allison 250-C18A or (500C) 400 shp (derated to 317 shp) 250-C20 turboshaft.

Performance: Max speed, 152 mph (244 km/h) at sea level; cruising speed, 135 mph (217 km/h); max inclined climb, 1,700 ft/min (8,6 m/sec); hovering ceiling (IGE), 8,200 ft (2 500 m); hovering ceiling (OGE), 5,300 ft (1 615 m); range, 377 mls (606 km).

Weights: Empty, 1,088 lb (493 kg); max take-off (normal), 2,550 lb (1 157 kg); (restricted), 3,000 lb (1 360 kg).

Dimensions: Rotor diameter, 26 ft 4 in (8,03 m); fuselage length, 23 ft 0 in (7,01 m); height, 8 ft 1½ in (2,48 m).

Notes: The Hughes 500 was designed (as Model 369) to meet the US Army LOH requirement, winning the competition in May 1965 (see *Military* volume, page 209). The first civil prototype flew early in 1967 and the 500C (certificated as the 369HS) has an uprated engine and better "hot and high" performance. The Hughes 500 is also built in Italy by Nardi and in Japan by Kawasaki, for both civil and military use.

Country of Origin: Soviet Union.

NATO Code Name: *Hormone.*

Type: Flying crane helicopter.

Power Plant: Two 900 shp Glushenkov GTD-3 turboshaft engines.

Performance: Max speed, 137 mph (220 km/h); cruising speed, 120 mph (193 km/h); service ceiling, 11,500 ft (3 500 m); normal range, 250 mls (400 km); max range, 405 mls (650 km).

Weights: Empty, 9,700 lb (4 400 kg); max payload, 4,400 lb (2 000 kg); max take-off, 16,100 lb (7 300 kg).

Dimensions: Rotor diameter, 51 ft 8 in (15,74 m); overall length, 32 ft 3 in (9,83 m); height, 17 ft 7½ in (5,37 m).

Notes: The Kamov design bureau evolved the Ka-25K from the anti-submarine Ka-25 (see *Military* volume, page 211) to provide a small flying crane helicopter, specialised for lifting large external loads. The main cabin can accommodate 12 passengers on folding seats, or freight. To facilitate the lifting and accurate delivery of externally-slung loads, there is a rearwards-facing cockpit under the nose, from which one of the pilots can control the helicopter through a limited range of flight manoeuvres.

KAMOV KA-26

The photograph above depicts the Kamov Ka-26, a general purpose helicopter that can also be flown as a "flying crane" with the fuselage pod removed

Country of Origin: Soviet Union.
NATO Code Name: Hoodlum.
Type: General purpose helicopter.
Power Plant: Two 325 hp Vedeneev M-14V-26 piston engines.
Performance: Max speed, 105 mph (170 km/h) at sea level; economical cruise, 68 mph (110 km/h); hovering ceiling (IGE), 4,265 ft (1 300 m); hovering ceiling (OGE), 2,625 ft (800 m); max range, 745 mls (1 200 km).
Weights: Empty (passenger version), 4,630 lb (2 100 kg), (agricultural), 4,885 lb (2 216 kg); max take-off, 7,165 lb (3 250 kg).
Dimensions: Rotor diameter, 42 ft 8 in (13,00 m); fuselage length, 25 ft 5 in (7,75 km); height, 13 ft 3½ in (4,05 m).
Notes: The Ka-26 was first flown in 1965 and has been built in large numbers to fulfil various tasks undertaken by the Soviet civil aviation authority Aeroflot. These duties include passenger transport, freight carrying (internal and external loads), air survey with cameras in the cabin; ambulance duties carrying two stretchers, two seated casualties and an attendant; geophysical surveys and agricultural duties.

KAWASAKI KH-4

The photograph above depicts a Kawasaki KH-4, this being a four-seat derivative of the Bell Model 47 produced in Japan primarily for the domestic market

Country of Origin: Japan.
Type: General purpose four-seat helicopter.
Power Plant: One 270 hp Lycoming TVO-435-D1A piston engine.
Performance: Max speed, 105 mph (169 km/h); cruising speed, 87 mph (140 km/h); max inclined climb, 850 ft/min (4,3 m/sec); hovering ceiling (IGE), 18,000 ft (5 485 m); hovering ceiling (OGE), 15,000 ft (4 570 m); max range, 214 mls (345 km).
Weights: Empty, 1,890 lb (857 kg); max take-off, 2,850 lb (1 292 kg).
Dimensions: Rotor diameter, 37 ft 1½ in (11,32 m); fuselage length, 32 ft 7¼ in (9,93 m); height, 9 ft 3½ in (2,84 m).
Notes: Kawasaki entered the helicopter field by acquiring a licence to build the Bell 47 in 1953, since when it has built some 240 examples of the US aircraft in four versions. The KH-4 was developed by Kawasaki from the Bell 47 with a larger cabin, more fuel and other changes. Over 200 had been built by the end of 1973, of which about three-quarters were for commercial use, mostly in Japan, and the remainder had been delivered for operation in the utility transport rôle by military users in Japan, Thailand, Korea and the Philippines.

The photograph above depicts a Bölkow BO-105C operated in the Gulf of Mexico by Petroleum Helicopters Inc, with flotation bags attached to the skids

Country of Origin: Federal Germany.

Type: Five–six seat general purpose helicopter.

Power Plant: Two 317 shp Allison 250-C18 or 400 shp -C20 turboshafts.

Performance: Max speed, 167 mph (270 km/h); max cruise, 144 mph (232 km/h); max inclined climb, 1,870 ft/min (9,5 m/sec); hovering ceiling (IGE), 8,925 ft (2 720 m); hovering ceiling (OGE), 5,000 ft (1 833 m); range (standard fuel), 388 mls (625 km); max range, 658 mls (1 060 km).

Weights: Empty, 2,447 lb (1 110 kg); max take-off, 5,070 lb (2 300 kg).

Dimensions: Rotor diameter, 32 ft 2¾ in (9,82 m); fuselage length, 28 ft 0½ in (8,55 m); height, 9 ft 9¾ in (2,98 m).

Notes: The BO 105 features a rigid non-articulated rotor, first flown on the second prototype on 16 February 1967. The third prototype, flown on 20 December 1967, had MAN-Turbo 6022 engines but all production aircraft have the Allison 250 engine, either the C18 (BO 205C) or C20 (BO 205D). Nearly 100 BO 205s had been delivered by the end of 1973. The BO 206, first flown on 25 September 1973, has a longer fuselage.

The photograph above depicts a Mil Mi-4, one of the first types of helicopters to be operated on a regular basis by the Soviet airline Aeroflot

Country of Origin: Soviet Union.

NATO Code Name: *Hound.*

Type: General purpose helicopter.

Power Plant: One 1,700 hp ASh-82V piston radial engine.

Performance: Max speed, 130 mph (210 km/h) at 5,000 ft (1 500 m); economical cruise, 99 mph (160 km/h); service ceiling, 18,000 ft (5 500 m); normal range, 155–250 mls (250–400 km).

Weights: Max take-off, 17,200 lb (7 800 kg).

Dimensions: Rotor diameter, 68 ft 11 in (21,0 m); fuselage length, 55 ft 1 in (16,80 m); overall height, 17 ft 0 in (5,18 m).

Notes: The Mi-4, which entered military service in 1953 and civil use a little later, is one of the most-produced of Soviet helicopters, although now superseded in production by the Mi-8 and other types. The basic civil version was designated Mi-4P and, as used by Aeroflot, carried 8–11 passengers. A special agricultural version was developed as the Mi-4S, both these being distinguished from the military versions in having square rather than round windows. A few Mi-4s have entered commercial service outside the Soviet Union, for example in Eastern European countries, Nepal and elsewhere.

MIL MI-6

The photograph above depicts a Soviet-built Mil Mi-8 operating in the German Democratic Republic, with external hoist fitted to handle outsize loads

Country of Origin: Soviet Union.
NATO Code Name: *Hook.*
Type: Heavy transport helicopter.
Power Plant: Two 5,500 shp Soloviev D-25V turboshafts.
Performance (at 93,700 lb/42 500 kg): Max speed, 186 mph (300 km/h); max cruise, 155 mph (250 km/h); service ceiling, 14,750 ft (4 500 m); range with 17,650-lb (8 000-kg) payload, 385 mls (620 km), with 9,920-lb (4 500-kg) payload and external tanks, 620 mls (1 000 km).
Weights: Empty, 60,055 lb (27 240 kg); normal take-off, 89,285 lb (40 500 kg); max take-off (for VTO), 93,700 lb (42 500 kg).
Dimensions: Rotor diameter, 114 ft 10 in (35,00 m); fuselage length, 108 ft 9½ in (33,16 m); height, 32 ft 4 in (9,86 m).
Notes: At the time of its public debut in the autumn of 1957, the Mi-6 was the World's largest helicopter, and it is still today the largest helicopter in commercial service. Although the majority of those built have probably been for military use (see *Military* volume, page 213), some Mi-6s are used by Aeroflot for heavy lift duties, such as transporting oil rig components, and to support forest fire-fighting teams.

MIL MI-8

The photograph above depicts the Mil Mi-6 in service with Aeroflot, this being the largest helicopter to achieve quantity production for commercial operation

Country of Origin: Soviet Union.
NATO Code Name: *Hip.*
Type: General-purpose transport helicopter.
Power Plant: Two 1,500 shp Izotov TB-2-117A turboshafts.
Performance (at 24,470 lb/11 100 kg): Max speed, 155 mph (250 km/h); max cruise, 140 mph (225 km/h); hovering ceiling (IGE), 5,900 ft (1 800 m); hovering ceiling (OGE), 2,625 ft (800 m); service ceiling, 14,760 ft (4 500 m); range with 6,615 lb (3 000 kg) of freight, 264 mls (425 km).
Weights: Empty (cargo), 15,787 lb (7 171 kg), (passenger), 16,352 lb (7 417 kg); normal take-off, 24,470 lb (11 100 kg); max take-off (for VTO), 26,455 lb (12 000 kg).
Dimensions: Rotor diameter, 69 ft 10¼ in (21,29 m); fuselage length, 59 ft 7 in (18,17 m); height, 18 ft 4½ in (5,60 m).
Notes: The Mi-8 has been in continuous production since 1964 for both civil and military tasks. The standard passenger version seats up to 28 in the cabin and the general utility version, designated Mi-8T, will seat 24 but has a quickly convertible interior and can carry freight internally and slung externally. There is also a *de luxe* 11-passenger model, the Mi-8 Salon.